PRENTICE-HALL SERIES IN MATHEMATICAL ECONOMICS

Donald V. T. Bear, *Series Editor*

Dennis J. Aigner
BASIC ECONOMETRICS

Arthur Benavie
MATHEMATICAL TECHNIQUES FOR ECONOMIC ANALYSIS

David A. Bowers and Robert N. Baird
ELEMENTARY MATHEMATICAL MACROECONOMICS

Michael D. Intriligator
MATHEMATICAL OPTIMIZATION AND ECONOMIC THEORY

Ronald C. Read
A MATHEMATICAL BACKGROUND FOR ECONOMISTS
AND SOCIAL SCIENTISTS

Menahem E. Yaari
LINEAR ALGEBRA FOR SOCIAL SCIENCES

Mathematical
Techniques
for Economic
Analysis

ARTHUR BENAVIE

Department of Economics
University of North Carolina

Mathematical Techniques for Economic Analysis

PRENTICE-HALL, INC., ENGLEWOOD CLIFFS, N.J.

For Bobbi

MATHEMATICAL TECHNIQUES FOR ECONOMIC ANALYSIS
by Arthur Benavie

© 1972 PRENTICE-HALL, INC., ENGLEWOOD CLIFFS, N. J.

Printed in the United States of America

ISBN : 0-13-562272-7
Library of Congress Catalog Card Number : 77-162350

10 9 8 7 6 5 4 3 2 1

PRENTICE-HALL INTERNATIONAL, INC., *London*
PRENTICE-HALL OF AUSTRALIA, PTY. LTD., *Sydney*
PRENTICE-HALL OF CANADA, LTD., *Toronto*
PRENTICE-HALL OF INDIA PRIVATE LIMITED, *New Delhi*
PRENTICE-HALL OF JAPAN, INC., *Tokyo*

Series Foreword

The Prentice-Hall Series in Mathematical Economics is intended as a vehicle for making mathematical reasoning and quantitative methods available to the main corpus of the undergraduate and graduate economics curricula.

The Series has been undertaken in the belief that the teaching of economics will, in the future, increasingly reflect the discipline's growing reliance upon mathematical and statistical techniques during the past 20 to 35 years and that mathematical economics and econometrics ought not to be "special fields" for undergraduates and graduate students, but that every aspect of economics education can benefit from the application of these techniques.

Accordingly, the Series will contain texts that cover the traditional substantive areas of the curriculum—for example, macroeconomics, microeconomics, public finance, and international trade—thereby offering the instructor the opportunity to expose his students to contemporary methods of analysis as they apply to the subject matter of his course. The composition of the early volumes in the Series will be weighted in favor of texts that offer the student various degrees of mathematical background, with the volumes of more substantive emphasis following shortly thereafter.

As the Series grows, it will contribute to the comprehensibility and quality of economics education at both the undergraduate and graduate levels.

DONALD V. T. BEAR, *Series Editor*

Contents

PART TWO

DYNAMIC ANALYSIS

Preface

This book was written for students of economics and professional economists who have had training in the fundamentals of the differential and integral calculus, matrix algebra, and differential or difference equations. It would be a useful addition to a study program in mathematical economics and economic theory following a one year course in mathematical economics. It might even be helpful in the beginning courses in mathematical economics.

Given the background assumed for the reader, the book is almost self-contained. All theorems are proved rigorously, but with the simplest mathematics. The few theorems which are not proved are accessible in lucid form elsewhere. The book may be thought of as an examination of how classical mathematical analysis is the foundation of analytical machinery indispensable to the economic theorist. The mappings throughout the book are assumed to be single valued and well behaved. Topological notions, which are also of importance in economic theory, are not developed in this volume.

The book can be outlined in a few sentences. The first chapter describes what a static economic model is, how comparative static analysis is carried out, what mathematical conditions guarantee the validity of this analysis, and how the correspondence principle yields comparative static information. The second chapter develops the Lagrange-Kuhn-Tucker Theory and demonstrates how fruitful this theory is in generating comparative static economic theorems. Chapter 3 spells out and mathematically justifies two solution techniques for linear differential and difference equation systems of any order. Chapter 4 states and proves some of the powerful Liapunov theorems pertaining to the stability characteristics of nonlinear as well as linear systems of differential and difference equations. Chapter 5 is an introduction to the problem of optimal control and contains a simple proof of a version of the maximum principle of Pontriagin, as well as an economic interpretation of the mathematical conditions stemming from this celebrated theorem.

Throughout the book, the development of each analytical technique is followed by exercises and examples from economics to illustrate how the technique is applied and to give the reader practice. It was not my intention to exhaust the economic applications of any technique, but rather to employ a few models from economics to illustrate each technique.

I have in the course of writing this book incurred an overwhelming debt of gratitude to D. V. T Bear. His comments and criticisms on the successive drafts were always correct, penetrating, patient, and challenging. It would be impossible for me to express adequately my feelings of gratitude to and admiration for him.

I also wish to thank J. P. Evans, F. J. Gould, R. J. Mackay, and L. E. Ruff for comments on portions of the manuscript, and to express my appreciation to S. N. Afriat and R. W. Pfouts for delightful conversations about mathematical economics. The initial stimulus for this book was an exciting seminar in mathematical economics conducted by R. E. Quandt at Princeton University in the Spring of 1965. My thanks to Miss Gayle A. Lamb, who expertly typed all drafts of the manuscript.

ARTHUR BENAVIE

PART I STATIC ANALYSIS

1 Comparative Static Analysis

1.1 ECONOMIC MODELS AND COMPARATIVE STATICS

Economic models consist of a set of functional relationships. The variables which are interrelated by the functions are classified either as *endogenous* or *exogenous*. An endogenous variable is determined by the model, while an exogenous variable is determined by forces outside of the model. An exogenous variable is thus by definition not affected by the endogenous variables. Of course, it is not correct simply to define a variable as exogenous and deduce that it is insulated from the endogenous variables. Rather, the opposite must be the case in constructing a model: A variable is understood to be independent of the endogenous variables and is *therefore* classified as exogenous. For example, the amount of rainfall is obviously independent of the demand, supply, and price of, say, corn. Rainfall would thus be exogenous in a model constructed to explain the demand, supply, and price of corn.

Suppose now that we mentally fix the values of all exogenous variables for some model, and suppose further that this set of values for the exogenous variables implies, via the functional relations, a set of values for the endogenous variables. We call this situation an *equilibrium*; the values assumed by the endogenous variables are called equilibrium values. Next, imagine that one or more of the exogeneous variables change values and remain at the new values. The question is, and this is a major concern of comparative static analysis— what will be the equilibrium change in each endogenous variable in response to the assumed changes in the exogenous variables?

To illustrate, and to aid in developing additional ideas, consider a model of a single market, say, the market for corn.

(1.1)

$$D = D(P, P_c, P_s, Y, X) \quad \text{(Demand equation)}$$
$$S = S(P, P_f, Z) \quad \text{(Supply equation)}$$
$$D = S \quad \text{(Equilibrium condition)}$$

where†

D = the quantity of corn demanded

S = the quantity of corn supplied

P = the price of corn

†To simplify, we have used a single letter for P_C, P_S, and P_f; these can be thought of as vectors without significantly affecting the discussion.

P_C = the price of a gross complement with corn (e.g., butter)

P_S = the price of a gross substitute for corn (e.g., potatoes)

Y = national income

P_f = the price of a productive factor used in the production of corn

X = any other variable which could affect D (e.g., a surrogate for preferences)

Z = any other variable which could affect S (e.g., rain or taxes)

and the behavioral assumptions are

$$\frac{\partial D}{\partial P} < 0, \frac{\partial D}{\partial P_C} < 0, \frac{\partial D}{\partial P_S} > 0, \frac{\partial D}{\partial Y} > 0, \frac{\partial S}{\partial P} > 0, \frac{\partial S}{\partial P_f} < 0$$

Equations (1.1), including the behavioral assumptions, constitute a model. The only thing missing is the *specification*, that is, *an explanation of why the behavioral assumptions are what they are.* For example, it is assumed that $\partial D/\partial P < 0$. The economist must explain why it is plausible that if P rises, with the other variables in the demand equation fixed, D will fall, and vice versa. An argument supporting this can be made on the basis of the substitution and income effects.† If P rises, corn is now more expensive vis-à-vis substitute (or rival) goods, thus consumers can be expected to increase the demand for substitutes at the expense of corn. This is the substitution effect. Also, a rise in P lowers real income for consumers and will thus diminish the demand for all normal goods, one of which we assume is corn. Consider the supply function where it is assumed that $\partial S/\partial P > 0$. This assumption stems from the theory of the perfectly competitive firm in the short run. This firm's marginal cost curve will eventually have a positive slope because of the law of diminishing returns. If the firm is a profit maximizer, the part of the marginal cost curve above the average variable cost curve will approximate the firm's supply curve. Thus, a rise in P will increase each firm's supply if average variable cost is covered at the new P. If the new P does not cover average variable cost, the firm will maintain a desired output of zero. The upshot of this argument is that $\partial S/\partial P > 0$, assuming that P is in a range where the average variable cost of at least one firm is being covered. The reader should provide a rationale for the other behavioral assumptions.

The partial derivatives expressing the behavioral assumptions of the model are called *structural parameters*, and equations (1.1) are called *structural equations*. Throughout this book we shall employ the following notation for structural parameters: D_P rather than $\partial D/\partial P$, S_P rather than $\partial S/\partial P$, and so on. We

---

†An argument leading to these effects and attempting to derive the sign of $\partial D/\partial P$ can also be derived from an assumption that consumers maximize utility subject to a budget constraint. We deal with this optimization argument in Chapter 2.

shall reserve the partial derivative notation $\partial Y/\partial X$ to apply to reduced form derivatives, a concept to be defined shortly.

Consider again the system in (1.1). The first equation determines D (given P, P_C, etc.), the second equation determines S (given P, P_f, etc.), and the equilibrium condition can be viewed as determining the value of P which equates D and S. We have three equations determining three unknowns—D, S, and P. Thus, the endogenous variables in this model are taken to be D, S, and P, and the others are assumed to be exogenous. Since it is quite unlikely that P_C and P_S actually will be unaffected by P, the assumption that P_C and P_S are exogenous is questionable. Adding the markets of these complementary and rival goods to the model is thus clearly called for. This addition would endogenize P_C and P_S.† The same point can be made with respect to P_f, although the defect probably is not as severe as with P_C and P_S. Considering Y as exogenous appears more defensible the smaller the markets analyzed are as a proportion of the national economy. If Z refers to, say, the amount of rainfall, we have as exogenous a variable as we ever will. Of course, in a meteorological model this variable might be one of the critical endogenous variables.

Having established that model (1.1) has glaring defects, we shall for simplicity continue the illustration pretending that it is a perfectly specified model. It is often convenient to write the structural equations in implicit form, which simply means transferring all the terms in (1.1) to the left side. This gives

$$(1.2) \qquad D - D(P, P_C, P_S, Y, X) = 0$$
$$S - S(P, P_f, Z) = 0$$
$$D - S = 0$$

The model can also be simplified by substituting the demand and supply equations into the equilibrium condition, giving (1.3), the excess demand for corn,

$$(1.3) \qquad D(P, P_C, P_S, Y, X) - S(P, P_f, Z) = 0$$

in which we now have one equation and one endogenous variable, P.

Let us now fix the values of the exogenous variables. Corresponding to these values, we *assume* the endogenous variables take on equilibrium values. We affix a superscript zero to express this equilibrium. Using (1.1) to illustrate, we have

$$D^0 = D(P^0, P_C^0, P_S^0, Y^0, X^0)$$
$$S^0 = S(P^0, P_f^0, Z^0)$$
$$D^0 = S^0$$

†We do this in section 1.7, example 1.2.

Now suppose that one or more of the exogenous variables change value and stay fixed at the new value. *Assuming that a unique new equilibrium exists*, we may write it as

$$D^1 = D(P^1, P_C^1, P_S^1, Y^1, X^1)$$
$$S^1 = S(P^1, P_f^1, Z^1)$$
$$D^1 = S^1$$

A major task of comparative static analysis is to find out as much as possible about the change in the endogenous variables (D, S, P) in response to a change in the exogenous variables (P_C, P_S, P_f, Y, X, Z).

The fundamental question which arises here is a main theme of this chapter. Can we be sure that a unique *new* equilibrium exists? Can we be certain that arbitrary values of the exogenous variables will generate unique values of the endogenous variables which satisfy (1.1)? In other words, can each endogenous variable be expressed as a unique function of the exogenous variables,

(1.4) $$D = \phi^1(P_C, P_S, Y, X, P_f, Z)$$
$$S = \phi^2(P_C, P_S, Y, X, P_f, Z)$$
$$P = \phi^3(P_C, P_S, Y, X, P_f, Z)$$

such that for arbitrary values assigned to the exogenous variables the resulting values of the endogenous variables will satisfy (1.1)?

Theorems from mathematical analysis, known as implicit function theorems, answer the question of when the functions in (1.4) are guaranteed to exist, and what the properties of these functions are. We shall state and prove these theorems in section 1.5; for now, we assume that such functions do exist.

The system in (1.4), where *each* endogenous variable is expressed as a function of *all* of the exogenous variables, is called the *reduced form*; the partial derivatives of the endogenous variables with respect to the exogenous variables are called the *reduced form derivatives*, or *multipliers*. We may restate the fundamental objective of comparative statics by using these concepts. Comparative static analysis is concerned with finding out as much as possible about the reduced form and its derivatives. Notice that a reduced form derivative, such as $\partial D/\partial Y$ from (1.4), tells us the *total equilibrium* change in an endogenous variable, in this case D, divided by the change in an exogenous variable, in this case Y, as ΔY converges to zero. In the language of economics we say $\partial D/\partial Y$ is the total equilibrium rate of change in D with respect to a change in Y.

If the reduced form exists, we say that we can *solve* for the endogenous variables in terms of the exogenous variables. However, *simply knowing that the reduced form exists does not tell us how we may solve explicitly for the endogenous variables.* For nonlinear structural systems, this may not only be an extremely difficult task, but may even be impossible in terms of such elementary functions as polynomial, trigonometric, or logarithmic. For linear systems, if the reduced form exists, it too will be linear, and the endogenous variables may be solved for explicitly. To illustrate this last point, we write (1.1) in linear form (1.5).

$$(1.5) \qquad D = a_{11}P + a_{12}P_C + a_{13}P_S + a_{14}Y + a_{15}X$$
$$S = a_{21}P + a_{22}P_f + a_{23}Z$$
$$D = S$$

where a_{ij} are the structural parameters and where $a_{11} < 0, a_{12} < 0, a_{13} > 0,$ $a_{14} > 0, a_{21} > 0, a_{22} < 0$. In matrix form (1.5) can be written

$$\begin{bmatrix} 1 & 0 & -a_{11} \\ 0 & 1 & -a_{21} \\ 1 & 1 & 0 \end{bmatrix} \begin{bmatrix} D \\ S \\ P \end{bmatrix} = \begin{bmatrix} a_{12}P_C + a_{13}P_S + a_{14}Y + a_{15}X \\ a_{22}P_f + a_{23}Z \\ 0 \end{bmatrix}$$

If the 3×3 matrix on the left side is nonsingular, then (D, S, P) can be solved for by premultiplying both sides by the inverse of this matrix. This solution is the reduced form

$$\begin{bmatrix} D \\ S \\ P \end{bmatrix} = \begin{bmatrix} 1 & 0 & -a_{11} \\ 0 & 1 & -a_{21} \\ 1 & -1 & 0 \end{bmatrix}^{-1} \begin{bmatrix} a_{12}P_C + a_{13}P_S + a_{14}Y + a_{15}X \\ a_{22}P_f + a_{23}Z \\ 0 \end{bmatrix}$$

Some efficient procedures for solving such systems (finding the indicated inverse) will be discussed in section 1.6.

  Returning to the general case, suppose we know that the reduced form of (1.1), which is (1.4), exists. Suppose further that, since (1.1) might be a nonlinear system, we may not know how to solve explicitly for the endogenous variables; in other words, we may not know precisely what the functions in (1.4) are. Pretend that we do not know what the functions in (1.4) look like. *Can we then solve for the reduced form derivatives even with this ignorance?* To see that under certain conditions we can, first substitute (1.4) into (1.2). This yields

$$(1.6) \qquad \phi^1(\ ) - D[\phi^3(\ ), P_C, P_S, Y, X] = 0$$
$$\phi^2(\ ) - S[\phi^3(\ ), P_f, Z] \qquad = 0$$
$$\phi^1(\ ) - \phi^2(\ ) \qquad\qquad\quad = 0$$

where the arguments (independent variables) have been left out of the reduced form functions ϕ^i for simplicity. Now if the chain rule applies† we can differentiate (1.6) with respect to any exogenous variable. *But*, simply because the equations in (1.6) equal zero in equilibrium does not mean that the derivative equals zero. These functions may be equal to zero only for certain values of the exogenous variables. If that is the case, we do not know what value a derivative of these equations will have. Example: $f(x) = x^2 + 4x = 0$ when $x = -4$. But $df(x)/dx = 2x + 4 \neq 0$, if $x \neq -2$, in particular, when $x = -4$. Clearly, if we do not know the value of the derivative of (1.6), we will not be able to solve for, say $(\partial D/\partial Y, \partial S/\partial Y, \partial P/\partial Y)$. On the other hand, if we knew that the expressions in (1.6) were *identically* zero for any values of the exogenous variables, in a neighborhood of the initial values, then any derivative would have to equal zero. (Example: $x^2 + 4x - x^2 - 4x = 0$.) As we shall demonstrate, this information is guaranteed by the implicit function theorem.‡ It assures us that if the structural equations have certain properties, the reduced form not only exists and has continuous first derivatives but, in addition, when it is substituted into the structural equations, the latter will be *identically* zero for *any* values of the exogenous variables in *some* neighborhood of the initial values. Thus, under this circumstance, we may set the derivative of (1.6) with respect to any exogenous variable equal to zero. Taking the derivative of (1.6) with respect to, say, Y gives, using the chain rule§

(1.7)
$$\frac{\partial D}{\partial Y} - D_P \frac{\partial P}{\partial Y} - D_Y = 0$$
$$\frac{\partial S}{\partial Y} - S_P \frac{\partial P}{\partial Y} = 0$$
$$\frac{\partial D}{\partial Y} - \frac{\partial S}{\partial Y} = 0$$

where the structural parameters, D_P, S_P, and D_Y are evaluated at the initial equilibrium. In matrix form, (1.7) is written as

$$\begin{bmatrix} 1 & 0 & -D_P \\ 0 & 1 & -S_P \\ 1 & -1 & 0 \end{bmatrix} \begin{bmatrix} \frac{\partial D}{\partial Y} \\ \frac{\partial S}{\partial Y} \\ \frac{\partial P}{\partial Y} \end{bmatrix} = \begin{bmatrix} D_Y \\ 0 \\ 0 \end{bmatrix}$$

†See section 1.4 for the theorem on the chain rule.
‡As indicated above, there are more than one. When we refer to *the* implicit function theorem we mean the general theorem which contains all the others. This is Theorem 1.8 in section 1.5.
§It follows that if the implicit function theorem is satisfied, the chain rule can be applied. See section 1.5.

Now, if the 3×3 matrix is nonsingular, we can solve for $(\partial D/\partial Y, \partial S/\partial Y, \partial P/\partial Y)$ as in the linear case. Will this matrix be nonsingular? As we shall see, the non-singularity of this matrix, which is called the *Jacobian matrix*, is one of the assumptions of the implicit function theorem; that is, when the implicit function theorem is applicable, (1.8) can be solved for $\partial D/\partial Y$, $\partial S/\partial Y$, and $\partial P/\partial Y$.†

Caution. Do not confuse the reduced form derivative $\partial D/\partial Y$ with the structural parameter D_Y, which unfortunately also is frequently, and correctly, denoted $\partial D/\partial Y$. The structural parameter D_Y is a partial derivative; the reduced form derivative $\partial D/\partial Y$ is a *total partial* derivative. The difference between them should be clear from the discussion in the text. The term D_Y is the change in D divided by the change in Y, as ΔY converges to zero, *holding everything else, including the other endogenous variables, fixed.* The reduced form derivative is the same ratio passing to the same limit, *with the other exogenous variables fixed, but with the endogenous variables adjusting to their new equilibrium.* The reduced form derivative is thus a partial total derivative, *partial* in the sense that all other exogenous variables are fixed, *total* in the sense that all other endogenous variables change as they must when all structural equations are assumed to be satisfied *simultaneously*.

1.2 MACROECONOMIC EXAMPLE

To illustrate these ideas further, consider a standard macroeconomic model.

$$(1.9) \quad \begin{array}{l} \text{Product} \\ \text{Market} \end{array} \left\{ \begin{array}{ll} C = C(Y_d, \alpha_1) & 0 < C_{Y_d} < 1 \\ I = I(Y, r, \alpha_2) & I_Y > 0, I_r < 0 \\ G = \bar{G} & \\ Y = Y_d + T & \\ T = \bar{T} + tY & 0 < t < 1 \\ Y = C + I + G & \end{array} \right.$$

$$\begin{array}{l} \text{Money} \\ \text{Market} \end{array} \left\{ \begin{array}{ll} M^* = M(r, Y, \alpha_3) & M_r < 0, M_Y > 0 \\ M = \bar{M} & \\ M = M^* & \end{array} \right.$$

where

---

†The assumption of nonsingularity of the Jacobian matrix as applied to (1.8) is that the demand and supply curves are not parallel, that is, $D_p \neq S_p$.

$C =$ Consumption spending

$I =$ Investment spending

$G =$ Government spending

$Y_d =$ Disposable income

$Y =$ National income

$T =$ Personal income taxes

$M^* =$ Demand for money

$M =$ Stock of money

$\alpha_i =$ Unspecified exogenous variables (also called shift parameters)

$r =$ The interest rate

A bar over a variable means exogenous.

We will now discuss this model briefly.[†] The first equation is the consumption function. The behavioral assumption is the usual one that C_{Y_d}, the marginal propensity to consume, is between zero and one. The rationale for this assumption is that in our society (and of course many others) studies of consumer attitudes indicate that an improvement in the standard of living is a positive goal. Thus, the desire exists to acquire goods, especially durable ones, as well as to build up financial reserves. A rise in disposable income offers an opportunity to take steps toward both. This means that an increment in disposable income will be used for both consumption and saving. Since disposable income is identical to consumption plus personal saving, the marginal propensity to consume out of disposable income is expected to be between zero and one. The element α_1 refers to any exogenous variable that might affect C, such as population growth, the age or geographical composition of population, wealth, expectations, and so on. Another endogenous variable that we could have included as an argument in the consumption function is the interest rate, r. The reason we excluded this variable is because its impact on C is theoretically and empirically ambiguous: A rise in r will increase the attractiveness of saving vis-à-vis consumption, and will thus generate a substitution of saving for consumption. On the other hand, a rise in r will reduce the level of saving required to provide a given future income stream. If one effect dominates the other, we have not been able to detect it in empirical work. Hence, we assume $C_r = 0$.

The second equation argues that a rise in Y will increase I, and a rise in r will depress I, and vice versa. A rise in Y could stimulate I through any of three routes. A rise in Y implies an increase in profits, which increases the funds available to business for investment spending. A rise in profits may also heighten optimism concerning the expected profitability of investment projects, thus providing an incentive for increasing I. Finally, a rise in Y implies a more intensive utilization of existing output capacity, thus stimulating I for the purpose of generating additional output capacity. A rise in r, on the other hand, increases the opportunity cost of funds that could be used for investment, hence marginal investment projects which appeared worthwhile before the rise in r may not seem worthwhile after it rises. The variable α_2 is any exogenous variable relevant to investment spending, for example, the pace of technological progress, population growth, expectations, the stock of capital, and so on.

The third equation states that G is exogenous. It is, however, an exogenous variable that is *controllable*, as compared to, say, technological progress, which usually is assumed not to be controllable. An exogenous variable that can be controlled is called a *policy instrument*. The fourth equation is an identity, saying that national income equals disposable income plus taxes. The next equation is not a behavioral equation like the first two; it is an *institutional* (or legal) functional relationship, showing the relationship between personal income taxes owed (and paid) and national income, given the tax laws characterized by $\bar{T}$ and t. We have made the equation linear since that is the usual way of expressing it. The symbols $\bar{T}$ and t can be considered as policy instruments, or, if assumed fixed for the course of an analysis, can be thought of as structural parameters. The next equation is the equilibrium condition in the product market stating that in equilibrium the intended national income (or output) generated by the business sector, Y, equals intended aggregate demand, $C + I + G$.

The first function in the money market is the demand for the stock of money considered as a function of the endogenous variables Y and r and our catchall exogenous variable α_3. A rise in r is assumed to diminish M^* for two reasons. First, the opportunity cost of holding money vis-à-vis other stocks of assets (in this model "bonds") rises when r does. Thus, the attractiveness of money diminishes relative to bonds, and the desired stock of money falls. Second, if the prevailing r is thought of by some financial investors as normal, then a rise in r may generate the expectation that r will fall (relative to the previous expectation) in the future. Since this is equivalent to expecting a capital gain (relative to before the change) on bonds, a portfolio rearrangement away from money and into bonds might result. Clearly, the second reason could operate the other way, a rise in r creating anticipation of a further rise. In the latter case, the sign of M_r would be ambiguous. Empirical evidence, however, is consistent with the notion that $M_r < 0$, which either suggests that the first two reasons are both operative, or that the opportunity cost argument dominates. The assumption that $M_Y > 0$ is based on the following reasoning. A rise in Y will increase the volume of transactions carried out by business and consumer units, and thus raise the level of cash balances required to carry out these transactions.

The next to last equation states that the supply of money is exogenous; it is also considered in this model to be a policy instrument. (Another way of formulating this equation is to make the supply of money a function of the interest rate and an exogenous component. An argument for this is that a rise in r increases the opportunity cost of excess reserves for the commercial banking system, thus depressing excess reserves, which raises the supply of money.) The last equation says that, in equilibrium, the supply of and demand for money are equal.

Notice that in the above discussion we mentioned a financial asset, bonds, which is a substitute for money. We did not spell out the equations for the bond market. This deletion is common in the literature, because if equilibrium states are the subject of investigation, an equilibrium in both the commodity and the money markets implies an equilibrium in the bond market, since the model is only considering goods, money, and bonds. This truism—that an equilibrium in any two markets must mean that the third is in equilibrium if the model has only three markets—is referred to as *Walras' Law.* The implication of this law is that any two of these markets can be used in the analysis, and the third can be dropped. Caution must be exercised in this regard, however, because the money and bond markets have some special interconnections: An increase in the supply of money constitutes an increase in the demand for bonds, and an increase in the supply of bonds implies an increase in the demand for money. We leave it to the reader to add the bond market and to verify that the analysis is not affected by selecting any two markets. (We suggest that both the demand and supply of bonds be made appropriate functions of r and Y, and that the supply of money and the exogenous component of the supply of bonds be incorporated into the demand for bonds and money, respectively.)

From this discussion, it follows that we may classify the variables in the structural equations (1.9) as

Endogenous: C, I, Y_d, Y, T, M^*, r

Exogenous: $\underbrace{\alpha_1, \alpha_2, \alpha_3}_{\text{Uncontrolled}}$ $\underbrace{\bar{M}, \bar{T}, t, \bar{G}}_{\text{Policy Instruments}}$

Notice that the model has as many equations as endogenous variables. The behavior of $C, I, Y_d, T,$ and M^* are explained by their respective equations; simultaneously, the values of Y and r are determined by the equilibrium conditions.

The model can be simplified by substituting all equations in the product and money markets into their respective equilibrium conditions, and eliminating T and Y_d. The result of these substitutions is

(1.10) $Y = C[(1 - t)Y - \bar{T}, \alpha_1] + I(Y, r, \alpha_2) + \bar{G}$

$\bar{M} = M(r, Y, \alpha_3)$

Observe that all endogenous variables except Y and r have been eliminated by these substitutions.

The reduced form is (to repeat) the endogenous variables expressed as functions of *all* the exogenous variables, which for (1.10) may be written as

$$(1.11) \qquad Y = Y(\alpha_1, \alpha_2, \alpha_3, \bar{M}, \bar{T}, t, \bar{G})$$
$$r = r(\alpha_1, \alpha_2, \alpha_3, \bar{M}, \bar{T}, t, \bar{G})$$

The reduced form of the full structural system (1.9) would be (1.11) and the other endogenous variables as functions of the same exogenous variables.† Examination of the partial derivatives in (1.11) is a major objective of comparative static analysis. These partial derivatives are the reduced form derivatives, or multipliers. For example $\partial Y/\partial G$ is called the government expenditure multiplier on Y, $\partial Y/\partial M$ the money multiplier on Y, and so on.

If (1.10) is linear, then we can usually solve for Y and r explicitly. Writing (1.10) in linear form, we have

$$Y = a_{11}[(1-t)Y - \bar{T}] + a_{12}\alpha_1 + a_{13}Y + a_{14}r + a_{15}\alpha_2 + \bar{G}$$
$$\bar{M} = a_{21}r + a_{22}Y + a_{23}\alpha_3$$

where $0 < a_{11} < 1, a_{13} > 0, a_{14} < 0, 0 < t < 1, a_{21} < 0, a_{22} > 0$, which in matrix form is

$$(1.12) \qquad \begin{bmatrix} 1 - a_{11}(1-t) - a_{13} & -a_{14} \\ a_{22} & a_{21} \end{bmatrix} \begin{bmatrix} Y \\ r \end{bmatrix} = \begin{bmatrix} -a_{11}\bar{T} + a_{12}\alpha_1 + \bar{G} + a_{15}\alpha_2 \\ \bar{M} - a_{23}\alpha_3 \end{bmatrix}$$

If the 2×2 matrix on the left, the Jacobian matrix, is nonsingular, we can solve (1.12) for (Y, r) and obtain the reduced form, and from that any reduced form derivative desired.

Suppose that we take the more general case, where (1.10) is allowed to be nonlinear. Then, although the implicit function theorem may guarantee the existence of (1.11), we may not (as we stressed in section 1.1) know how to go about obtaining explicit solutions for Y and r. In that case, we substitute (1.11) into (1.10) and express the result in implicit form, just as we substituted (1.4) into (1.2) in the case of the general model in section 1.1. This gives [deleting the arguments in (1.11)]

$$(1.13) \qquad Y(\ ) - C[(1-t)Y(\ ) - \bar{T}, \alpha_1] - I[Y(\ ), r(\ ), \alpha_2] - \bar{G} = 0$$
$$\bar{M} - M[r(\ ), Y(\ ), \alpha_3] = 0$$

†The remaining five reduced form expressions (C, I, Y_d, M, T) can be obtained simply by substituting (1.11) into the appropriate structural equations in (1.9).

If we know that these equations are identically zero in some neighborhood of the initial assumed values of the exogenous variables, and if we know that both (1.10) and (1.11) possess derivatives, we can differentiate (1.13) with respect to any exogenous variable, and set the derivative of each equation equal to zero. Suppose we differentiate (1.13) with respect to α_2. This gives, assuming the chain rule can be applied,

$$\frac{\partial Y}{\partial \alpha_2} - C_{Y_d}(1 - t)\frac{\partial Y}{\partial \alpha_2} - I_Y \frac{\partial Y}{\partial \alpha_2} - I_r \frac{\partial r}{\partial \alpha_2} - I_{\alpha_2} = 0$$

$$-M_r \frac{\partial r}{\partial \alpha_2} - M_Y \frac{\partial Y}{\partial \alpha_2} = 0$$

and in matrix form

(1.14)
$$\begin{bmatrix} 1 - C_{Y_d}(1 - t) - I_Y & -I_r \\ M_Y & M_r \end{bmatrix} \begin{bmatrix} \dfrac{\partial Y}{\partial \alpha_2} \\ \dfrac{\partial r}{\partial \alpha_2} \end{bmatrix} = \begin{bmatrix} I_{\alpha_2} \\ 0 \end{bmatrix}$$

We can solve for $(\partial Y/\partial \alpha_2, \partial r/\partial \alpha_2)$ if the Jacobian matrix in (1.14) is nonsingular, but, as we already pointed out, the nonsingularity of this matrix is one of the assumptions of the implicit function theorem. Notice once again that while *we may not actually be able to solve explicitly for Y and r, even knowing that such functions exist, we can, if the implicit function theorem is satisfied, solve for the reduced form derivatives.* The reader is encouraged to compute the analogue of (1.14) for other exogenous variables to verify that the Jacobian matrix is always the same matrix for this model.

1.3 A STANDARD FORMAT FOR ANALYZING STATIC MODELS

It is convenient to express the structural equations of *any* static model in a standard mathematical form. Consider (1.2) and (1.3) and the implicit form of (1.10), repeated here for convenience.

(1.2)
$$D - D(P, P_C, P_S, Y, X) = 0$$
$$S - S(P, P_f, Z) = 0$$
$$D - S = 0$$

(1.3)
$$D(P, P_C, P_S, Y, X) - S(P, P_f, Z) = 0$$

where (D, S, P) are endogenous and (P_C, P_S, Y, X, P_f, Z) are exogenous.

(1.10) $Y - C[(1 - t)Y - \bar{T}, \alpha_1] - I(Y, r, \alpha_2) - \bar{G} = 0$

$$\bar{M} - M(r, Y, \alpha_3) = 0$$

where (Y, r) are endogenous and $(\alpha_1, \alpha_2, \alpha_3, \bar{G}, \bar{M}, \bar{T}, t)$ are exogenous.
We can write these three structural equation sets, respectively, as

(1.15) $f^1(D, S, P; P_C, P_S, Y, X) = 0$

$$f^2(S, P; P_f, Z) = 0$$

$$f^3(D, S) = 0$$

(1.16) $f(P; P_C, P_S, Y, X, P_f, Z) = 0$

(1.17) $f^1(Y, r; \alpha_1, \alpha_2, t, \bar{T}, \bar{G}) = 0$

$$f^2(Y, r; \alpha_3, \bar{M}) = 0$$

where the semicolons separate the endogenous from the exogenous variables.

Consider next any static model.[†] Suppose the model has n endogenous variables $(x_1, x_2, \cdots, x_n)$ and s exogenous variables $(\alpha_1, \alpha_2, \cdots, \alpha_s)$. Assume also that we have as many equations as endogenous variables, as we did, by assumption, in the two illustrative models. We may then write the structural equations in the following way.

(1.18) $f^1(x_1, x_2, \ldots, x_n; \alpha_1, \alpha_2, \ldots, \alpha_s) = 0$

$$f^2(x_1, x_2, \ldots, x_n; \alpha_1, \alpha_2, \ldots, \alpha_s) = 0$$

$$\vdots \qquad\qquad\qquad\qquad \vdots$$

$$f^n(x_1, x_2, \ldots, x_n; \alpha_1, \alpha_2, \ldots, \alpha_s) = 0$$

We have included all endogenous and all exogenous variables in every equation. This does not mean that we assume that all variables belong to each equation. It is just a notational convenience, for if a variable really does not belong in an equation, then the partial derivative of that equation with respect to that variable is simply zero. (For example, if we know that x_2 does not belong in f^1 and that α_4 does not belong in f^5, then we know that $f^1_{x_2} = f^5_{\alpha_4} = 0$.)

The structural system (1.18) can also be written in the compact form

$$f(x; \alpha) = 0$$

where[‡] f is the vector function $(f^1, f^2, \ldots, f^n)$ and

†See P.A. Samuelson [47, chap. 2].
‡It is obvious from the context whether a vector is a column or row vector, so we shall not distinguish.

$$x = (x_1, \ldots, x_n)$$
$$\alpha = (\alpha_1, \ldots, \alpha_s)$$
$$0 = (0, \ldots, 0)$$

The Jacobian matrix of the functions f with respect to x is defined as

$$J_f(x) \equiv \begin{bmatrix} f^1_{x_1} & f^1_{x_2} & \cdots & f^1_{x_n} \\ f^2_{x_1} & f^2_{x_2} & & \\ \vdots & \vdots & & \vdots \\ f^n_{x_1} & f^n_{x_2} & \cdots & f^n_{x_n} \end{bmatrix}$$

The symbol for the Jacobian matrix is also sometimes written as $\partial(f^1, \ldots, f^n)/\partial(x_1, \ldots, x_n)$. The Jacobian is defined as the determinant of this matrix. To write the determinant we shall use $|J|$ or $|J_f(x)|$.

The reduced form of (1.18) can be written as

(1.19)
$$x_1 = \phi^1(\alpha_1, \ldots, \alpha_s)$$
$$\vdots \qquad \vdots$$
$$x_n = \phi^n(\alpha_1, \ldots, \alpha_s)$$

or $\qquad x = \phi(\alpha)$

where $\qquad \phi = (\phi^1, \ldots, \phi^n)$

Now, suppose we are assured that the reduced form exists, although, as we have emphasized, we may not know how to go about actually getting it. As we did in the above examples, we may substitute (1.19) into (1.18) yielding

$$f^1(\phi^1, \phi^2, \ldots, \phi^n; \alpha_1, \ldots, \alpha_s) = 0$$
$$\vdots \qquad\qquad\qquad \vdots$$
(1.20)
$$f^n(\phi^1, \phi^2, \ldots, \phi^n; \alpha_1, \ldots, \alpha_s) = 0$$

or $\qquad\qquad f(\phi; \alpha) = 0$

where f is now a vector function only of α, since the functions ϕ^i are functions only of α. We can designate an equilibrium by $f(\phi^0; \alpha^0) = 0$. As we asserted in the examples of the preceding sections, satisfaction of the assumptions of the implicit function theorem provides a guarantee not only that the reduced form exists, but that ϕ^i_j exists, $i = 1, 2, \ldots, n, j = 1, 2, \ldots, s$, and that $f(\phi; \alpha)$ is identically zero for α in some neighborhood of α^0. Assume now that some element of α, say α_k, changes from its initial value of α^0_k, where $1 \leq k \leq s$. If the new α_k is in a required neighborhood of α^0_k, f will stay at zero. (In fact, all the deductions of the implicit function theorem will be *local*, that is, holding *only* in some neighborhood of α^0.) Thus, we may differentiate (1.20) with respect to α_k, if the chain rule can be applied, which is also assured by the implicit function theorem. This gives

$$f^1_{x^0_1}\frac{\partial x_1}{\partial \alpha_k} + f^1_{x^0_2}\frac{\partial x_2}{\partial \alpha_k} + \cdots + f^1_{x^0_n}\frac{\partial x_n}{\partial \alpha_k} + f^1_{\alpha\ell} = 0$$

$$f^2_{x^0_1}\frac{\partial x_1}{\partial \alpha_k} + f^2_{x^0_2}\frac{\partial x_2}{\partial \alpha_k} + \cdots + f^2_{x^0_n}\frac{\partial x_n}{\partial \alpha_k} + f^2_{\alpha\ell} = 0$$

$$\vdots \qquad\qquad \vdots \qquad\qquad\qquad \vdots \qquad \vdots \qquad \vdots$$

$$f^n_{x^0_1}\frac{\partial x_1}{\partial \alpha_k} + f^n_{x^0_2}\frac{\partial x_2}{\partial \alpha_k} + \cdots + f^n_{x^0_n}\frac{\partial x_n}{\partial \alpha_k} + f^n_{\alpha\ell} = 0$$

or in matrix form

(1.21)

$$\begin{bmatrix} f^1_{x^0_1} & f^1_{x^0_2} & \cdots & f^1_{x^0_n} \\ f^2_{x^0_1} & & & \\ \vdots & \vdots & \vdots & \vdots \\ f^n_{x^0_1} & f^n_{x^0_2} & \cdots & f^n_{x^0_n} \end{bmatrix} \begin{bmatrix} \dfrac{\partial x_1}{\partial \alpha_k} \\ \dfrac{\partial x_2}{\partial \alpha_k} \\ \vdots \\ \dfrac{\partial x_n}{\partial \alpha_k} \end{bmatrix} = \begin{bmatrix} -f^1_{\alpha\ell} \\ -f^2_{\alpha\ell} \\ \vdots \\ -f^n_{\alpha\ell} \end{bmatrix}$$

where the superscript zero means that the partial derivatives are evaluated at the initial equilibrium (x^0, α^0). In more compact form,

$$J_f(x^0)\frac{\partial x}{\partial \alpha_k} = -f_{\alpha\ell}, \qquad 1 \le k \le s$$

where $J_f(x^0)$ is the Jacobian matrix of f evaluated at x^0, and where

$$\frac{\partial x}{\partial \alpha_k} \equiv \left(\frac{\partial x_1}{\partial \alpha_k}, \ldots, \frac{\partial x_n}{\partial \alpha_k}\right) \quad \text{and} \quad f_{\alpha\ell} \equiv (f^1_{\alpha\ell}, \ldots, f^n_{\alpha\ell})$$

The system (1.21) can be solved for the n-vector $\partial x/\partial \alpha_k$ if $J_f(x^0)$ is nonsingular. We have already stressed that this is one of the assumptions of the implicit function theorem. If the Jacobian matrix is nonsingular it will have an inverse $J_f^{-1}(x^0)$, so we can express the solution of the derivatives of the reduced form in the standard static model as

(1.22) $$\frac{\partial x}{\partial \alpha_k} = -J_f^{-1}(x^0)f_{\alpha\ell} \qquad 1 \le k \le s$$

Remarks. If a model with n endogenous variables contains n equations that are *functionally independent* in the n endogenous variables, we say the model is *complete*. Functional independence means that the Jacobian matrix is nonsingular. The determinant of the Jacobian matrix is sometimes called the functional determinant. We have already asserted that completeness is one of the assumptions required by the implicit function theorem. Thus, there is an intimate connection between the completeness of a model and the local existence of a differentiable reduced form. This point will be explored more fully in section 1.5, where we prove the implicit function theorems.

If a model contains n endogenous variables, it could of course contain $(n + r)$ equations. If the model is complete, then r of the equations will be functionally dependent, since the maximum number of linearly independent vectors in n-space, E^n, is n. The vectors referred to are the rows of the Jacobian. These rows of partial derivatives are called *gradient vectors*. The gradient vector of f^i is written

$$\nabla f^i \equiv (f^i_{x_1}, f^i_{x_2}, \ldots, f^i_{x_n})$$

The symbol ∇f^i is read "del f^i." To indicate that each component of the gradient vector is to be evaluated at x^0, we write $\nabla f^i(x^0)$.

A final point—if the implicit function theorem is satisfied, we then have a guarantee that a differentiable reduced form exists locally and that the procedure from (1.19) to (1.22) can be carried out. The opposite implication does not follow. That is, the ability to carry out the procedure and the local existence of a differentiable reduced form does *not* imply that the hypotheses of the implicit function theorem are satisfied. Thus, we say that the implicit function theorem is a sufficient but not a necessary condition for knowing that a locally differentiable reduced form of a static model exists.

1.4 SOME MATHEMATICAL PRELIMINARIES

Before proving the implicit function theorems, we shall need some mathematical background.†

We say that a real-valued function $z = f(x, y)$ is *differentiable* at a point (x^0, y^0) if f can be approximated in the neighborhood of (x^0, y^0) by a linear function, That is, if

(1.23) $f(x^0 + h, y^0 + k) = f(x^0, y^0) + Ah + Bk + \epsilon_1 h + \epsilon_2 k$

†The material in this and the following section was developed from Courant [13], Goursat and Hedrick [20], Apostol [4], and Protter and Morrey [46].

where A and B are independent of the variables h and k, and ϵ_1 and ϵ_2 go to zero as h and k go to zero. In other words, as h and k go to zero, $f(x^0 + h, y^0 + k)$ converges to the linear function $f(x^0, y^0) + Ah + Bk$. Thus, at the point $(x^0 + h, y^0 + k)$ it is possible to represent $f(x^0 + h, y^0 + k)$ approximately by $f(x^0, y^0) + Ah + Bk$.

If we assume that f can be approximated this way, it follows immediately that $\partial f/\partial x$ and $\partial f/\partial y$ exist at (x^0, y^0) and further that $\partial f/\partial x = A, \partial f/\partial y = B$ at $x = x^0, y = y^0$. To see this, set $k = 0$ and write (1.23) as

$$\frac{f(x^0 + h, y^0) - f(x^0, y^0)}{h} = A + \epsilon_1$$

Since ϵ_1 goes to zero with h and A is independent of h, the left side has a limit as $h \to 0$ and that limit is A. Thus, since the limit of the left side is, by definition, $\partial f/\partial x$, we see that $\partial f/\partial x = A$ at (x^0, y^0). The same argument applies to $\partial f/\partial y$ and B. Hence, if a function is differentiable its partial derivatives exist.

Assuming that f is differentiable at (x^0, y^0), we can rewrite (1.23) as

$$f(x^0 + h, y^0 + k) - f(x^0, y^0) \simeq \frac{\partial f(x^0, y^0)}{\partial x} h + \frac{\partial f(x^0, y^0)}{\partial y} k$$

(where $\simeq$ means is approximately equal to)

The left side of this expression is called the *increment* of the function and is denoted as Δz. The right side is the linear part of that increment. We call this linear part the *differential* (or the *total differential*) of the function and write it as dz or df. Thus

$$dz = \frac{\partial f(x^0, y^0)}{\partial x} h + \frac{\partial f(x^0, y^0)k}{\partial y}$$

and if we let the increments $h = dx$ and $k = dy$, which are said to be the differentials of the independent variables, we have as the expression for the differential of f evaluated at (x^0, y^0)

(1.24)
$$dz = \frac{\partial f(x^0, y^0)}{\partial x} dx + \frac{\partial f(x^0, y^0)}{\partial y} dy, \quad \text{or}$$

$$dz = f_x(x^0, y^0) \, dx + f_y(x^0, y^0) \, dy$$

The same argument can be extended to functions of n variables.

The differential is an approximation to the increment as we have just seen. The *mean value theorem* provides an exact relationship between the increment and the partial derivatives f_x and f_y.

THEOREM 1.1   THE MEAN VALUE THEOREM

IF $f(x, y)$ HAS CONTINUOUS FIRST PARTIAL DERIVATIVES, THAN FOR SOME θ BE-
TWEEN ZERO AND ONE

(1.25) $f(x^0 + h, y^0 + k) - f(x^0, y^0)$
$$= f_x(x^0 + \theta h, y^0 + \theta k)h + f_y(x^0 + \theta h, y^0 + \theta k)k$$

We shall prove this theorem in Chapter 2 as a special case of the Taylor
Theorem. Notice that the statement of the theorem implies that f is defined
in a neighborhood of (x^0, y^0), that is, (x^0, y^0) is an *interior point* of the set
over which f is defined. This is true because h and k are not restricted in sign.
Also notice that the derivatives are evaluated somewhere on a *line segment*
joining (x^0, y^0) and $(x^0 + h, y^0 + k)$. Calling these two end points u and v, we
define a line segment as the set of all points satisfying the equation $\theta u +
(1 - \theta)v$ where $0 \leq \theta \leq 1$.† This definition holds for u and v in n-space, E^n.
The extension of the mean value theorem to E^n is obvious.

If a function $f(x, y)$ has continuous first partial derivatives f_x and f_y, we
say that $f(x, y)$ is *continuously differentiable*, or, $f \in C^1$. The definition holds
of course when f is a function of n variables.

THEOREM 1.2

IF $f(x, y) \in C^1$ AT AN INTERIOR POINT OF THE DOMAIN OF f, THEN f IS DIFFER-
ENTIABLE AT THAT POINT.

PROOF:

An interesting point here is that *while differentiability implies the existence of first partial derivatives, the reverse is not necessarily true.* The
theorem says that to guarantee differentiability, we must assume that f
possesses *continuous* first partial derivatives at the point in question.
The proof is a simple consequence of the mean value theorem. Consider
(1.25). The continuity of f_x and f_y means that as $h \to 0, k \to 0, f_x \to
f_x(x^0, y^0)$ and $f_y \to f_y(x^0, y^0)$ with $f_x = f_x(x^0, y^0)$ and $f_y = f_y(x^0, y^0)$ when
$h = k = 0$. Thus we can rewrite (1.25) as

$$f(x^0 + h, y^0 + k) - f(x^0, y^0) = [f_x(x^0, y^0) + \epsilon_1]h + [f_y(x^0, y^0) + \epsilon_2]k$$

where $\epsilon_1 \to 0$ and $\epsilon_2 \to 0$ as $h \to 0$ and $k \to 0$. Clearly, the increment can
be approximated by the linear function on the right, hence f is differenti-
able at (x^0, y^0).

Q.E.D.

†This implies that the domain of f must be *convex*; that is, if u and v belong to the
domain, so must the line segment joining u and v.

THEOREM 1.3

IF $f(x, y)$ IS CONTINUOUS OVER A CLOSED AND BOUNDED SET R, THEN f IS BOUND-
ED ON R AND THERE IS AT LEAST ONE POINT IN R WHERE f TAKES ON A MAXIMUM
VALUE, AND AT LEAST ONE POINT WHERE f TAKES ON A MINIMUM VALUE.† THE MAXI-
MUM OR MINIMUM MAY OCCUR ON THE BOUNDARY OF R. THIS THEOREM IMMEDIATELY
IMPLIES THAT IF $f(x, y) \in C^1$ ON R, THEN f_x AND f_y ARE BOUNDED ON R.

THEOREM 1.4

IF $f(x, y)$ HAS BOUNDED PARTIAL DERIVATIVES IN A CONVEX SET R, THEN f IS
CONTINUOUS EVERYWHERE IN R.

PROOF:

The proof follows immediately from the mean value theorem. Consider
(1.25). Since there exists a positive number M which exceeds the absolute
values of the partial derivatives on the right, we can deduce that

$$|f(x^0 + h, y^0 + k) - f(x^0, y^0)| \leq M(|h| + |k|)$$

Since it is clearly possible to make the left side as small as desired by
choosing sufficiently small values of h and k, the continuity of $f(x, y)$ at
(x^0, y^0) is proved.

Q.E.D.

THEOREM 1.5   THE CHAIN RULE

SUPPOSE THAT $z = f(x, y)$ IS A DIFFERENTIABLE FUNCTION, AND $x = x(r, s)$ AND
$y = y(r, s)$ ARE ALSO DIFFERENTIABLE FUNCTIONS. THEN, THE COMPOSITE (OR COM-
POUND) FUNCTION

$$z = f[x(r, s), y(r, s)] = F(r, s)$$

IS ALSO A DIFFERENTIABLE FUNCTION OF r AND s, AND ITS PARTIAL DERIVATIVES ARE
GIVEN BY

$$\frac{\partial z}{\partial r} = \frac{\partial f}{\partial x}\frac{\partial x}{\partial r} + \frac{\partial f}{\partial y}\frac{\partial y}{\partial r} = f_x x_r + f_y y_r$$

$$\frac{\partial z}{\partial s} = \frac{\partial f}{\partial x}\frac{\partial x}{\partial s} + \frac{\partial f}{\partial y}\frac{\partial y}{\partial s} = f_x x_s + f_y y_s$$

†This is a straightforward extension of the extreme value theorem for functions of
one variable, the proof of which is simple but lengthy. See Apostol [4, Chap. 8, Section 8].

PROOF:

To establish that the composite function F is differentiable, write the increment of the differentiable functions x and y, letting the increments of the independent variables be denoted by Δr and Δs. This gives

$$(1.26) \qquad \Delta x = x_r \Delta r + x_s \Delta s + \epsilon_1 \Delta r + \epsilon_2 \Delta s$$
$$\Delta y = y_r \Delta r + y_s \Delta s + \delta_1 \Delta r + \delta_2 \Delta s$$

where

$$\epsilon_1 \text{ and } \delta_1 \to 0 \text{ as } \Delta r \to 0$$
$$\epsilon_2 \text{ and } \delta_2 \to 0 \text{ as } \Delta s \to 0$$

Now if the quantities x and y undergo changes Δx and Δy, the function $z = f(x, y)$ is subject to an increment of the form

$$\Delta z = f_x \Delta x + f_y \Delta y + \gamma_1 \Delta x + \gamma_2 \Delta y$$

where

$$\gamma_1 \to 0 \text{ as } \Delta x \to 0$$
$$\gamma_2 \to 0 \text{ as } \Delta y \to 0$$

Substituting (1.26) into the last expression gives

$$(1.27) \qquad \Delta z = (f_x x_r + f_y y_r)\Delta r + (f_x x_s + f_y y_s)\Delta s + \epsilon \Delta s + \delta \Delta r$$

where

$$\delta = (f_x + \gamma_1)\epsilon_1 + (f_y + \gamma_2)\delta_1 + \gamma_1 x_r + \gamma_2 y_r$$
$$\epsilon = (f_x + \gamma_1)\epsilon_2 + (f_y + \gamma_2)\delta_2 + \gamma_1 x_s + \gamma_2 y_s$$

Clearly, $\delta \to 0$ and $\epsilon \to 0$ as $\Delta r \to 0$ and $\Delta s \to 0$. Therefore, the composite function is differentiable. Using (1.27), we may also establish the chain rule. Setting $\Delta s = 0$, dividing by Δr, and taking the limit as $\Delta r \to 0$ gives the formula for $\partial z / \partial r$. The expression for $\partial z / \partial s$ is found analogously. The results is easily extended to more variables.†

Q.E.D.

We next prove that a compound function is continuous if it is made up of continuous functions.

†The chain rule is also valid if f is differentiable and the functions x and y possess first derivatives at the point in question.

THEOREM 1.6

IF THE FUNCTION $z = f(x, y)$ IS CONTINUOUS IN THE SET S, AND THE FUNCTIONS $x = x(r, s)$ AND $y = y(r, s)$ ARE CONTINUOUS IN THE SET R, THEN THE COMPOSITE FUNCTION $z = f[x(r, s), y(r, s)]$ IS CONTINUOUS IN R.

PROOF:

Let (r^0, s^0) be an interior point in R, and let y^0 and x^0 be the corresponding values of y and x. Then, for any $\epsilon > 0$

$$|f(x, y) - f(x^0, y^0)| < \epsilon$$

provided that

$$|x - x^0| < \delta, |y - y^0| < \delta$$

is satisfied, where δ is a sufficiently small positive number depending on ϵ. But, by the continuity of the functions x and y, the last inequalities are satisfied for any $\delta > 0$ if

$$|r - r^0| < \gamma, |s - s^0| < \gamma$$

where $\gamma > 0$ depends on δ.

Q.E.D.

THEOREM 1.7 THEOREM OF BOLZANO

SUPPOSE THAT $f(x)$ IS CONTINUOUS AT EVERY POINT ON SOME CLOSED INTERVAL $[a, b]$ AND THAT $f(a)$ AND $f(b)$ HAVE OPPOSITE SIGNS. THEN THERE IS AT LAST ONE POINT c IN THE OPEN INTERVAL (a, b) SUCH THAT $f(c) = 0$.

PROOF:

Suppose that $f(a) < 0$ and $f(b) > 0$. We then find the largest x (there may of course be many) for which $f(x) = 0$. Let R be the set of all points in (a, b) such that $f(x) \leq 0$. Since f is continuous and $f(a) < 0$ by assumption, it follows from the definition of continuity that R cannot be empty. Also, R is bounded above since, by assumption $R \subset [a, b]$. By the least-upper-bound axiom for the real number system, every nonempty bounded set of real numbers possesses a least upper bound, that is, the smallest of these numbers which are at least as large as any number in the set. Let c be that number. Then, $c \geq x$ for all $x \in R$. We shall demonstrate that if c is the least upper bound of R, then $f(c) = 0$. We do this by showing that $f(c)$ cannot be positive or negative.

Suppose $f(c) > 0$. Then, by the continuity of f, there exists an interval $(c - \delta, c + \delta)$ around c such that $f(x) > 0$ for all x in this interval. Clearly

$c - \delta$ is an upper bound of R, which contradicts the assumption that c is a *least* upper bound.

Suppose $f(c) < 0$. Then, by the continuity of f, there exists an interval $(c - \delta, c + \delta)$ such that $f(x) < 0$ for all x in this interval. Thus $(c + \delta) \in R$, which contradicts the assumption that c is an upper bound.

The argument is similar for $f(a) > 0$ and $f(b) < 0$.

Q.E.D.

By a simple extension of the theorem of Bolzano we obtain the intermediate value theorem.

THEOREM 1.8   INTERMEDIATE VALUE THEOREM

LET f BE A CONTINUOUS FUNCTION ON THE CLOSED INTERVAL $[a, b]$. CONSIDER ANY TWO POINTS x_1 AND x_2 IN $[a, b]$. SUPPOSE $x_1 < x_2$ AND $f(x_1) \neq f(x_2)$. THEN f TAKES ON EVERY VALUE BETWEEN $f(x_1)$ AND $f(x_2)$ SOMEWHERE IN $[x_1, x_2]$.

PROOF:

For definiteness let $f(x_1) < f(x_2)$ and let k be *any* number such that $f(x_1) < k < f(x_2)$. Next, define a function g on $[x_1, x_2]$ such that

$$g(x) = f(x) - k$$

Thus, $g(x_1) < 0$, $g(x_2) > 0$, and since g is continuous on $[x_1, x_2]$ we can apply Bolzano's theorem, which says that there exists a number c in the open interval (x_1, x_2) such that $g(c) = 0$, which by definition of g says that $f(c) = k$.

Q.E.D.

1.5   IMPLICIT FUNCTION THEOREMS

Consider a specific relation in the form

(1.28) $F(x, y) = 0$

A set of points which satisfy (1.28) is called a locus of the equation. We are interested in determining under what conditions this equation gives y as a function of x or x as a function of y.

EXAMPLE:

$F(x, y) = x^2 + 3xy + 5y - 2x - 8 = 0$,   hence $y = (8 + 2x - x^2)/(3x + 5)$ and y is expressed as a function of x.

However, even in cases where the algebra can be performed, a function may not be obtainable. For example, $9x^2 + 4y^2 - 36 = 0$ may be solved for y to give $y = \pm 3/2\sqrt{4 - x^2}$ and y is clearly not represented as a function of x.

A relation of the form $F(x, y) = 0$ may have a complicated locus, such as the one in Figure 1-1. Consider the point Q where the slope of the locus is positive in a small neighborhood of the point. In a small neighborhood of Q we can see that y is a function of x and x is a function of y. But if we make

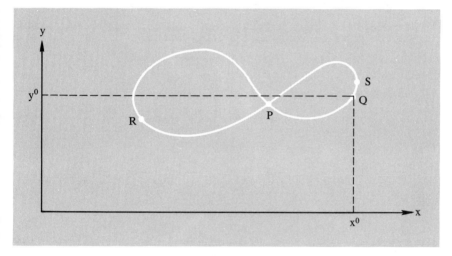

Fig. 1-1

the neighborhood too large, the statement becomes false. Consider the point S. In a small neighborhood, x is a function of y but y is not a function of x, because given values of x can be seen to correspond to more than one value of y. The point P shows the locus intersecting itself, thus neither x nor y can be expressed as functions of each other. In a small neighborhood of the point R, x can be expressed as a function of y and vice versa.

Consider the point $Q(x^0, y^0)$ in the relation $F(x, y) = 0$ represented in Figure 1-1. Suppose that in a very small neighborhood of x^0 we represent y as a function of x.

(1.29) $$y = f(x)$$

If we substitute (1.29) into (1.28) we have

(1.30) $$F[x, f(x)] = 0$$

which is an identity in the postulated neighborhood. Thus, if the chain rule applies, we get

(1.31) $$F_x + F_y f'(x) = 0, \qquad f' \equiv \frac{df}{dx}$$

and if $F_y \neq 0$ we obtain

(1.32) $$f'(x) = -\frac{F_x}{F_y}$$

The first implicit function theorem may thus be described as one which states the conditions under which (1.28) may be put into the form (1.29) in some neighborhood of x^0, and which states the conditions under which the formulae in (1.31) and (1.32) are valid.

We now prove the first implicit function theorem.

THEOREM 1.9

ASSUME THE FUNCTION $F(x, y) \in C^1$ ON A REGION AND SUPPOSE THAT

$$F(x^0, y^0) = 0, F_y(x^0, y^0) \neq 0$$

THEN THERE EXISTS A NEIGHBORHOOD R OF x^0 AND ONE AND ONLY ONE f SUCH THAT, LETTING $y = f(x), x \in R$,

(a) $y^0 = f(x^0)$. IN ADDITION, FOR EACH x IN R THERE EXISTS A UNIQUE y WHICH SATISFIES $F(x, y) = 0$. THUS, $F[x, f(x)] \equiv 0$ ON R.

(b) THE FUNCTION f IS CONTINUOUSLY DIFFERENTIABLE FOR ALL $x \in R$.

PROOF:

(a). For definiteness, assume that $F_y(x^0, y^0) > 0$. By definition of a continuous function, if $F_y(x^0, y^0) > 0$, there must be some neighborhood of (x^0, y^0) within which $F_y(x, y) > 0$. This neighborhood may be very small, but if F_y is continuous there must be such a neighborhood. Call it S and think of it as a rectangle with (x^0, y^0) in the middle. It follows that if we fix x at any point in S, $F(x, y)$ is an increasing function of y in S. Since by assumption $F(x^0, y^0) = 0$, we see that

$$F(x^0, y^0 + k) > 0, F(x^0, y^0 - k) < 0 \quad \text{for} \quad y^0 \pm k \in S, k > 0.$$

From Theorems 1.3 and 1.4 we know that a continuously differentiable function is continuous. Thus, $F(x, y)$ is continuous in S. Therefore, for fixed values of x in some neighborhood of x^0, say $|x - x^0| < h$, it follows that

$$F(x, y^0 + k) > 0, F(x, y^0 - k) < 0$$

According to the Bolzano theorem, $F(x, y)$ must assume the value zero for some y between $y^0 + k$ and $y^0 - k$, for each x in the prescribed neighborhood. And since $F_y > 0$, there can only be one such value of y for each x. We have thus established the existence of the unique function $y = f(x)$ for $|x - x^0| < h$. Call this interval R and notice that it must lie in the rectangle S. And since for each $x \in R$ the function f determines a y which sets $F(x, y) = 0$, we may write

$$F[x, f(x)] \equiv 0 \quad \text{for all} \quad x \in R$$

(b). Next, we must prove that f is a continuous function at x^0, that is, for any $\epsilon > 0$ there exists a δ, which depends on ϵ, such that

$$|f(x) - f(x^0)| < \epsilon \quad \text{when} \quad |x - x^0| < \delta$$

The values of $f(x)$ in the proof have been restricted by the values of k. Selecting any $k^1 < k$ and going through the existence proof once again, we will obtain the same function f defined on another (perhaps smaller) interval $|x - x^0| < h^1$. Since k^1 can be any number, let it be ϵ in the definition of continuity; letting $h^1 = \delta$ we have shown that f is continuous at x^0. By repetition of this argument, f can be shown to be continuous for all $x \in R$.

Since $F \in C^1$ in R by assumption, F is differentiable at (x^0, y^0) by Theorem 1.2. Writting $\Delta f = f(x^0 + \Delta x) - f(x^0)$, we have

$$0 = F[x^0 + \Delta x, f(x^0 + \Delta x)] - F[x^0, f(x^0)]$$
$$= F_x(x^0, y^0)\Delta x + F_y(x^0, y^0)\Delta f + \epsilon_1 \Delta x + \epsilon_2 \Delta f$$

and

$$\frac{\Delta f}{\Delta x} = -\frac{F_x + \epsilon_1}{F_y + \epsilon_2} \quad \text{at} \quad (x^0, y^0)$$

Since f is continuous at x^0, Δf goes to zero as Δx does. Since F is differentiable at (x^0, y^0), ϵ_1 and $\epsilon_2 \to 0$ as Δx and $\Delta f \to 0$. Thus, as $\Delta x \to 0$ the left side goes to $f'(x^0)$ and the right side to $-F_x/F_y$. Therefore, $f'(x^0)$ exists, and furthermore it is continuous at x^0 because F_x and F_y are continuous by assumption. The same argument demonstrates that $f \in C^1$ for all $x \in R$.

Q.E.D.

A few points about the theorem should be emphasized.
Using Figure 1–1, the theorem deduces certain things about $F(x, y) = 0$ only for a small portion of its locus, for example, only for that part of its locus inside of a rectangle about Q. The rectangle can be arbitrarily small but if it is too large the theorem may not hold.

There is nothing in the theorem that determines low big this rectangle can be, in other words, how far the domain of f can be extended.

This is a pure existence theorem, in that it tells us when f exists but it does not provide us with any method for finding the particular function f. With obvious modifications, these points apply to all implicit function theorems

The first implicit function theorem can be extended with no difficulty to any number of variables. The proof is not affected in any significant way. The reader should reread the theorem and proof simply assuming that x is an n-vector and thus, for example, $F_x \equiv (F_{x_1}, F_{x_2}, \cdots, F_{x_n})$. The variable $y \equiv x_1$ would then be implicitly defined as $y = f(x_2, x_3, \cdots, x_n)$.

Next, we prove an implicit function theorem for a system of two equations in four unknowns.

THEOREM 1.10

SUPPOSE THAT

$$f^i(x_1, x_2, \alpha_1, \alpha_2) \in C^1, f^i(x_1^0, x_2^0, \alpha_1^0, \alpha_2^0) = 0, i = 1, 2$$

AND THAT

$$|J_f(x^0)| \equiv \begin{vmatrix} f^1_{x_1} & f^1_{x_2} \\ f^2_{x_1} & f^2_{x_2} \end{vmatrix} \neq 0$$

THEN THERE EXISTS A NEIGHBORHOOD R OF (α_1^0, α_2^0) AND ONE AND ONLY ONE PAIR OF FUNCTIONS ϕ^1 AND ϕ^2 DEFINED ON R SUCH THAT, LETTING $x_1 = \phi^1(\alpha_1, \alpha_2)$ AND $x_2 = \phi^2(\alpha_1, \alpha_2)$

(i) $x_i^0 = \phi^i(\alpha_1^0, \alpha_2^0)$ $i = 1, 2$

(ii) $f^i(\phi^1, \phi^2, \alpha_1, \alpha_2) \equiv 0$ ALL (α_1, α_2) IN R $i = 1, 2$

(iii) ϕ^1 AND ϕ^2 ARE CONTINUOUSLY DIFFERENTIABLE ON R

Notice that for each $(\alpha_1, \alpha_2) \in R$, there is a unique solution for x_1 and x_2 of the equations $f^i(x_1, x_2, \alpha_1, \alpha_2) = 0$. We define this solution as the functional relations $\phi^1(\alpha_1, \alpha_2)$ and $\phi^2(\alpha_1, \alpha_2)$.

PROOF:

Since $|J_f(x^0)| \neq 0$, it follows that $f^1_{x_1}$ and $f^2_{x_1}$ cannot both be zero.

Suppose that $f^1_{x_1} \neq 0$. From a simple extension of the previous theorem there exists a neighborhood S of $(x_2^0, \alpha_1^0, \alpha_2^0)$ and one and only one function H on S, given by $x_1 = H(x_2, \alpha_1, \alpha_2)$, such that

(iv) $$x_1^0 = H(x_2^0, \alpha_1^0, \alpha_2^0)$$

(v) $$f^1(H, x_2, \alpha_1, \alpha_2) \equiv 0 \quad \text{on} \quad S$$

(vi) $$H \in C^1 \quad \text{on} \quad S$$

Substituting the function H into f^2, we may define

$$K(x_2, \alpha_1, \alpha_2) \equiv f^2(H, x_2, \alpha_1, \alpha_2)$$

where K is defined on the same S that H is. By Theorems 1.2 and 1.5, the chain rule can be used to differentiate K with respect to x_2, since both f^2 and H are differentiable. This gives, using (v),

$$K_{x_2} = f_{x_1}^2 H_{x_2} + f_{x_2}^2$$

$$= f_{x_1}^2 \left(-\frac{f_{x_2}^1}{f_{x_1}^1} \right) + f_{x_2}^2 = \frac{f_{x_1}^1 f_{x_2}^2 - f_{x_1}^2 f_{x_2}^1}{f_{x_1}^1}$$

Evaluating K_{x_2} at $(x_2^0, \alpha_1^0, \alpha_2^0)$ we have that

$$K_{x_2}(x_2^0, \alpha_1^0, \alpha_2^0) = \frac{|J_f(x^0)|}{f_{x_1^0}^1}$$

which by assumption is not zero.

With this last result we can apply a simple extension of the first implicit function theorem to $K(x_2, \alpha_1, \alpha_2)$, since we also know that $K \in C^1$ and that $K(x_2^0, \alpha_1^0, \alpha_2^0) = 0$. This tells us that there exists a neighborhood R of (α_1^0, α_2^0) and one and only one function ϕ^2, given by $x_2 = \phi^2(\alpha_1, \alpha_2)$ on R, such that

(vii) $$x_2^0 = \phi^2(\alpha_1^0, \alpha_2^0)$$

(viii) $$K(\phi^2, \alpha_1, \alpha_2) \equiv 0 \text{ on } R$$

(ix) $$\phi^2 \in C^1 \text{ on } R$$

(Obviously $R \subset S$, since K is only defined on S.)

Now substitute ϕ^2 into $H(x_2, \alpha_1, \alpha_2)$ and $f^1(H, x_2, \alpha_1, \alpha_2) = 0$ and notice that (iv), (v), and (vi) remain true on R with this substitution. In the case of H, this gives

$$x_1 = H(\phi^2, \alpha_1, \alpha_2) \text{ on } R$$

which we may rewrite as

$$x_1 = \phi^1(\alpha_1, \alpha_2) \text{ on } R$$

It is easy to see that the theorem is established. For, recalling the definition of K as f^2 on R, conditions (vii), (viii), and (ix) are identical with (i), (ii), and (iii), for $i = 2$. And, replacing H in (iv), (v) and (vi) with ϕ^1 on R, and x_2 in (v) with ϕ^2 on R, we see that (i), (ii), and (iii) are satisfied for $i = 1$, being identical to (iv), (v), and (vi).

The proof is similar when $f^1_{x_1^0} = 0$, but $f^2_{x_1^0} \neq 0$.

Q.E.D.

We next extend these implicit function theorems to any number of variables and equations, as long as the number of equations is strictly less than the number of variables. The following theorem states the result in full generality.

THEOREM 1.11   THE IMPLICIT FUNCTION THEOREM: GENERAL CASE

SUPPOSE THAT

$$f^i(x_1, \ldots, x_n, \alpha_1, \ldots, \alpha_s), i = 1, \ldots, n$$

ARE CONTINUOUSLY DIFFERENTIABLE AT A POINT $(x^0, \alpha^0) = (x_1^0, \ldots, x_n^0, \alpha_1^0, \ldots, \alpha_s^0)$. ALSO ASSUME THAT THE VECTOR-VALUED FUNCTION $f(x^0, \alpha^0) = 0$ WHERE $f = (f^1, f^2, \ldots, f^n)$ AND THAT

$$|J_f(x^0)| \equiv \begin{vmatrix} f^1_{x_1^0} & f^1_{x_2^0} & \cdots & f^1_{x_n^0} \\ f^2_{x_1^0} & f^2_{x_2^0} & \cdots & f^2_{x_n^0} \\ \vdots & \vdots & & \vdots \\ f^n_{x_1^0} & f^n_{x_2^0} & \cdots & f^n_{x_n^0} \end{vmatrix} \neq 0$$

THEN THERE EXISTS A NEIGHBORHOOD R OF $(\alpha_1^0, \alpha_2^0, \cdots, \alpha_s^0)$ AND ONE AND ONLY ONE VECTOR-VALUED FUNCTION $\phi = (\phi^1, \cdots, \phi^s)$ DEFINED ON R, LETTING $x = \phi(\alpha)$, SUCH THAT

(i) $x^0 = \phi(\alpha^0)$, THAT IS

$$x_i^0 = \phi^i(\alpha_1^0, \alpha_2^0, \ldots, \alpha_s^0) \quad i = 1, 2, \ldots, n$$

(ii) $f[\phi(\alpha), \alpha] \equiv 0$ ALL $\alpha \in R$

(iii) $\phi \in C^1$ ON R

Notice that for $\alpha \in R$ there is a unique solution of $f(x, \alpha) = 0$. We define this solution as $x = \phi(\alpha)$.

PROOF:

We shall prove the theorem by induction on n, the number of equations.†
That is, we shall assume that the theorem holds for $n - 1$ equations and
will demonstrate that it therefore is valid for n.

By assumption the $n \times n$ Jacobian does not vanish at (x^0, α^0). Thus, at
least one of the $(n - 1)$-dimensional cofactors in the expansion of $|J_f(x^0)|$
does not vanish.‡ Suppose without loss of generality that it is the determinant obtained by deleting the last row and the last column of $J_f(x^0)$.
That is, assume that

$$|J_f(\bar{x}^0)| \equiv \begin{vmatrix} f^1_{x^0_1} & f^1_{x^0_2} & \cdots & f^1_{x^0_{n-1}} \\ \vdots & \vdots & & \vdots \\ f^{n-1}_{x^0_1} & f^{n-1}_{x^0_2} & \cdots & f^{n-1}_{x^0_{n-1}} \end{vmatrix} \neq 0$$

Now, we invoke the induction hypothesis. That is, we assume that
the theorem holds for $(f^1, \ldots, f^{n-1})$. This implies that there exists a
neighborhood S of $(x^0_n, \alpha^0_1, \ldots, \alpha^0_s)$ and one and only one vector-valued
function $H = (H^1, \cdots, H^{n-1})$ defined on S such that

(a) $x^0_i = H^i(x^0_n, \alpha^0_1, \ldots, \alpha^0_s) \qquad i = 1, 2, \ldots, n - 1$

(b) $f^i[H(x_n, \alpha), x_n, \alpha] \equiv 0$ on $S \qquad i = 1, 2, \ldots, n - 1$

(c) $H \in C^1$ on S

Substitute H into $f^n(x, \alpha)$, which gives

(d) $f^n[H(x_n, \alpha), x_n, \alpha] \equiv g(x_n, \alpha)$ on S

Since $f^n \in C^1$ by assumption and $H \in C^1$ by the induction hypothesis,
we are assured that $\partial g / \partial x_n$ exists on S, by theorems 1.2 and 1.5.

The strategy now is to prove that

$$\frac{\partial g}{\partial x_n} \neq 0 \quad \text{at} \quad (x^0_n, \alpha^0)$$

If this is true, we can apply the simple extension of the first implicit function theorem to g, which tells us that there exists a neighborhood R of α^0
and one and only one function ψ defined in this neighborhood such that

†See Theorem A1.1. in the appendix for a proof of the induction theorem. Notice
that we have already established the theorem for $n = 2$ in Theorem 1.10.

‡That at least one $(n - 1)$-dimensional subdeterminant of J does not vanish follows
from the cofactor expansion of J. A renumbering of the functions and/or the variable permits the assumption in the next sentence.

$$x_n^0 = \psi(\alpha^0)$$

$$g[\psi(\alpha), \alpha] \equiv 0 \text{ on } R$$

$$\psi \in C^1 \text{ on } R$$

Substituting ψ into (a) and (b) and defining ϕ as (H, ψ) on R, the general theorem is easily seen as established.

To prove that $\partial g / \partial x_n \neq 0$ at (x_n^0, α^0), consider the partial derivative of (d) with respect to x_n

(e) $$\frac{\partial g}{\partial x_n} = \frac{\partial f^n}{\partial x_1}\frac{\partial H^1}{\partial x_n} + \frac{\partial f^n}{\partial x_2}\frac{\partial H^2}{\partial x_n} + \cdots + \frac{\partial f^n}{\partial x_{n-1}}\frac{\partial H^{n-1}}{\partial x_n} + \frac{\partial f^n}{\partial x_n}$$

Next, differentiate the $n - 1$ equations in (b) with respect to x_n, which partial derivatives must all be zero in S, since these functions are identically zero in S by the induction hypothesis. This gives for $i = 1, 2, \ldots, n - 1$

(f) $$\frac{\partial f^i}{\partial x_1}\frac{\partial H^1}{\partial x_n} + \frac{\partial f^i}{\partial x_2}\frac{\partial H^2}{\partial x_n} + \cdots + \frac{\partial f^i}{\partial x_{n-1}}\frac{\partial H^{n-1}}{\partial x_n} + \frac{\partial f^i}{\partial x_n} = 0$$

Equations (e) and (f) can be written in matrix form as

$$
\begin{bmatrix}
f^1_{x_1} & f^1_{x_2} & \cdots & f^1_{x_{n-1}} & 0 \\
f^2_{x_1} & f^2_{x_2} & \cdots & f^2_{x_{n-1}} & 0 \\
\vdots & \vdots & & \vdots & \vdots \\
f^n_{x_1} & f^n_{x_2} & \cdots & f^n_{x_{n-1}} & -1
\end{bmatrix}
\begin{bmatrix}
\dfrac{\partial H^1}{\partial x_n} \\[2mm]
\dfrac{\partial H^2}{\partial x_n} \\[2mm]
\vdots \\[2mm]
\dfrac{\partial H^{n-1}}{\partial x_n} \\[2mm]
\dfrac{\partial g}{\partial x_n}
\end{bmatrix}
= -
\begin{bmatrix}
f^1_{x_n} \\[2mm]
f^2_{x_n} \\[2mm]
\vdots \\[2mm]
f^n_{x_n}
\end{bmatrix}
$$

Solving for $\partial g / \partial x_n$ by Cramer's rule gives

$$\frac{\partial g}{\partial x_n} = \frac{|J_f(x)|}{|J_f(\bar{x})|}$$

which by assumption is not zero at (x^0, α^0).[†]

Q.E.D.

[†]One might imagine that if the Jacobian is nonsingular over some region, that the region itself might be the neighborhood of equilibrium over which the theorem holds. This, however, is not true. There must be additional conditions on the Jacobian to make the theorem a global rather than a local statement. One such condition of interest for Economics is that all the principal minors of the Jacobian be positive. See Gale and Nikaido [18].

1.6 NUMERICAL SOLUTION TECHNIQUES

We have demonstrated that if the implicit function theorem is satisfied, the standard format for solving static models developed in section 1.3 is justified. This procedure led us to equations (1.21) and (1.22). Let us rewrite (1.21) in a simpler form as

$$Ax = b$$

where A is the Jacobian matrix, x is the n-vector $(\partial x_1/\partial \alpha_k, \ldots, \partial x_n/\partial \alpha_k)$, and b is the n-vector $-(f_{\alpha_k}^1, \ldots, f_{\alpha_k}^n)$. We referred to (1.22), that is, $x = A^{-1}b$, as the solution, but how can we solve for x numerically?

One method is Cramer's rule, which involves replacing the inverse by the adjoint of the Jacobian divided by its determinant. This procedure is useful in economic theory and is efficient for numerical computations when the system is small. For large n, however, Cramer's rule is inefficient for numerical computation because of the enormous amount of labor involved in evaluating the $n + 1$ determinants. A more efficient technique for numerical solutions in the Gaussian reduction or elimination method, and a modification of it called the Gauss-Jordan method. Both of these schemes are iterative procedures—that is, they involve a series of steps. Both are useful for machine computation. They also provide a beautiful entré to the theory of linear equation systems. We explore them in this section.

First we illustrate both methods, using a simple system of equations

(1.33) $2x_1 + x_2 + 4x_3 = 16$

(1.34) $3x_1 + 2x_2 + x_3 = 10$

(1.35) $x_1 + 3x_2 + 3x_3 = 16$

where

$$A = \begin{bmatrix} 2 & 1 & 4 \\ 3 & 2 & 1 \\ 1 & 3 & 3 \end{bmatrix}$$
$$x = (x_1, x_2, x_3)$$
$$b = (16, 10, 16)$$

The Gaussian method eliminates x_1 from (1.34) and (1.35) by using (1.33); then, x_2 is eliminated from the new (1.35) by using the modified (1.34). Equation (1.35) now can be solved for x_3, with the result substituted into the modified (1.34), which gives a solution of x_2. Finally, the solutions of x_2 and x_3 are substituted into (1.33), which yields x_1. The steps involved are not unique.

Applying this procedure, we may eliminate x_1 from (1.34) and (1.35) by dividing (1.33) by 2 and then adding the new (1.33) multiplied by -3 to (1.34), and adding the new (1.33) multiplied by -1 to (1.35). This gives

(1.33') $$x_1 + \tfrac{1}{2} x_2 + 2x_3 = 8$$
(1.34') $$\tfrac{1}{2} x_2 - 5x_3 = -14$$
(1.35') $$\tfrac{5}{2} x_2 + x_3 = 8$$

To eliminate x_2 from the new (1.35), (1.35'), multiply (1.34') by -5 and add to (1.35'), which gives

(1.33') $$x_1 + \tfrac{1}{2} x_2 + 2x_3 = 8$$
(1.34') $$\tfrac{1}{2} x_2 - 5x_3 = -14$$
(1.35*) $$26x_3 = 78$$

Notice that we have triangularized the system by these operations. We can now immediately obtain $x_3 = 3$ and can solve for x_1 and x_2 by backward substitution, that is, by substituting this value into (1.33') and (1.34'), giving $x_1 = 1$ and $x_2 = 2$.

While the Gauss method triangularizes the system, the Gauss-Jordan method diagonalizes it. The first step in the Gauss-Jordan method is the same as the Gauss procedure—(1.33) is used to eliminate x_1 from (1.34) and (1.35). In the next step, the new (1.34), (1.34'), is used to eliminate x_2 from the new (1.33) and (1.35). Finally, the modified (1.35) is used to eliminate x_3 from the newest (1.34) and (1.33). Begin with equations (1.33'), (1.34'), and (1.35'). To eliminate x_2 from (1.33') and (1.35') multiply (1.34') by -1 and add the resulting equation to (1.33'); then multiply (1.34') by -5 and add to (1.35'). The result is

(1.33*) $$x_1 + 7x_3 = 22$$
(1.34') $$\tfrac{1}{2} x_2 - 5x_3 = -14$$
(1.35*) $$26x_3 = 78$$

Finally, using (1.35*) to eliminate x_3 from both (1.33*) and (1.34'), we multiply (1.35*) by $-7/26$ and add to (1.33*), and then multiply (1.35*) by $5/26$ and add to (1.34'). The result is the diagonal form

$$x_1 = 1$$
$$\tfrac{1}{2} x_2 = 1$$
$$26x_3 = 78$$

Observe that, with both of these procedures, it would have been convenient simply to remove the x's altogether and to have operated on just the coefficients. Then, the original system could be written as the *augmented matrix* $[A, b]$

$$\begin{bmatrix} 2 & 1 & 4 & 16 \\ 3 & 2 & 1 & 10 \\ 1 & 3 & 3 & 16 \end{bmatrix}$$

The first stage of the Gauss method would look like

$$\begin{bmatrix} 1 & \frac{1}{2} & 2 & 8 \\ 0 & \frac{1}{2} & -5 & -14 \\ 0 & \frac{5}{2} & 1 & 8 \end{bmatrix}$$

and the triangular form would be

$$\begin{bmatrix} 1 & \frac{1}{2} & 2 & 8 \\ 0 & \frac{1}{2} & -5 & -14 \\ 0 & 0 & 26 & 78 \end{bmatrix}$$

1681683

The procedure would be similar for the Gauss-Jordan method.

Some questions about these methods probably have occurred to the reader. First, why do they generate the correct solutions? How do we know that, in the midst of all of these operations, we are not getting a set of solutions different from the original system? We can answer that question this way: What exactly did we do to the original system? First, we divided equations by nonzero constants. Clearly, that operation does not alter a solution. Second, we multiplied equations by nonzero constants and added the result to another equation. This does not affect the solutions either, for if a given set of values for an x vector satisfies two equations, the same set of values must satisfy the sum of two equations, since equals added to equals are equal. There is also a third operation that we may need to employ, although we did not use it in the above examples, and that is simply to interchange any two equations, such as making the first equation the third one and vice versa. Obviously, that operation will have no affect on the solutions either.

The operations just described are called *elementary row operations*, and they are so important that we shall repeat them with reference to the augmented matrix:

1. Multiplying a row by a nonzero constant.
2. Multiplying a row by a nonzero constant and adding the result to another row.
3. Interchanging two rows.

The iterative procedures are thus seen to be a sequence of elementary row operations applied to the augmented matrix [A, b].

Another question that may arise is, what do we do if the coefficient of x_1 is zero in the first equation, and we cannot then use that equation (row) to eliminate x_1 from the other equations (rows)? The answer is simply to use elementary row operation 3. to replace the first row with one that has a nonzero coefficient for x_1, and then proceed as before. Suppose that after the first step the second row finds the coefficient of x_2 to be zero, for example

$$\begin{bmatrix} 1 & \frac{1}{2} & 2 & 8 \\ 0 & 0 & -5 & -14 \\ 0 & \frac{5}{2} & 1 & 8 \end{bmatrix}$$

Obviously, if we are using the Gauss-Jordan method, we cannot use the second row to eliminate the coefficients of x_2 in the first and third rows, nor can we employ the second step of the Gauss method and use the second row to eliminate the coefficient of x_2 from the third row. However, interchanging the second and third rows

$$\begin{bmatrix} 1 & \frac{1}{2} & 2 & 8 \\ 0 & \frac{5}{2} & 1 & 8 \\ 0 & 0 & -5 & -14 \end{bmatrix}$$

we can now continue to a solution with either method. With the Gauss method we already have the triangular form, and all we need to do is the backward substitution. With the Gauss-Jordan, we proceed as usual.

Another question that might have occurred to the reader concerns what we do if after, say, the first step the coefficients of both x_1 and x_2 are eliminated from the second and third rows, so that the augmented matrix presents this ugly picture.

$$\begin{bmatrix} 1 & \frac{1}{2} & 2 & 8 \\ 0 & 0 & 1 & 8 \\ 0 & 0 & -5 & -14 \end{bmatrix}$$

This tells us that $x_3 = 8$ and $x_3 = 14/5$. Understandably, a system which exhibits such a malady is called *inconsistent*. The theorist must go back to the structural equations to find his error in specifying the model, for he apparently posited that the same variable was governed by contradictory laws. A solution in such a case is impossible.†

†Technically, this condition is described by saying that the rank of [A, b] exceeds the rank of [A]. Consistency requires that the two ranks be the same.

Suppose we make the system consistent but still leave the four zeros there, for example

(1.36)
$$\begin{bmatrix} 1 & \frac{1}{2} & 2 & 8 \\ 0 & 0 & 1 & 8 \\ 0 & 0 & 2 & 16 \end{bmatrix}$$

The system is consistent, but another problem presents itself. Substituting $x_3 = 8$ into the first equation we see that $x_1 + \frac{1}{2} x_2 = -8$. Now we have an infinity of solutions for x_1 and x_2. What is the trouble? As we shall explain, it is that A is singular, that is, it has a zero determinant. We thus do not have a complete system, for the structural equations are not functionally independent and a critical assumption of the implicit function theorem is not met. How do we know that A is singular? The first three columns in (1.36) are not A, but A transformed by elementary row operations. Maybe A itself is nonsingular.

One way of answering this question is to observe that *elementary row (or column) operations do not affect the nonsingularity or singularity of a matrix.* That is, if A has a nonzero (zero) determinant, the application of elementary operations to A which triangularize or diagonalize or do anything else to it will not generate a matrix that has a zero (nonzero) determinant. This point can easily be demonstrated by using a few elementary rules of determinants. Consider again the first elementary row operation, multiplying a row by a nonzero constant. This action simply multiplies the value of the determinant by the same constant. To see this, simply expand the determinant by cofactors along the altered row and factor out the constant. This operation cannot make a nonzero determinant zero, or a zero determinant nonzero. Next, consider the second operation, multiplying a row by a nonzero constant and adding the result to another row. This operation does not even change the value of the determinant. We illustrate with a 3×3 A matrix written

$$A = \begin{bmatrix} a_{11} & a_{12} & a_{13} \\ a_{21} & a_{22} & a_{23} \\ a_{31} & a_{32} & a_{33} \end{bmatrix}$$

Now multiply, say, the second row by $\lambda \neq 0$ and add the result to, say, the third row. This gives

$$A^* = \begin{bmatrix} a_{11} & a_{12} & a_{13} \\ a_{21} & a_{22} & a_{23} \\ a_{31} + \lambda a_{21}, & a_{32} + \lambda a_{22}, & a_{33} + \lambda a_{23} \end{bmatrix}$$

Taking the determinant of this last matrix, expanding by the last row, we have

$$|A^*| = (a_{31} + \lambda a_{21})A_{31} + (a_{32} + \lambda a_{22})A_{32} + (a_{33} + \lambda a_{23})A_{33}$$

where A_{3i} is the cofactor of a_{3i}, $i = 1, 2, 3$.

Hence,

$$|A^*| = a_{31}A_{31} + a_{32}A_{32} + a_{33}A_{33} + \lambda[a_{21}A_{31} + a_{22}A_{32} + a_{23}A_{33}]$$

$$= |A| + \lambda \begin{vmatrix} a_{11} & a_{12} & a_{13} \\ a_{21} & a_{22} & a_{23} \\ a_{21} & a_{22} & a_{23} \end{vmatrix}$$

$$= |A|$$

by the property that a determinant with two identical rows is zero. The exercise is carried out as easily when A is an $n \times n$ matrix. Finally, the last elementary operation, interchanging any two rows, simply changes the sign of the determinant.

We have thus established that any matrices generated by applying elementary row operations to a nonsingular (singular) matrix must be nonsingular (singular). The same point obviously holds for elementary column operations. Any set of matrices which can be transformed into each other by elementary row and/or column operations are called *equivalent* matrices.

It is now easy to demonstrate that if the A matrix is nonsingular, the Gauss-Jordan method is always able to diagonalize it, that is, transform it into a matrix with zeros everywhere except for nonzero elements along the principal diagonal. Each of these elements can then, by an elementary operation, be converted to a one, which in fact is the final step of the solution. How do we know that the diagonal matrix may not have zeros as some of the diagonal elements? We know because A is assumed nonsingular. The determinant of a diagonal matrix is the product of the diagonal elements. If any of these diagonal elements turned out to be zero, the diagonal matrix would have a zero determinant. This would mean that a sequence of elementary row operations on a nonsingular A would produce a singular diagonal matrix. But we know by the above discussion that this is impossible. By the same reasoning, we can apply the Gauss procedure to triangularize a nonsingular A, that is, to transform it into a matrix with zeros below the main diagonal, nonzeros in *all* the places along the main diagonal, and assorted elements above the main diagonal.†

What if A is singular? Then the largest nonvanishing minor in A will be, say, $r \times r$ with $r < n$, where A is $n \times n$. To simplify the discussion, assume that by row and column interchanges this nonsingular $r \times r$ submatrix A^* has been placed in the upper left corner of A. Now apply the Gauss procedure to

†Such a matrix is called upper triangular. The determinant of a triangular matrix, like the determinant of a diagonal matrix, is simply the product of its diagonal elements.

this matrix. What will we get? We know that A^* can be triangularized because it is nonsingular. After that, we can use the diagonal elements of the triangularized A^* to eliminate *all* elements below A^* (for example, to eliminate a_{nr} multiply a_{rr} of the triangular matrix by a_{nr}/a_{rr} and subtract from the nth row). So far, we have transformed A into

$$\left[\begin{array}{c|c} A^{**} & A_1 \\ \hline 0 & A_2 \end{array}\right]$$

where A^{**} is $r \times r$ and triangular, 0 is an $(n - r) \times r$ submatrix with all zeros, and A_1 and A_2 are submatrices of order $r \times (n - r)$ and $(n - r) \times (n - r)$, respectively. Can we say anything about A_1 or A_2? Yes, we can say that all the elements of A_2 must be zero! If any element of A_2 is not zero, we can, by row and column interchanges involving the last $(n - r)$ rows and columns, bring that element to the upper left corner of A_2, which would yield nonzero elements in the first $r + 1$ diagonal places and give us a nonsingular $(r + 1) \times (r + 1)$ submatrix in the upper left corner of the transformed A. This contradicts our assumption that the largest nonvanishing minor of A is $r \times r$, since we have done nothing to A except elementary row and column operations which we know do not affect the singularity or nonsingularity of any submatrix of A. To sum up: By triangularizing the nonsingular $r \times r$ submatrix in the upper left corner of A and then using the diagonal elements of this triangular submatrix A^{**} to eliminate all the elements below A^{**}, we have transformed A into

$$\left[\begin{array}{c|c} A^{**} & A_1 \\ \hline 0 & 0 \end{array}\right]$$

where the elements in A_1 can be any numbers. Suppose we had performed all of these operations on the augmented matrix $[A, b]$. The final form of the Gauss procedure would then be

$$\left[\begin{array}{c|c|c} A^{**} & A_1 & b_1 \\ \hline 0 & 0 & b_2 \end{array}\right]$$

where b_1 is an r-subvector and b_2 an $(n - r)$-subvector. What can be said about b_1 or b_2? Clearly, if the system is to be consistent, b_2 must be zero, while b_1 can have any numbers. The final form is thus

$$\left[\begin{array}{c|c|c} A^{**} & A_1 & b_1 \\ \hline 0 & 0 & 0 \end{array}\right]$$

if the system is consistent. The Gauss-Jordan method continues from this point. The diagonal elements in A^{**} can be used to eliminate all elements above the main diagonal of A^{**}. The final form of the Gauss-Jordan procedure would thus be, assuming consistency,

$$\left[\begin{array}{c|c|c} I & A_1^* & b_1^* \\ \hline 0 & 0 & 0 \end{array}\right]$$

where I is an $r \times r$ unit matrix, A_1^* is $r \times (n-r)$, and b_1^* is $r \times 1$. Clearly, if A is singular the solution cannot be unique, for we have $x_i, i = 1, 2, \ldots, r$, solved for in terms of $(x_{r+1}, x_{r+2}, \ldots, x_n)$. Only by fixing the values of last $(n-r)$ variables can we solve uniquely for the first r variables.

As an example, consider (1.36) with the third row eliminated by the second, and the second and third columns interchanged, which gives as the final form of the Gauss procedure

$$\begin{bmatrix} 1 & 2 & \frac{1}{2} & 8 \\ 0 & 1 & 0 & 8 \\ 0 & 0 & 0 & 0 \end{bmatrix}$$

and the final form for the Gauss-Jordan as

$$\begin{bmatrix} 1 & 0 & \frac{1}{2} & -8 \\ 0 & 1 & 0 & 8 \\ 0 & 0 & 0 & 0 \end{bmatrix}$$

If A *is nonsingular, the Gauss-Jordan method is in fact a premultiplication of* $Ax = b$ *by the inverse of* A, A^{-1}. This procedure is computationally a most efficient method of generating the inverse of A for large A. To see why this is so, observe that *any elementary row operation performed on* A *is precisely the same thing as first performing the same operation on the unit matrix and then using this matrix, called an elementary matrix, to premultiply* A. The same point holds for column operations, except that the operation is performed on the columns of the unit matrix and then the elementary matrix is used to post-multiply A. Thus, a sequence of, say, q elementary row operations performed on A can be written as q elementary matrices premultiplying A, that is

$$E_q \cdots E_2 E_1 A$$

where $E_i, i = 1, \ldots, q$ are the elementary matrices. Suppose then that the q elementary row operations transform A into a unit matrix, I. Then we may write

$$E_q \cdots E_2 E_1 A = I$$

and writing the q elementary matrices multiplied together as the matrix E we write

$$EA = I$$

and clearly $E = A^{-1}$. Hence, the Gauss-Jordan technique premultiplies $Ax = b$ by A^{-1}, but does so step by step. The elementary row operations performed on the augmented matrix $[A, b]$ convert that matrix into $[I, A^{-1}b]$ where the last column yields the reduced form derivatives, that is, the solution. To obtain A^{-1} itself, all we need is EI, that is, we perform the same sequence of elementary row operations on the unit matrix that we performed on A to transform it into the unit matrix.

Exercises

Find the solutions, if any, of the following systems of equations. Use elementary row operations.

1.
$$6x_1 - 2x_3 + 4x_3 - 6 = 0$$
$$2x_1 + 2x_2 + x_3 - 2 = 0$$
$$4x_1 - 12x_2 + 4x_3 - 16 = 0$$

Answer. Inconsistent.

2.
$$2x_1 + 3x_2 - x_3 = -15$$
$$6x_1 + 10x_2 + 4x_3 = 0$$
$$7x_1 + 11x_2 = -30$$
$$2x_1 + 6x_2 + 6x_3 = 22$$

Answer. $x_1 = 2, x_2 = -4, x_3 = 7$

3.
$$6x_2 - 9x_3 = 6$$
$$4x_1 - 4x_2 + 8x_3 = -8$$
$$3x_1 - 2x_2 + 4x_3 = -5$$

Answer. $x_1 = -1, x_2 = 1, x_3 = 0$

4. Find a solution if one exists.

a.
$$x_1 + x_2 = 1$$
$$4x_1 + 6x_2 = 3$$
$$2x_1 + 3x_2 = 2$$

b.
$$x_1 + x_2 = 1$$
$$4x_1 + 6x_2 = 3$$
$$2x_1 + 4x_2 = 1$$

Answer. (a) is inconsistent

(b) $x_2 = -1/2, x_1 = 3/2$

Example 1.1 The Corn Market

Consider the model of the corn market discussed in section 1.1, systems (1.5) or (1.8). We shall work with (1.8), which is rewritten here for convenience:

$$
\begin{bmatrix} 1 & 0 & -D_p \\ 0 & 1 & -S_p \\ 1 & -1 & 0 \end{bmatrix}
\begin{bmatrix} \dfrac{\partial D}{\partial Y} \\ \dfrac{\partial S}{\partial Y} \\ \dfrac{\partial P}{\partial Y} \end{bmatrix}
=
\begin{bmatrix} D_Y \\ 0 \\ 0 \end{bmatrix}
$$

This can easily be solved by Cramer's rule, but for practice we shall solve it by the Gauss and Gauss-Jordan methods. The augmented matrix of this system is

$$
\begin{bmatrix} 1 & 0 & -D_p & D_Y \\ 0 & 1 & -S_p & 0 \\ 1 & -1 & 0 & 0 \end{bmatrix}
$$

Subtract row one from row three

$$
\begin{bmatrix} 1 & 0 & -D_p & D_Y \\ 0 & 1 & -S_p & 0 \\ 0 & -1 & D_p & -D_Y \end{bmatrix}
$$

Add row two to row three. This yields the triangular form,

$$
\begin{bmatrix} 1 & 0 & -D_p & D_Y \\ 0 & 1 & -S_p & 0 \\ 0 & 0 & (D_p - S_p) & -D_Y \end{bmatrix}
$$

We can now obtain the solution by backward substitution, which yields

$$\frac{\partial P}{\partial Y} = \frac{-D_Y}{D_p - S_p}$$

$$\frac{\partial S}{\partial Y} = \frac{-S_p D_Y}{D_p - S_p}$$

$$\frac{\partial D}{\partial Y} = D_Y - \frac{D_p D_Y}{D_p - S_p} = \frac{-S_p D_Y}{D_p - S_p}$$

Diagonalizing the triangular form, divide the last row by $(D_p - S_p)$

$$\begin{bmatrix} 1 & 0 & -D_p & D_Y \\ 0 & 1 & -S_p & 0 \\ 0 & 0 & 1 & \dfrac{-D_Y}{D_p - S_p} \end{bmatrix}$$

Multiply the last row by S_p and add to the second row. Then multiply the last row by D_p and add to the first row. This yields the diagonal form, which in the notation of the last section is $[I, A^{-1}b]$, where the solution vector (the vector of the partial derivatives of the three endogenous variables with respect to income, Y) is the column vector $A^{-1}b$,

$$\begin{bmatrix} 1 & 0 & 0 & D_Y - \dfrac{D_Y D_p}{D_p - S_p} \\ 0 & 1 & 0 & -\dfrac{S_p D_Y}{D_p - S_p} \\ 0 & 0 & 1 & -\dfrac{D_Y}{D_p - S_p} \end{bmatrix}$$

and where the solutions check with those obtained by the Gauss method. Observe that if we take the behavioral assumptions of this model, namely, $D_Y > 0$, $D_p < 0$, $S_p > 0$, the signs of the reduced form derivatives are unambiguously determined as

$$\frac{\partial P}{\partial Y} > 0, \frac{\partial S}{\partial Y} = \frac{\partial D}{\partial Y} > 0$$

Example 1.2 Three Interconnected Markets

Suppose we expand this model by explicitly considering two other markets, one for a good assumed to be a gross substitute to the consumer for corn and the other for a commodity assumed to be a gross complement to the consumer for corn. Pretending that butter is the complement and potatoes the rival, construct a model for each market as we did in section 1.1. To diminish the size of the Jacobian with which we shall have to work, substitute the demand and supply equations into the equilibrium condition and construct the excess demand functions in each market. This reduces the dimension of the system from nine to three—three excess demand functions in three endogenous variables consisting of the prices of the three goods. This gives three equations like (1.3). Using the same symbols as in the standard format, we define

$$x_1 = \text{Price of corn}$$
$$x_2 = \text{Price of butter}$$
$$x_3 = \text{Price of potatoes}$$
$$\alpha_1 = \text{National income}$$
$$\alpha_2 = \text{Price of a productive factor}$$

and we have the structural equations

(1.37)
$$f^1(x_1, x_2, x_3: \alpha_1, \alpha_2) = 0$$
$$f^2(x_1, x_2, x_3: \alpha_1, \alpha_2) = 0$$
$$f^3(x_1, x_2, x_3: \alpha_1, \alpha_2) = 0$$

where f^i, $i = 1, 2, 3$, is the excess demand for the ith good. Notice that we did not include the shift parameters, that is, the exogenous variables that fall into the category of "any other variable that could affect a particular endogenous variable." It is convenient to leave them out until we wish to assume that one of them changes. We could have treated α_1 and α_2 this way, bringing them into the structural relations only when we wish to investigate the impact of a change in their value on the endogenous variables (x_1, x_2, x_3). Suppose, for example, that we want to examine the impact on the system (1.37) of a change in some kind of tax or subsidy to corn producers. We can then call this tax or subsidy α_3 and insert it into f^1 in (1.37) and reason that $f^1_{\alpha_3}$ is positive for a tax and negative for a subsidy, because such a tax (subsidy) reduces (increases) supply.

The behavioral assumptions about (1.37) are as follows:

(a) Corn Market. $(f^1_{x_1}, f^1_{x_2}, f^1_{x_3})$ have the signs $(-, -, +)$. The first sign is obvious and the next two are the definitions of gross complementarity and substitutability, since we are assuming for simplicity that x_2 and x_3 have no influence on the supply of corn.†

(b) Butter Market. $(f^2_{x_1}, f^2_{x_2}, f^2_{x_3})$ have the signs $(-, -, -)$, where we assume that the last sign is negative, indicating that butter and potatoes are assumed to be complements.

---

†We shall also make analogous assumptions about the other markets.

(c) Potato Market. $(f^3_{x_1}, f^3_{x_2}, f^3_{x_3})$ have the signs $(+, -, -)$.

Suppose we wish to analyze the impact on (x_1, x_2, x_3) of a tax or subsidy to, say, corn producers. Ignoring α_1 and α_2, which are assumed fixed for this exercise, we could rewrite (1.37) as

(1.38) $f^i(x_1, x_2, x_3; \alpha_3) = 0$ $i = 1, 2, 3$

where α_3 is the tax or subsidy to corn and $f^2_{\alpha_3} = f^3_{\alpha_3} = 0$, that is, a change in α_3 is assumed not to affect the excess demand for butter or potatoes *given* (x_1, x_2, x_3).

Assuming the implicit function theorem holds, we may differentiate (1.38) with respect to α_3, and we obtain the analogue of (1.21).

(1.39)
$$
\begin{bmatrix} f^1_{x_1} & f^1_{x_2} & f^1_{x_3} \\ f^2_{x_1} & f^2_{x_2} & f^2_{x_3} \\ f^3_{x_1} & f^3_{x_2} & f^3_{x_3} \end{bmatrix}
\begin{bmatrix} \dfrac{\partial x_1}{\partial \alpha_3} \\ \dfrac{\partial x_2}{\partial \alpha_3} \\ \dfrac{\partial x_3}{\partial \alpha_3} \end{bmatrix}
=
\begin{bmatrix} -f^1_{\alpha_3} \\ 0 \\ 0 \end{bmatrix}
$$

The system is easy to solve by Cramer's rule, but we shall work through some of the iterative procedures. Rewriting (1.39) as $Ax = b$, we can write the augmented matrix $[A, b]$ as

$$
\begin{bmatrix} a_{11} & a_{12} & a_{13} & b_1 \\ a_{21} & a_{22} & a_{23} & 0 \\ a_{31} & a_{32} & a_{33} & 0 \end{bmatrix}
$$

Divide the first row by a_{11}. Next, multiply the new first row by a_{21} and subtract from the second row. Then multiply the first row by a_{31} and subtract form the third row. The result is

$$
\begin{bmatrix} 1 & \dfrac{a_{12}}{a_{11}} & \dfrac{a_{13}}{a_{11}} & \dfrac{b_1}{a_{11}} \\ 0 & a_{22} - \dfrac{a_{21}a_{12}}{a_{11}} & a_{23} - \dfrac{a_{21}a_{13}}{a_{11}} & -\dfrac{b_1 a_{21}}{a_{11}} \\ 0 & a_{32} - \dfrac{a_{31}a_{12}}{a_{11}} & a_{33} - \dfrac{a_{31}a_{13}}{a_{11}} & -\dfrac{a_{31}b_1}{a_{11}} \end{bmatrix}
$$

and rewriting the variables to simplify gives

$$
\begin{bmatrix} 1 & b_{12} & b_{13} & b_{14} \\ 0 & b_{22} & b_{23} & b_{24} \\ 0 & b_{32} & b_{33} & b_{34} \end{bmatrix}
$$

Divide the second row by b_{22}. Then multiply the new second row by b_{32} and subtract from the third row. This yields the triangular form

$$
\begin{bmatrix}
1 & b_{12} & b_{13} & b_{14} \\
0 & 1 & \dfrac{b_{23}}{b_{22}} & \dfrac{b_{24}}{b_{22}} \\
0 & 0 & \left(b_{33} - \dfrac{b_{32}b_{23}}{b_{22}}\right) & \left(b_{34} - \dfrac{b_{32}b_{24}}{b_{22}}\right)
\end{bmatrix}
$$

Thus

$$
\frac{\partial x_3}{\partial \alpha_3} = \frac{b_{22}b_{34} - b_{32}b_{24}}{b_{33}b_{22} - b_{32}b_{23}}
$$

or in terms of the structural parameters

(1.40) $$\frac{\partial x_3}{\partial \alpha_3} = \frac{b_1[a_{21}a_{32} - a_{22}a_{31}]}{|A|}$$

The remaining labor is left for the reader.

The interesting question now is, can we establish the sign of, say, $\partial x_3/\partial \alpha_3$, given our assumptions about the signs of the structural parameters? The term in brackets can be seen to be positive. The term b_1, which is $-f^1_{\alpha_3}$ in (1.39), is negative if α_3 is a tax and positive if α_3 is a subsidy. The denominator is the determinant of the Jacobian matrix in (1.39). Inspecting that determinant, we can see that the sign is in doubt. Thus, without further information we cannot make any clear-cut qualitative statement about the response of (x_1, x_2, x_3) to α_3, or indeed to a change in any exogenous variable, for that determinant will be present in every solution. We shall have more to say about this crucial problem in section 1.8 in discussing Samuelson's Correspondence Principle, where under certain conditions the needed information as to the sign of $|A|$ can be discovered. We shall also provide another possible way of attacking this problem in the discussion of optimization theory in Chapter 2. Given just the equipment and assumptions that we have so far, however, we can do no better than to generate expressions like (1.40) and perhaps compute the sign of the numerator.†

Consider (1.38) again. Suppose it is a linear system and we had econometric estimates of the structural parameters, which indicated that (1.39) could be written (assuming α_3 to be a tax)

---

†Notice we cannot even derive the sign of the numerator of $\partial x_1/\partial \alpha_3$ from the signs of the structural parameters.

$$\begin{bmatrix} -3 & -1 & 1 \\ -\frac{1}{2} & -1 & -2 \\ 1 & -1 & -3 \end{bmatrix} \begin{bmatrix} \dfrac{\partial x_1}{\partial \alpha_3} \\ \dfrac{\partial x_2}{\partial \alpha_3} \\ \dfrac{\partial x_3}{\partial \alpha_3} \end{bmatrix} = \begin{bmatrix} -2 \\ 0 \\ 0 \end{bmatrix}$$

Working out the iterative method, we have (the reader might wish to employ different sequences of operations)

$$\begin{bmatrix} 1 & -1 & -3 & 0 \\ -\frac{1}{2} & -1 & -2 & 0 \\ -3 & -1 & 1 & -2 \end{bmatrix}$$

$$\begin{bmatrix} 1 & -1 & -3 & 0 \\ 0 & -\frac{3}{2} & -3\frac{1}{2} & 0 \\ 0 & -4 & -8 & -2 \end{bmatrix}$$

$$\begin{bmatrix} 1 & -1 & -3 & 0 \\ 0 & -\frac{3}{2} & -3\frac{1}{2} & 0 \\ 0 & 0 & \frac{4}{3} & -2 \end{bmatrix}$$

$$\begin{bmatrix} 1 & -1 & -3 & 0 \\ 0 & 1 & \frac{7}{3} & 0 \\ 0 & 0 & 1 & -\frac{3}{2} \end{bmatrix}$$

where backward substitution in the Gaussian procedure begins. Diagonalizing, we have

$$\begin{bmatrix} 1 & -1 & -3 & 0 \\ 0 & 1 & 0 & \frac{7}{2} \\ 0 & 0 & 1 & -\frac{3}{2} \end{bmatrix}$$

$$\begin{bmatrix} 1 & -1 & 0 & -\frac{9}{2} \\ 0 & 1 & 0 & \frac{7}{2} \\ 0 & 0 & 1 & -\frac{3}{2} \end{bmatrix}$$

$$\begin{bmatrix} 1 & 0 & 0 & -1 \\ 0 & 1 & 0 & \frac{7}{2} \\ 0 & 0 & 1 & -\frac{3}{2} \end{bmatrix}$$

In economic terminology, this tells us that a unit increase in a tax on corn production will lower the equilibrium price of corn by one unit, raise the price of butter by 7/2 units, and lower the price of potatoes by 3/2 units.

> *Remark.* This example implies that there are goods other than the three being studied. At least one other good must exist; otherwise, the Jacobian in (1.39) is a singular matrix. If there are only three goods in the economy, the value of the excess demands in any two markets determines the value of the excess demand that must obtain in the third market. This is called Walras' law. Mathematically, it means that there exists a set of prices (x_1, x_2, x_3) not all zero, which can be used as weights to set a linear combination of the rows in the Jacobian in (1.39) equal to zero. Thus, the rank of the Jacobian is two, which means that in the analysis one market may be dropped, for the solutions of the included markets must satisfy the excluded market. Also, in order to obtain unique solutions for two markets, the solution of the third must be considered exogenous; for example, if three prices are to be solved, one must be made exogenous and given a value before the other two can be solved uniquely. The price made exogenous is usually given a value of one and called the numeraire. This point as applied to (1.38) would mean that we would drop f^3 and set $x_3 = 1$. Illustrating this with $Ax = b$, suppose that all dependent equations have been dropped so that A is $r \times n$, x is an n-vector, b is an r-vector, and $r < n$. Partition A into $[A_1, A_2]$ where A_1 is $r \times r$, and A_2 is $r \times (n - r)$. Partition x conformably into (x_1, x_2), where x_1 is an r-subvector and x_2 is an $(n - r)$-subvector. If the columns of A have been arranged so that the first r columns are linearly independent, then A_1 is nonsingular. We may now write $Ax = b$ as
>
> $$A_1 x_1 + A_2 x_2 = b$$
>
> hence
>
> $$x_1 = -A_1^{-1} A_2 x_2 + A_1^{-1} b$$
>
> We see that to solve x_1 uniquely we must consider x_2 to be exogenous. If $r = n - 1$, x_2 would be a scalar, and we could give it a value of one and call it the numeraire when x is a price vector.

Example 1.3 A Macro Model

Consider the model in (1.9) and (1.10). We may solve for the linear case in (1.12), or for the more general case in (1.14), which assumes a change in α_2, some exogenous variable affecting investment. We shall work with (1.14), and repeat that system here:

$$
\begin{bmatrix}
1 - C_{Yd}(1-t) - I_Y & -I_r \\
M_Y & M_r
\end{bmatrix}
\begin{bmatrix}
\dfrac{\partial Y}{\partial \alpha_2} \\
\dfrac{\partial r}{\partial \alpha_2}
\end{bmatrix}
=
\begin{bmatrix}
I_{\alpha_2} \\
0
\end{bmatrix}
$$

Solving for $\partial Y / \partial \alpha_2$ gives

$$
\frac{\partial Y}{\partial \alpha_2} = \frac{M_r I_{\alpha_2}}{|J|}
$$

where $|J|$ is the determinant of the Jacobian matrix evaluated at the equilibrium. Can we find the sign of $\partial Y / \partial \alpha_2$? The numerator should be no problem. If α_2 is, say, an index of technological progress, then I_{α_2} should be positive. We know that M_r is assumed to be negative. The determinant is

$$
M_r(1 - E_Y) + I_r M_y
$$

where $E \equiv$ aggregate demand and $E_Y \equiv C_{Y_d}(1 - t) + I_Y$, which is the marginal propensity to spend. If we assume, as is frequently done, that $0 < E_Y < 1$, then $|J| < 0$. If we are not willing to put an upper constraint on E_Y and are only willing to say that it is positive, then $|J|$ is indeterminate pending further information. In the next section we shall see, given some additional plausible assumptions, that $|J|$ must be negative.

Remark. It is often convenient to think of a shift parameter such as α_2 as the exogenous or autonomous part of investment itself. Thus, I_{α_2} would be the partial derivative of investment with respect to autonomous investment and would therefore equal one by definition. Also, $\partial Y / \partial \alpha_2$ would be reinterpreted accordingly: In economic terminology, it would be the equilibrium response of Y to a unit change in exogenous I.

Suppose we write this macro model, making specific assumptions about the nonlinearities in the investment and money demand functions while assuming that the consumption and tax functions are linear. The symbols and behavioral assumptions will be those in section 1.2. We write†

(1.41) $C = a_{11} + a_{12}(Y - T)$

(1.42) $I = (a_{21} - a_{22}r^2)^{1/2} + a_{23}Y$

(1.43) $T = \bar{T} + tY$

†See Brems [10, Chap. 35].

(1.44) $G = \bar{G}$

(1.45) $Y = C + I + G$

(1.46) $M^* = a_{31} Y + \dfrac{a_{32}}{r - a_{33}}$

(1.47) $M = \bar{M}$

(1.48) $M = M^*$

where the endogenous variables are (C, I, Y, T, M^*, r), and the policy instruments are $(\bar{M}, \bar{T}, t, \bar{G})$. The symbols a_{11}, a_{21}, and a_{32} can be interpreted as the exogenous components of C, I, and M^*, respectively, so that, for example, a_{11} is autonomous consumption spending. If, in the course of analysis, a_{11}, a_{21}, and a_{32} do not change, we can think of them as structural parameters. If they do change, we can treat them as shift parameters or exogenous variables, if we do not wish explicitly to include in the model the exogenous variables that are producing the changes in these exogenous components. Thinking of them as structural parameters for the moment, we state the behavioral assumptions of the model to be that all a_{ij} are positive and $0 < t < 1$. The I function can be seen to be concave from below[†] and the M^* function convex from below for $r > a_{33}$, where a_{33} can be interpreted as a liquidity trap. Such a shape for the I schedule implies that the higher the level of r, the more sensitive is I to changes in r, which could be rationalized by arguing that the higher the level of r, the more variations in it are perceived and taken account of.[‡] The argument supporting the convex shape of the money demand schedule can be found in almost any text on Macroeconomics.

Substituting (1.41) through (1.44) into (1.45), and (1.46) and (1.47) into (1.48) gives

(1.49) $[1 - a_{23} - (1 - t)a_{12}]Y + a_{12}\bar{T} - \bar{G} - a_{11}$

             $- (a_{21} - a_{22}r^2)^{1/2} = 0$

(1.50) $\bar{M} - a_{31} Y - \dfrac{a_{32}}{r - a_{33}} = 0$

which is the analogue of (1.13), and constitutes the structural relations of the model where all endogenous variables except Y and r have been eliminated by substitution. Suppose that we displace the equilibrium expressed in (1.49) and (1.50) by changing, say, $\bar{G}$. Assuming the implicit function theorem holds, we differentiate (1.49) and (1.50) with respect to $\bar{G}$, which gives

---

[†]This only holds over a range of r such that $(a_{21} - a_{22}r^2)$ is positive.
[‡]See Hansen [25].

$$(1.51) \quad \begin{bmatrix} (1 - \alpha) & \dfrac{a_{22}r}{\sqrt{a_{21} - a_{22}r^2}} \\[3ex] -a_{31} & \dfrac{a_{32}}{(r - a_{33})^2} \end{bmatrix} \begin{bmatrix} \dfrac{\partial Y}{\partial \bar{G}} \\[3ex] \dfrac{\partial r}{\partial \bar{G}} \end{bmatrix} = \begin{bmatrix} 1 \\[3ex] 0 \end{bmatrix}$$

where $\alpha \equiv a_{23} + (1 - t)a_{12}$, and where the Jacobian matrix is evaluated at the initial equilibrium.

Suppose now that we have the following econometric estimates for the structural parameters of the model, where the dollar magnitudes are in billions.

$$\begin{aligned} \alpha &= & .7 \\ a_{21} &= & 457 \\ a_{22} &= & 10{,}000 \\ a_{31} &= & .5 \\ a_{33} &= & .02 \\ a_{32} &= & 2 \\ a_{12} &= & .75 \\ a_{11} &= & 49 \end{aligned}$$

Notice that since $\bar{T}$ and t are fixed for this exercise, we may interpret them as structural parameters as well as policy instruments. Their values would also be estimated. The value of t is contained in α. Suppose that

$$\bar{T} = 100$$

Since $\bar{M}$ is a policy instrument and we are assuming that it is fixed, we may take its initial value, say

$$\bar{M} = 160$$

Finally, to solve for an equilibrium Y and r, we need the initial value of $\bar{G}$, say

$$\bar{G} = 100$$

Solving (1.49) and (1.50), we find one pair of equilibrium values of (Y, r) to be $(320, .04)$. Substituting $r = .04$ and the necessary structural parameter estimates into (1.51), we get

$$\begin{bmatrix} .3 & 19.0 \\[3ex] -.5 & 5000.0 \end{bmatrix} \begin{bmatrix} \dfrac{\partial Y}{\partial \bar{G}} \\[3ex] \dfrac{\partial r}{\partial \bar{G}} \end{bmatrix} = \begin{bmatrix} 1 \\[3ex] 0 \end{bmatrix}$$

which, when solved, yields

$$\frac{\partial Y}{\partial \bar{G}} \simeq 3.3 \qquad \frac{\partial r}{\partial \bar{G}} \simeq .00003$$

We may interpret these reduced form derivatives, or multipliers, as saying that a one billion dollar rise in government spending will raise equilibrium national income by about \$ 3.3 billion, and the equilibrium average interest rate about 3/1,000 of 1 per cent.

Example 1.4 Leontief (input-output) Model

Suppose we divide the economy into four producing sectors and imagine that the output of sector i is demanded not only by itself (for example, the steel industry demands steel) but by the other three sectors, and also demanded by exogenous sectors which are taken to be the consumer plus the government plus foreign sectors. We assume that the demand by the producing sectors depends on their level of output. We can therefore write the demand function for the product of the ith sector as

$$x_i^* = f^i(x_1, x_2, x_3, x_4; \alpha_i) \qquad i = 1, 2, 3, 4$$

where x_i is the production of the ith sector and α_i is the exogenous demand for the product of the ith sector. Since the production of the ith sector is defined as being distributed among these five outlets, we may set $x_i = x_i^*$. Writing the system in its usual linear form we have

$$x_i = a_{i1}x_1 + a_{i2}x_2 + a_{i3}x_3 + a_{i4}x_4 + \alpha_i$$

or in matrix form

(1.52) $$x = Ax + \alpha$$

where

$$x = (x_1, x_2, x_3, x_4)$$
$$\alpha = (\alpha_1, \alpha_2, \alpha_3, \alpha_4)$$
$$A = \begin{bmatrix} a_{11} & \cdots & a_{14} \\ \vdots & & \vdots \\ a_{41} & \cdots & a_{44} \end{bmatrix}$$

where the input coefficients a_{ij}, $i, j = 1, 2, 3, 4$ are nonnegative and are interpreted as the product of the ith sector required per unit output of the jth sector.

In the structural equations (1.52) the endogenous variables are x, the exogenous variables α, and the structural parameters are the elements of A. The reduced form of this system is

$$(1.53) \qquad\qquad\qquad x = (I - A)^{-1}\alpha$$

which obviously requires that the Jacobian matrix for this model, $(I - A)$, be nonsingular. If one of the exogenous variables, say α_2, changes, the solution is

$$(1.54) \qquad
\begin{bmatrix}
\dfrac{\partial x_1}{\partial \alpha_2} \\[2mm]
\dfrac{\partial x_2}{\partial \alpha_2} \\[2mm]
\dfrac{\partial x_3}{\partial \alpha_2} \\[2mm]
\dfrac{\partial x_4}{\partial \alpha_2}
\end{bmatrix}
= (I - A)^{-1}
\begin{bmatrix}
0 \\ 1 \\ 0 \\ 0
\end{bmatrix}$$

One problem with the input-output system (1.53) is that the solution must not contain any negative elements. We may have a nonsingular matrix $(I - A)$ and be able to solve for x, but obtain a nonsense solution involving negative production levels for some industries. To assure a nonnegative solution of (1.53) for any exogenous demand vector $\alpha \geq 0$, with at least one element of α nonzero, it is obvious that $(I - A)^{-1}$ must have all nonnegative elements. A necessary and sufficient condition for $(I - A)^{-1}$ to be positive is that all the principal minors of $(I - A)$ be positive. This is called the Hawkins-Simon Theorem,[†] which assumes the matrix A is indecomposable, that is, A cannot be transformed by interchanges (permutations) of the *same* rows and columns into the form

$$\begin{bmatrix} A_1 & A_2 \\ 0 & A_3 \end{bmatrix}$$

where A_1 and A_3 are square submatrices on the main diagonal and not necessarily of the same order. A sufficient condition for a nonnegative and indecomposable matrix to satisfy the Hawkins-Simon Theorem is that all column sums of the matrix should not exceed one and at least one column sum should be less than one.[‡]

Another question is the existence of fixed amounts of inputs such as labor, which are not included in the production sectors in (1.53). If a_{0i} is the amount of labor required for one unit of output of sector $i = 1, 2, 3, 4$, and if α_0 is the

†See Morishima [37, pp. 15-17], Lancaster [32, Chap. 6].
‡See Solow [48].

autonomous demand for labor, then the model in (1.53) must satisfy the constraint

(1.55) $$a_{01}x_1 + a_{02}x_2 + a_{03}x_3 + a_{04}x_4 \leq L - \alpha_0$$

where L = the supply of labor. Clearly, for any nonnegative x which satisfies (1.53), we can find some scalar multiple λx which satisfies (1.55). Thus, the *scale* of α must be constrained, and the real problem in the input-output model is whether a nonnegative α of any *proportion* can be satisfied by a nonnegative x (nonnegative implying at least one positive element).

Ignoring constraints, consider a 3×3 input matrix with input coefficients

$$A = \begin{bmatrix} .2 & .1 & .1 \\ .1 & .2 & .1 \\ .1 & .1 & .2 \end{bmatrix}$$

and suppose the exogenous demand α is

$$\alpha = (.1, .2, .1)$$

Since A is indecomposable and nonnegative and its columns all add up to less than one, the Hawkins-Simon condition is satisfied and we know that $x \geq 0$, $x \neq 0$ for all $\alpha \geq 0, \alpha \neq 0$.

Checking the leading principal minors of $(I - A)$ directly we see that

$$(I - A) = \begin{bmatrix} .8 & -.1 & -.1 \\ -.1 & .8 & -.1 \\ -.1 & -.1 & .8 \end{bmatrix}$$

has leading principal minors

$$.8, \begin{vmatrix} .8 & -.1 \\ -.1 & .8 \end{vmatrix}, \begin{vmatrix} .8 & -.1 & -.1 \\ -.1 & .8 & -.1 \\ -.1 & -.1 & .8 \end{vmatrix}$$

which are all positive.

Employing the Gaussian procedure to solve $(I - A)x = \alpha$, we write the augmented matrix $[(I - A), \alpha]$ with each row multiplied by -10, and the first and third rows interchanged, which gives

$$\begin{bmatrix} 1 & 1 & -8 & -1 \\ 1 & -8 & 1 & -2 \\ -8 & 1 & 1 & -1 \end{bmatrix}$$

Subtract the first row from the second, and multiply the first row by 8 and add to the third. This gives

$$\begin{bmatrix} 1 & 1 & -8 & -1 \\ 0 & -9 & 9 & -1 \\ 0 & 9 & -63 & -9 \end{bmatrix}$$

Add the second row to the third, then divide the second row by -9. We now have

$$\begin{bmatrix} 1 & 1 & -8 & -1 \\ 0 & 1 & -1 & \frac{1}{9} \\ 0 & 0 & -54 & -10 \end{bmatrix}$$

Thus, $x_3 = 10/54$. Substituting into the other equations yields $x_2 = 8/27$ and $x_1 = 730/54$.

1.8 THE CORRESPONDENCE PRINCIPLE

The correspondence principle employs dynamic analysis to supply information which may not be obtainable when working only with the static model. The procedure is to select a dynamic counterpart of a static model, assume the dynamic model to be stable, derive the implications of the stability assumption for the structural parameters, and then employ the information in the static analysis. To demonstrate the process we begin with the structural equations representing any static model expressed in (1.18), rewritten here as

$$(1.56) \qquad f^i(x_1, x_2, \ldots, x_n; \alpha_1, \alpha_2, \ldots, \alpha_s) = 0 \qquad i = 1, 2, \ldots, n$$

where the x's are endogenous variables and the α's are exogenous variables. Whether the system (1.56) is a macro or a micro model, the f^i can be considered excess demand equations, as we illustrated in section 1.7. Now suppose that we construct a plausible dynamic counterpart of (1.56). The most common dynamic model constructed for this purpose† is one that assumes that the rate at which x_i changes from period t to period $t + 1$ is a positive function of the amount of excess demand prevailing in the ith market in period t.‡ Approximating this positive function with a linear function, we say that the rate of change in x_i is

---

†See Samuelson [47, Chap. 9], Patinkin [41], Kuenne [31, Chap. 8], and Baumol [7, pp. 373-378].

‡The variable x_i is assumed to be the variable determined by demand and supply in the ith market, thus x_i is the variable which equilibrates the ith market.

a constant fraction of the excess demand in the ith market. We may write this assumption as

(1.57) $x_{i,t+1} - x_{i,t} = K_i f^i(x_{1,t}, \ldots, x_{n,t}: \alpha_{1,t}, \ldots, \alpha_{s,t})$ $i = 1, 2, \ldots, n$

where the K_i are positive constants and the f^i are excess demand functions. The system (1.57) is the dynamic counterpart of (1.56). If there is no excess demand, $f^i = 0$, and x_i is the same in period $t + 1$ as in period t. If there is positive (negative) excess demand, $f^i > 0 \, (<0)$ and x_i in period $t + 1$ is greater (less) than x_i in period t. It is a bit more convenient to write (1.57) in differential equation form, which is equivalent to letting the length of the time period converge to zero. This gives

(1.58) $\dot{x}_i = K_i f^i(x_1, x_2, \ldots, x_n; \alpha_1, \alpha_2, \ldots, \alpha_s)$ $i = 1, 2, \ldots, n$

where $\dot{x}_i$ is the derivative of x_i with respect to time. The reader should verify that the results which follow using (1.58) would also stem from (1.57).

Suppose that (1.58) is in equilibrium. Then

(1.59) $0 = K_i f^i(x^0; \alpha^0)$ $i = 1, 2, \ldots, n$

where $x = (x_1, \ldots, x_n), \alpha = (\alpha_1, \ldots, \alpha_s)$, and the superscript zero indicates equilibrium. Next assume that x is not in equilibrium while α is still fixed at α^0. This can be written as

(1.60) $\dot{x}_i = K_i f^i(x; \alpha^0)$ $i = 1, 2, \ldots, n$ $x \neq x^0$

Subtracting (1.59) from (1.60) gives

$$\dot{x}_i = K_i[f^i(x; \alpha^0) - f^i(x^0; \alpha^0)] \qquad i = 1, 2, \ldots, n$$

Assuming as usual that all excess demand functions f^i are differentiable, we may approximate the term in backets with the total differential of f^i evaluated at (x^0, α^0). (See section 1.4.) This yields

$$\dot{x}_i = K_i[f^i_{x_1^0}(x_1 - x_1^0) + f^i_{x_2^0}(x_2 - x_2^0) + \cdots + f^i_{x_n^0}(x_n - x_n^0)]$$
$$i = 1, 2, \ldots, n$$

where $f^i_{x_j^0}$ are the partial derivatives of f^i with respect to x_j evaluated at the point of equilibrium (x^0, α^0). In matrix form we write this differential equation system as

(1.61) $\dot{x} = KJ(x - x^0)$

where $\dot{x} = (\dot{x}_1, \ldots, \dot{x}_n)$, K is a diagonal matrix with K_i as the ith diagonal element, J is the Jacobian matrix of the functions $(f^1, f^2, \ldots, f^n)$ evaluated at equilibrium [see section 1.3, where we labeled this matrix $J_f(x^0)$], and

$$(x - x^0) = (x_1 - x_1^0, x_2 - x_2^0, \ldots, x_n - x_n^0)$$

The general solution of (1.61) is the sum of the solution of the homogeneous part $\dot{x} = KJx$, often called the transient solution, and any solution of (1.61), called a particular solution.† For a particular solution we can let x equal the n-vector of constants z. Substituting z into (1.61) gives

$$0 = KJz - KJx^0$$

hence

$$z = x^0$$

Since we are interested in the stability of (1.61), our concern is with the transient solution, that is, the solution of the homogeneous part of (1.61). Labeling KJ as A, we may write a solution of $\dot{x} = Ax$ as $x = ce^{\lambda t}$, where c is an n-vector of constants and λ is a root to be solved for. Substituting $ce^{\lambda t}$ for x in $\dot{x} = Ax$ gives

$$\lambda c e^{\lambda t} = A c e^{\lambda t}$$

or, since $e^{\lambda t} \neq 0$

(1.62) $\lambda c = Ac$

which says that

(1.63) $(A - \lambda I)c = 0$

The system in (1.62) or (1.63) is called the eigenvalue problem: A vector c is sought which is mapped by the matrix A into some scalar multiple of itself. The vector c is called the eigenvector (also latent or characteristic vector) and λ is the eigenvalue (also latent or characteristic root) which corresponds to the eigenvector c.

We wish to obtain a nontrivial solution of (1.63), that is, a vector c which is not the zero vector. If we are able to obtain one, say, C_i, and if the corresponding eigenvalue is, say, λ_i, then

$$(A - \lambda_i I)C_i = 0$$

and $C_i e^{\lambda_i t}$ satisfies $\dot{x} = Ax$ and is by definition a solution.

†See Baumol [7, Chap. 14].

However, in order to obtain a nontrivial solution of (1.63), $(A - \lambda I)$ must be a singular matrix. This means that λ must assume a value which sets $|A - \lambda I| = 0$. This determinant is called the characteristic determinant and the matrix $(A - \lambda I)$ is the characteristic matrix of A. Thus, we must solve $|A - \lambda I| = 0$, the characteristic equation, for λ. If A is an $n \times n$ matrix, then the characteristic equation is easily seen to be a polynomial of the nth degree in λ. There will be n values of λ, not necessarily distinct, which will satisfy the characteristic equation. Assume that these n values of λ are distinct.[†] Corresponding to each of these eigenvalues λ_i is an eigenvector C_i, $i = 1, 2, \ldots, n$. We therefore have n solutions of $\dot{x} = Ax$: $C_i e^{\lambda_i t}$, $i = 1, 2, \ldots, n$. Given these n solutions, it is easy to establish that any linear combination of these solutions is also a solution. We may now write the solution of $\dot{x} = Ax$ as x^* where

$$ x^* = P_1 e^{\lambda_1 t} C_1 + P_2 e^{\lambda_2 t} C_2 + \cdots + P_n e^{\lambda_n t} C_n $$

where P_i is a nonzero constant, $i = 1, 2, \ldots, n$, and x^* is an n-vector which is a function of time.

It is easy to verify that if the real parts of all the eigenvalues are negative, than $x^* \to 0$ as $t \to \infty$, and the system (1.61) is stable, for x converges to x^0 as time passes.[‡] Let us assume that the system is stable. Let C be the matrix with columns composed of the eigenvectors $(C_1, C_2, \ldots, C_n)$. We prove in Theorem A1.2 of the appendix that if the eigenvalues are distinct, then C, called the modal matrix, is nonsingular. By multiplication, it can be immediately established that

$$ AC = CD $$

where

$$ D = \begin{bmatrix} \lambda_1 & 0 & \cdots & 0 \\ 0 & \lambda_2 & & \vdots \\ \vdots & \vdots & & \vdots \\ 0 & 0 & \cdots & \lambda_n \end{bmatrix} $$

Since C is nonsingular

$$ C^{-1} AC = D $$

Thus

[†]We deal with the problem of multiple roots in Chapter 3, and also provide there the mathematical background for the statement that the characteristic equation will have n roots, not necessarily distinct.

[‡]See Baumol [7, Chap. 14].

$$|C^{-1}AC| = |D| = \prod_{i=1}^{n} \lambda_i$$

and since the determinant of a matrix product equals the product of the determinants of the matrices,[†]

$$|C^{-1}AC| = |C^{-1}| \, |A| \, |C| = |A|$$

and we have that

$$|A| = \prod_{i=1}^{n} \lambda_i$$

Recalling that by definition $A = KJ$, we have

(1.64) $$|K| \, |J| = \prod_{i=1}^{n} \lambda_i$$

which is the desired result. It indicates that if all the roots have negative real parts, then the sign of the Jacobian can be determined. The sign of $|K|$ must be positive, since K is a diagonal matrix with all positive elements. The right side of (1.64) must have a positive sign if n is even and a negative sign if n is odd. The reason is that if the characteristic equation has the complex root $a + bi$ of some multiplicity, it must also have the conjugate root $a - bi$ of the same multiplicity.[‡] Thus, there will always be an even number of complex roots and their product must be positive. It follows that the right side of (1.64) will have a positive sign if n is even and a negative sign if n is odd. Therefore, $|J|$ is positive when n is even, and negative when n is odd. This was the information we were after.[§]

Supplied with this new information, we can strengthen the results obtained in our economic examples. Consider Example 1.2. We were not able to establish the sign of $\partial x_3/\partial \alpha_3$ in (1.40) because we could not deduce the sign of the Jacobian, $|A|$, from the structural parameters. From the correspondence principle we can say that, if it is plausible that the rate of price increase in each market is a positive function of the excess demand in that market, then the Jacobian must have a negative sign if the system is stable. Thus, in solving (1.39) in Example 1.2, we can now see that

$$\frac{\partial x_3}{\partial \alpha_3} > 0 \frac{\partial x_2}{\partial \alpha_3} > 0$$

where

[†]This proposition is proved as Theorem A1.3 in the appendix. The proof that $|C^{-1}| = |C|^{-1}$ is left to the reader.

[‡]We prove this in Theorem 3.16.

[§]Notice that if the system is stable, the Jacobian of the static model is not zero, and one critical assumption of the implicit function theorem is satisfied.

α_3 is a tax on corn producers

x_3 is the price of potatoes

x_2 is the price of butter

That is, an increase in a tax on corn producers will raise the price of the complement butter, and also raise the price of the rival of corn, potatoes. (Recall that butter and potatoes are supposed complements.) What about the response of the price of corn, x_1? Solving (1.39) for $\partial x_1 / \partial \alpha_3$, we have

$$\frac{\partial x_1}{\partial \alpha_3} = \frac{-f^1_{\alpha_3}(f^2_{x_2}f^3_{x_3} - f^3_{x_2}f^2_{x_3})}{|J|}$$

where $|J|$ is the determinant of the Jacobian matrix in (1.39). We know from the correspondence principle that $|J| < 0$. Since α_3 is a tax $-f^1_{\alpha_3}$ is also negative. The sign of the term in parenthesis appears to be in doubt, since the four structural parameters are negative. But this term is the minor of the element in the first row and first column of the Jacobian matrix of (1.39). Expanding the determinant of the Jacobian matrix by the first row gives

$$f^1_{x_1}J_{11} - f^1_{x_2}J_{12} + f^1_{x_3}J_{13} < 0$$

where J_{1i} is the minor of the element in the first row and ith column, $i = 1, 2, 3$. Recalling that the signs of the elements in this Jacobian are

$$\begin{bmatrix} - & - & + \\ - & - & - \\ + & - & - \end{bmatrix}$$

we see that

$$-f^1_{x_2}J_{12} + f^1_{x_3}J_{13} > 0$$

Thus

$$f^1_{x_1}J_{11} < 0$$

and since $f^1_{x_1} < 0$ it follows that J_{11} must be positive, that is,

$$f^2_{x_2}f^3_{x_3} > f^3_{x_2}f^2_{x_3}$$

We may therefore deduce that

$$\frac{\partial x_1}{\partial \alpha_3} > 0$$

where the correspondence principle not only gave us the sign of the Jacobian but also helped us to determine the sign of the relevant minor. Clearly, when the system is larger, the correspondence principle will in general not be able to help deduce the signs of the various subdeterminants.†

Consider the numerical example of the same three markets in Example 1.2. Recall that the value of the Jacobian was 2. We see now that the results obtained in that calculation were probably nonsensical, and that static analysis could not be applied given the numbers assumed for the structural parameters, which were

$$
\begin{bmatrix}
-3 & -1 & 1 \\
-\frac{1}{2} & -1 & -2 \\
1 & -1 & -3
\end{bmatrix}
$$

The reason for these assertions is that this system is not stable, if the dynamic counterpart of the static model assumed in the correspondence principle is plausible. If it were stable, the Jacobian determinant would have to be negative. Of course, the reverse does not follow: The determinant could be negative and the model unstable in a 3×3 system. In general, *stability implies the sign of the determinant, while the sign of the determinant can only imply instability.*

Next, consider the macro model in Example 1.3, where we were attempting to evaluate the sign of

$$
\frac{\partial Y}{\partial \alpha_2} = \frac{M_r I_{\alpha_2}}{|J|}
$$

where

$$
|J| = M_r(1 - E_Y) + I_r M_Y
$$

and

$$
E_Y = C_{Y_d}(1 - t) + I_Y
$$

[See symbols in (1.9).] Recall that α_2 is a shift parameter in the investment function, and we interpret it as any exogenous variable affecting investment, such as an index of technological progress, or we may think of it as simply autonomous investment. With any interpretation, we will usually know the sign of I_{α_2}; say it is positive. The sign of M_r is negative, as explained in section 1.2. Now if we assume that the marginal propensity to spend, E_Y, is between zero and one, as is often done, we can deduce that

†See Patinkin [42].

$$\frac{\partial Y}{\partial \alpha_2} > 0$$

since $I_r < 0$ and $M_Y > 0$.

Using the correspondence principle, we deduce that $|J| < 0$, that is,

$$M_r(1 - E_Y) + I_r M_Y < 0, \qquad \text{or}$$

$$E_Y < 1 + \frac{I_r M_Y}{M_r}$$

if the dynamic counterpart of this static model is stable. Constructing the dynamic counterpart in this case involves taking the system as expressed in (1.10). Moving Y and $\bar{M}$ to the right side gives

$$C(\quad) + I(\quad) + \bar{G} - Y = 0$$
$$M(\quad) - \bar{M} = 0$$

These are excess demand functions. If we are now willing to assume as plausible that the rate of increase in Y and r are positive functions of the excess demands in these markets, we have in linear form

$$\dot{Y} = K_1[C(\quad) + I(\quad) + \bar{G} - Y]$$
$$\dot{r} = K_2[M(\quad) - \bar{M}]$$

where K_1 and K_2 are positive constants. Following the same reasoning as in the general discussion, we deduce that $|J| < 0$. The evaluation of other reduced form derivatives is left to the reader.

One criticism leveled at the correspondence principle† is that a plausible dynamic counterpart of a particular model may *not* result in a matrix of K's that is diagonal. A nondiagonal K matrix would be required if it were assumed that the rate of change of x_i depended on the excess demands in all or some of the other markets, and not just on the excess demand in the ith market. This assumption would change (1.58) to

$$\dot{x}_i = \sum_{j=1}^{n} K_{ij} f^j(x, \alpha) \qquad i = 1, 2, \ldots, n$$

The argument would proceed in similar fashion from that point until (1.64); hawever, the sign of $|K|$ would not necessarily be known, since K would not be diagonal. Thus, the sign of $|J|$ would remain a mystery.

The question then is, is it plausible to assume that the rate of change in x_i depends on anything but the excess demand in the ith market? To assume

†See Patinkin [41, App. to Chap. 12].

so is to suppose that the amount of excess demand in, say, the jth market $j \neq i$, can influence x_i, *given the amount of excess demand in the ith market.* But this is equivalent to assuming that forces other than the demand and supply for the ith good influence the price of the ith good, or that the demand and supply for national output (money) in our macro model is not the only determinant of national output (the price of money). Since the variable in question is free to act as an equilibrating variable, and since demand and supply subsume all influences on such a variable by definition, it does not seem plausible to argue that the rate of change of such a variable depends upon anything other than the excess demand in *that* variable's market. Obviously, the excess demands in various markets are interconnected. But this fact is expressed in a diagonal K matrix in that a change in the excess demand in market X will affect a variable determined by demand and supply in market Y by changing the excess demand in market Y. To argue for a nondiagonal K matrix is to argue that a change in the excess demand in matrix X will affect a variable determined by demand and supply in market Y independently of the excess demand in market Y.† This argument does not seem to be a valid criticism of the correspondence principle.

On the other hand, the correspondence principle assumes that a particular type of dynamic model is a reasonable counterpart to a static model, a dynamic model characterized by the rate of change of each variable being a function of the excess demand for that variable. But this type of dynamic model might not be a plausible counterpart to a static model. The dynamic model required might be of a different kind. Suppose, for example, that the markets always are in equilibrium in each period, and thus excess demand is always zero for that period. At the same time the demand and/or supply variables in the model could depend on the values of variables in the present and in past periods. Such a model is quite different from the one assumed in the usual process of applying the correspondence principle. Or suppose that the rate of change of each variable depends on its excess demand in periods t, $t-1$, and $t-2$. It is certainly possible that the excess demand either is eliminated within the selected time period, or is not eliminated and influences the equilibrating variable for more than one period into the future. Even in such cases some correspondence may be found between the dynamic model assumed stable and properties of the static model. The correspondence might be different, however, from that typically deduced from the correspondence principle. We shall go into the question of more general types of dynamic models in Chapter 3; we shall develop the stability theory for these models in Chapter 4.

†Patinkin [41, pp. 342-344] appears mistaken on this point. He sets up a nondiagonal K matrix in a two equation model where the price level and the interest rate are determined by excess demands in the goods and money markets. Then (p. 344) he adopts the "Keynesian Assumption" that "an excess demand in the money market affects only the rate of interest" and not the price level, which assumption he feels legitimates a diagonal K matrix. Thus, in his view, a diagonal K matrix is only plausible when the excess demand in one market does not affect the variable in the other market.

THEOREM A1.1   PRINCIPLES OF FINITE INDUCTION

THERE ARE TWO SUCH PRINCIPLES.

First Principle of Finite Induction. SUPPOSE THAT TO EACH POSITIVE INTEGER n THERE CORRESPONDS A PROPOSITION $p(n)$ WHICH IS EITHER TRUE OR FALSE. IF $p(1)$ IS SHOWN TO BE TRUE, AND IF THE *assumption* FOR ANY POSITIVE INTEGER k THAT $p(k)$ IS TRUE *implies* THAT $p(k+1)$ IS TRUE, THEN $p(n)$ IS TRUE FOR ALL POSITIVE INTEGERS n.

Second Principle of Finite Induction. SUPPOSE THAT $p(1)$ IS PROVEN TO BE TRUE, AND SUPPOSE THAT, FOR *any* POSITIVE INTEGER m, THE ASSUMPTION THAT $p(k)$ IS TRUE FOR ALL $k < m$ *implies* THAT $p(m)$ ITSELF IS TRUE, THEN $p(n)$ IS TRUE FOR ALL POSITIVE INTEGERS n.

PROOF:

We shall prove the second principle, the proof of the first principle involves precisely the same reasoning. The proof is by contradiction. Let S be the set of positive integers for which $p(n)$ is false. Now S does not contain 1, for we assume that $p(1)$ has been proven true. Next we assume that S contains some smallest integer (this axiom is called the well-ordering principle); call this integer m. Thus, $p(k)$ must be true for any $k < m$. We now assume that the implication can be made that $p(m)$ is true, which contradicts that $m \in S$. It follows that S must contain no positive integers and is therefore empty.

Q.E.D.

THEOREM A1.2

IF AN $n \times n$ MATRIX A HAS n DISTINCT EIGENVALUES, THEN THE n EIGENVECTORS WHICH CORRESPOND TO THESE EIGENVALUES ARE LINEARLY INDEPENDENT.

PROOF:

Let $z_1, \ldots, z_n$ be the eigenvectors which correspond to the distinct eigenvalues $r_1, \ldots, r_n$. Thus, by definition

$$(1.65) \qquad Az_i = r_i z_i \qquad i = 1, \ldots, n$$

The proof is carried out by obtaining a contradiction. Assume that there exists a set of p linearly dependent eigenvectors, where $p \le n$. Let this set be $(z_1, \ldots, z_{p-1}, z_p)$, where $(z_1, \ldots, z_{p-1})$ are assumed without loss of generality to be linearly independent. Then there exists (by definition of linear dependence) a set of scalars $(\alpha_1, \ldots, \alpha_p)$ not all zero such that

$$(1.66) \qquad \alpha_1 z_1 + \cdots + \alpha_{p-1} z_{p-1} + \alpha_p z_p = 0$$

In particular, $\alpha_p \neq 0$, for if it were zero (1.66) could only be true if $\alpha_1 = \alpha_2 = \cdots = \alpha_{p-1} = 0$, since $(z_1, \ldots, z_{p-1})$ are linearly independent by assumption. Next, premultiply (1.66) by A and then substitute (1.65). This gives

$$(1.67) \qquad \alpha_1 r_1 z_1 + \cdots + \alpha_{p-1} r_{p-1} z_{p-1} + \alpha_p r_p z_p = 0$$

Multiply (1.66) by r_p, which yields

$$(1.68) \qquad \alpha_1 r_p z_1 + \cdots + \alpha_{p-1} r_p z_{p-1} + \alpha_p r_p z_p = 0$$

Subtracting (1.68) from (1.67) we have

$$(1.69) \qquad \alpha_1(r_1 - r_p)z_1 + \cdots + \alpha_{p-1}(r_{p-1} - r_p)z_{p-1} = 0$$

Since $(z_1, \ldots, z_{p-1})$ are linearly independent, (1.69) implies that

$$(1.70) \qquad \alpha_i(r_i - r_p) = 0 \qquad i = 1, \ldots, p - 1$$

Since $(r_i - r_p) \neq 0, i = 1, \ldots, p - 1$, by assumption, (1.70) implies

$$(1.71) \qquad \alpha_i = 0 \qquad i = 1, \ldots, p - 1$$

which from (1.66) implies that $\alpha_p = 0$, but this contradicts the assumption that there exists p linearly dependent eigenvectors, $p \leq n$.

$$\text{Q.E.D.}$$

THEOREM A1.3

Suppose that A and B are $n \times n$ nonsingular matrices. Then,

$$|AB| = |A||B|$$

Proof:

It is easy to verify the lemma that

$$|EA| = |E||A|$$

where E is an elementary matrix, that is, a unit matrix with one of the three elementary operations having been performed on its rows. It follows that if $E_i, i = 1, \ldots, n$, are elementary matrices

$$(1.72) \qquad |E_1 \cdots E_n A| = |E_1||E_2| \cdots |E_n||A|$$

by induction.

Next, any nonsingular matrix can be expressed as the product of elementary matrices,† thus

(1.73) $$|A| = |E_1 \cdots E_n| = |E_1| \cdots |E_n|$$

Let

(1.74) $$|AB| = |E_1 \cdots E_n B|$$

By (1.72) we can write (1.74) as

(1.75) $$|AB| = |E_1||E_2| \cdots |E_n||B|$$

and by (1.73)

$$|AB| = |A||B|$$

Q.E.D.

Comment. If A or B is singular, the theorem still holds. Suppose A is singular, then $|A| = 0$, and whether B is singular or not $|A||B| = 0$. If A is singular, its rank is less than n. It follows that AB must have rank less than n, hence $|AB| = 0$. This follows from Theorem 3.22, which says that rank $(AB) \leq \min \{\text{rank } A, \text{rank } B\}$.

†This fact is immediately deducible from the last paragraph of section 1.6.

2 Optimization Theory

The economic theorist attempts to discover how a complex system responds qualitatively to various exogenous disturbances. In the language of the previous chapter, he wants to find out as much as possible about the signs of the reduced form derivatives or multipliers. So far we have appealed to two kinds of economic arguments to help us. First, we have employed our understanding of the motives and aspirations of the economic actors in a particular cultural context to provide persuasive explanations of the qualitative responses that could be expected to various stimuli. We called this specification, and the fruits were the behavioral assumptions of the model, that is, the signs of the structural parameters. Second, we constructed a reasonable dynamic counterpart to a static model, assumed stability, and then were able to deduce additional information relevant to our objective. This process is Samuelson's correspondence principle.

In this chapter, we explore a rich third source which provides some powerful weapons in the theorist's arsenal—the theory of optimizing activity. Many economic models derive from the assumption that economic units are maximizing or minimizing something, be it utility, profits, product, or cost. This optimization process usually occurs in the presence of constraints, such as income, resources, and production functions.

We shall develop some of the fundamental mathematical machinery for analyzing problems of optimization subject to constraints, and we shall provide illustrations of the way in which these techniques can complement those of the previous chapter in generating economic models and information about these models.

2.2 UNCONSTRAINED OPTIMIZATION

Before developing the fundamentals of constrained optimization, we will explore the theory of unconstrained optimization, for the latter will be used to generate the former. Our objective in this section is to derive necessary and sufficient conditions for the optimization of a function of several variables. Fundamental to this development is the famous Taylor theorem, which we present and prove.†

†See Courant [13].

THEOREM 2.1   TAYLOR'S THEOREM

LET $f(x)$ BE A FUNCTION OF ONE VARIABLE AND DEFINED AT $x = a$. SUPPOSE THAT $f \in C^n$ OVER SOME INTERVAL[†] OF WHICH a IS ONE ENDPOINT AND x IS THE OTHER ENDPOINT. THEN

$$f(x) = f(a) + f'(a)(x - a) + \frac{f''(a)}{2!}(x - a)^2 + \cdots$$

$$+ \frac{f^{n-1}(a)}{(n - 1)!}(x - a)^{n-1} + R_n$$

WHERE THE REMAINDER R_n IS GIVEN BY

$$R_n = \int_a^x \frac{(x - t)^{n-1}}{(n - 1)!} f^n(t)\, dt$$

AND WHERE

$$f' \equiv \frac{df}{dx}$$

$$f'' \equiv \frac{d^2f}{dx^2}$$

$$\vdots$$

$$f^n \equiv \frac{d^nf}{dx^n}$$

PROOF:

Observe that the following statement is true by the fundamental theorem of calculus.[‡]

(2.1) $$f(x) - f(a) = \int_a^x f'(t)\, dt$$

To the integral, we now apply integration by parts. Recall that, given $w(t)$ and $u(t)$

$$\frac{d}{dt}(u \cdot w) = w\frac{du}{dt} + u\frac{dw}{dt}$$

and by the fundamental theorem of calculus

[†]Recall that $f \in C^n$ means that the nth derivative of f is continuous. By theorems 1.2 and 1.4, if $f \in C^n$ all lower order derivatives, including f, are continuous.

[‡]See Yamane [51, pp. 136–139] and Courant [13, Vol. I, pp. 114–117].

$$u \cdot w \Big|_a^x = \int_a^x \left(w \frac{du}{dt} \right) dt + \int_a^x \left(u \frac{dw}{dt} \right) dt$$

or

(2.2) $$\int_a^x \left(u \frac{dw}{dt} \right) dt = u \cdot w \Big|_a^x - \int_a^x \left(w \frac{du}{dt} \right) dt$$

In (2.2) let $u = f'(t)$ and $w = -(x - t)$. Thus

(2.3) $$\int_a^x f'(t) \, dt = -f'(t)(x - t) \Big|_a^x$$

$$- \int_a^x - (x - t) f''(t) \, dt$$

$$= f'(a)(x - a) + \int_a^x (x - t) f''(t) \, dt$$

Notice that the left side of (2.3) equals the right side of (2.1). We may rewrite (2.3) as

(2.4) $$f(x) = f(a) + f'(a)(x - a) + \int_a^x (x - t) f''(t) \, dt$$

which proves the theorem for $n = 2$.
Again, apply integration by parts to the integral in (2.4), where we define

$$u = f''(t) \quad \text{and} \quad w = \frac{-(x - t)^2}{2}$$

This gives, for $\int_a^x (x - t) f''(t) \, dt$,

(2.5) $$\int_a^x f''(t) \frac{dw}{dt} \, dt = \frac{-(x - t)^2}{2} f''(t) \Big|_a^x$$

$$- \int_a^x \frac{-(x - t)^2}{2} f'''(t) \, dt$$

$$= \frac{(x - a)^2}{2} f''(a) + \frac{1}{2} \int_a^x (x - t)^2 f'''(t) \, dt$$

We may now write (2.4) as

(2.6) $$f(x) = f(a) + f'(a)(x - a) + \frac{f''(a)(x - a)^2}{2}$$

$$+ \frac{1}{2} \int_a^x (x - t)^2 f'''(t) \, dt$$

Notice that we have proved the theorem for $n = 3$. To complete the proof we employ induction. We now assume that the theorem is true for $n - 1$, that is,

$$(2.7) \qquad f(x) = f(a) + f'(a)(x - a) + \frac{f''(a)(x - a)^2}{2!} + \cdots$$

$$+ \frac{f^{n-2}(a)(x - a)^{n-2}}{(n - 2)!} + R_{n-1}$$

where

$$R_{n-1} = \int_a^x \frac{(x - t)^{n-2}}{(n - 2)!} f^{n-1}(t)\, dt$$

From (2.7) we now must deduce that if f^n is continuous on the interval, then the theorem holds. Notice that (2.7) and the theorem differ only in the last couple of terms, so if we can shown that the last term of (2.7) is identical to the last two terms of the theorem, we will have proved the theorem. To do this we need only apply integration by parts to R_{n-1}. Rewrite R_{n-1} as

$$\int_a^x f^{n-1}(t) \frac{dw}{dt}\, dt$$

where

$$u = f^{n-1}(t)$$

and

$$w = -\frac{(x - t)^{n-1}}{(n - 1)!}, \quad \text{hence,} \quad \frac{dw}{dt} = \frac{(x - t)^{n-2}}{(n - 2)!}$$

and applying integration by parts gives

$$\int_a^x f^{n-1}(t) \frac{dw}{dt}\, dt = -\frac{f^{n-1}(t)(x - t)^{n-1}}{(n - 1)!} \bigg|_a^x$$

$$- \int_a^x -\frac{(x - t)^{n-1}}{(n - 1)!} f^n(t)\, dt$$

$$= \frac{f^{n-1}(a)(x - a)^{n-1}}{(n - 1)!} + \int_a^x \frac{(x - t)^{n-1}}{(n - 1)!} f^n(t)\, dt$$

that is,

$$R_{n-1} = \frac{f^{n-1}(a)(x-a)^{n-1}}{(n-1)!} + R_n$$

Q.E.D.

For our purpose it is convenient to establish another form of the remainder R_n, a form named after Lagrange.

THEOREM 2.2

THE REMAINDER IN TAYLOR'S THEOREM MAY ALSO BE WRITTEN AS

$$R_n = \frac{f^n(c)(x-a)^n}{n!}$$

WHERE c IS A NUMBER IN THE OPEN INTERVAL (a, x).

PROOF:

Since f^n is by assumption continuous on the interval $[a, x]$, then by Theorem 1.3 there must exist points M and m in that interval where f^n assumes its maximum and minimum values, respectively. Suppose that $f^n(M)$ is greater than $f^n(m)$. It follows that $t \in [a, x]$ implies

(2.8) $$f^n(m) \leq f^n(t) \leq f^n(M)$$

By the intermediate value theorem,† the middle term assumes all values between its maximum and minimum as t takes on all values in $[a, x]$. For definiteness, assume that $a < x$, thus $x - t \geq 0$ and

$$\frac{(x-t)^{n-1}}{(n-1)!} \geq 0$$

We now multiply (2.8) by this expression and integrate over the interval, which yields

(2.9) $$\int_a^x \frac{(x-t)^{n-1}}{(n-1)!} f^n(m)\, dt < R_n < \int_a^x \frac{(x-t)^{n-1}}{(n-1)!} f^n(M)\, dt$$

where the strict inequalities hold because the intermediate value theorem asserts that strict inequalities must hold in (2.8) over portions of $[a, x]$. Since $f^n(m)$ and $f^n(M)$ are constants, we can take them outside the integral signs, and after a painless integration we have

$$\frac{f^n(m)(x-a)^n}{n!} < R_n < \frac{f^n(M)(x-a)^n}{n!}$$

†See Theorem 1.8.

Since $(x - a)^n/n!$ is a constant, and $f^n(t)$ is assumed to be a continuous function for $t \in [a, x]$, we use the intermediate value theorem once again to deduce that there exists a value of t, say c, such that

$$\frac{f^n(c)(x - a)^n}{n!} = R_n$$

and where c is a number in the open interval (m, M), hence $c \in (a, x)$. Had we assumed, prior to (2.8), that $f(m) = f(M)$, then (2.8) and (2.9) would have been equalities and the theorem would have followed easily.

Q.E.D.

We have thus established that if $f \in C^n$ on $[a, x]$, then we may write the Taylor formula as

$$(2.10) \quad f(x) = f(a) + f'(a)(x - a) + \frac{f''(a)(x - a)^2}{2} + \cdots$$

$$+ \frac{f^n(c)(x - a)^n}{n!}$$

where $c \in (a, x)$. If we now let $n = 1$, we write the theorem as

$$(2.11) \quad f(x) = f(a) + f'(c)(x - a)$$

which is the mean value theorem or the theorem of the mean for a function of one variable. It will also be useful to let $n = 2$, which gives

$$(2.12) \quad f(x) = f(a) + f'(a)(x - a) + \frac{f''(c)(x - a)^2}{2}$$

Observe that the c's in (2.10), (2.11), and (2.12) are not, in general, the same number, although all of them do lie in the open interval (a, x). Also, it is usually not possible to compute the exact value of c.†

We may now use these results to derive the fundamental conditions for an unconstrained extremum (that is, maximum or minimum) for functions of one variable.

Definitions. We say that $f(x)$ has a *local* maximum at a point x^0, if $f(x) \leq f(x^0)$ for all x in a neighborhood of x^0, which may be very small. If the inequality holds for a neighborhood which covers the entire domain over which f is defined, we say that $f(x)$ has a *global* maximum at x^0. Similar definitions hold for a minimum. When the weak inequality in

†What is the value of c in (2.11) and (2.12) if f is linear and quadratic, respectively?

these definitions can be replaced with a strong inequality, we have a unique (sometimes called "strong") maximum or minimum in the neighborhood.

THEOREM 2.3 NECESSARY CONDITION AND SUFFICIENT CONDITIONS FOR A LOCAL EXTREMUM

LET $f(x) \in C^n$ ON THE OPEN INTERVAL (a, b) AND CONSIDER AN INTERIOR POINT c, THAT IS, $a < c < b$. THEN:

(a) IF f HAS A LOCAL EXTREMUM AT c, IT IS NECESSARY THAT $f'(c) = 0$.

(b) THE CONDITIONS $f'(c) = 0$ AND $f''(c) > 0(f''(c) < 0)$ ARE SUFFICIENT TO ESTABLISH THAT f HAS A UNIQUE LOCAL MINIMUM (MAXIMUM) AT c.

(c) THE CONDITIONS $f'(c) = f''(c) = \cdots = f^{n-1}(c) = 0$, AND $f^n(c) > 0$ $(f^n(c) < 0)$ WITH n EVEN, ARE SUFFICIENT TO ESTABLISH THAT f HAS A UNIQUE LOCAL MINIMUM (MAXIMUM) AT c. THESE CONDITIONS WITH n ODD ARE SUFFICIENT TO ESTABLISH THAT f DOES NOT POSSESS A LOCAL MAXIMUM OF MINIMUM AT c.†

PROOF:

(a) Applying the theorem of the mean, expressed in (2.11), we have

$$f(x) = f(c) + f'(d)(x - c)$$

where $x \in (a, b)$ and $d \in (x, c)$, or

$$(2.13) \qquad f(x) - f(c) = f'(d)(x - c)$$

Now, if f has a local maximum at c, then

$$f(x) - f(c) \leq 0$$

for all x in some neighborhood of c. Therefore, by (2.13), if f has a local maximum at c, then

$$(2.14) \qquad f(x) - f(c) - f'(d)(x - c) \leq 0$$

Imagine that $f'(c)$ is, say, positive. Then, since $f'(c)$ is assumed continuous at c, there must be a neighborhood of c, which may be very small, such that $f'(x) > 0$ for all x in this neighborhood. If x is chosen in this neighborhood, then d must also be in this neighborhood. Then $f'(d) > 0$. But in (2.14), $(x - c)$ can be either positive or negative, which means that $f'(d)(x - c)$ can be either positive or negative. Hence, we have contradicted our assumption that f has a local maximum at c. Conversely, suppose that $f'(c) < 0$. By the same continuity argument, $f'(d) < 0$, and, since f is assumed to have a local maximum at c, (2.14) must hold. But (2.14)

†This condition defines a point of inflection of f at c.

cannot hold if $f'(d) < 0$, because $(x - c)$ can be either positive or negative. Again we have a contradiction. We thus conclude that if $f(c)$ is assumed to be a local maximum, it is impossible for $f'(c)$ to be either positive or negative. The same argument follows for a local minimum. And (a) of the theorem has been established, requiring only that $f \in C^1$ on (a, b).

(b) Applying the Taylor theorem with $n = 2$, equation (2.12), in this context gives

$$f(x) - f(c) = f'(c)(x - c) + \frac{f''(d)(x - c)^2}{2}$$

According to the assumptions of (b), $f'(c) = 0$ and $f''(c) > 0$. Thus, the last expression can be written as

(2.15) $$f(x) - f(c) = \frac{f''(d)(x - c)^2}{2}$$

Since f'' is assumed continuous at c, there exists a neighborhood of c in which $f''(x) > 0$ for all x in this neighborhood. Let x be in this neighborhood. Therefore, the right side of (2.15) is positive for all x in this neighborhood of c, which implies $f(x) > f(c)$ in this neighborhood. We see that if $f'(c) = 0$ and $f''(c) > 0$, then f enjoys a unique local minimum at c. The reasoning is similar for $f'(c) = 0$ and $f''(c) < 0$. Hence, (b) of the theorem has been proved, requiring only that $f \in C^2$ on (a, b).

(c) Consider the conditions of (c) and the Taylor formula in (2.10). Together they give

(2.16) $$f(x) - f(c) = \frac{f^n(d)(x - c)^n}{n!}$$

If $f^n(c) > 0$ and n even, by the continuity argument $f^n(d) > 0$ in some interval of c, hence the right side of (2.16) is positive, for all x in some neighborhood of c. Thus, f in this case must have a unique local minimum at c. If $f^n(c) > 0$ and n is odd, the right side of (2.16) must change signs, being positive for $x > c$ and negative for $x < c$; therefore, f cannot have a local minimum or maximum at c. The argument is similar if $f^n(c) < 0$. Finally, if all derivatives vanish at c, we see from (2.16) that f is a stationary point at c, but f could be a local maximum or minimum or neither at c.

Q.E.D.

An example $y = x^3$ is given in Figure 2-1, where all derivatives vanish

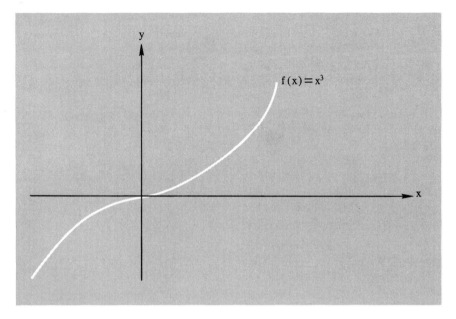

$f(x) = x^3$

Fig. 2-1

at $x = 0$, but $f(0)$ is neither a local maximum nor a minimum, but an inflection point.

It is a simple matter to extend these results to a function of n variables. Let x be the n-vector $(x_1, x_2, \ldots, x_n)$. Suppose that the real-valued function $f(x)$ takes on a local maximum at $x^0 = (x_1^0, x_2^0, \ldots, x_n^0)$. Describe a neighboring point of x^0 as $x^0 + th$ where t is a variable number and $h = (h_1, h_2, \ldots, h_n)$ is a fixed and arbitrary vector with elements not all zero, that is,

$$x^0 + th = (x_1^0 + th_1, x_2^0 + th_2, \ldots, x_n^0 + th_n)$$

We say that f has a local maximum at x^0 if $f(x^0 + th) \leq f(x^0)$ for all h and t is some neighborhood of zero. The definition is analogous for a local minimum. Now, define a real-valued function of one variable $g(t)$ as

$$g(t) = f(x^0 + th)$$

hence

$$g(0) = f(x^0)$$

Clearly, if f takes on a local maximum at x^0, g takes on a local maximum at $t = 0$. Observe also that $g(t)$ is a composite function, made up of $f(x)$

and $x_i(t) = x_i + th_i$, $i = 1, 2, \ldots, n$; thus, by Theorems 1.5 and 1.6, if $f \in C^n$ so will g, since the functions $x_i(t)$ clearly do.

Since g is a function of one variable, we may apply Theorem 2.3 to it and obtain necessary and sufficient conditions for the unconstrained maximum or minimum of a function of n variables. We state the result as a theorem.

THEOREM 2.4   NECESSARY CONDITION AND SUFFICIENT CONDITIONS FOR A LOCAL EXTREMUM FOR A FUNCTION OF n VARIABLES

LET $f(x) \in C^n$ ON A CONVEX SET R IN E^n, AND ASSUME THAT x^0 IS AN INTERIOR POINT OF R. THEN:

(a) IF f HAS A LOCAL MAXIMUM OR MINIMUM AT x^0, IT IS NECESSARY THAT THE GRADIENT OF f EVALUATED AT x^0 BE THE ZERO VECTOR, THAT IS $\nabla f(x^0) = 0$.

(b) THE CONDITIONS $\nabla f(x^0) = 0$ AND $d^2 f(x^0) > 0 (d^2 f(x^0) < 0)$ ARE SUFFICIENT TO ESTABLISH THAT f HAS A UNIQUE LOCAL MINIMUM (MAXIMUM) AT x^0. (THE SYMBOL $d^2 f(x^0)$ IS THE SECOND DIFFERENTIAL OF f EVALUATED AT x^0.)

(c) THE CONDITIONS $\nabla f(x^0) = 0$ AND $d^2 f(x^0) = d^3 f(x^0) = \cdots = d^{n-1} f(x^0) = 0$ AND $d^n f(x^0) > 0 (d^n f(x^0) < 0)$ WITH n EVEN, ARE SUFFICIENT TO ESTABLISH THAT f HAS A UNIQUE LOCAL MINIMUM (MAXIMUM) AT x^0. THESE CONDITIONS WITH n ODD ARE SUFFICIENT TO ESTABLISH THAT f DOES NOT POSSESS A LOCAL MAXIMUM OR MINIMUM AT x^0. IF THE DIFFERENTIALS OF EVERY ORDER VANISH AT x^0, THEN WE ONLY HAVE A NECESSARY CONDITION THAT f HAS A LOCAL MAXIMUM OR MINIMUM AT x^0, BUT WE HAVE NO GUARANTEE.

PROOF:

(a) By the definition of $g(t)$, this assertion is equivalent to the assumption that $g(t)$ has a local maximum or minimum at $t = 0$. By (a) of Theorem 2.3, this implies that $g'(0)$, and differentiating g with respect t, at $t = 0$, gives†

$$(2.17) \qquad g'(0) = \sum_1^n f_i(x^0) h_i = 0 \equiv \nabla f(x^0) h = 0$$

where

$$f_i(x_0) \equiv \frac{\partial f(x^0)}{\partial x_i} \quad \text{and} \quad \nabla f(x^0) \equiv (f_1(x^0), \ldots, f_n(x^0))$$

Notice that $g'(0) = df(x^0)$. Since the h_i are arbitrary, (2.17) implies that $f_i(x^0) = 0, i = 1, 2, \ldots, n$. That is, $\nabla f(x^0)$ is the zero vector, and (a) has been established.

---

†The chain rule can be applied to $g(t)$ by Theorem 1.2. Differentiation to the nth order is similarly justified since $g \in C^n$.

(b) By (b) of Theorem 2.3 as applied to $g(t)$, the conditions $g'(0) = 0$ and $g''(0) > 0$ are sufficient to establish that g has a local minimum at $t = 0$. Computing $g''(0)$ gives

$$(2.18) \qquad g''(0) = \sum_{i=1}^{n} \sum_{j=1}^{n} f_{ij}(x^0) h_i h_j > 0, \quad \text{where} \quad f_{ij}(x^0) \equiv \frac{\partial^2 f(x^0)}{\partial x_i \partial x_j}$$

Observing that $g''(0) = d^2 f(x^0)$, we see that (b) is established for a minimum. The argument for a maximum is parallel, with the sign in (2.18) being negative.

(c) This follows analogously from (c) of Theorem 2.3, and the fact that $g^i(0) = d^i f(x^0), i = 1, \ldots, n$. It is seldom used in economics and we shall not elaborate on it further.

Q.E.D.

Remark. An expression such as the one on the right side of (2.18) is called a *quadratic form*. It can be written in matrix form as $h'Hh$ where $h = (h_1, h_2, \cdots, h_n)$ and the matrix H has $f_{ij}(x^0)$ in the ith row and jth column. This matrix of second order partial derivatives is called the *Hessian* matrix. By a well-known theorem on partial derivatives, if $f(x) \in C^2$ then $f_{ij} = f_{ji}$†; therefore, the Hessian is a symmetric matrix. If $h'Hh > 0(<0)$ for all $h \neq 0$, we say that the quadratic form is *positive (negative)* definite. This is precisely what (b) of the theorem says: If $\nabla f(x^0)$ is the zero vector, and if the quadratic form evaluated at x^0 is positive (negative) definite, then f is guaranteed to have a local minimum (maximum) at x^0. It should be clear that if the quadratic form $h'Hh$ is *indefinite*, that is, positive for some h and negative for others, then we have neither a maximum nor a minimum at x^0, but a saddle point. If the quadratic form is positive (negative) *semidefinite*, that is, for all $h \neq 0$, $h'H_f(x^0)h \geq 0(\leq0)$, we do not have a sufficient condition for a local minimum (maximum). The reason is that although H is semidefinite at x^0, there is no reason why H may not be indefinite at a point in every neighborhood of x^0. In the case of definiteness, the continuity of H rules out this possibility. It follows that when the Hessian is semidefinite at a suspected extreme point, Theorem 2.4 cannot be used; use of the Taylor theorem requires that g'' be positive or negative in a neighborhood of zero which implies that $h'Hh > 0(<0)$ in a neighborhood of x^0. However, $h'H_f(x^0)h \geq 0(\leq0)$ *is* a necessary condition for a local minimum (maximum).

---

†See Courant [13, Vol. II, p. 55]. The theorem stems directly from the mean value theorem. The Hessian is often written $H_f(x^0)$, that is, the Hessian of f evaluated at x^0. See appendix for further comments on quadratic forms.

It is a fundamental result in matrix analysis† that H is a *positive definite matrix if and only if all of its naturally ordered principal minors are positive; that* H *is a negative definite matrix if and only if all of its naturally ordered principal minors of order* k *have sign* $(-1)^k$. The naturally ordered principal minors are found as follows:

$$\begin{vmatrix} f_{11} & f_{12} & f_{13} & \cdots & f_{1n} \\ f_{21} & f_{22} & f_{23} & \cdots & f_{2n} \\ f_{31} & f_{32} & f_{33} & \cdots & f_{3n} \\ \vdots & \vdots & \vdots & & \vdots \\ f_{n1} & f_{n2} & f_{n3} & \cdots & f_{nn} \end{vmatrix}$$

where $f_{ij} \equiv \partial^2 f/(\partial x_i \partial x_j)$ is the ijth element of H. We may, therefore, use this condition on the signs of the principal minors of H at x^0 in lieu of $d^2f = h'Hh \gtrless 0$ in (b) of the theorem. If H is not too large, the determinantal condition may be useful.

Example 2.1

Find the extreme points of

$$f(x_1, x_2) = \frac{x_1^3}{3} + \frac{x_2^2}{2} + x_1 x_2 - 3x_1 + 3x_2$$

The necessary conditions are

$$f_1 = x_1^2 + x_2 - 3 = 0$$
$$f_2 = x_2 + x_1 + 3 = 0$$

which yields the solutions $(-2, -1)$ and $(3, -6)$.

The Hessian of f is

$$H = \begin{bmatrix} f_{11} & f_{12} \\ f_{21} & f_{22} \end{bmatrix} = \begin{bmatrix} 2x_1 & 1 \\ 1 & 1 \end{bmatrix}$$

and the Hessian evaluated at these two suspected extreme points is

$$H(-2, -1) = \begin{bmatrix} -4 & 1 \\ 1 & 1 \end{bmatrix}$$

$$H(3, -6) = \begin{bmatrix} 6 & 1 \\ 1 & 1 \end{bmatrix}$$

†See Hadley [21, Chap. 7].

The principal minors of $H(-2, -1)$ are -4 and -5, which indicates that H at this point is indefinite, and we therefore have a saddle point. The principle minors of $H(3, -6)$ are 6 and 5, which implies that H at this point is positive definite. The point $(3, -6)$ is thus a local minimum.

Example 2.2

Find the extreme points of

$$f(x_1, x_2, x_3) = -2x_1^2 + 2x_1 x_2 - 2x_2^2 - x_3^2$$

The necessary conditions are

$$f_1 = -4x_1 + 2x_2 = 0$$
$$f_2 = 2x_1 - 4x_2 = 0$$
$$f_3 = -2x_3 = 0$$

which yields the unique solution $(0, 0, 0)$. Computing the Hessian at this point gives

$$H(0, 0, 0) = \begin{bmatrix} -4 & 2 & 0 \\ 2 & -4 & 0 \\ 0 & 0 & -2 \end{bmatrix}$$

and the principal minors are $-4, 12$, and -24. Hence $(0, 0, 0)$ is a local maximum.†

We can now easily prove the mean value theorem for functions of n variables, which we employed in section 1.4 to prove several theorems. Expanding the function $g(t)$ around $t = 0$, and letting the n in the Taylor formula equal one, we have

$$g(t) = g(0) + g'(c)t$$

where $c \in (0, t)$. Since by definition $g(t) = f(x^0 + th)$, we can write this equation in terms of f. Letting $t = 1$, we have

(2.19) $$f(x^0 + h) = f(x^0) + df(x^0 + ch)$$
$$0 < c < 1$$

which yields the theorem of the mean, or the Taylor theorem for a function of several variables, with the n of that theorem equal to one. Notice that the

---

†This point, in fact, is also a global maximum, and f itself is a negative definite quadratic form. We shall pursue this point in our discussion of convex and concave functions in section 2.6.

point $x^0 + ch$ is on a line segment between x^0 and $x^0 + h$, that is, $x^0 + ch$ is a *convex combination* of these points, for

$$(x^0 + ch) = (1 - \lambda)x^0 + \lambda(x^0 + h)$$

where $0 \le \lambda \le 1$; in fact, $\lambda = c$. This point underlines the *assumption* of the Taylor theorem that f be defined on a convex set, for if x^0 and $x^0 + h$ belong to the domain of f, it is necessary that the line segment between them also belong. Observe also that x^0 must be an interior point of the domain of f. Thus, we either define the Taylor theorem on an open set, which by definition makes x^0 an interior point if it belongs to that set, or we may define f on a closed set and specify that x^0 be an interior point.

Alternatively, we can write (2.19) as

(2.20) $$f(x^0 + h) = f(x^0) + \nabla f(x^0 + ch) \cdot h$$

where the last term indicates the inner product of the gradient of f, evaluated at the point $(x^0 + ch)$, and h.

Recalling (2.18) and the remark on quadratic forms, we can write the Taylor theorem for functions of several variables with $n = 2$ as follows. Writing (2.12) for $g(t)$ gives

$$g(t) = g(0) + g'(0)t + \frac{g''(c)t^2}{2}$$

$$c \in (0, t)$$

and substituting $g(t) = f(x^0 + th)$ into this expression, and setting $t = 1$, yields

(2.21) $$f(x^0 + h) = f(x^0) + df(x^0) + \frac{d^2 f(x^0 + ch)}{2}$$

$$c \in (0, 1)$$

or

(2.22) $$f(x^0 + h) + f(x^0) + \nabla f(x^0) \cdot h + \frac{h' H h}{2}$$

where the Hessian matrix H is evaluated at the point $(x^0 + ch)$. The number $0 < c < 1$ in (2.21) and (2.22) is in general not the same as the c in (2.19) and (2.20). By similar reasoning, the analogue of (2.10) for functions of several variables can be computed.

In concluding this section, we emphasize some points that should be kept in mind when applying these methods. First, solution of the necessary conditions locates only potential *interior* extrema. If f is defined on a closed set, extreme points on the boundary will not be picked up by the above techniques, and other methods must be used. Second, these methods assume that f has continuous partial derivatives of the required order on the interior of the domain. Any points at which f is not well-behaved will not be considered by these methods as candidates for extrema. Finally, if the Hessian of f at a possible extreme point is semidefinite, this generally tells us nothing. However, if all higher than second order derivatives vanish identically in a neighborhood of a point, then the semidefiniteness of the Hessian at the point, in conjunction with the necessary condition, provides a sufficient condition for a local extrema. The reason for this is that if all higher than second order derivatives vanish in a neighborhood of a point, then the Hessian must be a fixed matrix in this neighborhood; in other words, the elements of the Hessian, which are second order derivatives, must be constants in a neighborhood where all higher than second order derivatives are identically zero. If the Hessian is a fixed matrix in a neighborhood of x^0, we see from (2.22) that if $\nabla f(x^0) = 0$, and if the quadratic form is positive (negative) semidefinite at x^0, then

$$f(x) - f(x^0) = \frac{h' H_f(x^0 + ch)h}{2} = \frac{h' H_f(x^0)h}{2} \geq 0(\leq 0)$$

(where $x = x^0 + h$) where the second equality holds because H_f is invariant with respect to x in a neighborhood of x^0. For the Hessian in this neighborhood, the quadratic form is by assumption nonnegative (nonpositive) for all h. Hence, f assumes a local minimum (maximum) at x^0.

As an illustration of this point, consider the general second-order polynomial

$$f(x) = \tfrac{1}{2} x'Ax - c'x$$

where A is a symmetric $n \times n$ matrix. The necessary condition for an extreme point is

$$\nabla f(x) = Ax - c = 0$$

and the Hessian of f is the matrix A. Now if A is nonsingular, there is a unique candidate for an extremum,

$$x^0 = A^{-1}c$$

and we then investigate the definiteness of A to get further information. If A is nonsingular it cannot be semidefinite.[†] On the other hand, if A is singular, $\nabla f(x) = 0$ has an infinity of solutions if the system is consistent. If, in addition, A is semidefinite, then any solution x^0 to $\nabla f(x) = 0$ is a local extremum, for in the Taylor expansion about x^0 we have from (2.22) that

†See Hadley [21, Chap. 7].

$$f(x^0 + h) - f(x^0) = \frac{h'Hh}{2}$$

where the Hessian is evaluated in a neighborhood of x^0. But in this example the Hessian is A, which is invariant with respect to x. Thus, if A is positive semidefinite we have

$$f(x^0 + h) - f(x^0) = \frac{h'Ah}{2} \geq 0$$

for all $h \neq 0$, and we see that x^0, in this case, is in fact a global minimum, though clearly not unique. Similarly, if A is negative semidefinite, x^0 is a global maximum. By the same argument, if A is nonsingular and positive or negative definite, we have a unique x^0, and by the strong equality in the last expression, x^0 is a unique global minimum or maximum.

2.3 CONSTRAINED OPTIMIZATION

We now use the above results to establish the Lagrange method for analyzing the problem of maximizing or minimizing $f(x_1, x_2, \ldots, x_n)$ subject to a certain number of side conditions or constraints $g^i(x_1, x_2, \ldots, x_n) = 0$, $i = 1, 2, \ldots, r < n$.† The function f is called the *objective function*. In what follows, we let $x \equiv (x_1, x_2, \ldots, x_n)$.

Definitions. Frequent use will be made of a function $L(x, \lambda)$, formed by taking a linear combination of the objective function and the r constraint functions

$$L(x, \lambda) = f(x) - \sum_{r=1}^{r} \lambda_i g^i(x)$$

where $\lambda \equiv (\lambda_1, \lambda_2, \ldots, \lambda_r)$ and where the λ's are called *Lagrange multipliers*. Notice that there is one Lagrange multiplier for each constraint. The function $L(x, \lambda)$ is called the *Lagrangian function*.

The following theorem provides a necessary condition and a sufficient condition for f to have a local extremum subject to the constraints $g^i(x) = 0$, $i = 1, 2, \ldots, r$.

†If $r = n$, and the constraints are functionally independent, the problem is trivial, since there is only one point that satisfies the constraints. If $r = n$ and the constraints are not independent, we can drop the dependent ones, which gives less constraints than variables.

THEOREM 2.5   LAGRANGE MULTIPLIER THEOREM

LET f BE A REAL-VALUED FUNCTION SUCH THAT $f \in C^2$ ON AN OPEN SET R OF E^n. LET $g^1(x)$, $g^2(x)$, ..., $g^r(x)$ BE $r < n$ REAL-VALUED FUNCTIONS SUCH THAT $g \equiv$ $(g^1, \ldots, g^r) \in C^2$ ON R. LET S BE THAT SUBSET OF R ON WHICH g VANISHES; THAT IS, IF $x \in S$, THEN $g(x)$ IS THE ZERO VECTOR. ASSUME ALSO THAT SOME $r \times r$ SUB-MATRIX OF THE JACOBIAN ASSOCIATED WITH THE CONSTRAINT FUNCTIONS IS NONSING-ULAR AT $x^0 \in S$. THAT IS, WE ASSUME, WITHOUT LOSS OF GENERALITY, THAT THE FOLLOWING JACOBIAN MATRIX OF $g(x)$ IS NONSINGULAR AT x^0.

$$J_g(x^0) \equiv \begin{bmatrix} g_1^1(x^0) & g_2^1(x^0) & \cdots & g_r^1(x^0) \\ \vdots & & & \vdots \\ g_1^r(x^0) & & \cdots & g_r^r(x^0) \end{bmatrix}$$

WHERE $g_j^i(x^0) \equiv \partial g^i(x^0)/\partial x_j$.

(a) IF f ASSUMES A LOCAL EXTREMUM AT $x^0 \in S$, THEN THERE EXIST r REAL AND UNIQUE NUMBERS $\lambda_1^0, \lambda_2^0, \ldots, \lambda_r^0$ SUCH THAT THE FOLLOWING n EQUATIONS ARE SATIS-FIED.

(2.23)
$$L_j(x^0, \lambda^0) \equiv f_j(x^0) - \sum_{i=1}^{r} \lambda_i^0 g_j^i(x^0) = 0$$

$$j = 1, 2, \ldots, n$$

WHERE

$$L_j(x^0, \lambda^0) \equiv \frac{\partial L(x^0, \lambda^0)}{\partial x_j}$$

$$f_j(x^0) \equiv \frac{\partial f(x^0)}{\partial x_j}$$

Remark.   The equations in (2.23) may be expressed more compactly with gradient notation,

(2.24) $$\nabla L(x^0, \lambda) \equiv \nabla f(x^0) - \sum_{i=1}^{r} \lambda_i^0 \nabla g^i(x^0) = 0$$

that is, the gradient of the Lagrangian function at (x^0, λ^0) equals the zero vector.

(b) THE CONDITIONS $\nabla L(x^0, \lambda^0) = 0$, $g(x^0) = 0$, AND†

(2.25) $$\sum_{i=1}^{n} \sum_{j=1}^{n} L_{ij}(x^0, \lambda^0) h_i h_j < 0(>0)$$

†$L_{ij}(x^0, \lambda^0) \equiv f_{ij}(x^0) - \sum_{s=1}^{r} \lambda_s^0 g_{ij}^s(x^0)$ where $L_{ij}(x^0, \lambda^0) \equiv \dfrac{\partial^2 L(x^0, \lambda^0)}{\partial x_i \partial x_j}$

FOR ALL $h = (h_1, h_2, \ldots, h_n)$ SUCH THAT

(2.26) $\sum_{j=1}^{n} g_j^i(x^0)h_j = 0 \qquad i = 1, 2, \ldots, r$

ARE SUFFICIENT TO ESTABLISH THAT f HAS A LOCAL MAXIMUM (MINIMUM) AT THE POINT $x^0 \in S$.

Remark. The portion of the sufficient condition in (2.25) and (2.26) can be seen as a negative or positive quadratic form (2.25), subject to a set of linear constraints (2.26). Let L be the symmetric matrix or order $n \times n$ of the quadratic (2.25), with L_{ij} as ijth element, and let G be the $r \times n$ matrix of first order partial derivatives of the constraint functions with g_j^i as the ijth element. We can now write (b) compactly as

(2.27)   (i) $\nabla L = 0$ and $g = 0$
       (ii) $h'Lh < 0(>0)$ subject to
       (iii) $Gh = 0$
       with (i), (ii), and (iii) evaluated at (x^0, λ^0)
$\Rightarrow$ $f(x^0)$ is a local maximum (minimum) with $g(x^0) = 0$

Notice that $\nabla L(x^0, \lambda^0) \equiv \nabla f(x^0) - \lambda' G(x^0)$, where λ' is the row vector $(\lambda_1^0, \cdots, \lambda_r^0)$.

PROOF:

(a) The argument rests on the implicit function theorem.† By assumption, the vector-valued function $g \in C^1$ on the open set R and $x^0 \in R$ is a point for which $g(x^0) = 0$ and for which $|J_g(x^0)| \neq 0$. These are the assumptions of the implicit function theorem. Hence, there exists an $(n - r)$-dimensional neighborhood R_0 of $(x_{r+1}^0, x_{r+2}^0, \ldots, x_n^0)$ and a unique differentiable vector-valued function $\phi = (\phi^1, \phi^2, \ldots, \phi^r)$ defined on R_0, where

(2.28) $x_i = \phi^i(x_{r+1}, \ldots, x_n) \qquad$ on R_0

such that $\phi \in C^1$, and that

$x_i^0 = \phi^i(x_{r+1}^0, \ldots, x_n^0) \qquad i = 1, 2, \ldots, r$

and

(2.29) $g^i(\phi^1, \ldots, \phi^r, x_{r+1}, \ldots, x_n) \equiv 0 \quad$ on $R_0 \quad i = 1, 2, \ldots, r$

Substituting ϕ into the objective function f gives a function F defined on R_0,

†See section 1.5.

(2.30) $\qquad F(x_{r+1}, \ldots, x_n) \equiv f(\phi^1, \ldots, \phi^r, x_{r+1}, \ldots, x_n)$

Now, (a) assumes that f takes on a local extremum at x^0, which implies by (2.28) and (2.30) that F has a local extremum at $(x^0_{r+1}, \cdots, x^0_n)$, which is an interior point of R_0. Furthermore, F has an unconstrained local extremum at this point since the $(n - r)$ arguments of F can vary independently in R_0, because by (2.29) the constraints are identically zero on R_0. We can therefore apply Theorem 2.4, the necessary condition for a local extremum, and deduce that, at x^0

(2.31) $\qquad F_i \equiv \sum_{k=1}^{r} f_k \phi_i^k + f_i = 0 \qquad i = r + 1, \ldots, n$

By the implicit function theorem, the $\phi^k \in C^1$, and therefore we can apply the chain rule to the r equations in (2.29) and set the derivatives equal to zero, which yields, at x^0

(2.32) $\qquad \sum_{k=1}^{r} g_k^s \phi_i^k + g_i^s = 0 \qquad \begin{matrix} s = 1, \ldots, r \\ i = r + 1, \ldots, n \end{matrix}$

Next, for a given i, multiply each of the corresponding equations in (2.32) by an arbitrary number λ_s, $s = 1, \ldots, r$, and sum these r equations over s. This gives

(2.33) $\qquad \sum_{s=1}^{r} \sum_{k=1}^{r} \lambda_s g_k^s \phi_i^k + \sum_{s=1}^{r} \lambda_s g_i^s = 0 \qquad i = r + 1, \ldots, n$

Now subtract (2.33) from (2.31), which yields

(2.34) $\qquad \sum_{k=1}^{r} \left(f_k - \sum_{s=1}^{r} \lambda_s g_k^s \right) \phi_i^k + \left(f_i - \sum_{s=1}^{r} \lambda_s g_i^s \right) = 0$

$$i = r + 1, \ldots, n$$

The question becomes, is there a unique $\lambda = (\lambda_1, \ldots, \lambda_r)$ such that, at x^0,

(2.35) $\qquad f_k - \sum_{s=1}^{r} \lambda_s g_k^s = 0 \qquad k = 1, \ldots, r$

is satisfied? The answer is clearly yes, because the Jacobian matrix of the constraints $J_g(x^0)$ is by assumption nonsingular. We can write (2.35) as

(2.36) $\qquad \begin{bmatrix} g_1^1(x^0) & g_1^2(x^0) & \cdots & g_1^r(x^0) \\ \vdots & & & \vdots \\ g_r^1(x^0) & & \cdots & g_r^r(x^0) \end{bmatrix} \begin{bmatrix} \lambda_1 \\ \vdots \\ \lambda_r \end{bmatrix} = \begin{bmatrix} f_1 \\ \vdots \\ f_r \end{bmatrix}$

which yields a unique solution λ^0, since the matrix in (2.36) is the transpose of $J_g(x^0)$. Then, using (2.35) in (2.34), we see that

$$f_i - \sum_{s=1}^{r} \lambda_s^0 g_i^s = 0 \qquad i = r+1, \ldots, n$$

which, in conjunction with (2.35), establishes (a) of the theorem.[†]
(b) Consider (2.31) again and compute F_{ij}—all partial derivatives still evaluated at x^0—

$$(2.37) \quad F_{ij} = \sum_{k=1}^{r} f_k \phi_{ij}^k + \sum_{k=1}^{r} \phi_i^k \left(\sum_{p=1}^{r} f_{kp} \phi_j^p + f_{kj} \right) + \sum_{p=1}^{r} f_{ip} \phi_j^p + f_{ij}$$

$$i, j = r+1, \ldots, n$$

Performing the same differentiation on the constraints [see (2.29) and (2.32)] gives, at x^0

$$(2.38) \quad \sum_{k=1}^{r} g_k^s \phi_{ij}^k + \sum_{k=1}^{r} \phi_i^k \left(\sum_{p=1}^{r} g_{kp}^s \phi_j^p + g_{kj}^s \right) + \sum_{p=1}^{r} g_{ip}^s \phi_j^p + g_{ij}^s = 0$$

$$s = 1, \ldots, r$$
$$i, j = r+1, \ldots, n$$

Next, for a given i and j, multiply each of the corresponding r equations in (2.38) by λ_s^0 and sum over s; then subtract this from (2.37). The resulting expression after rearranging terms is

$$(2.39) \quad F_{ij} = \sum_{k=1}^{r} \left(f_k - \sum_{s=1}^{r} \lambda_s^0 g_k^s \right) \phi_{ik}^k$$
$$+ \sum_{k=1}^{r} \sum_{p=1}^{r} \left(f_{kp} - \sum_{s=1}^{r} \lambda_s^0 g_{kp}^s \right) \phi_i^k \phi_j^p$$
$$+ \sum_{k=1}^{r} \left(f_{kj} - \sum_{s=1}^{r} \lambda_s^0 g_{kj}^s \right) \phi_i^k$$
$$+ \sum_{p=1}^{r} \left(f_{ip} - \sum_{s=1}^{r} \lambda_s^0 g_{ip}^s \right) \phi_j^p$$
$$+ f_{ij} - \sum_{s=1}^{r} \lambda_s^0 g_{ij}^s \qquad i, j = r+1, \ldots, n$$

Notice that the first term on the right is zero by the first assumption in (b).
Next, define

[†]Notice that the proof of (a) required only that f and $g \in C^1$.

$$h_k = \sum_{i=r+1}^{n} \phi_i^k h_i \qquad k = 1, 2, \ldots, r$$

and

$$h_p = \sum_{j=r+1}^{n} \phi_j^p h_j \qquad p = 1, 2, \ldots, r$$

where h_i, $i = r + 1, \ldots, n$, are arbitrary but not all zero, and compute from (2.39)

$$\sum_{i=r+1}^{n} \sum_{j=r+1}^{n} F_{ij} h_i h_j$$

which yields, at x^0

$$(2.40) \qquad \sum_{i=r+1}^{n} \sum_{j=r+1}^{n} F_{ij} h_i h_j = \sum_{i=1}^{n} \sum_{j=1}^{n} \left(f_{ij} - \sum_{s=1}^{r} \lambda_s^0 g_{ij}^s \right) h_i h_j$$

Now, by assumption (2.25) of (b), the right side of (2.40) is, say, negative for all h such that (2.26) is satisfied. But we can demonstrate that we have defined h in such a way that it will always satisfy (2.26). Assuming that we can prove this, the theorem is completed by the following argument. The first assumption in (b) implies $F_i = 0$ at x^0 [see (2.31)]. If the right side of (2.40) satisfies assumptions (2.25) and (2.26) of (b), the left side of (2.40) is a negative definite quadratic form, since the h_i, $i = r + 1, \ldots, n$ are arbitrary numbers not all zero. Thus, by (b) of Theorem 2.4, F is guaranteed to take on a local maximum on R_0 at x^0. By the definition of F in (2.30), f must therefore take on a local maximum on R_0 at x^0. Since x^0 is assumed to satisfy the constraints (i.e., since $R_0 \subset S$), part (b) of the theorem has been established.

It only remains to be demonstrated that h satisfies the set of linear equations in (2.26). Recall that we defined h_k as

$$h_k \equiv \sum_{i=r+1}^{n} \phi_i^k h_i \qquad k = 1, \ldots, r$$

where the h_i, $i = r + 1, \ldots, n$ are arbitrary constants not all zero. Consider next (2.32)

$$\sum_{k=1}^{r} g_k^s \phi_i^k + g_i^s = 0 \qquad \begin{array}{l} s = 1, \ldots, r \\ i = r + 1, \ldots, n \end{array}$$

Now multiply this expression by h_i and sum over i

(2.41) $\sum\limits_{i=r+1}^{n} \left(\sum\limits_{k=1}^{r} g_k^s \phi_i^k + g_i^s \right) h_i = 0$

$= \sum\limits_{k=1}^{r} \left(\sum\limits_{i=r+1}^{n} \phi_i^k h_i \right) g_k^s + \sum\limits_{i=r+1}^{n} g_i^s h_i = 0 \qquad s = 1, \dots, r$

which by definition of h_k gives

(2.42) $\sum\limits_{k=1}^{r} g_k^s h_k + \sum\limits_{i=r+1}^{n} g_i^s h_i = 0 \qquad s = 1, \dots, r$

but this is precisely the set of linear equations in (2.26). Notice that (2.42) can be solved uniquely for h_k, $k = 1, \dots, r$, since the Jacobian matrix of the constraints is nonsingular at x^0. Thus, given an arbitrary and not all zero set of values for h_i, $i = r + 1, \dots, n$, a unique set of values is determined for h_k, $k = 1, \dots, r$, such that $h = (h_1, \dots, h_n)$ satisfies (2.26), or $Gh = 0$ in (2.27).

Q.E.D.

Remark. Consider (2.23) and (2.24) in (a) of Theorem 2.5. We can write this necessary condition [see (2.27)] as

$$\nabla L = \nabla f - \lambda' G = 0 \qquad (\text{at } x^0, \lambda^0)$$

This implies that, at x^0, ∇f must be linearly dependent on the r rows of G in order for $f(x^0)$ to be a local extremum satisfying the side conditions. If ∇f is linearly independent of the rows of G at x^0, the necessary condition $\nabla L = 0$ cannot hold, since by the definition of linear independence there cannot exist a set of numbers $(1, \lambda_1^0, \dots, \lambda_r^0)$ such that $\nabla L = 0$. Observe also that if $r = 1$, the necessary condition becomes the familiar tangency condition

$$f_i = \lambda^0 g_i \qquad i = 1, \dots, n$$

where λ^0 is a scalar and g the single constraint.

We now wish to express the sufficiency condition (2.27) in a different form, one frequently used in the literature. Consider the following matrix

$$\hat{H} \equiv \begin{bmatrix} L & G' \\ G & 0 \end{bmatrix}$$

referred to as a *bordered Hessian*, where L is the $n \times n$ matrix with ijth element

$$L_{ij} \equiv f_{ij} - \sum_{s=1}^{r} \lambda_s g_{ij}^s$$

and G is the $r \times n$ matrix of first order partial derivatives of the constraint functions, with g_j^i as the ijth element. The matrix G' is the transpose of G, and 0 is an $r \times r$ matrix of zeros. In the following theorem, derivatives all are evaluated at x^0 and $\lambda = \lambda^0$.

THEOREM 2.6

(i) $\left.\begin{array}{l} h'Lh > 0 \\ \text{WHEN } Gh = 0 \end{array}\right\} \Rightarrow$ EVERY APPROPRIATELY OBTAINED PRINCIPAL MINOR OF $|\hat{H}|$ OF ORDER GREATER THAN $2r$ WILL HAVE SIGN $(-1)^r$

(ii) $\left.\begin{array}{l} h'Lh < 0 \\ \text{WHEN } Gh = 0 \end{array}\right\} \Rightarrow$ EVERY APPROPRIATELY OBTAINED PRINCIPAL MINOR OF $|\hat{H}|$ OF ORDER $n+r-i$ WILL HAVE SIGN $(-1)^{n-i}, 0 \le i \le n - r - 1$

BY APPROPRIATELY OBTAINED MINOR, WE MEAN THAT MINOR OBTAINED BY DELETING ANY SET OF i ROWS AND *corresponding* COLUMNS FROM THE *first* n ROWS AND COLUMNS OF $|\hat{H}|$, WHERE $0 \le i \le n - r - 1$. KEEP IN MIND THAT n IS THE NUMBER OF VARIABLES AND r THE NUMBER OF CONSTRAINTS.†

In the next theorem we establish the meaning of the Lagrange multiplier. To do this, it is convenient to write the constraints as

$$g^i(x) = b_i \qquad i = 1, \ldots, r$$

where the b's are constants.

THEOREM 2.7

If (b) OF THEOREM 2.5 HOLDS, THEN

$$\frac{\partial f(x^0)}{\partial b_k} = \lambda_k^0 \qquad k = 1, \ldots, r$$

WHICH SAYS THAT THE LAGRANGE MULTIPLIER FOR CONSTRAINT i IS THE RATE AT WHICH THE OPTIMUM VALUE OF THE OBJECTIVE FUNCTION CHANGES WITH RESPECT TO CHANGES IN THE kTH CONSTRAINT QUANTITY, b_k.

PROOF:

Write the necessary conditions for a constrained local extremum

†See appendix for a proof; see also (2.27).

$$f_j - \sum_{i=1}^{r} \lambda_i^0 g_j^i = 0 \qquad j = 1, \ldots, n$$

$$g^i = b_i \qquad i = 1, \ldots, r$$

These are $(n + r)$ equations in $(n + 2r)$ variables (x, λ, b) where $b = (b_1, \ldots, b_r)$. Since f and $g \in C^2$ by assumption, we can show, by using the implicit function theorem, that these equations implicitly define the $(n + r)$ variables x and λ as differentiable functions of the r variables b, if the appropriate Jacobian is nonsingular. But that critical Jacobian is none other then the bordered Hessian $\hat{H}$, which by theorem 2.6 is shown to be nonsingular at (x^0, λ^0). Writing the reduced form gives the differentiable functions

$$x = x(b), \qquad \lambda = \lambda(b)$$

in an r-dimensional neighborhood about b. Now substitute $x(b)$ into the objective function $f(x)$, and since both f and $x(b)$ are differentiable functions we can apply the chain rule to the composite function $f[x(b)]$.† Differentiating with respect to b_k gives, at x^0

$$\frac{\partial f}{\partial b_k} = \sum_{j=1}^{n} f_j \frac{\partial x_j}{\partial b_k}$$

From the necessary conditions, $f_j = \sum_{i=1}^{r} \lambda_i^0 g_j^i$, so that

(2.43)
$$\frac{\partial f}{\partial b_k} = \sum_{j=1}^{n} \left(\sum_{i=1}^{r} \lambda_i g_j^i \right) \frac{\partial x_j}{\partial b_k}$$

$$= \sum_{i=1}^{r} \lambda_i \left(\sum_{j=1}^{n} g_j^i \frac{\partial x_j}{\partial b_k} \right)$$

But substituting $x(b)$ into the constraints $g^i = b_i$ and differentiating with respect to b_k, we see that

$$\sum_{j=1}^{n} g_j^i \frac{\partial x_j}{\partial b_k} = \begin{cases} 0 \text{ if } i \neq k \\ 1 \text{ if } i = k \end{cases}$$

Substituting into (2.43) gives, at x^0

$$\frac{\partial f}{\partial b_k} = \lambda_k^0$$

Q.E.D.‡

†In the literature of consumer theory, the composite function $f[x(b)] = g(b)$ is called the *indirect* objective function.
‡Notice that had we originally written the Lagrangian function with a plus, the Lagrange multipliers would have been the negative of what we obtained, and this last equation would have had a minus in front of the Lagrange multiplier. Obviously, the result is the same.

We see from this theorem that the Lagrange multipliers are much more than mere numbers brought in to help establish the conditions which prevail at a constrained extreme point. They have an important economic interpretation which emerges naturally from the problem. The multiplier λ_k^0 is the rate of change in the objective function, with x optimally selected, with respect to a change in b_k, the kth constraint. It is, loosely speaking, the value to the optimizer of a small change in the kth constraint, with this value measured in the units of the objective function. Often, in economic problems, b_k is the amount of some resource available for use. The Lagrange multiplier λ_k^0 is then referred to as the "shadow price" or marginal value imputed to a unit of that resource, measured in the units in which the objective function is measured. If, for example, $\lambda_k^0 > 0$, this means that a "small" increase in the kth resource increases the value of the objective function. Clearly, in equilibrium, the unit cost, or price, of the resource will have to equal λ_k^0, otherwise the maximizer can gain by increasing or decreasing the rate of use of that resource. In this context the necessary condition

$$f_j(x^0) = \sum_{i=1}^{r} \lambda_i^0 g_j^i(x^0)$$

has the familiar interpretation that for f to be at a constrained maximum at x^0, it is necessary that the "marginal benefit" of the jth "activity" [i.e., $f_j(x^0)$] equal the marginal imputed cost of that activity $\left[\text{i.e., } \sum_{i=1}^{n} \lambda_i^0 g_j^i(x^0)\right]$.

If λ^0 turns out to be zero, then $f_j(x^0) = 0$, and the conditions for an unconstrained and a constrained extremum coincide. In this sense, the constraints are seen to be not binding, and the Hessian which must be bordered is simply the Hessian of f. In verifying the sufficient condition in such a case, however, the border must still appear in computing the principal minors.

In concluding this section, we emphasize certain aspects of this method that should be kept in mind. As in the theory of unconstrained optimization, the technique does not detect possible extrema on the boundary of the domain of f. Only interior points are scanned by the method. In addition, the functions must have continuous derivatives to the appropriate order to be considered by this method as a candidate for an extreme point. Thus, for boundary points and points at which f and g are not well behaved, other methods must be employed to establish maxima or minima. Further, the analysis in this section deals only with local extrema, of which there may be many. Finally, if there is no $r \times r$ nonsingular submatrix of $G(x^0)$, the method does not work.

Example 2.3 Consumer Theory

In the theory of consumer behavior, it is customarily assumed that the consumer is a *rational* animal. This postulate of rationality means that the consumer is assumed to make choices among available alternatives in such a way that he derives the greatest possible satisfaction. He is supposed to be cognizant of all existing alternatives and capable of evaluating them. All information concerning the satisfaction which the consumer derives from available bundles of commodities is incorporated into his preference or *utility function.*

His utility function is a mathematical expression of his ranking of available commodity bundles. This function associates with each bundle of goods a real number. If a bundle of goods A corresponds with a higher number than another bundle B, the consumer derives more satisfaction from A than B, and we say that the consumer prefers A to B. If two commodity bundles are mapped into the same number by the utility function, the consumer derives the same utility from both bundles and is said to be indifferent between them.

Thus, we begin with the consumer ranking all bundles of available goods in order of his preference. The ranking involves preferring bundle A to B, or preferring B to A, or being indifferent between A and B. Then a function is constructed which expresses this rank ordering. We require this utility function to map every bundle of goods into a real number such that the higher the number, the greater the satisfaction; if two bundles yield the same utility, they correspond to the same number. *This function is not unique. Any other function which captures the rank ordering of the consumer will serve the economic analyst just as well.* As long as the function selected is consistent with the rankings of the consumer, it is a bona fide utility function. There are an infinity of utility functions that can represent a given rank ordering by a consumer. We will show that the analysis of consumer behavior is not affected by the utility function selected, as long as the function is faithful to the ordering.

Suppose that the commodity bundles (A, B, C, D) are mapped into the numbers $(10, 20, 20, 30)$ by a certain utility function. This tells us that this consumer derives more utility from B then from A, the same utility from C as from B, and more utility from D than from $C, B,$ or A. Does the utility function tell us that the *addition* to utility by switching from A to B or C is the same as that from switching from B or C to D? Not according to our requirements of the function; it is only required to express *ranking*. To compare *additions* to utility, the consumer would have to be assumed to be able to assign numbers that represent the *amount* of utility he derives from a bundle, once the units of measurement are agreed upon. In modern consumer theory we only assume an *ordinal* utility function, one that ranks; we do not assume a *cardinal* utility measure, one that registers the amount of utility. A cardinal utility function would imply that increments to utility can be measured and thus compared. An ordinal utility function simply indicates that utility is higher or lower, but does not purport to indicate how much utility change has occurred. Therefore, in the above numbers, an ordinal function does not pretend that the utility increment in going from A to B or C can be compared with the utility increment in moving from B or C to D. Hence, the ranking of (A, B, C, D) could just as well be represented by ordinal utility functions which yielded the numbers $(1, 2, 2, 3)$ or $(5, 70, 70, 600)$.

It follows that in ordinal utility theory the idea of the *rate* of change in utility is meaningless, and familiar notions of diminishing, constant, or increasing marginal utility make absolutely no sense. It does make sense to talk about positive, negative, or zero marginal utility, for these obviously would be invariant with respect to any ordinal utility function that reflected the rankings of a consumer. On the other hand, the rate of utility change is clearly not invariant with respect to ordinal utility functions that reflect a consumer's rankings. Even though ordinality has humbler assumptions than cardinality, the behavior of the consumer can be explained as well with an ordinal as with a cardinal utility function. We shall prove this shortly.

Let us express a utility function of a consumer who consumes n commodities as

$$(2.44) \qquad z = f(x_1, x_2, \ldots, x_n)$$

where $x = (x_1, x_2, \ldots, x_n)$ is the vector of the amounts consumed of the n goods. The function f maps a commodity bundle x into the real number z, which we call a utility index. We shall assume that $f \in C^2$, and that an increase in x_i, $i = 1, \ldots, n$ will increase the value of z. In other words, we suppose that the consumer is not satiated with any good, hence $f_i > 0$, $i = 1, \ldots, n$, over the domain which concerns us. The partial derivatives f_i are referred to as marginal utilities, with the understanding that their magnitudes have no meaning, only their signs.†

We emphasized above that a utility function is not unique. We could form a new utility index z^* which would reflect the same ranking by the consumer as does z. Let us write this new utility index as the composite function

$$(2.45) \qquad z^* = F[f(x)], \quad F' > 0 \quad F \in C^2$$

---

†The ratios also have meaning, since $\dfrac{dx_i}{dx_j}\Big|_{z=\text{constant}} = \dfrac{-f_j}{f_i}$, which is the rate at which the consumption of the ith good must change in response to a change in the consumption of the jth good in order for z to be fixed. We define $\left|\dfrac{dx_i}{dx_j}\right|$ as the marginal rate of substitution.

We can think of F as any real-valued function with $F' \equiv (\partial F/\partial f) > 0$. It should be apparent that (2.44) and (2.45) represent the same ranking by the consumer, and that we therefore have an infinity of utility functions that reflect this consumer, since F is *any* function with the above properties. To see that the same ordering is represented by F as by f, consider commodity bundles x^1, x^2, and x^3. Then

$$f(x^1) = f(x^2) \longleftrightarrow F[f(x^1)] = F[f(x^2)]$$

since F is a function, and

$$f(x^3) > f(x^2) \longleftrightarrow F[f(x^3)] > F[f(x^2)]$$

since $F' > 0$. A function $F(f)$ such that $F' > 0$ is said to be a monotonic transformation of f or an increasing monotonic function of f.

Next, we assume that the consumer is rational, that is, he desires to find that vector x^0 which will maximize his utility index z or z^*. He is constrained by his income, however, so we must write his income or budget constraint. We write this as

$$(2.46) \qquad\qquad M = \sum_{i=1}^{n} P_i x_i$$

where M is the money income available to him over the period of analysis, and $P_i, i = 1, \ldots, n$ is the price at which he purchases the ith good. We assume all prices to be strictly positive.† The right side of (2.46), is then, the expenditure by the consumer on the n goods.

Working for the moment with the original utility function (2.44), we can express this constrained maximization problem as

$$\text{maximizing } z = f(x)$$

$$\text{subject to } M = \sum_{1}^{n} P_i x_i$$

Forming the Lagrangian function for this problem, we have

$$(2.47) \qquad\qquad L(x, \lambda) = f(x) - \lambda \left(\sum_{1}^{n} P_i x_i - M \right)$$

By the Lagrange multiplier theorem,‡ if f assumes a local maximum at the point x^0, where x^0 is an interior point of the domain of f, and satisfies (2.46),

---

†This will assure the rank condition for the constraint needed below.

‡In this case, without loss of generality, the Jacobian matrix of the constraint would be $P_1 > 0$.

and if a Jacobian matrix of the constraint of order one† is nonsingular at x^0, then there exists a unique number λ^0 such that the following n equations are satisfied:

$$(2.48) \qquad L_i(x^0, \lambda^0) = f_i(x^0) - \lambda^0 P_i = 0 \qquad i = 1, \ldots, n$$

This system of equations along with (2.46) constitutes $n + 1$ equations in $2n + 2$ variables (x, λ, P, M) where $P = (P_1, \ldots, P_n)$. We may think of these $n + 1$ equations as the structural relations of this model and write them in the standard form (see section 1.3)

$$(2.49) \qquad f^i(x, \lambda; P, M) = 0 \qquad i = 1, \ldots, n + 1$$

where the exogenous variables in this model are P and M, and the endogenous variables are x and λ. Fixing the values of the exogenous variables at (P^0, M^0), we can express the equilibrium at the local maximum as

$$(2.50) \qquad f^i(x^0, \lambda^0; P^0, M^0) = 0 \qquad i = 1, \ldots, n + 1$$

We now apply the implicit function theorem. We know that $f^i \in C^1$, $i = 1$, $\ldots, n + 1$, since $L(x, \lambda) \in C^2$, and if, in addition to (2.50), the $(n + 1) \times (n + 1)$ Jacobian matrix

$$(2.51) \qquad \frac{\partial(f^1, \ldots, f^{n+1})}{\partial(x_1, \ldots, x_n, \lambda)} \equiv \begin{bmatrix} f_{11} & f_{12} & \cdots & f_{1n} & -P_1 \\ f_{21} & & & & \vdots \\ \vdots & & & & \\ f_{n1} & & \cdots & f_{nn} & -P_n \\ -P_1 & & \cdots & -P_n & 0 \end{bmatrix}$$

is nonsingular at (x^0, λ^0), we may then deduce the existence of an $(n + 1)$-dimensional neighborhood R_0 of (P^0, M^0) and a unique and differentiable set of functions $\phi^1, \ldots, \phi^{n+1}$, defined on R_0, such that

$$(2.52) \quad (\mathrm{i}) \quad x_i^0 = \phi^i(P^0, M^0) \qquad\qquad\qquad i = 1, \ldots, n$$

$$(\mathrm{ii}) \quad \lambda^0 = \phi^{n+1}(P^0, M^0)$$

$$(\mathrm{iii}) \quad x_i \equiv \phi^i(P, M) \quad \text{on } R_0 \qquad\quad i = 1, \ldots, n$$

$$(\mathrm{iv}) \quad \lambda \equiv \phi^{n+1}(P, M) \quad \text{on } R_0$$

$$(\mathrm{v}) \quad f^i(\phi^1, \ldots, \phi^{n+1}; P, M) \equiv 0 \quad \text{on } R_0 \qquad i = 1, \ldots, n + 1$$

The reduced form equations in (2.52) (iii) are the consumer's demand functions

†See Theorem 2.5.

for the n goods. A major objective of consumer theory is to obtain as much information as possible about these functions and the reduced form derivatives

$$\frac{\partial x_i}{\partial P_j}, \frac{\partial x_i}{\partial M} \qquad i, j = 1, \ldots, n$$

which express the optimal rate of change in the amount consumed of the ith good with respect to a change in the price of the jth good or income. For $i = j$, the reduced form derivatives are the slopes of the demand functions as normally drawn in textbooks. In general, we wish to find out about the signs of these reduced form derivatives, given the assumptions about the utility function and the optimizing nature posited for the consumer.

We know from the previous chapter that if the assumptions of the implicit function theorem hold, then we can derive the reduced form derivatives by differentiating (2.52) (v) with respect to any exogenous variable, and, since (2.52) (v) is identically zero for all (P, M) in a neighborhood R_0 of (P^0, M^0), this derivative will be zero. Differentiating with respect to P_i, $i = 1, \ldots, n$, and recalling that (2.52) (v) is standard form for $(\phi^1, \ldots, \phi^{n+1})$ substituted into (2.46) and (2.48), we obtain

(2.53)
$$
\begin{bmatrix}
f_{11} & f_{12} & \cdots & f_{1n} & -P_1^0 \\
\vdots & & & \vdots & \vdots \\
f_{n1} & & \cdots & f_{nn} & -P_n^0 \\
-P_1^0 & & \cdots & -P_n^0 & 0
\end{bmatrix}
\begin{bmatrix}
\dfrac{\partial x_1}{\partial P_i} \\
\vdots \\
\dfrac{\partial x_n}{\partial P_i} \\
\dfrac{\partial \lambda}{\partial P_i}
\end{bmatrix}
=
\begin{bmatrix}
0 \\
\vdots \\
\lambda^0 \\
\vdots \\
x_i^0
\end{bmatrix}
$$

where the Jacobian is evaluated at (x^0, λ^0) and where the vector on the right has λ^0 in the ith place, x_i^0 as the last element, and zeros elsewhere. Solving for $\partial x_j/\partial P_i$, we have by Cramer's rule the famous Slutsky equations

(2.54)
$$\frac{\partial x_j}{\partial P_i} = \frac{\lambda^0 J_{ij} + x_i^0 J_{n+1,j}}{|J|} \qquad i, j = 1, \ldots, n$$

where $|J|$ is the determinant of the Jacobian matrix in (2.53), J_{ij} is the cofactor of the ijth element in the Jacobian, and $J_{n+1,j}$ is the cofactor of the $(n + 1, j)$th element in the Jacobian. Notice that if $i = j$, the cofactor J_{ii} is a principal minor of $|J|$.

So far, we can say nothing about the signs in (2.54). In fact, we have no assurance that we can derive these derivatives, for we *assumed* that the critical Jacobian was nonsingular at (x^0, λ^0).

Next, differentiate (2.52) (v) with respect to M. This yields

$$(2.55) \quad \begin{bmatrix} f_{11} & f_{12} & \cdots & f_{1n} & -P_1 \\ \vdots & & & \vdots & \vdots \\ f_{n1} & & \cdots & f_{nn} & -P_n \\ -P_1 & & \cdots & -P_n & 0 \end{bmatrix} \begin{bmatrix} \dfrac{\partial x_1}{\partial M} \\ \vdots \\ \dfrac{\partial x_n}{\partial M} \\ \dfrac{\partial \lambda}{\partial M} \end{bmatrix} = \begin{bmatrix} 0 \\ \vdots \\ 0 \\ -1 \end{bmatrix}$$

and again by Cramer's rule

$$(2.56) \qquad \frac{\partial x_j}{\partial M} = \frac{-J_{n+1,j}}{|J|} \qquad j = 1, \ldots, n$$

This result yields a piece of information about (2.54), for we can substiture (2.56) into (2.54), which gives

$$\frac{\partial x_j}{\partial P_i} = \frac{\lambda^0 J_{i,j}}{|J|} - x_i^0 \left(\frac{\partial x_j}{\partial M} \right) \qquad i, j = 1, \ldots, n$$

To gain another bit of information about (2.54), suppose we derive $\partial x_j / \partial P_i$ under the assumption that no change in the utility index z is permitted. In other words, we wish to compute the rate of change in x_j with respect to a change in P_i with the utility level of the consumer fixed. To do this, substitute the reduced form functions $(\phi^1, \ldots, \phi^n)$ into the utility function $z = f(x)$ and differentiate the composite function

$$z = f(\phi^1, \ldots, \phi^n)$$

with respect to P_i, holding z fixed. This gives

$$(2.57) \qquad 0 = f_1 \frac{\partial x_1}{\partial P_i} + \cdots + f_n \frac{\partial x_n}{\partial P_i}$$

where the f_i are evaluated at x^0. Next, consider (2.48), the necessary conditions for x^0 to be a local constrained maximum. Substituting (2.48) into (2.57) gives

$$(2.58) \qquad 0 = \lambda^0 \left(P_1^0 \frac{\partial x_1}{\partial P_i} + \cdots + P_n^0 \frac{\partial x_n}{\partial P_i} \right)$$

By Theorem 2.7 we know that, at the optimum, λ^0 is the marginal utility of income, and therefore λ^0 should be positive. Thus, the term in parentheses in (2.58) must be zero. But this term is the negative of the left side of the last equation of (2.53). It follows that if we compute $\partial x_j / \partial P_i$ with the utility level of the consumer fixed, we get (2.53) with one difference, the last element in the vector on the right being zero. Solving, we have

(2.59) $$\left(\frac{\partial x_j}{\partial P_i}\right)_{z \text{ fixed}} = \frac{\lambda^0 J_{ij}}{|J|} \qquad i, j = 1, \dots, n$$

which happens, elegantly, to be the first term in (2.54). Using (2.56) and (2.59) in (2.54), we can write the Slutsky equations as

(2.60) $$\frac{\partial x_j}{\partial P_i} = \left(\frac{\partial x_j}{\partial P_i}\right)_{z \text{ fixed}} - x_i^0 \left(\frac{\partial x_j}{\partial M}\right) \qquad i, j = 1, \dots, n$$

The first term on the right of (2.60) is the *substitution effect*, or the rate at which the consumer changes the optimal amount consumed of the jth good in response to a change in the price of the ith good, assuming that he is held to the same indifference surface.† The second term in (2.60) is the *income effect*, or the residual variability. To see the economic meaning of this term we must inquire into the significance of x_i^0 in (2.60). Consider the consumer at his initial equilibrium x^0, faced with prices P^0. The cost of x^0 at P^0, C_0, is

$$C_0 = \sum_1^n P_i^0 x_i^0$$

Now, mentally hold this consumer at x^0 and change one of the prices, perhaps increasing P_i^0 to P_i^1. The cost of x^0 must now rise to C_1 where

$$C_1 = \sum_{\substack{j=1 \\ j \neq i}}^n P_j^0 x_j^0 + P_i^1 x_i^0$$

Subtracting C_0 from C_1 gives

$$C_1 - C_0 = (P_i^1 - P_i^0)x_i^0, \text{ or}$$
$$\Delta C = \Delta P_i x_i^0$$

This rise in price, which increases the cost of x^0 by $C_1 - C_0$, *is precisely the same in impact as if the consumer were to suffer a reduction in income by* ΔC, for it would require a rise in his income of ΔC to enable him to purchase x^0 at the new prices. Therefore, we can replace ΔC with $-\Delta M$, and write

$$\frac{-\Delta M}{\Delta P_i} = x_i^0$$

or in the limit as $\Delta P_i \to 0$, we have

$$\frac{\partial M}{\partial P_i} = -x_i^0$$

---

†The process of holding him to the same utility level or indifference surface is referred to as a compensating income variation.

and substituting this for $-x_i^0$ in (2.60) we have

$$(2.61) \qquad \frac{\partial x_j}{\partial P_i} = \left(\frac{\partial x_j}{\partial P_i}\right)_{z \text{ fixed}} + \left(\frac{\partial M}{\partial P_i}\right)\left(\frac{\partial x_j}{\partial M}\right) \qquad i, j = 1, \ldots, n$$

which shows that the income effect is the rate at which x_j responds to a change in M multiplied by the rate at which M changes with respect to a change in P_i.

Let us now assume that conditions exist which guarantee that x^0 is a local maximum. These conditions were spelled out in (b) of Theorem 2.5 or in the equivalent determinantal form in Theorem 2.6. Consider the bordered Hessian employed in Theorem 2.6, which is precisely the Jacobian of this example.† Thus, if the conditions in Theorem 2.6 hold, we know immediately that the Jacobian is nonsingular at x^0 and the assumptions of the implicit function theorem hold.‡ We also know from Theorem 2.6 that every appropriately obtained principal minor of $|J|$ or order $n + 1 - i$ will have sign $(-1)^{n-i}$, $0 \leq i \leq n - 2$. Consider then the substitution effect

$$\left(\frac{\partial x_i}{\partial P_i}\right)_{z \text{ fixed}} = \frac{\lambda^0 J_{ii}}{|J|} \qquad i = 1, \ldots, n$$

We *now* can say that this term must be negative, since $\lambda^0 > 0$, the sign of $|J|$ is $(-1)^n$, and the sign of the principal minor of $|J|$, J_{ii}, will be $(-1)^{n-1}$.

Another way to achieve this result is to rewrite (2.53), with z fixed, in partitioned matrix form as

$$(2.62) \qquad \begin{bmatrix} H & -P^0 \\ (-P^0)' & 0 \end{bmatrix} \begin{bmatrix} \dfrac{\partial x}{\partial P_i} \\ \dfrac{\partial \lambda}{\partial P_i} \end{bmatrix} = e_i$$

where

H is the $n \times n$ matrix whose ijth element is $f_{ij}(x^0)$

$P^0 = (P_1^0, \ldots, P_n^0)$ is a column vector

$\dfrac{\partial x}{\partial P_i} = \left(\dfrac{\partial x_1}{\partial P_i}, \ldots, \dfrac{\partial x_n}{\partial P_i}\right)$ with z fixed

$e_i = (0, \ldots, \lambda^0, \ldots, 0)$ with λ^0 in the ith place

Multiplying both sides by the transpose of

†This, of course, is always true.
‡Hence, we can justify deriving the reduced form derivatives referred to as Slutsky's equations.

$$\begin{bmatrix} \dfrac{\partial x}{\partial P_i} \\[2ex] \dfrac{\partial \lambda}{\partial P_i} \end{bmatrix}$$

gives

$$\left(\frac{\partial x}{\partial P_i}\right)' H\left(\frac{\partial x}{\partial P_i}\right) - \left(\frac{\partial x}{\partial P_i}\right)' P^0 \frac{\partial \lambda}{\partial P_i}$$

$$- \frac{\partial \lambda}{\partial P_i} (P^0)' \left(\frac{\partial x}{\partial P_i}\right) = \lambda^0 \left(\frac{\partial x_i}{\partial P_i}\right)$$

Comparing this expression with (2.58), we see that the last two terms on the left must be zero. But by (b) of Theorem 2.5 the quadratic form on the left is negative, which yields again the result that

$$\left(\frac{\partial x_i}{\partial P_i}\right)_{z \text{ fixed}} < 0 \qquad i = 1, \ldots, n$$

Unfortunately, we cannot, in the general case, derive the signs of any other reduced form derivatives from the assumptions employed in this section. All we can say is that the substitution effect in $\partial x_i / \partial P_i$ is negative. We can say nothing about the signs of $\partial x_j / \partial M$ or $\partial x_j / \partial P_i$ except to classify them.[†] The "law" of downward sloping demand therefore does not hold.

There are, however, other interesting propositions that can be deduced from this theory. We can demonstrate that:

(a) *Maximizing z in (2.44) subject to the budget constraint is equivalent to maximing z* in (2.45) subject to that constraint.* Recall that z^* is a monotonic transformation of the original utility index z.

(b) *Not all of the i goods can be complements.* Goods i and j are defined as complements if [see (2.54) and (2.61)]

$$\left(\frac{\partial x_j}{\partial P_i}\right)_{z \text{ fixed}} = \frac{\lambda^0 J_{ij}}{|J|} < 0$$

and

$$\left(\frac{\partial x_i}{\partial P_j}\right)_{z \text{ fixed}} = \frac{\lambda^0 J_{ji}}{|J|} < 0$$

Notice the amazing fact that these two expressions are identical, since J is

[†]If $\partial x_i / \partial M$ is positive (negative), the ith good is said to be normal (inferior); if $dx_i / \partial P_i$ is positive, the good is called a *Giffen* good.

symmetric. The two goods are said to be *substitutes* if these expressions are positive; the goods are *independent* if the expressions are zero.[†]

PROOF OF (a):

The strategy here is to show that if the sufficient conditions which imply that x^0 is a local maximum hold with the utility function $z = f(x)$, then the sufficient conditions will also be satisfied at x^0 using $z^* = F[f(x)]$, $F' > 0$. Thus, a local maximum x^0 is shown to be invariant with respect to monotonic transformations of a utility function.

If the sufficient conditions hold for x^0 to be a local maximum in the original problem of

$$\text{maximizing } z = f(x)$$

$$\text{subject to } M = \sum_1^n P_i^0 x_i$$

then [see (2.48) and (2.62)] there exists a unique λ^0 such that at x^0

(2.63) $\qquad\qquad f_i - \lambda^0 P_i^0 = 0 \qquad i = 1, \ldots, n$

and

(2.64) $\qquad\qquad h'Hh < 0 \quad \text{when} \quad h'P^0 = 0$

Next, consider the point x^0 when the problem is to

$$\text{maximize } z^* = F[f(x)], F' > 0$$

$$\text{subject to } M = \sum_1^n P_i^0 x_i$$

If the sufficient conditions for x^0 to be a local maximum are satisfied for this problem, then there exists a unique λ^* such that, at x^0,

(2.65) $\qquad\qquad F_i - \lambda^* P_i^0 - 0 \qquad i = 1, \cdots, n$

and

(2.66) $\qquad\qquad h'H^*h < 0 \quad \text{when} \quad h'P^0 = 0$

where H^* has F_{ij} as its ijth element.

[†]In Chapter 1 we spoke of substitutes and complements in the "gross" sense, that is, $\partial x_j/\partial P_i, i \neq j$, which contains both the substitution and the income effects, as in the Slutsky equation. When z is held fixed, the adjective "Hicksian" is sometimes appended to substitutes and complements.

The question then is, are the sufficient conditions for both problems equivalent? From (2.65) we have that

$$F'f_i - \lambda^* P_i^0 = 0 \qquad i = 1, \cdots, n$$

thus

$$f_i - \left(\frac{\lambda^*}{F'}\right) P_i^0 = 0$$

which shows that (2.63) $\longleftrightarrow$ (2.65), with

$$\lambda^0 = \frac{\lambda^*}{F'}$$

Next, observe that the ijth element of H^* in (2.66) is

$$F_{ij} = f_j F'' f_i + F' f_{ij} \qquad i, j = 1, \cdots, n$$

Thus, we can write

$$(2.67) \qquad h' H^* h = F'' \sum_{i,j=1}^{n} (f_j h_j)(f_i h_i) + F' h' H h$$

Notice that $\sum_1^n h_i f_i$, by (2.63), is equal to

$$\lambda^0 h' P^0$$

which is constrained to be zero by (2.64). So the first term on the right of (2.67) must be zero, and we have demonstrated that (2.64) $\longleftrightarrow$ (2.66).

PROOF OF (b):
If all goods are complements, then

$$\left(\frac{\partial x_i}{\partial P_j}\right)_{z \text{ fixed}} = \frac{\lambda^0 J_{ji}}{|J|} > 0 \qquad \begin{array}{l} j = 1, \cdots, n \\ 1 \leq i \leq n \\ i \neq j \end{array}$$

Fixing i, multiply each of these n terms by the corresponding P_j and sum over j. This gives

$$(2.68) \qquad \frac{\lambda^0}{|J|} (J_{1i} P_1 + J_{2i} P_2 + \cdots + J_{ni} P_n)$$

But, observing the matrix in (2.53), we see that the expression in parentheses is the expansion of the determinant of this matrix by alien cofactors, that is, the cofactors of the elements in the ith column, $1 \leq i \leq n$, are multiplied by the elements in the $(n + 1)$st column. Thus, the expression in (2.68) must be zero. But, given the result that

$$\frac{J_{ii}}{|J|} < 0$$

it is impossible that all the other terms in (2.68) could also be negative, that is, that all the goods could be complements.

EXAMPLE:

Suppose that we can represent the utility function of a consumer for three goods as

$$z = x_1^2 x_2^2 x_3^2$$

and the budget constraint is

$$P_1 x_1 + P_2 x_2 + P_3 x_3 = M$$

where

$$M = 18, P_1 = 1, P_2 = 2, P_3 = 1$$

Find the local maxima of z subject to the budget constraint for strictly positive (x_1, x_2, x_3).

The Lagrangian function is

$$L(x, \lambda) = x_1^2 x_2^2 x_3^2 - \lambda \left(\sum_1^3 P_i x_i - M \right)$$

The necessary conditions are

$$\frac{\partial L}{\partial x_1} = 2x_1 x_2^2 x_3^2 - \lambda = 0$$

$$\frac{\partial L}{\partial x_2} = 2x_2 x_1^2 x_3^2 - 2\lambda = 0$$

$$\frac{\partial L}{\partial x_3} = 2x_3 x_1^2 x_2^2 - \lambda = 0$$

To solve for potential local maxima, substitute the first equation of the necessary conditions into both the second and third equations, eliminating λ

$$2x_2 x_1^2 x_3^2 - 4x_1 x_2^2 x_3^2 = 0$$
$$2x_3 x_1^2 x_2^2 - 2x_1 x_2^2 x_3^2 = 0$$

or

$$2x_2 x_1 x_3^2 (x_1 - 2x_2) = 0$$
$$2x_3 x_1 x_2^2 (x_1 - x_3) = 0$$

and ignoring zero solutions, these equations imply that

$$x_1 = 2x_2 = x_3$$

Substituting into the budget equation, eliminating x_2 and x_3, gives

$$3x_1 = 18$$

hence

$$(x_1^0, x_2^0, x_3^0) = (6, 3, 6)$$

To see if the sufficient conditions for a local maximum are satisfied at this point, compute the bordered Hessian [see (2.53) and (2.62)]

$$\begin{bmatrix} H & -P \\ P' & 0 \end{bmatrix} = \begin{bmatrix} 2x_2^2 x_3^2 & 4x_1 x_2 x_3^2 & 4x_1 x_2^2 x_3 & -1 \\ 4x_1 x_2 x_3^2 & 2x_1^2 x_3^2 & 4x_2 x_1^2 x_3 & -2 \\ 4x_1 x_2^2 x_3 & 4x_3 x_1^2 x_2 & 2x_1^2 x_2^2 & -1 \\ -1 & -2 & -1 & 0 \end{bmatrix}$$

Evaluating it at $(6, 3, 6)$ gives

$$\begin{bmatrix} 648 & 2592 & 1296 & -1 \\ 2592 & 2592 & 2592 & -2 \\ 1296 & 2592 & 648 & -1 \\ -1 & -2 & -1 & 0 \end{bmatrix}$$

which can be checked either by computing the appropriate principal minors, or by computing

$$h'Hh \text{ subject to } P'h = 0$$

to see whether the quadratic form is negative, given the linear constraint. Doing the latter, the quadratic form is

$$h'Hh = 648(h_1^2 + 4h_2^2 + h_3^2 + 8h_1 h_2 + 4h_1 h_3 + 8h_2 h_3)$$

Substituting into this expression $P'h$, which in this case is

$$h_1 + 2h_2 + h_3 = 0$$

and eliminating h_2 gives

$$648(-2h_1^2 - 4h_1h_3 - 2h_3^2)$$

or

$$-1296(h_1 + h_3)^2$$

which is negative for all (h_1, h_3).

Next, compute the Slutsky equation. This requires differentiating the necessary conditions and the constraint with respect to, say, P_2, evaluating at $(x_1^0, x_2^0, x_3^0) = (6, 3, 6)$. The differentiation gives [see (2.53)]

$$\begin{bmatrix} 648 & 2592 & 1296 & -1 \\ 2592 & 2592 & 2592 & -2 \\ 1296 & 2592 & 648 & -1 \\ -1 & -2 & -1 & 0 \end{bmatrix} \begin{bmatrix} \dfrac{\partial x_1}{\partial P_2} \\[2mm] \dfrac{\partial x_2}{\partial P_2} \\[2mm] \dfrac{\partial x_3}{\partial P_2} \\[2mm] \dfrac{\partial \lambda}{\partial P_2} \end{bmatrix} = \begin{bmatrix} 0 \\ \lambda^0 \\ 0 \\ 3 \end{bmatrix}$$

where λ^0 can be computed from the necessary conditions to be 3888. The remaining labor is straightforward. The reader might wish to verify that the substitution effects are negative,[†] and to compute the various reduced form derivatives.

Example 2.4 Production Theory

Consider a firm which produces a single product and uses several inputs. Assume that the firm is a profit maximizer and does not affect the prices of its inputs by varying the rate of input use. The problem of maximizing output subject to a given expenditure on inputs, or, equivalently, the problem of minimizing the expenditure on inputs at a given output, is mathematically parallel to the analysis of the consumer in the previous example.

[†]Remember, only the substitution effects in $\partial x_i/\partial P_i$ must be negative; the signs of the substitution effects in $\partial x_i/\partial P_j$, $i \neq j$, will determine whether the two goods are substitutes, complements, or independent.

The analogue of the consumer's utility function is the firm's production function, and the analogue of the budget equation is the cost equation. The rational consumer wants to maximize his utility from a given amount spent on consumption, while the rational enterpreneur wants to maximize his output from a given expenditure on inputs, this being a necessary step toward maximizing profits.

We can thus retrace the argument in the theory of the consumer and develop the theory of production. Equation (2.44) would be the production function, with z as output and x as the vector of amounts used of the n inputs. A difference between the utility function and the production function is that output can easily be measured, while utility cannot. Hence, once measurement units are chosen, z is a cardinal measure of output, the partial derivatives of various orders and mixes have unambiguous meanings, and monotonic transformations of z are not legitimate.†

Redefining the symbols in (2.46) gives us the cost equation, where M is now variable cost and P_i is the price or unit cost of the ith input.

We can write the problem either as one of maximizing z subject to (2.46), where M is a *given* variable cost, or as one of minimizing M subject to *a* given z. By the former approach, (2.47) would have the same appearance, and the Lagrange multiplier would be the reciprocal of the marginal cost of output. The reduced form equation (2.52) (iii) would be the demand for the ith input as a function of the exogenous variables, input prices, and amount spent on inputs; (2.52) (iv) would be the inverse of the marginal cost as a function of the same exogenous arguments. To obtain the cost functions of the firm, we simply substitute (2.52) (iii) into the cost equation, which gives the variable cost as a function of input prices and output; fixing input prices, we have the total variable cost curve of the firm.

The rest of the analysis is formally quite similar to consumer theory. Notice, however, that the Slutsky equation (2.54) does not have the significance in production theory that it does in consumer theory, for in production theory (2.54) would express the rate at which the demand for the jth input changes in response to a change in the price of the ith input, *at a given variable cost*.‡ But the firm is not constrained to a given level of variable cost as the consumer is restricted to a given income. Therefore, the expression in (2.54) does not express the *full* adjustment in demand for the jth input, because it does not contain the adjustment in variable cost itself in the profit-maximizing response of the firm to a change in the ith input price. Another way of stating this point is to say that, in the production model, either variable cost or output is an exogenous variable, depending on whether the maximization or minimization

†Unless the transformation F is proportional—i.e., $F[f(x)] = af(x)$, where a is a positive constant—in which case there is simply a change in the units in which output is measured.

‡Or at a given output when the minimization approach is taken.

approach is taken to the problem; in order to obtain the full response of x_j to P_i, both would have to be endogenous. To make them so, we need simply introduce the next step in the firm's assumed optimization process, the maximization of profits. To see this, consider the approach of maximizing z subject to fixed M, which makes M exogenous.†

Substitute the reduced form equations (2.52) (iii), the demand functions for the inputs, into the production function and the cost equation, giving

$$z = f[\phi(P, M)]$$

and

$$M = \sum_1^n P_i \phi^i(P, M)$$

where

$$\phi = (\phi^1, \ldots, \phi^n)$$

Now define profits, π, as

$$\pi = P^* f[\phi(P, M)] - \sum_1^n P_i \phi^i(P, M)$$

where P^* is the price of output.‡ At this point, by assuming that the firm chooses M so as to maximize π, we have endogenized M, for it is now a decision variable for the firm. If the firm selects M so as to maximize π, we obtain the necessary condition that

$$\frac{\partial \pi}{\partial M} = 0$$

which can be written in general form as

$$G(M; P^*, P) = 0$$

where M is endogenous and P^* and P are exogenous. If the sufficient condition for a maximum holds, then

$$\frac{\partial^2 \pi}{\partial M^2} = G_M < 0$$

---

†The argument beginning here assumes M endogenous and z exogenous, which stems from the minimization approach.
‡This variable could be endogenized without affecting the argument.

which means that we can use the implicit function theorem on G to guarantee the local existence of the differentiable function

$$M = M(P^*, P)$$

Substituting this into (2.52) (iii) gives

$$x_i = \phi^i[P, M(P^*, P)] \qquad i = 1, \dots, n$$

Now we can compute the full response of x_j to a change in P_i, a response which includes the response in M, that is

$$\frac{\partial x_j}{\partial P_i} = \frac{\partial \phi^j}{\partial P_i} + \frac{\partial \phi^j}{\partial M} \frac{\partial M}{\partial P_i}$$

The Slutsky equation in (2.54) only contains the first term on the right of the last expression, for (2.54) assumes M to be exogenous, hence fixed with respect to changes in P_i.

Example 2.5 The Paretian Contract Surface

Suppose we have m consumers and n goods in fixed supply for the time period under analysis. Write the utility function of each consumer as

$$z_i = f^i(x^i) \qquad i = 1, \dots, m$$

where $x^i \equiv (x_1^i, x_2^i, \dots, x_n^i)$ is the vector of the amounts of the n goods consumed by the ith consumer, and z_i is the utility index of the ith consumer. Write the supply constraints as

$$\sum_{i=1}^{m} x_j^i = b_j^0 \qquad j = 1, \dots, n$$

where x_j^i is the amount of the jth good consumed by the ith consumer, and b_j^0 is the fixed supply of the jth good.

The problem is to find a point on the Paretian contract surface, that is, a set of vectors $(x^1, \dots, x^m) = x$, such that no consumer can have more utility without some consumer having less. To find such a point, we must maximize the utility of any one consumer, while fixing the utility levels of all the others. Suppose we maximize z_1, fixing the remaining utility levels at $z_2^0, \dots, z_m^0$; then the Lagrangian function can be written

$$L(x, \lambda, \Gamma) = f^1(x^1) + \sum_{i=2}^{m} \lambda_i(z_i^0 - f^i(x^i)) + \sum_{j=1}^{n} \Gamma_j\left(b_j^0 - \sum_{i=1}^{m} x_j^i\right)$$

where

$$x \equiv (x^1, x^2, \ldots, x^m) \equiv (x_1^1, \ldots, x_n^1; \ldots; x_1^m, \ldots, x_n^m)$$

$$\lambda = (\lambda_2, \ldots, \lambda_m)$$

$$\Gamma = (\Gamma_1, \ldots, \Gamma_n)$$

By the Lagrange multiplier theorem, if f^1 assumes a local maximum at the point $\bar{x} = (\bar{x}^1, \cdots, \bar{x}^m)$, where $\bar{x}$ is an interior point of the domain of $(f^1, \cdots, f^m)$, and if a Jacobian matrix of the $n + m - 1$ constraints

(2.69)
$$z_i^0 = f^i(x^i) \qquad i = 2, \ldots, m$$

$$\sum_{i=1}^{m} x_j^i = b_j^0 \qquad j = 1, \ldots, n$$

in the nm variables $(x^1, \cdots, x^m)$ is nonsingular at $\bar{x}$, then there exists a unique (λ^0, Γ^0) such that, at $\bar{x}$, the following system of nm equations is satisfied:

(2.70)
$$\frac{\partial L}{\partial x_j^i} = f_{x_j^1}^1 - \Gamma_j^0 = 0 \qquad j = 1, \ldots, n$$

$$\frac{\partial L}{\partial x_j^i} = -\lambda_i^0 f_{x_j^i}^i - \Gamma_j^0 = 0 \qquad \begin{array}{l} i = 2, \ldots, m \\ j = 1, \ldots, m \end{array}$$

By eliminating the Lagrange multipliers, we obtain the well-known result†

(2.71)
$$\frac{f_{x_j^i}^i}{f_{x_s^i}^i} = \frac{f_{x_j^k}^k}{f_{x_s^k}^k} \qquad \begin{array}{l} i, k = 1, \ldots, m \\ j, s = 1, \ldots, n \end{array}$$

which says that, at the optimal point $\bar{x}$, it is necessary that the ratio of the marginal utilities of any two goods, viz., the marginal rate of substitution, be the same for all consumers.

The economic meaning of the λ^0 and Γ^0 in this problem is interesting; Γ_j^0 is the rate at which the optimum value of the marginal utility of the first consumer changes with respect to a change in the supply of the jth good, and λ_i^0 is the optimal response of f^1 to a change in the utility index of consumer i, $i \neq 1$. We expect λ_i^0 to be negative, because an increase in the utility index of consumer i, $i \neq 1$, requires that consumer one receive less goods, all other utility indices and supplies fixed, of course.‡ Γ_j^0 should be positive, since any increase in the amount available of the jth good must benefit consumer one, if z_i is fixed, $i \neq 1$.

Consider next the necessary conditions (2.70) and the constraints (2.69) which in general form we may write as

---

†It is necessary that the number of variables exceed the number of constraints, which, in this problem, requires that $m > 1$ if $n > 1$.

‡We are still assuming that no consumer is satiated with any good at the optimal point.

$$F^i(x^1, \ldots, x^m, \lambda, \Gamma; b^0, z^0) = 0$$

$$b^0 \equiv (b_1^0, \ldots, b_n^0)$$

$$z^0 \equiv (z_2^0, \ldots, z_m^0)$$

where i goes from 1 to $2n + (n + 1)(m - 1)$ and there are $2(n + m - 1) + mn$ variables. The exogenous variables are b^0 and z^0, and the others are endogenous. If the appropriate Jacobian matrix is nonsingular, then differentiable reduced form equations, expressing the endogenous variables in terms of b and z, are guaranteed to exist and to satisfy (2.69) and (2.70) identically in a neighborhood about (b^0, z^0). Substituting the reduced form equations into (2.69) and (2.70), we can derive the reduced form derivatives

$$\frac{\partial x_j^i}{\partial b_k} \qquad \begin{array}{l} i = 1, \ldots, m \\ j = 1, \ldots, n \\ k = 1, \ldots, n \end{array}$$

that is, the optimal rate of response of the ith consumer's consumption of the jth good with respect to a change in the amount available of the kth good.†

The Jacobian of this model, which is also the bordered Hessian, with $n = m = 2$, is

$$
\begin{bmatrix}
f_{x_1^1 x_1^1}^1 & f_{x_2^1 x_1^1}^1 & 0 & 0 & -1 & 0 & 0 \\
f_{x_1^1 x_2^1}^1 & f_{x_2^1 x_2^1}^1 & 0 & 0 & 0 & -1 & 0 \\
0 & 0 & -\lambda^0 f_{x_1^2 x_1^2}^2 & -\lambda^0 f_{x_2^2 x_1^2}^2 & -1 & 0 & -f_{x_1^2}^2 \\
0 & 0 & -\lambda^0 f_{x_1^2 x_2^2}^2 & -\lambda^0 f_{x_2^2 x_2^2}^2 & 0 & -1 & -f_{x_2^2}^2 \\
-1 & 0 & -1 & 0 & 0 & 0 & 0 \\
0 & -1 & 0 & -1 & 0 & 0 & 0 \\
0 & 0 & -f_{x_1^2}^2 & -f_{x_2^2}^2 & 0 & 0 & 0
\end{bmatrix}
$$

and differentiating (2.69) and (2.70) with respect to, say, b_2, yields this matrix premultiplying

$$\left(\frac{\partial x_1^1}{\partial b_2}, \frac{\partial x_2^1}{\partial b_2}, \frac{\partial x_1^2}{\partial b_2}, \frac{\partial x_2^2}{\partial b_2}, \frac{\partial \Gamma_1}{\partial b_2}, \frac{\partial \Gamma_2}{\partial b_2}, \frac{\partial \lambda}{\partial b_2} \right)$$

which will equal $(0, 0, 0, 0, 0, -1, 0)$. This reveals that even if the sufficiency condition is assumed, none of the signs of the reduced form derivatives, in general, can be deduced. The reason is that only one of the derivatives, $\partial \Gamma_2 / \partial b_2$, has a principal minor in the numerator, when solved by Cramer's rule.

†Analysis of the other reduced form derivatives is left for the reader.

But that principal minor is obtained by deleting the second last row and column from the bordered Hessian, which is *not* an appropriately derived minor,† so nothing is known a priori about its sign.

Suppose now that we introduce a social welfare function F, which implies that any set of utility levels of the consumers is mapped into a social welfare index W; thus

$$W = F(f^1, \ldots, f^m)$$

where we would naturally expect that $F_i > 0$, $i = 1, \ldots, m$. The problem is now one of maximizing W subject to the supply constraints

$$\sum_{i=1}^{m} x_j^i = b_j^0 \qquad j = 1, \ldots, n$$

The Lagrangian function for this problem is

$$L(x, \lambda) = F(f^1, \ldots, f^m) + \sum_{j=1}^{n} \Gamma_j \left(b_j^0 - \sum_{i=1}^{m} x_j^i \right)$$

and the necessary conditions for a local maximum are that a unique Γ^0 exists which, at the maximum, satisfies

$$F_i f_{x_j^i}^i - \Gamma_j^0 = 0 \qquad \begin{array}{l} i = 1, \ldots, m \\ j = 1, \ldots, n \end{array}$$

hence

$$\frac{F_i f_{x_j^i}^i}{F_k f_{x_j^i}^k} = \frac{F_i f_{x_s^i}^i}{F_k f_{x_s^i}^k} \qquad \begin{array}{l} j, s = 1, \ldots, n \\ i, k = 1, \ldots, m \end{array}$$

or

$$\frac{f_{x_j^i}^i}{f_{x_s^i}^i} = \frac{f_{x_j^i}^k}{f_{x_s^i}^k} \qquad \begin{array}{l} i, k = 1, \ldots, m \\ j, s = 1, \ldots, n \end{array}$$

which is identical to (2.71). This result was expected, because the previous problem provided the conditions characterizing *any* point on the contract surface, and this problem yields that point on the surface which maximizes social welfare. Again letting $n = m = 2$, we see that the Jacobian for this problem is

†See Theorem 2.6.

$$\begin{bmatrix} (F_1f^1_{x_1})_{x_1} & (F_1f^1_{x_1})_{x_1} & (F_1f^1_{x_1})_{x_1} & (F_1f^1_{x_1})_{x_1} & -1 & 0 \\ (F_1f^1_{x_1})_{x_1} & (F_1f^1_{x_1})_{x_1} & (F_1f^1_{x_1})_{x_1} & (F_1f^1_{x_1})_{x_1} & 0 & -1 \\ (F_2f^2_{x_1})_{x_1} & (F_2f^2_{x_1})_{x_1} & (F_2f^2_{x_1})_{x_1} & (F_2f^2_{x_1})_{x_1} & -1 & 0 \\ (F_2f^2_{x_1})_{x_1} & (F_2f^2_{x_1})_{x_1} & (F_2f^2_{x_1})_{x_1} & (F_2f^2_{x_1})_{x_1} & 0 & -1 \\ -1 & 0 & -1 & 0 & 0 & 0 \\ 0 & -1 & 0 & -1 & 0 & 0 \end{bmatrix}$$

where

$$(F_i f^i_{x_j})_{x_l} \equiv F_i f^i_{x_j x_l} + F_{is} f^i_{x_j} f^s_{x_l}$$

For the same reason as in the previous problem, we are not able in general to derive the signs of any reduced form derivatives by employing the sufficiency conditions for a maximum.

Example 2.6 Optimization and a Macroeconomic Model

Consider the macroeconomic model discussed in section 1.2. In linear form, the model collapsed to two equations expressing equilibrium in the goods and money markets, respectively:

(2.72) $Y = a_{11}(1 - t)Y - a_{11}\bar{T} + a_{12}\alpha_1 + a_{13}Y + a_{14}r + a_{15}\alpha_2 + \bar{G}$

$\bar{M} = a_{21}r + a_{22}Y + a_{23}\alpha_3$

Now suppose that we introduce a welfare or utility function for a national policy maker, and assume that this function is the following quadratic

(2.73) $W = \frac{1}{2}[w_1(Y - \hat{Y}^0)^2 + w^2(\bar{G} - \hat{G}^0)^2$
$+ w_3(r - \hat{r}^0)^2 + w_4(\bar{G} - T)^2]$

where $\hat{Y}^0 = $ target income

$\hat{G}^0 = $ target government spending

$\hat{r}^0 = $ target interest rate

$W = $ the disutility index of the policy maker

$w_i > 0, i = 1, \ldots, 4$

This function purports to describe the preferences of a national political leader. According to (2.73), he wants Y, $\bar{G}$ and r to achieve the desired levels $\hat{Y}^0$, $\hat{G}^0$, and $\hat{r}^0$; and he wants the national budget to be balanced.

It is a simple matter to work out the properties of this preference function.

The marginal rate of substitution between, say, $\bar{G}$ and Y at $(\bar{G}, Y^0)$ can be seen to be

$$\frac{d\bar{G}}{dY} = -\frac{w_1(Y^0 - \hat{Y}^0)}{w_2(\bar{G}^0 - \hat{G}^0)}$$

where W is, of course, assumed to be fixed. Thus, if $Y^0 > \hat{Y}^0$ and $\bar{G}^0 > \hat{G}^0$, an increment in Y requires a reduction in $\bar{G}$ to keep the policy maker at the same level of utility. This ratio at, say, $(Y^1, \bar{G}^0)$ where $Y^1 > Y^0$, is a larger negative magnitude than at $(Y^0, \bar{G}^0)$, expressing the fact that the reduction in $\bar{G}$ required by an increment in Y must be larger the farther Y is from the target Y^0. The greater the priority in eliminating the discrepancy between Y and $\hat{Y}^0$, the larger the negative magnitude of $d\bar{G}/dY$; that is, the larger is w_1, the greater the reduction in $\bar{G}$ per unit increase in Y in order to keep W at the same level (still assuming $Y > \hat{Y}^0$ and $\bar{G} > \hat{G}^0$). The reader can generate the remaining properties, which are similar to the ones mentioned.

The problem, then, is to minimize W subject to the model in (2.72). In general form, we may write the Lagrangian function for this problem as†

$$L(Y, r, \bar{G}, \bar{T}, \bar{M}, \lambda_1, \lambda_2) = W(Y, \bar{G}, r, \bar{T}) + \lambda_1 g^1(Y, r, \bar{T}, \bar{G}) + \lambda_2 g^2(Y, r, \bar{M})$$

where g^1 and g^2 refer to the implicit form of the first and second equations in (2.72), respectively, and (λ_1, λ_2) are Lagrange multipliers. (The α's have been deleted.) To apply the sufficient conditions of the Lagrange multiplier theorem,‡ we must be assured that $(W, g^1, g^2) \in C^2$, which is clearly true in this case, and we must be able to assume that a 2×2 Jacobian matrix of the constraint functions g^1 and g^2 is nonsingular at the constrained minimum. Consider the following Jacobian matrix of (2.72)

$$\begin{bmatrix} 1 - \beta & -a_{14} \\ -a_{22} & -a_{21} \end{bmatrix}$$

where $\beta \equiv a_{11}(1 - t) + a_{13}$, and is the marginal propensity to spend. This was the matrix whose determinant we were able to sign in the discussion of the correspondence principle in section 1.8. Thus, we may assume that g^1 and g^2 are functionally independent in this problem. It follows by (a) of the Lagrange multiplier theorem that if W assumes a local constrained extremum at the interior point $(Y^0, r^0, \bar{G}^0, \bar{T}^0, \bar{M}^0)$, there exist real and unique numbers λ_1^0 and λ_2^0 such that the following five equations are satisfied:§

---

†We have excluded the marginal tax rate, t, as a choice variable because it turns out the $\partial L/\partial t = Y(\partial L/\partial \bar{T})$, which means that in the necessary conditions for a constrained minimum we cannot obtain functionally independent equations for T and t. We shall thus consider t as a structural parameter in this problem.

‡See Theorem 2.5.

§Recall that $T = \bar{T} + tY$.

(2.74) $\dfrac{\partial L}{\partial Y} = w_1(Y^0 - \hat{Y}^0) - w_4 t(\bar{G}^0 - \bar{T}^0 - tY^0)$

$\qquad\qquad + \lambda_1^0(1 - \beta) - a_{22}\lambda_2^0 = 0$

$\dfrac{\partial L}{\partial r} = w_3(r^0 - \hat{r}^0) - \lambda_1^0 a_{14} - \lambda_2^0 a_{21} = 0$

$\dfrac{\partial L}{\partial \bar{G}} = w_2(\bar{G}^0 - \hat{G}^0) + w_4(\bar{G}^0 - \bar{T}^0 - tY^0) - \lambda_1^0 = 0$

$\dfrac{\partial L}{\partial \bar{T}} = -w_4(\bar{G}^0 - \bar{T}^0 - tY^0) + \lambda_1^0 a_{11} = 0$

$\dfrac{\partial L}{\partial \bar{M}} = \lambda_2^0 = 0$

In general form we can write (2.74) and the implicit form of (2.72) as

(2.75) $$f(Y, r, \bar{G}, \bar{T}, \bar{M}, \lambda_1, \lambda_2; \hat{Y}, \hat{r}, \hat{G}) = 0$$

where

$$f \equiv (f^1, \ldots, f^7)$$

where the targets are exogenous and the other seven variables endogenous in this model. We may consider (2.75) as the structural relations of the model.

By the implicit function theorem, if the Jacobian matrix

$$\frac{\partial(f^1, \ldots, f^7)}{\partial(Y, r, \bar{G}, \bar{T}, \bar{M}, \lambda_1, \lambda_2)}$$

is nonsingular at the constrained local extremum, then there exists a three-dimensional neighborhood of $(\hat{Y}^0, \hat{r}^0, \hat{G}^0)$ and a set of unique and differentiable function $(\phi^1, \ldots, \phi^7)$ defined on this neighborhood as

(2.76) $$z = \phi(\hat{Y}, \hat{r}, \hat{G})$$

where

$$\phi \equiv (\phi^1, \ldots, \phi^7)$$
$$z \equiv (Y, r, \bar{G}, \bar{T}, \bar{M}, \lambda_1, \lambda_2)$$

such that

$$f(\phi; \hat{Y}, \hat{r}, \hat{G}) = 0$$

identically in this neighborhood.

The objective of this analysis is to derive the reduced form equations (2.76), if possible, and to obtain as much information as we can about the reduced form derivatives, such as $\partial Y/\partial \hat{Y}$, $\partial \bar{G}/\partial \hat{r}$ and so on.

Since we are working with linear structural equations, we can derive the reduced form if the Jacobian matrix of (2.75) is nonsingular. Writing (2.75) in matrix form, we have

$$(2.77) \quad \begin{bmatrix} (w_1 + w_4 t^2) & 0 & -w_4 t & w_4 t & 0 & (1-\beta) & -a_{22} \\ 0 & w_3 & 0 & 0 & 0 & -a_{14} & -a_{21} \\ -w_4 t & 0 & (w_2 + w_4) & -w_4 & 0 & -1 & 0 \\ w_4 t & 0 & -w_4 & w_4 & 0 & a_{11} & 0 \\ 0 & 0 & 0 & 0 & 0 & 0 & 1 \\ (1-\beta) & -a_{14} & -1 & a_{11} & 0 & 0 & 0 \\ -a_{22} & -a_{21} & 0 & 0 & 1 & 0 & 0 \end{bmatrix} \begin{bmatrix} Y^0 \\ r^0 \\ \bar{G}^0 \\ \bar{T}^0 \\ \bar{M}^0 \\ \lambda_1^0 \\ \lambda_2^0 \end{bmatrix}$$

$$= \begin{bmatrix} w_1 \hat{Y}^0 \\ w_3 \hat{r}^0 \\ w_2 \hat{G}^0 \\ 0 \\ 0 \\ 0 \\ 0 \end{bmatrix}$$

Notice that, as usual, this Jacobian matrix is the bordered Hessian which plays such a prominent role in the sufficient conditions for a constrained optimum in Theorem 2.6.†

If we assume that the sufficient conditions for a local constrained minimum hold, then by Theorem 2.6 we know that the Jacobian matrix in (2.77) is invertible. We also know that the determinant of the matrix in (2.77) has the sign $(-1)^2 > 0$, and that any principal minor of this matrix obtained by deleting any one of the first five rows and columns also has a positive sign.‡

Premultiplying both sides of (2.77) by the inverse of the Jacobian matrix, we obtain the reduced form equations, which yield the solution for $(Y^0, r^0, \bar{G}^0, \bar{T}^0, \bar{M}^0, \lambda_1^0, \lambda_2^0)$ in terms of $(\hat{Y}^0, \hat{r}^0, \hat{G}^0)$. We can then differentiate the reduced

---

†The matrix L of Theorem 2.6 is, in this case. the 5×5 submatrix in the upper left corner of (2.77); G is here the 2×5 matrix, which is the last two rows and first five columns of (2.77). The transpose of G, G' is the last two columns and first five rows of (2.77).

‡Instead of *assuming* that the sufficient conditions hold, we could investigate the appropriate minors of (2.77) to see what, if any, conditions on the structural parameters and welfare function weights will satisfy the sufficiency condition. We leave this to the interested reader.

form equations with respect to any of the targets and try to evaluate the rate of change in the optimal value of the five choice variables with respect to a change in any of these target values. The satisfaction of the sufficiency condition immediately tells us that $\partial Y/\partial \hat{Y}$, $\partial r/\partial \hat{r}$, and $\partial \bar{G}/\partial \hat{G}$ are all positive, by applying Cramer's rule and the determinantal conditions of Theorem 2.6.

2.5 THE KUHN-TUCKER THEOREM (NECESSARY CONDITIONS)

We now extend our results on constrained optimization to allow for the possibility of inequality constraints and other restrictions on the decision variables. That is, we may wish to require that $g^i(x) \leq b_i^0$ instead of just the strict equalities $g^i(x) = b_i^0$. In addition, instead of permitting x to vary over the entire domain of the objective function f, we might wish to restrict the choice variables in some way. For example, we might wish to confine our attention to those values of x which are nonnegative or nonpositive, or to those x such that $x \geq a^0$ or $x \leq b^0$, or even some combination of these types of constraints. Optimization problems with these kinds of restrictions and constraints constitute the subject matter of *nonlinear programming*.

The standard form of a nonlinear programming problem is

maximize $f(x)$

subject to $g^i(x) \leq b_i^0$ $i = 1, 2, \ldots, v$

$g^i(x) = b_i^0$ $i = v + 1, \ldots, m$

$x \geq 0$

Any mixture of inequalities in the constraint functions and restrictions on the choice variables can easily be transformed into this standard form. For example, suppose the problem is to

maximize $\phi(y)$

subject to $h^i(y) \leq b_i^0$ $i = 1, \ldots, p$

$h^i(y) \geq c_i^0$ $i = p + 1, \ldots, v$

$h^i(y) = b_i^0$ $i = v + 1, \ldots, m$

$y_j \geq a_j^0$ $j = 1, \ldots, k$

$y_j \leq d_j^0$ $j = k + 1, \ldots, n$

By defining $x_j = y_j - a_j^0$ for $j = 1, \ldots, k$ and $x_j = d_j^0 - y_j$ for $j = k + 1$, $\ldots, n$, we convert the last two sets of restrictions, to $x \geq 0$. Moreover, the

second set of constraints can be written $-h^i(y) \leq -c_i^0$ for $i = p+1, \ldots, v$.
Next, define

$$f(x) \equiv \phi(y) \equiv \phi(x_1 + a_1^0, \ldots, x_k + a_k^0, d_{k+1}^0 - x_{k+1}, \ldots, d_n^0 - x_n)$$

and similarly

$$g^i(x) \equiv h^i(y) \qquad i = 1, \ldots, p, v+1, \ldots, m$$
$$g^i(x) \equiv -h^i(y) \qquad i = p+1, \ldots, v$$

Substituting the above definitions for y into the last two expressions, we have
the standard form of the nonlinear programming problem.

We now transform the standard form into an equivalent problem, which
will allow us to use the classical results developed in section 2.3. Consider the
problem

$$\text{maximize } f(x)$$
$$\text{subject to } g^i(x) + x_{si} = b_i^0 \qquad i = 1, \ldots, v$$
$$g^i(x) = b_i^0 \qquad i = v+1, \ldots, m$$
$$x_j - y_j = b_{m+j}^0 \qquad j = 1, \ldots, n$$
$$(x_s, y) \geq 0$$

where $x_s \equiv (x_{s1}, \ldots, x_{sv})$
$y \equiv (y_1, \ldots, y_n)$
$b^0 \equiv (b_1^0, \ldots, b_{m+n}^0)$

In the last set of constraints, it is understood that $b_{m+j}^0 = 0$. Notice that this
problem is equivalent to the standard form. What we have done is to add to
the standard form two sets of nonnegative "slack variables" x_s and y. Instead
of $g^i(x) \leq b_i^0$, we require that $g^i(x) + x_{si} = b_i^0$. Thus, if $g^i(x) < b_i^0, x_{si}$ is positive and takes up the slack between the availability of the ith "resource" b_i^0 and
its "use," $g^i(x)$. In addition, we have replaced $x_j \geq 0$ with $x_j - y_j = 0$, so
that, when $x_j > 0, y_j > 0$ also. Notice that *we have liberated* x *from its nonnegativity restriction by requiring instead that* y *be nonnegative.* We have enlarged the decision vector by these transformations to (x, x_s, y), but the objective function now has the *unrestricted* variables x as its arguments. Observe
that we have converted the standard form into a problem which is almost the
Lagrange problem. In the transformed problem we have equalities instead of
inequalities, and the restrictions on the decision variables x of the standard
problem have been replaced with similar restrictions on the new variables y.
The restrictions on x_s and y of the transformed problem constitute the only
difference between this problem and the Lagrange problem.

Consider now a feasible point x^0, that is, a point which satisfies the constraints. Some of the components of x^0 will be positive, and the rest will be zero. Without loss of generality, we can assume that $x_j^0 > 0$ for $j = 1, \ldots, n_1$ and $x_j^0 = 0$ for $j = n_1 + 1, \ldots, n$. Thus, the number of nonzero components in the decision vector x^0 is n_1. Given the restrictions $x_j - y_j = b_{m+j}^0$ for $j = 1, \ldots, n$, where $b_{m+j}^0 = 0$, we can deduce that $y_j^0 > 0$ for $j = 1, \ldots, n_1$ and $y_j^0 = 0$ for $j = n_1 + 1, \ldots, n$.

Next, consider the constraints $g^i(x) + x_{si} = b_i^0$ for $i = 1, \ldots, v$. For a particular point x^0, it may be true that for some i, $g^i(x^0) < b_i^0$ (that is, $x_{si}^0 > 0$) and for other i, $g^i(x^0) = b_i^0$ (that is, $x_{si}^0 = 0$). Again without loss of generality, we may assume that, corresponding to x^0, $x_{si}^0 > 0$ for $i = 1, \ldots, v_1$, and $x_{si}^0 = 0$ for $i = v_1 + 1, \ldots, v$, with $0 \le v_1 \le v$. Thus, from the m constraints $g^i(x) \le b_i^0$, we are assuming that, at the point x^0, the first v_1 constraints are not binding (satisfied with an inequality) and the remaining $m - v_1$ constraints are binding (satisfied with equality).

Next, suppose that f assumes a local maximum at the feasible point x^0. *Since x^0 is a given point, we can avoid dealing with noninterior points by eliminating as variables from the problem the zero components of x_s and y.* In other words, we *assume* that there exists a neighborhood of the point $b^0 = (b_1^0, \ldots, b_{m+n}^0)$ for which x^0 is a local maximum, such that the components of x_s and y which were zero at b^0 remain zero in a neighborhood of b^0.† *With this assumption we have converted the problem into the classical Lagrange problem,* for the local maximum occurs at the *interior* point (x^0, x_s^0, y^0) of the expanded domain of f, where x_s and y now have v_1 and n_1 components, respectively. We are thus now dealing with a problem in $(n + v_1 + n_1)$ variables (x, x_s, y) with $(m + n)$ equality constraints, that is

$$\max f(x)$$
$$\text{subject to} \quad b_i^0 - x_{si} - g^i(x) = 0 \quad i = 1, , \ldots v_1$$
$$b_i^0 - g^i(x) = 0 \quad i = v_1 + 1, \ldots, m$$
$$b_{m+j}^0 + y_j - x_j = 0 \quad j = 1, \ldots, n_1$$
$$b_{m+j}^0 - x_j = 0 \quad j = n_1 + 1, \ldots, n$$

Using this statement of the problem, we can now prove the following theorem, which gives the necessary conditions for a local maximum of the nonlinear programming problem.‡

†The other variables can of course be imagined as assuming new optimal values as b takes on a value in this neighborhood of b^0. More on this point will follow.
‡This proof is adapted from that given in G. Hadley [22, Chap. 6]. The auther benefited greatly from a proof of the this theorem communicated to him by D.V.T. Bear.

THEOREM 2.8   KUHN-TUCKER NECESSARY CONDITIONS

LET f AND $g^i (i = 1, \ldots, m)$ BE REAL-VALUED FUNCTIONS DEFINED ON A SET $S \subset E^n$. DEFINE THE SET $R \subset S$ AS THE SET OF x VECTORS WHICH SATISFY THE CONSTRAINTS IN THE STANDARD PROBLEM.

ASSUME THE FOLLOWING:

1. THE POINT x^0 IS A LOCAL MAXIMUM OF $f(x)$ ON R.

2. $f, g^i \in C^2$ ON $R, i = 1, \ldots, m$.

3. THE $(m + n)$ CONSTRAINTS ARE FUNCTIONALLY INDEPENDENT AT THE POINT (x^0, x_s^0, y^0), WHERE x^0 HAS n COMPONENTS AND x_s^0 AND y^0 HAVE v_1 AND n_1 POSITIVE COMPONENTS, RESPECTIVELY.

4. THERE EXIST, IN A NEIGHBORHOOD OF b^0, DIFFERENTIABLE FUNCTIONS $x(b)$, $y(b)$, $x_s(b)$, AND $\lambda(b)$† THAT IDENTICALLY SATISFY THE CONSTRAINTS AND THE NECESSARY CONDITIONS SPELLED OUT BELOW IN (i), (ii), AND (iii). THE COMPONENTS OF (x_s, y) WHICH ARE ZERO AT b^0 REMAIN IDENTICALLY ZERO IN A NEIGHBORHOOD OF b^0.

UNDER THE ABOVE CONDITIONS, IT FOLLOWS THAT THERE EXISTS A UNIQUE SET OF LAGRANGE MULTIPLIERS $\lambda^0 = (\lambda_1^0, \ldots, \lambda_m^0)$ SUCH THAT

(a) $$f_j(x^0) - \sum_{i=1}^{m} \lambda_i^0 g_j^i(x^0) \leq 0 \qquad j = 1, \ldots, n$$

WHERE THE EQUALITY HOLDS IF $x_j^0 > 0$ AND WHERE $\leq$ HOLDS IF $x_j^0 = 0$; AND

(b) $$\lambda_i^0 \geq 0 \text{ FOR } i = 1, \ldots, v$$

WHERE THE EQUALITY HOLDS IF $g^i(x^0) < b_i^0$ AND WHERE $\geq$ HOLDS IF $g^i(x^0) = b_i^0$. ALSO, FOR $i = v + 1, \ldots, m, \lambda_i^0 \gtreqless 0$, THAT IS, λ_i^0 IS UNRESTRICTED FOR THE EQUALITY CONSTRAINTS $g^i(x) = b_i^0$.

Remark. Notice that (a) can also be written as

(a′) $$f_j(x^0) - \sum_{i=1}^{m} \lambda_i^0 g_j^i(x^0) \leq 0 \qquad j = 1, \ldots, n$$

and

$$\sum_{j=1}^{n} x_j^0 \left[f_j(x^0) - \sum_{i=1}^{m} \lambda_i^0 g_j^i(x^0) \right] = 0$$

†Here λ refers to the $(m + n)$ Lagrangian multipliers corresponding to the $(m + n)$ constraints.

Moreover, an alternative way of expressing (b) is

(b')
$$\lambda_i^0 \geq 0 \qquad i = 1, \ldots, v$$
$$\lambda_i^0 \gtreqless 0 \qquad i = v + 1, \ldots, m$$

and

$$\sum_{i=1}^{m} \lambda_i^0 [b_i^0 - g^i(x^0)] = 0$$

Remark. This theorem is not generally used to *locate* a local maximum of f on R, for that would require advance knowledge of v_1 and n_1. The principal value of the theorem is that it provides a theoretical *characterization* of a local maximum. Conceivably, one could use the theorem to find and compare all local maxima by trying all possible combinations of zero decision variables and inactive constraints. The theorem has, however, been of great importance in developing numerical procedures for solving quadratic programming problems.†

PROOF:

By hypothesis 1, together with the discussion immediately preceding this theorem, a local maximum occurs at the interior point (x^0, x_s^0, y^0) of the expanded domain of f, and the $(m + n)$ constraints are functionally independent at this point. We can, therefore, apply the Lagrange multiplier theorem. The Lagrangian function in this case is

$$L(x, x_s, y, \lambda) = f(x) + \sum_{i=1}^{v_1} \lambda_i(b_i^0 - x_{si} - g^i(x))$$
$$+ \sum_{i=v_1+1}^{m} \lambda_i(b_i^0 - g^i(x)) + \sum_{j=1}^{n_1} \lambda_{m+j}(b_{m+j}^0 + y_j - x_j)$$
$$+ \sum_{j=n_1+1}^{n} \lambda_{m+j}(b_{m+j}^0 - x_j)$$

and by the Lagrange multiplier theorem we know that there exist $(m + n)$ unique real numbers $\lambda_1^0, \ldots, \lambda_m^0, \lambda_{m+1}^0, \ldots, \lambda_{m+n}^0$ such that the following equations hold:

(i) $\dfrac{\partial L}{\partial x_j} = f_j(x^0) - \displaystyle\sum_{i=1}^{m} \lambda_i^0 g_j^i(x^0) - \lambda_{m+j}^0 = 0 \qquad j = 1, \ldots, n$

(ii) $\dfrac{\partial L}{\partial x_{si}} = -\lambda_i^0 = 0 \qquad i = 1, \ldots, v_1$

(iii) $\dfrac{\partial L}{\partial y_j} = \lambda_{m+j}^0 = 0 \qquad j = 1, \ldots, n_1$

†See Hadley [22, Chap. 7].

All that remains is to determine the signs of $\lambda_i^0 (i = v_1 + 1, \ldots, m)$ and $\lambda_{m+j}^0 (j = n_1 + 1, \ldots, n)$. The strategy here is to verify that an earlier theorem, Theorem 2.7, in which it was shown that

$$\frac{\partial f[x^0(b^0)]}{\partial b_i} = \lambda_i^0$$

is applicable in the present situation; we then deduce the sign of this partial derivative and thereby obtain the sign of λ_i^0. Employing assumption 4, and following the reasoning of Theorem 2.7, it follows that $\partial f(x^0)/\partial b_i = \lambda_i^0$, for $i = 1, \ldots, m + n$.†

Next, consider any $i \in \{v_1 + 1, \ldots, v\}$ and assume an increase in b_i^0 to $b_i^0 + \delta$, with $\delta > 0$. Then, any x which satisfies $g^i(x) \leq b_i^0$ must also satisfy $g^i(x) \leq b_i^0 + \delta$. That is, the feasible set R has been enlarged to R', where $R \subset R'$.

Hence,

$$\max_{x \,\in\, R'} f(x) \geq \max_{x \,\in\, R} f(x)$$

It follows from this that

$$\frac{\partial f(x^0)}{\partial b_i} = \lambda_i^0 \geq 0 \qquad i = v_1 + 1, \ldots, v$$

A similar argument establishes that $\lambda_{m+j}^0 \leq 0$ for $j = n_1 + 1, \ldots, n$,‡ and that $\lambda_i^0 \gtreqless 0$, for $i = v + 1, \ldots, m$.§

Substituting (iii) into (i), and using the fact that $\lambda_{m+j}^0 \leq 0$ for $j = n_1 + 1, \ldots, n$ in (i), we thus obtain

†Given the second part of assumption 4, a sufficient condition for the first part of assumption 4 is that the Jacobian of (i), (ii), (iii), and the constraints is nonsingular at $(x^0, x_s^0, y^0, \lambda^0)$. Then, by the implicit function theorem, we may express (x, x_s, y, λ) as differentiable functions of b in a neighborhood about b^0; these functions satisfy (i), (ii), (iii), and the constraints identically in this neighborhood. If we do not assume the second part of 4, then $\partial f(x^0)/\partial b_i$ might not only be discontinuous, that is, the right and lefthand derivatives might not be equal, but will also in general not be equal to λ_i^0. The validity of this point becomes clear in going through the reasoning of Theorem 2.7 for this problem. Perhaps the most interesting equestion here is the precise relationship between our assumptions 3 and 4 and the "constraint qualification" assumed by Kuhn and Tucker in their argument to obtain the necessary conditions. To the author's knowledge, no such analysis has been made. For a good discussion linking several different constraint qualifications, see Arrow, Hurwicz, and Uzawa [6], and Mangasarian [34].

‡Observe that if we were concerned with minimizing f, the reasoning in this paragraph would imply the opposite inequalities:

$$\lambda_i^0 \leq 0 (i = v_1 + 1, \ldots, v), \lambda_{m+j}^0 \geq 0 (j = n_1 + 1, \ldots, n)$$

§Recall that for $i = v + 1, \ldots, m$, $g^i(x) = b_i^0$. Since these are equality constraints, there is no way to evaluate the effect of a change in b_i on the feasibility set, hence on f. Thus, λ_i for $i = v + 1, \ldots, m$ are unrestricted.

$$f_j(x^0) - \sum_{i=1}^{m} \lambda_i^0 g_j^i(x^0) = 0 \qquad j = 1, \ldots, n_1$$

and

$$f_j(x^0) - \sum_{i=1}^{m} \lambda_i^0 g_j^i(x^0) \leq 0 \qquad j = n_1 + 1, \ldots, n$$

which is conclusion (a) of the theorem. Combining (ii) with the fact that $\lambda_i^0 \geq 0$ for $i = v_1 + 1, \ldots, v$, we obtain

$$\lambda_i^0 = 0 \qquad i = 1, \ldots, v_1$$
$$\lambda_i^0 \geq 0 \qquad i = v_1 + 1, \ldots, v$$
$$\lambda_i^0 \gtreqless 0 \qquad i = v + 1, \ldots, m$$

which is conclusion (b) of the theorem.

Q.E.D.

These Kuhn-Tucker necessary conditions contain the necessary conditions of the classical Lagrange problem where the optimum must be an interior point, as a special case. For activities (such as consuming the jth good or using the jth input) which are optimally at a positive level, we do have an interior point, and the Kuhn-Tucker conditions are identical with the classical conditions. Recall that the economic interpretation of these conditions is that the incremental benefit $(f_j(x^0))$ is equal to the incremental cost of that activity $\left(\sum_{i=1}^{m} \lambda_i^0 g_j^i(x^0)\right)$. For activities which are optimally operated at a zero level, with negative levels ruled out, we have a boundary or a corner solution which is not covered by the Lagrange multiplier theorem. For such activities, the economic meaning of the Kuhn-Tucker conditions is that the incremental return must be less than or equal to the incremental cost. In those cases where $f_j(x^0) < \sum_{i=1}^{m} \lambda_i^0 g_j^i(x^0)$, it would pay to reduce the level of the jth activity even further; but x_j^0 is already zero, and the nonnegativity restrictions prevent such a reduction. Recalling our earlier interpretation of the Lagrange multiplier, λ_i^0, as the "shadow price" of the ith resource, we see that if a particular resource is not fully used at the optimum, that is, $g^i(x^0) < b_i^0$, it follows that $\lambda_i^0 = 0$. Or the ith resource is a free good, and hence its shadow price is zero.

2.6 CONVEX AND CONCAVE FUNCTIONS

Our next objective is to develop the sufficient conditions for a global maximum of f subject to the equality and inequality constraints of the previous section. These conditions involve the assumption that f be a *concave function* and that the g^i be *concave* or *convex functions*. In this section, we will define these concepts and some useful theorems involving them. We develop the sufficient conditions in section 2.7.

In the theory of optimization, concave and convex functions are particularly interesting.† If a function can be shown to be convex over the whole region for which it is defined, it follows that any local minimum of this function is also a global minimum. It can also be demonstrated that a positive semidefinite quadratic form is a convex function. By similar argument, it can be shown that if a function is concave, any local maximum is a global maximum, and a negative semidefinite quadratic form is a concave function on E^n.

Definitions. A function $f(x)$ is said to be a convex function over the convex set‡ X if for any two points x_1 and x_2 in X and for all $\lambda, 0 \leq \lambda \leq 1$,

$$f[\lambda x_1 + (1 - \lambda)x_2] \leq \lambda f(x_1) + (1 - \lambda)f(x_2)$$

A function $f(x)$ is defined as a concave function over the convex set X if for any two points x_1 and x_2 in X and for all $\lambda, 0 \leq \lambda \leq 1$,

$$f[\lambda x_1 + (1 - \lambda)x_2] \geq \lambda f(x_1) + (1 - \lambda)f(x_2)$$

Notice that if f is concave, then $-f$ must be convex, and vice versa. In E^3, a convex function would look typically like a bowl, and a concave function would look like an upside-down bowl. These definitions say that if a function is convex (concave), the value of the function at some point between x_1 and x_2, $\lambda x_1 + (1 - \lambda)x_2$, is less than or equal to (greater than or equal to) the value at $\lambda x_1 + (1 - \lambda)x_2$ of a line segment joining $f(x_1)$ and $f(x_2)$.§ Figures 2–2 and 2–3 illustrate a convex and concave function of a single variable. If these definitions are altered to exclude the possibility of equality, and if λ is restricted to the open interval, $0 < \lambda < 1$, we say that the functions are *strictly* concave or convex. The function in Figure 2–2 is convex but not strictly convex for $x \leq x^0$, and is strictly convex for $x \geq x^0$. The function is Figure 2–3 is strictly concave. Notice that a linear function $z = cx$ (where c is a constant) is both convex and concave.∥ Hence, in Figure 2–2, $f(x)$ for $x \leq x^0$, is concave as well as convex. Clearly, a linear function cannot be strictly convex or concave. Notice that the definitions of convex and concave functions require that f

---

†See Hadley [22, Chap. 3].

‡Recall that a convex set X in E^n is a set of points such that for any two points x_1 and x_2 in X, it follows that the point $z = \lambda x_1 + (1 - \lambda)x_2$ is also in X, for all λ such that $0 \leq \lambda \leq 1$. The point z is said to be a *convex combination* of x_1 and x_2; geometrically, z lies on the line segment connecting x_1 and x_2.

§Recall that a line segment between any two points x_1 and x_2 in E^n is defined as the set of points mapped by $\lambda x_1 + (1 - \lambda)x_2$, as λ takes on all values between zero and one.

∥This is true because $c[\lambda x_1 + (1 - \lambda)x_2] = \lambda(cx_1) + (1 - \lambda))cx_2$. Therefore, replacing the equality by either $\leq$ or $\geq$ results in a true statement.

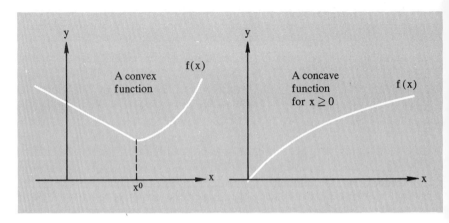

Fig. 2-2   Fig. 2-3

be defined on a convex set, since if f is defined at x_1 and x_2, the definitions assume that f is defined at any point which is a convex combination of x_1 and x_2.

THEOREM 2.9

If $f(x)$ IS A CONVEX FUNCTION, ANY LOCAL MINIMUM OF f IS A GLOBAL MINI-MUM.

PROOF:

Suppose that f assumes a local minimum at point x^0 and a global minimum at a point x^*. We shall demonstrate that it is impossible that $f(x^*) < f(x^0)$. Assume that $f(x^*) < f(x^0)$. Since f is convex, it follows that, for all λ such that $0 \le \lambda \le 1$

$$f[\lambda x^* + (1 - \lambda)x^0] \le \lambda f(x^*) + (1 - \lambda)f(x^0)$$

If $f(x^*) < f(x^0)$, then

$$f[\lambda x^* + (1 - \lambda)x^0] < \lambda f(x^0) + (1 - \lambda)f(x^0) = f(x^0)$$

Now imagine that λ is made arbitrarily close to zero, hence the point $\lambda x^* + (1 - \lambda)x^0$ is arbitrarily close to x^0. It follows, by the last inequality, that we have contradicted the assumption that f assumes a local minimum at x^0. Therefore, $f(x^*) = f(x^0)$.

Q.E.D.

THEOREM 2.10

(a) IF f IS A CONVEX FUNCTION AND TAKES ON GLOBAL MINIMA AT x^0 AND x^*, THEN ALL POINTS ON THE LINE SEGMENT JOINING x^* AND x^0 ARE ALSO GLOBAL MINIMA.

(b) IF f IS A STRICTLY CONVEX FUNCTION, THEN IT IS IMPOSSIBLE FOR f TO ASSUME A GLOBAL MINIMUM AT MORE THAN ONE POINT.

PROOF:

(a) Let $z = \lambda x^* + (1 - \lambda)x^0$ for $0 \leq \lambda \leq 1$. Then, since f is convex and $f(x^*) = f(x^0)$, we have that

$$f(z) \leq \lambda f(x^*) + (1 - \lambda)f(x^0) = f(x^*) = f(x^0)$$

If the strict inequality holds, we have contradicted the assumption that $f(x^*)$ and $f(x^0)$ are global minima. Hence, $f(z) = f(x^*) = f(x^0)$; if there are two global minima, there are an infinity of them. Notice that we have also established that the set of points at which f assumes a global minimum is a convex set.†

(b) Let f take on a global minimum at x^* and x^0. Forming again the inequality in (a), we see that the equality cannot hold, because f is assumed to be strictly convex. Therefore, the assumption of more than one minimum runs into the immediate contradiction that $f(z) < f(x^*)$.‡

Q.E.D.

The last two theorems apply word-for-word to concave functions and maxima, with appropriate changes in sign.

THEOREM 2.11

A POSITIVE (NEGATIVE) SEMIDEFINITE QUADRATIC FORM IS A CONVEX (CONCAVE) FUNCTION ON E^n.

PROOF:

We shall prove the theorem for a positive semidefinite quadratic form. Let $f(x) = x'Ax \geq 0$ for all $x \neq 0$. Choose any two points x_1 and x_2 and let

---

†A single point is also a convex set.

‡It is easy to establish from these arguments that if f is convex on a closed and bounded convex set, then f cannot have a strong local maximum at an interior point. See Hadley [22, pp. 91-93].

$z = \lambda x_2 + (1 - \lambda)x_1$ where $0 \leq \lambda \leq 1$. By the definition of a convex function, we need to prove that

$$z'Az \leq \lambda x_2'Ax_2 + (1 - \lambda)x_1'Ax_1$$

By the definition of z

$$z'Az = [\lambda x_2 + (1 - \lambda)x_1]'A[\lambda x_2 + (1 - \lambda)x_1]$$
$$= x_1'Ax_1 + 2\lambda(x_2 - x_1)'Ax_1 + \lambda^2(x_2 - x_1)'A(x_2 - x_1)$$

Since $0 \leq \lambda \leq 1$ and $x'Ax \geq 0$, it follows that

$$\lambda(x_2 - x_1)'A(x_2 - x_1) \geq \lambda^2(x_2 - x_1)'A(x_2 - x_1)$$

Therefore,

$$z'Az \leq x_1'Ax_1 + 2\lambda(x_2 - x_1)'Ax_1 + \lambda(x_2 - x_1)'A(x_2 - x_1)$$

and multiplying out the right side we see that the theorem is proved. The argument for a negative semidefinite quadratic form is similar.

Q.E.D.

Notice that if the quadratic form is positive definite, that is, $x'Ax > 0$ for $x \neq 0$, then it follows in the last proof for $0 < \lambda < 1$ and $x_1 \neq x_2$ that

$$\lambda(x_2 - x_1)'A(x_2 - x_1) > \lambda^2(x_2 - x_2)'A(x_2 - x_1)$$

hence,

$$z'Az < \lambda x_2'Ax_2 + (1 - \lambda)x_1'Ax_1$$

which shows that $f(x) = x'Ax$ is a strictly convex function on E^n. Similarly, if $f(x) = x'Ax$ is negative definite, then it is a strictly concave function on E^n.

2.7   THE KUHN-TUCKER THEOREM (SUFFICIENT CONDITIONS)

In this section it will be convenient to rewrite the necessary conditions of the Kuhn-Tucker theorem in gradient notation. Letting $L(x, \lambda) \equiv f(x) + \sum_{i=1}^{m} \lambda_i(b_i^0 - g^i(x))$, we may restate conditions (a) and (b) as

(a) $\qquad$ $\nabla_x L(x^0, \lambda^0) \leq 0$ and $\nabla_x L(x^0, \lambda^0) x^0 = 0$

(b) $\qquad$ $\nabla_\lambda L(x^0, \lambda^0) \geq 0$ and $\nabla_\lambda L(x^0, \lambda^0) \lambda^0 = 0$

where

$x_j^0 > 0$ for $j = 1, \ldots, n_1$; $x_j^0 = 0$ for $j = n_1 + 1, \ldots, n$;

$\lambda_i^0 \geq 0$ for $i = 1, \ldots, v$; and λ_i^0 is unrestricted for $i = v + 1, \ldots, m$

$$\nabla_x L(x^0, \lambda^0) \equiv \left(\frac{\partial L(x^0, \lambda^0)}{\partial x_1}, \ldots, \frac{\partial L(x^0, \lambda^0)}{\partial x_n} \right)$$

$$\nabla_\lambda L(x^0, \lambda^0) \equiv \left(\frac{\partial L(x^0, \lambda^0)}{\partial \lambda_1}, \ldots, \frac{\partial L(x^0, \lambda^0)}{\partial x_m} \right)$$

Now we shall develop conditions which are sufficient for f to assume a global maximum at the feasible point x^0, that is, at a point x^0 such that $g^i(x^0) \leq b_i^0$ for $i = 1, \ldots, v$, and $g^i(x^0) = b_i^0$ for $i = v + 1, \ldots, m$. We again refer to the feasible set of x-vectors as R, that is

$$R = \{x | g^i(x) \leq b_i^0 \text{ for } i = 1, \ldots, v; \ g^i(x) = b_i^0 \text{ for } i = v + 1, \ldots, m\}$$

As we shall see, *if* f(x) *is a concave function for* x ≥ 0 *and if the* g^i(x) *are either convex or concave functions as required by the sign of* λ_i^0, *it follows that a point* x^0 *which satisfies the necessary conditions for a local maximum also satisfies the sufficient conditions for a global maximum.* In other words, with these restrictions on the concavity of $f(x)$ and the convexity or concavity of $g^i(x)$, the necessary conditions are also sufficient. We shall also demonstrate that *the sufficient conditions for a global maximum hold at* x^0 *if the Lagrangian function* L(x, λ) *has a global saddle point at* (x^0, λ^0), *for* $x \in R$ *and* λ_i *nonnegative for* $i = 1, \ldots, v$ *and unrestricted for* $i = v + 1, \ldots, m$. We shall refer to this restriction on λ throughout by saying that $\lambda \in W$. By a global saddle point at (x^0, λ^0) we mean that

(2.78) $\qquad$ $L(x, \lambda^0) \leq L(x^0, \lambda^0) \leq L(x^0, \lambda)$

for $x \in R$ and $\lambda \in W$. The argument for a global minimum would be identical, except that concave and convex would be interchanged, the inequalities in the saddle point would be reversed, and the inequalities in the necessary conditions would be reversed, except, of course, that x would still be nonnegative and belong to R.

A concept which will be useful in what follows is that of a *supporting hyperplane*. We say that $L(x, \lambda)$ has supporting hyperplanes at (x^0, λ^0), given the above restrictions on (x, λ), if

(2.79) $\qquad$ $L(x, \lambda^0) \leq L(x^0, \lambda^0) + \nabla_x L(x^0, \lambda^0)(x - x^0)$

and

(2.80) $L(x^0, \lambda) \geq L(x^0, \lambda^0) + \nabla_\lambda L(x^0, \lambda^0)(\lambda - \lambda^0)$

The vectors ∇_x and ∇_λ are called *support gradients* of $L(x, \lambda)$ at (x^0, λ^0). For a function L of a single variable x, we write (2.79) as

$$L(x) \leq L(x^0) + L'(x^0)(x - x^0), \text{ or}$$
$$\frac{L(x) - L(x^0)}{x - x^0} \leq L'(x^0)$$

which says that the slope of L at x^0 is at least as great as the slope of the secant through the points $[x^0, L(x^0)]$ and $[x, L(x)]$. Geometrically, this is shown in Figure 2–4, where the dotted line is the supporting line at x^0, which clearly has a larger slope than the secant through $[x^0, L(x^0)]$ and $(\hat{x}, L(\hat{x}))$, where $\hat{x}$ can be any other x over the domain of L.

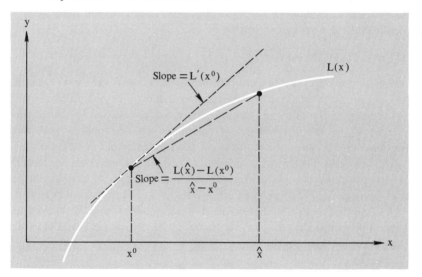

Fig. 2-4

Our strategy will be as follows. We will show that if $L(x, \lambda)$ has a global saddle point at (x^0, λ^0), then x^0 is a global maximum for f subject to the constraints. Next, we will prove that if $L(x, \lambda)$ has supporting hyperplanes at (x^0, λ^0), and if the necessary conditions hold, then $L(x, \lambda)$ has a global saddle point at (x^0, λ^0). Finally, we will demonstrate that if f is concave and the $g^i(x)$ are either concave or convex functions as required by the sign of λ_i^0, then $L(x, \lambda)$ has supporting hyperplanes at (x^0, λ^0). Throughout, it is assumed that $x \in R$ and $\lambda \in W$. Schematically, we can express these assertions, which constitute the message of the theorems to follow, as[†]

†Notice that if f takes on a global maximum at x^0, then the necessary conditions must hold, and if, in addition, either (2.79) and (2.80) hold, or the required concavity-convexity conditions hold, then $L(x, \lambda)$ has a global saddle point at (x^0, λ^0).

$$\left.\begin{array}{l} f \text{ concave and} \\ g^i \text{ convex or} \\ \text{concave depending} \\ \text{on sign of } \lambda_i^0 \end{array}\right\} \Rightarrow \left.\begin{array}{l} \text{(a) and (b)} \\ (2.79) \text{ and } (2.80) \end{array}\right\} \Rightarrow (2.78) \Rightarrow \begin{array}{l} f(x^0) \\ \text{is a global} \\ \text{maximum} \\ \text{of } f(x) \text{ on } R \end{array}$$

THEOREM 2.12

IF (x^0, λ^0) IS A GLOBAL SADDLE POINT OF $L(x, \lambda)$, THEN f ASSUMES A GLOBAL MAXIMUM ON R AT x^0.

PROOF:

By the hypothesis that (x^0, λ^0) is a saddle point of $L(x, \lambda)$ and the definition of $L(x, \lambda)$, we have that

$$f(x) + \sum_{i=1}^m \lambda_i^0(b_i^0 - g^i(x)) \leq f(x^0) + \sum_{i=1}^m \lambda_i^0(b_i^0 - g^i(x^0)) \leq f(x^0)$$

$$+ \sum_{i=1}^m \lambda_i(b_i^0 - g^i(x^0))$$

By definition of a global saddle point $x \in R$, thus, $(b_i^0 - g^i(x)) \geq 0$ for $i = 1, \ldots, v$, and $(b_i^0 - g^i(x)) = 0$ for $i = v + 1, \ldots, m$. Since $\lambda \in W$, $\lambda_i \geq 0$, for $i = 1, \ldots, v$ and λ_i is unrestricted for $i = v + 1, \ldots, m$. The right-hand inequality holds for all $\lambda_i \geq 0, i = 1, \ldots, v$, hence

$$\sum_{i=1}^m \lambda_i^0(b_i^0 - g^i(x^0)) = 0$$

Moreover, $x \in R, \lambda \in W$ also implies that

$$\sum_{i=1}^m \lambda_i^0(b_i^0 - g^i(x)) \geq 0$$

thus, from the left-hand inequality of the saddle point statement (2.78)

$$f(x) \leq f(x^0) \qquad x \in R$$

$$\text{Q.E.D.}$$

THEOREM 2.13

IF (a), (b), (2.79), AND (2.80) HOLD, THEN $L(x, \lambda)$ HAS A GLOBAL SADDLE POINT AT (x^0, λ^0).

PROOF:

By (a)

$$\nabla_x L(x^0, \lambda^0)x^0 = 0 \quad \text{and} \quad \nabla_x L(x^0, \lambda^0) \leq 0$$

Thus

$$\nabla_x L(x^0, \lambda^0)(x - x^0) = \nabla_x L(x^0, \lambda^0)x$$

Since $x \geq 0, \nabla_x(x^0, \lambda^0)x \leq 0$, it follows that

$$\nabla_x L(x^0, \lambda^0)(x - x^0) \leq 0$$

If (2.79) holds, we deduce from this inequality that

$$L(x, \lambda^0) \leq L(x^0, \lambda^0) \qquad x \in R$$

and we have proved the left-hand inequality in (2.78).
Next, we see from (b) that

$$\nabla_\lambda L(x^0, \lambda^0)(\lambda - \lambda^0) = \nabla_\lambda L(x^0, \lambda^0)\lambda$$

Since $x^0 \in R$, the last $(m - v)$ components of $\nabla_\lambda L(x^0, \lambda^0) = 0$, and the first v components are nonnegative. Moreover, $\lambda \in W$, which means that its last $(m - v)$ components are $\gtreqless 0$, and its first v components are nonnegative. Therefore,

$$\nabla_\lambda L(x^0, \lambda^0)(\lambda - \lambda^0) \geq 0$$

Now, if (2.80) holds, the last inequality implies that

$$L(x^0, \lambda^0) \leq L(x^0, \lambda) \qquad \lambda \in W$$
$$\text{Q.E.D.}$$

THEOREM 2.14

If $L(x, \lambda^0)$ IS A CONCAVE FUNCTION ON R, AND $L(x^0, \lambda)$ IS A CONVEX FUNCTION ON W, THEN (2.79) AND (2.80), RESPECTIVELY, MUST HOLD.

PROOF:
If $L(x, \lambda^0)$ is concave on R, then for $x, x^0 \in R$ and $0 \leq \alpha \leq 1$

$$L(\alpha x + (1 - a)x^0, \lambda^0) \geq \alpha L(x, \lambda^0) + (1 - \alpha)L(x^0, \lambda^0), \text{ or}$$

$$(2.81) \qquad L(x^0 + \alpha(x - x^0), \lambda^0) - L(x^0, \lambda^0) \geq \alpha[L(x, \lambda^0) - L(x^0, \lambda^0)]$$

Applying Taylor's theorem to the left side gives

$$(2.82) \qquad L(x^0 + \alpha(x - x^0), \lambda^0) - L(x^0, \lambda^0) = \alpha\nabla_x(\hat{x}, \lambda^0)(x - x^0)$$

where $\hat{x} = x^0 + \theta\alpha(x - x^0)$ and $\theta \in (0, 1)$, and substituting (2.82) into (2.81) and canceling α gives

(2.83) $\nabla_x(\hat{x}, \lambda^0)(x - x^0) \geq L(x, \lambda^0) - L(x^0, \lambda^0)$

Since (2.83) is true for all $\alpha \in (0, 1)$, and since, for each α, the corresponding θ is bounded [since $\theta \in (1, 0)$], it follows that (2.82) remains true in the limit as $\alpha \to 0$, hence $\hat{x} \to x^0$. Taking that limit establishes (2.79). The second statement is proved in identical fashion.

Q.E.D.

By putting the three previous theorems together, we have in fact proved the following.

THEOREM 2.15   KUHN-TUCKER SUFFICIENT CONDITIONS

IF (a) AND (b) HOLD, AND IF $f(x)$ IS CONCAVE FOR $x \in R$, WHILE $g^i(x)$ IS CONVEX IF $\lambda_i^0 > 0$ AND CONCAVE IF $\lambda_i^0 < 0$ FOR $i = 1, \ldots, m$, THEN $f(x^0)$ IS A GLOBAL MAXIMUM OF $f(x)$ ON R.

PROOF:

By hypothesis and the definition of $L(x, \lambda)$, it follows that $L(x, \lambda^0)$ is concave. This stems from the fact (easily proven) that the sum of convex functions is convex, and that the negative of a convex function is concave. Moreover, $L(x^0, \lambda)$ is a linear function, hence it must be convex (and concave) for all λ.

It follows, from Theorem 2.14, that (2.79) and (2.80) hold, which, with the assumption about (a) and (b), establishes that $L(x, \lambda)$ has a global saddle point (relative to R, W) at (x^0, λ^0), by Theorem 2.13; hence, by Theorem 2.12, $f(x^0)$ is a global maximum of $f(x)$ on R.†

2.8 EXAMPLES

Example 2.7   A Nonlinear Programming Problem‡

Consider a company which produces automobiles and trucks. Suppose that the demand functions for these are

---

†The results in this section apply, of course, to the Lagrange problem; we have thus stated the sufficient conditions for a global maximum (and minimum) for that problem. These theorems go through even more easily for the classical Lagrange problem, since the necessary conditions together with the equality constraints imply that the support gradients ∇_x and ∇_λ are zero vectors at (x^0, λ^0).

‡See Dorfman, Samuelson, and Solow [14, Chaps. 6 and 8].

$$P_1 = 625 - \frac{x_1}{60}$$

$$P_2 = 250$$

where

$P_1 =$ the price of automobiles

$P_2 =$ the price of trucks

$x_1 =$ the sales of automobiles

$x_2 =$ the sales of trucks

Next, we assume that this company utilizes the following inputs in carrying out these two production processes or "activities." The production of one automobile per month uses up 0.004 per cent of the company's capacity of metal-stamping equipment, 0.003 per cent of engine-assembly capacity, and 0.00444 per cent of automobile-assembly capacity. The production of one truck per month requires as inputs 0.00286 per cent of metal-stamping capacity, 0.006 per cent of engine-assembly capacity, and 0.00667 per cent of truck-assembly capacity.

If we let x_1 denote the production (and sales) of automobiles per month, and x_2 the number of trucks, we can use this data to write

$0.004x_1 + 0.00286x_2 =$ per cent utilization of metal-stamping capacity

$0.003x_1 + 0.006x_2 =$ per cent utilization of engine-assembly capacity

$0.00444x_1 =$ per cent utilization of automobile-assembly capacity

$0.00667x_2 =$ per cent utilization of truck-assembly capacity

Since the capacity limitation is 100 per cent for each input, we may write the constraint functions for the firm as†

$$0.004x_1 + 0.00286x_2 \leq 100$$

$$0.003x_1 + 0.006x_2 \leq 100$$

$$0.00444x_1 \leq 100$$

$$0.00667x_2 \leq 100$$

---

†Notice the simplifying assumptions that have been made. The *total* capacity requirement is directly proportional to the number of automobiles made, and the same is assumed for trucks. Also, while automobiles and trucks compete for the available capacity, it is supposed that they do not interfere with each other. That is, the total capacity requirement for any production program (any x_1 and x_2) is simply the sum of the requirements for both. These assumptions are typical of linear programming models of the firm.

We do not permit the production of negative amounts, so we require that x_1, $x_2 \geq 0$.

Now, assume that this firm desires to maximize its revenue function

$$(2.84) \qquad r(x_1 x_2) = P_1 x_1 + P_2 x_2 = x_1 \left(625 - \frac{x_1}{60} \right) + 250 x_2$$

$$= 625 x_1 + 250 x_2 - \frac{x_1^2}{60}$$

The problem is simple enough for us to use the Kuhn-Tucker theorem constructively. Assume, as a first try, that only the first constraint is effective at the optimum and that the others are not, and that both x_1^0 and x_2^0 are strictly positive. The Kuhn-Tucker theorem tells us that the Lagrange multipliers for the last three constraints must be zero, hence we can write the Lagrangian expression as

$$L = r(x_1, x_2) + \lambda_1 (0.004 x_1 + 0.0286 x_2 - 100)$$

and computing the partial derivatives

$$\frac{\partial L}{\partial x_1} = 625 - \frac{x_1}{30} + 0.004 \lambda_1 = 0$$

$$\frac{\partial L}{\partial x_2} = 250 + 0.00286 \lambda_1 = 0$$

which, along with the first equality constraint, enables us to solve for (x_1, x_2, λ_1). The result is $x_1 = 8{,}250$, $x_2 = 23{,}450$, $\lambda_1 = -87{,}500$. Substituting this candidate for an optimal solution into the constraints shows that this solution is not feasible, 'for it requires approximately 165 per cent of the available engine-assembly capacity. Trying again, we assume that only the second constraint is binding and that the optimal values of x_1 and x_2 are strictly positive. Following the same procedure, we obtain as a potential optimum $x_1 = 15{,}000$, $x_2 = 9{,}167$, and $\lambda_2 = -41{,}667$. It is easily seen to be feasible. The question is, is this solution a global maximum?

Applying the results of the previous section, we know that if the necessary conditions hold at a point, and if, in addition, the objective function is concave and the constraint functions are concave or convex, depending on the sign of the Lagrange multiplier, then the candidate point is guaranteed to be a global maximum subject to the constraints.† In this problem, the constraint functions

---

†Another route is to investigate whether support hyperplanes exist at the point which satisfies the necessary conditions.

are linear, hence they are both concave and convex. The question then becomes, is the objective function (2.84) a concave function? Observe that this function can be written as the sum of the quadratic form whose matrix is

$$\begin{bmatrix} -\dfrac{1}{\sqrt{60}} & 0 \\ 0 & 0 \end{bmatrix}$$

and the linear function $625x_1 + 250x_2$. Clearly, the quadratic form is negative semidefinite, hence by Theorem 2.11, and by the fact that the sum of concave functions is a concave function, we deduce that the objective function in this problem is a concave function, and therefore the suspected point is a constrained global maximum.

Example 2.8   A Multiproduct Firm†

SYMBOLS:

$X_i = i$th product produced by the firm, $i = 1, \ldots, n$

$Y_{ij} = j$th variable factor used in ith product, $j = 1, \ldots, m$

$W_j = $ price of the jth variable factor

$Z_{it} = t$th fixed factor used in ith product, $t = 1, \ldots, p$

$Z_t = $ stock of tth fixed factor

$K = $ cost of switching fixed factor between products

$F = $ fixed cost

MODEL:

$$(2.85) \qquad \sum_{i=1}^{n} Z_{it} \leq Z_t, \, Z_{it} \geq 0$$

This says that the firm can allot to all n products not more than its total stock of the tth fixed factor, and that its allocation to each product must be nonnegative.

$$(2.86) \qquad X_i = f_i(Y_{i1}, \ldots, Y_{im}; Z_{i1}, \ldots, Z_{ip}) \qquad Y_{ij} \geq 0, Z_{it} \geq 0$$

Production of the ith product is a function of the nonnegative quantities of the variable and the fixed factors allocated to the ith product.

$$(2.87) \qquad K = K(Z_{11}, \ldots, Z_{1p}, Z_{21}, \ldots, Z_{2p}, \ldots, Z_{n1}, \ldots, Z_{np})$$

†See Pfouts [44].

where $\partial K/\partial Z_{ij} > 0$ is the cost of switching a small quantity of fixed input j to the production of product i.

(2.88) $\sum_i \sum_j W_j Y_{ij}$ is variable cost

The problem is to minimize cost at some set of outputs subject to (2.85) and (2.86), that is

Minimize $\sum_i \sum_j W_j Y_{ij} + K(\ ) + F$

subject to $\bar{X}_i - f_i(Y_{i1}, \ldots, Y_{im}, Z_{i1}, \ldots, Z_{ip}) = 0 \qquad i = 1, 2, \ldots, n$

and

$$\sum_{i=1}^n Z_{it} - Z_t \leq 0, t = 1, 2, \ldots, P, Y_{ij} \geq 0, Z_{it} \geq 0$$

(where $\bar{X}_i$ is a fixed amount of product i).

We may apply the Kuhn-Tucker theorem to this problem. Set up the Lagrangian expression

(2.89) $L = \sum_{i=1}^n \sum_{j=1}^m W_j Y_{ij} + K(\ ) + F$

$$+ \sum_{i=1}^n \lambda_i [\bar{X}_i - f_i(Y_{i1}, \ldots, Y_{im}, Z_{i1}, \ldots, Z_{ip})]$$

$$+ \sum_{t=1}^p \Gamma_t \left(Z_t - \sum_{i=1}^n Z_{it} \right)$$

where λ_i and Γ_t are Lagrangian multipliers. The necessary conditions for cost minimization subject to constraints (2.85) and (2.86) are

(2.90) $\dfrac{\partial L}{\partial Y_{ij}} = W_j - \lambda_i^0 \dfrac{\partial X_i}{\partial Y_{ij}} \geq 0 \qquad i = 1, \ldots, n, j = 1, \ldots, m$

(2.91) $\dfrac{\partial L}{\partial Z_{it}} = \dfrac{\partial K}{\partial Z_{it}} - \lambda_i^0 \dfrac{\partial X_i}{\partial Z_{it}} - \Gamma_t^0 \geq 0 \qquad i = 1, \ldots, n, t = 1, \ldots, p$

(2.92) $\displaystyle\sum_{j=1}^m \dfrac{\partial L}{\partial Y_{ij}} Y_{ij}^0 = \sum_{t=1}^p \dfrac{\partial L}{\partial Z_{it}} Z_{it}^0 = 0 \qquad i = 1, \ldots, n$

(2.93) $\displaystyle\sum_{t=1}^p \Gamma_t^0 \left(\sum_{i=1}^n Z_{it}^0 - Z_t \right) = 0$

where the superscript zero indicates the optimal value. Before interpreting these results, observe that total cost is generally assumed to be a convex function, and the production function is generally assumed to be concave. Given these assumptions, it follows from the analysis of the previous section that we have a global minimum at the point which satisfies conditions (2.90) through (2.93), or, equivalently, the Lagrangian function possessess a global saddle point at this critical value. In other words, *any* constrained minimum point (local or global) must satisfy conditions (2.90) through (2.93); if *in addition* to these conditions, it can be assumed that the cost function is convex and the production function concave, we are guaranteed that this point will be a global minimum subject to constraints (2.85) and (2.86).† (This assumes $\lambda_i^0 > 0$. Why may we assume that?)

From (2.90) and (2.92), it follows that if $Y_{ij}^0 > 0$, then the equality in (2.90) must hold. Thus, if $Y_{ij}^0 > 0$ and $Y_{ik}^0 > 0$, the familiar marginal condition holds that

$$(2.94) \qquad \frac{1}{W_j}\frac{\partial X_i}{\partial Y_{ij}} = \frac{1}{W_k}\frac{\partial X_i}{\partial Y_{ik}}$$

which says that at the optimum an additional dollar spent on variable input j produces the same increment to output i as an extra dollar spent on input k. On the other hand, if, at the optimum, *none* of the jth variable input is used to produce output i, and *some* of the kth variable input is used for output i, it follows that

$$(2.95) \qquad \frac{1}{W_j}\frac{\partial X_i}{\partial Y_{ij}} \leq \frac{1}{W_k}\frac{\partial X_i}{\partial Y_{ik}}$$

because (2.90) for Y_{ij}^0 is greater than or equal to zero, while (2.90) for Y_{ik}^0 is zero.

This tells us that at the optimum an additional dollar spent on the jth variable input adds not more to output i then another dollar spent on variable input k. Even if the inequality holds, however, it is not possible to reallocate dollars from j to k, since $Y_{ij}^0 = 0$, and negative amounts of input use (that is, "production" of the input) are not allowed by assumption. Notice that if both Y_{ij}^0 and Y_{ik}^0 are strictly positive, then

$$(2.96) \qquad \lambda_i^0 = W_j\left(\frac{\partial X_i}{\partial Y_{ij}}\right)^{-1} = W_k\left(\frac{\partial X_i}{\partial Y_{ik}}\right)^{-1}$$

which says that λ_i^0 equals the marginal input cost of product i for any variable input used in product i.

Moreover, from the analysis of the necessary Kuhn-Tucker conditions, we also know that λ_i^0 is the addition to variable input cost per unit increase in the production of product i. On the other hand, for any input not used in product i, (2.96) will hold with the inequality $\leq$. Hence, the marginal input cost of

†To guarantee that the optimum is unique, we must assume *strict* concavity and convexity.

product i for any input optimally utilized at a positive rate, which equals the marginal cost of product i, must be less than or equal to the marginal input cost of any input optimally used at a zero rate.

Next, consider (2.91) rewritten as

$$(2.97) \qquad \frac{\partial K}{\partial Z_{it}} - \lambda_i^0 \frac{\partial X_i}{\partial Z_{it}} \geq \Gamma_t^0 \qquad \begin{array}{l} i = 1, \ldots, n \\ t = 1, \ldots, p \end{array}$$

if $Z_{it}^0 > 0$, the equality in (2.97) will hold. In this case, (2.97) says that the Lagrange multiplier Γ_t^0 equals the difference between the change in variable input cost and the switching cost resulting from an increment of the tth fixed input to the production of product i. That is, allocating more of the fixed factor Z_t to the production of the ith good incurs a switching cost, $\partial K / \partial Z_{it}$, but also permits a reduction in the variable inputs employed for that good, since the production of the ith good is fixed. The *net* cost of this is the difference between the switching cost and the saving in variable cost, and it is given by the Lagrange multiplier Γ_t^0. Moreover, from the Kuhn-Tucker necessary conditions we know that Γ_t^0 is nonpositive and is the derivative of cost with respect to the tth fixed input at the optimum. Recalling the reasoning employed in the necessary conditions, $\Gamma_t^0 \leq 0$ because an increase in Z_t expands the feasibility region and allows the objective function (cost) to assume at least as small a value as before.

If $Z_{it}^0 = 0$, then (2.97) holds with the weak inequality. This says that the net cost of allocating a fixed input to product i, given that optimally this input is not used for product i, is at least as great as the net cost of allocating another fixed input to product i, where this other input *is* optimally used for product i. If, at the optimum, there is unused capacity in the tth fixed input, then $\Gamma_t^0 = 0$. Thus, if $\Gamma_t^0 = 0$ and $Z_{it}^0 > 0$, the left side of (2.97) will equal zero. That is, if optimal excess capacity exists for input t and if this input is optimally used to produce i, then the net cost of allocating an increment of input t to product i is zero at the optimum. If there is no excess capacity for input t at the optimum, implying that $\Gamma_t^0 \leq 0$, and if $Z_{it}^0 > 0$, then this net cost is nonpositive, that is, the switching cost is less than or equal to the saving in variable input cost at the optimum.

Other analytical possibilities are left to the reader.

2.9 APPENDIX

Before proving Theorem 2.6, we shall mention a few results on quadratic forms.†

†See Yamane [51, Chap. 11] and Hadley [21, Chap. 7].

Allowing h to vary over all of E^n, the values assumed by the quadratic form $h'Lh$ are called the *range* of the quadratic form. Now, if R is a nonsingular matrix and we define $h = Ry$, then for every y there is a unique h, and vice versa. Thus, we can replace h with Ry in the quadratic form and not affect its range, that is, with $R'LR = B$,

$$h'Lh = y'By$$

and the range of both quadratic forms is the same. We see that *under a nonsingular transformation of variables, the range of a quadratic form is not affected.* If R is singular, this result will not hold in general. For example, if R is the zero matrix and we define $h = Ry$, then it is true that

$$h'Lh = y'By$$

but if L is not a zero matrix, the range of $h'Lh$ will have been affected, since after this transformation $h'Lh$ can only equal zero.

Another important fact about *nonsingular transformations of variables* is that they *do not alter the positive or negative definiteness of a quadratic form.* That is, if $h'Lh > 0(<0)$ for all $h \neq 0$, then $y'By > 0(<0)$ for all $y \neq 0$ where $h = Ry$, $B = R'LR$, and R is nonsingular. It is easy to establish this property. We know that the range of both quadratic forms is the same. We also know that $y'By$ ranges over the nonnegative numbers as y takes on all values on E^n. The only question then is, does $y'By$ ever become zero for $y \neq 0$? Since $h'Lh = 0$ only when $h = 0$, and since $y = R^{-1}h$, if follows that $y = 0$ is the only value of y for which h, hence $y'By$, will equal zero. It can be similarly shown that semidefinite and indefinite quadratic forms remain semidefinite and indefinite, respectively, under a nonsingular transformation of variables.

Recalling that an *orthogonal* matrix is a matrix† R such that $R'R = I$, a basic result‡ is that *every symmetric matrix can be transformed by an orthogonal matrix into a diagonal matrix.* That is, if C is symmetric, there exists an orthogonal matrix R such that

$$R'CR = D$$

where D is a diagonal matrix. The matrix used to diagonalize C has as its columns an orthogonal set of eigenvectors for C. The elements on the diagonal of D are the eigenvalues of C. C *is positive definite, if and only if all its eigenvalues are positive.* C *is positive semidefinite, if and only if all of its eigenvalues are nonnegative and at least one is zero;* in this case the number of positive

†These results only refer to real matrices, that is, matrices with real numbers. An orthogonal matrix can never be singular.

‡For lucid proofs of the following important properties of quadratic forms, see Hadley [21, pp. 236–263].

eigenvalues will equal the rank of C and the remaining elements on the diagonal of D will be zeros. It follows from these observations that the quadratic form

$$h'Ch$$

can be diagonalized† by an orthogonal transformation of variables

$$h = Ry$$

such that

$$h'Ch = y'R'CRy = y'Dy = \sum_1^r \lambda_i y_i^2$$

where R is orthogonal, D is diagonal, and the λ's are the eigenvalues of C. If C is positive definite, $\lambda_i > 0, i = 1, \ldots, r$, and $r = n$, if C is an $n \times n$ matrix. If C is positive semidefinite, its rank must be less than n, say, r, and $\lambda_i > 0$, $i = 1, \ldots, r < n$ and $\lambda_i = 0$ for $i = r + 1, \ldots, n$. One more property we shall use is that *a necessary and sufficient condition for $x'Cx$ to be positive definite is that all the principal minors of C be positive*, that is

$$c_{kk} > 0, \begin{vmatrix} c_{kk} & c_{kj} \\ c_{jk} & c_{jj} \end{vmatrix}, \begin{vmatrix} c_{kk} & c_{kj} & c_{ki} \\ c_{jk} & c_{jj} & c_{ji} \\ c_{ik} & c_{ij} & c_{ii} \end{vmatrix} > 0, \cdots, |C| > 0$$

where $(k, j, i, \ldots ,)$ is any permutation of the set of integers $(1, 2, \ldots , n)$, and where c_{ij} is the ijth element of C. These determinants, in other words, can be obtained by deleting any arbitrary set of rows, up to $n - 1$ of them, and deleting the corresponding set of columns. In the resulting determinant, any two rows can be interchanged if the same columns are also interchanged, without, of course, affecting the sign of the determinant.

We are now ready for the theorem that links Theorems 2.5 and 2.6.

THEOREM A2.1   FINSLER‡

$$\left.\begin{array}{c} h'Lh > 0 \\ \text{WHEN} \\ Gh = 0 \end{array}\right\} \Rightarrow \begin{array}{l}\text{THERE EXISTS A POSITIVE NUMBER} \\ \lambda \text{ SUCH THAT } L + \lambda G'G \text{ IS POSITIVE DEFINITE} \end{array}$$

WHERE

† If C is not symmetric, the matrix of the quadratic form can always be made so, for $h'Ch = h' \dfrac{C + C'}{2} h$ and $(C + C')$ is symmetric.

‡ See Bellman [8, Chap. 5].

$$G \quad \text{IS} \quad r \times n$$

$$L \quad \text{IS} \quad n \times n$$

PROOF:

Let $G'G = C$. This matrix is $n \times n$, symmetric, and clearly positive semi-definite.† Let $h = Py$, where P is an orthogonal matrix selected so that

$$(2.98) \qquad h'Ch = y'P'CPy = \sum_1^r \lambda_i y_i^2 \qquad \lambda_i > 0$$

where $C = G'G$. Apply the same orthogonal transformation to L, which gives

$$(2.99) \qquad h'Lh = y'P'LPy = \sum_{i,j=1}^n h_{ij} y_i y_j$$

where h_{ij} is the ijth element of $P'LP$. If $Gh = 0$, $h'Ch = 0$. Thus, if $h'Lh > 0$ when $Gh = 0$, it follows that $y_i, i = 1, \ldots, r$ must be zero. Hence

$$(2.100) \qquad \sum_{i,j=r+1}^n h_{ij} y_i y_j > 0$$

for arbitrary $y_i, i = r + 1, \ldots, n$, not all zero; that is, the quadratic form in (2.100) is positive definite.

Next, let $y = Sx$ where S is the orthogonal matrix

$$S = \begin{bmatrix} I & 0 \\ 0 & \hat{S} \end{bmatrix}$$

where I is $r \times r$, $\hat{S}$ is $(n - r) \times (n - r)$, and $\hat{S}$ is constructed so that it will transform (2.100) into the sum of squares

$$\sum_{i=r+1}^n \lambda_i x_i^2 \qquad \lambda_i > 0$$

Applying this transformation to (2.99) gives

$$(2.101) \qquad h'Lh = x'(S'P'LPS)x = \sum_{i,j=1}^r w_{ij} x_i x_j$$

$$+ 2 \sum_{i=1}^r \sum_{j=r+1}^n w_{ij} x_i x_j + \sum_{i=r+1}^n \lambda_i x_i^2$$

†See Mirsky [36, p. 155]. This matrix is called a Gram matrix and it can be shown that if the rank of G is r, so is the rank of C. We shall therefore assume that C has r positive eigenvalues.

where w_{ij} is the ijth element of $S'P'LPS$. Applying the same transformation to (2.98) gives

$$(2.102) \qquad h'Ch = \sum_{i=1}^{r} \lambda_i x_i^2 \qquad \lambda_i > 0$$

Multiplying (2.102) by λ of the theorem and adding to (2.101) gives

$$(2.103) \qquad h'(L + \lambda C)h = \sum_{i,j=1}^{r} w_{ij} x_i x_j$$

$$+ 2\sum_{i=1}^{r} \sum_{j=r+1}^{n} w_{ij} x_i x_j + \sum_{i=r+1}^{n} \lambda_i x_i^2 + \lambda \sum_{i=1}^{r} \lambda_i x_i^2$$

and we must prove that this expression is positive for all $h \neq 0$. To do so, let $\lambda = 3r\Gamma$. This definition allows us to write the last element in (2.103) as the sum of

$$\sum_{j=1}^{r} \sum_{i=1}^{r} \Gamma \lambda_i x_i^2 + \sum_{j=1}^{r} \sum_{i=1}^{r} \Gamma \lambda_j x_j^2 + \sum_{j=r+1}^{n} \sum_{i=1}^{r} \frac{r\Gamma}{n-r} \lambda_i x_i^2$$

and to write the second last term in (2.103) as

$$\sum_{i=1}^{r} \sum_{j=r+1}^{n} \frac{1}{r} \lambda_j x_j^2$$

Substituting these expressions into (2.103), and rearranging, we can write

$$(2.104) \qquad h'(L + \lambda C)h = \sum_{i,j=1}^{r} [\Gamma \lambda_i x_i^2 + w_{ij} x_i x_j + \Gamma \lambda_j x_j^2]$$

$$+ \sum_{j=r+1}^{n} \sum_{i=1}^{r} \left[\frac{r\Gamma}{n-r} \lambda_i x_i^2 + 2w_{ij} x_i x_j + \frac{1}{r} \lambda_j x_j^2 \right]$$

which is clearly positive definite for sufficiently large Γ (thus λ) [recalling that $(n - r) > 0$, and $\lambda_i > 0, i = 1, \cdots, n$].

$$\text{Q.E.D.}$$

PROOF OF THEOREM 2.6:†

The proof is by construction. Consider the constructed matrices

$$M_1 = \begin{bmatrix} L & \lambda G' \\ G & -I \end{bmatrix}$$

where L is $n \times n$, G is $r \times n$, G' is the transpose of G, I is $r \times r$, and λ is a scalar.

†This proof follows Lancaster [32, pp. 301–304].

$$M_2 = \begin{bmatrix} I & 0 \\ G & I \end{bmatrix}$$

which is partitioned conformably to postmultiply M_1. Thus

$$M_1 M_2 = \begin{bmatrix} L + \lambda G' G & \lambda G' \\ 0 & -I \end{bmatrix}$$

Calling the last matrix M_3, we have

$$|M_1||M_2| = |M_3|$$

and, since $|M_2| = 1$, we have

(2.105)
$$\begin{vmatrix} L & \lambda G' \\ G & -I \end{vmatrix} = \begin{vmatrix} L + \lambda G' G & \lambda G' \\ 0 & -I \end{vmatrix}$$

Since the unit matrix in M_3 is $r \times r$, we can expand $|M_3|$ by its bottom row r times, which gives

$$|M_3| = (-1)^r |L + \lambda G' G|$$

Thus

$$\begin{vmatrix} L & \lambda G' \\ G & -I \end{vmatrix} = (-1)^r |L + \lambda G' G|$$

Next, transform $|M_1|$ by multiplying the last r columns by $1/\lambda$ and the result by λ^r so as not to change the value of $|M_1|$. The result is

$$\begin{vmatrix} L & \lambda G' \\ G & -I \end{vmatrix} = \lambda^r \begin{vmatrix} L & G' \\ G & \left(-\dfrac{1}{\lambda}\right)I \end{vmatrix}$$

Therefore, we may now write $|M_1| = |M_3|$ in (2.105) as

(2.106)
$$\lambda^r \begin{vmatrix} L & G' \\ G & \left(-\dfrac{1}{\lambda}\right)I \end{vmatrix} = (-1)^r |L + \lambda G' G|$$

For sufficiently large λ, the sign of $|M_1|$ will be the same as the sign of the determinant of the bordered Hessian $\hat{H}$, where we recall that

$$\hat{H} \equiv \begin{bmatrix} L & G' \\ G & 0 \end{bmatrix}$$

Now, if $h'Lh > 0$ when $Gh = 0$, then by Finsler's theorem there exists a sufficiently large λ such that $L + \lambda G'G$ is positive definite. Hence, $|L + \lambda G'G| > 0$, and the right side of (2.106) has sign $(-1)^r$, which implies that the determinant on the left of (2.106) has sign $(-1)^r$. Therefore, the sign of the determinant of $\hat{H}$ is $(-1)^r$.

To prove the rest of the theorem, we need simply to repeat this argument for the principal minors in (2.106). Set any element of h, say the first, equal to zero. This deletes the first row and column of L in the quadratic form $h'Lh$, and it deletes the first column of G in $Gh = 0$. Now assume again that $h'Lh > 0$ when $Gh = 0$, with the first element of h set to zero. Again applying Finsler's theorem, we deduce that the principal minor of $L + \lambda G'G$ obtained by deleting the first row and column is positive. Using (2.106), we see that the same principal minor in $\hat{H}$ has sign $(-1)^r$.

This argument can be repeated by setting two elements in h equal to zero, three elements equal to zero, and so on. The maximum number of elements in h that we can set equal to zero is $n - r - 1$, because the $r \times n$ matrix G has rank r by assumption. Therefore, were we to set $n - r$ elements in h equal to zero, we could not assume that $h'Lh > 0$ for $Gh = 0$, because the only remaining set of r elements in h which could make $Gh = 0$ would be the zero elements.

We have thus proved (i) of Theorem 2.6: If $h'Lh > 0$ for $Gh = 0$, then any *appropriately determined* minor of $\hat{H}$ will have sign $(-1)^r$. By appropriately determined we mean that the principal minor must be obtained, from among the *first* n rows and columns of $\hat{H}$, by deleting any collection of i rows and corresponding columns of $\hat{H}$ for $0 \leq i \leq n - r - 1$.

To prove statement (ii) of Theorem 2.6, simply replace L with $-L$ in the above argument. By Finsler's theorem we have, for sufficiently large $\lambda > 0$

$$\left.\begin{array}{c} h'Lh < 0 \\ \text{when} \\ Gh = 0 \end{array}\right\} \Rightarrow \begin{array}{c} -L + \lambda G'G \\ \text{is positive} \\ \text{definite} \end{array}$$

By precisely the same argument as above, we establish that if $h'Lh < 0$ when $Gh = 0$, then the appropriately obtained principal minors of

$$|\hat{\hat{H}}| \equiv \begin{vmatrix} -L & G' \\ G & 0 \end{vmatrix}$$

have sign $(-1)^r$. The strategy now is to establish the sign relationships between the relevant principal minors of $\hat{H}$ and $\hat{\hat{H}}$.

Let us denote an appropriately obtained principal minor of $\hat{H}$ and $\hat{\hat{H}}$ of order $n + r - i$ as

$$|\hat{H}_{n+r-i}| \quad \text{and} \quad |\hat{\hat{H}}_{n+r-i}|$$

where $0 \le i \le n - r - 1$. Keep in mind that this minor has been obtained by deleting any set of i rows and corresponding columns from the first n rows and columns of $\hat{H}$ and $\hat{\hat{H}}$.

Multiply the first $n - i$ columns of this principal minor $\hat{\hat{H}}$ by (-1); then multiply the last r rows by (-1); finally, multiply the minor by $(-1)^{n+r-i}$ to preserve its original sign. The result of these operations is that

$$|\hat{\hat{H}}_{n+r-i}| = (-1)^{n+r-i}|\hat{H}_{n+r-i}|$$

But we know that

$$|\hat{\hat{H}}_{n+r-i}| \overset{\text{sgn}}{=} (-1)^r$$

Thus

$$(-1)^{n+r-i}|\hat{H}_{n+r-i}| \overset{\text{sgn}}{=} (-1)^r$$

Multiplying both sides by $(-1)^{n-i-r}$ gives

$$(-1)^{2(n-i)}|\hat{H}_{n+r-i}| \overset{\text{sgn}}{=} (-1)^{n-i}$$

and since $(-1)^{2(n-i)}$ will always be positive, we see that

$$|\hat{H}_{n+r-i}| \overset{\text{sgn}}{=} (-1)^{n-i} \qquad 0 \le i \le n - r - 1$$

Q.E.D.

PART II DYNAMIC ANALYSIS

3 Techniques for Dynamic Economic Models

Dynamic economic models usually take the form of a system of linear difference or differential equations. It is the purpose of this chapter to develop some techniques for solving such systems† and to examine the theoretical foundations of these techniques.

The type of system that we shall focus on can be expressed in matrix notation as follows:

$$(3.1) \quad \begin{bmatrix} A_{11}(Q) & A_{12}(Q) & \cdots & A_{1m}(Q) \\ \cdot & \cdot & & \cdot \\ \cdot & \cdot & & \cdot \\ \cdot & \cdot & & \cdot \\ A_{m1}(Q) & & \cdots & A_{mm}(Q) \end{bmatrix} \begin{bmatrix} y_1 \\ y_2 \\ \vdots \\ y_m \end{bmatrix} = \begin{bmatrix} f_1(t) \\ f_2(t) \\ \vdots \\ f_m(t) \end{bmatrix}$$

where $A_{ij}(Q)$ are polynomials of any degree in either the differential operator or the shift operator, $(y_1, \ldots, y_m)$ are the dependent variables understood to be functions of time, and $(f_1(t), \ldots, f_m(t))$ are functions of time, with time

---

†We shall assume that the reader is conversant with single-equation techniques. If not, we recommend the lucid treatment in Baumol [7, Chaps. 9–13]. Other recommended sources on this level are Allen [3, Chaps. 5 and 6], Yamane [51, Chap. 8]. and Goldberg [19].

designated by t. We shall denote the differential operator as D and the shift operator as E, where by definition

$$Dx \equiv \frac{dx}{dt} \qquad\qquad Ex_t \equiv x_{t+1}$$

$$D^2 x \equiv D(Dx) \equiv \frac{d^2 x}{dt^2} \qquad E^2 x_t \equiv E(Ex_t) \equiv x_{t+2}$$

$$\vdots \qquad\qquad\qquad \vdots$$

This system may be written compactly as

(3.2) $$A(Q)y = f(t)$$

where $A(Q)$ is the $m \times m$ matrix in (3.1), $y = (y_1, \ldots, y_m)$, and $f(t) = (f_1(t), \ldots, f_m(t))$.

Example 3.1

Consider the dynamic Keynesian model written in difference equation form with the following arbitrarily selected lag structure.†

†See section 1.2 for a discussion of the static version of this model.

149

(i) $\qquad\qquad C_t = a_{11} + a_{12}Y_t + a_{13}Y_{t-1}$

(ii) $\qquad\qquad I_t = a_{21} + a_{22}Y_t + a_{23}Y_{t-1} + a_{24}r_{t-1} + a_{25}r_{t-2}$

(iii) $\qquad\qquad Y_t = C_t + I_t$

(iv) $\qquad\qquad M_t^* = a_{31}Y_t + a_{32}Y_{t-1} + a_{33}r_t + a_{34}r_{t-1}$

(v) $\qquad\qquad M_t = a_{41}$

(vi) $\qquad\qquad M_t = M_t^*$

where $\qquad\qquad Y = $ income

$\qquad\qquad\qquad r = $ interest rate

$\qquad\qquad\qquad C = $ consumption

$\qquad\qquad\qquad I = $ investment

$\qquad\qquad\qquad M^* = $ demand for money

$\qquad\qquad\qquad M = $ supply of money

Substituting (i) and (ii) into (iii), and (iv) and (v) into (vi), and advancing the dates on all variables in the resulting equations by two periods, we have (where E is the shift operator)

(vii)
$$\begin{bmatrix} b_{11}E^2 - b_{12}E & -a_{24}E - a_{25} \\ a_{31}E^2 + a_{32}E & a_{33}E^2 + a_{34}E \end{bmatrix} \begin{bmatrix} y_t \\ r_t \end{bmatrix} = \begin{bmatrix} b_{13} \\ a_{41} \end{bmatrix}$$

where
$$b_{11} \equiv 1 - a_{12} - a_{22}$$
$$b_{12} \equiv a_{13} + a_{23}$$
$$b_{13} \equiv a_{11} + a_{21}$$

Our objective is to find a solution of this system. That is, we seek functions of time alone (given the parameter values), $y(t)$ and $r(t)$, which identically satisfy these two equations for all $t = 0, 1, \ldots$, and which satisfy specified initial conditions $y(0) = y_0$, $r(0) = r_0$.

Problem. What would (vii) look like if (iii) and (vi) were changed to

(iii′) $\qquad\qquad Y_t - Y_{t-1} = k_1(C_{t-1} + I_{t-1} - Y_{t-1})$

(vi′) $\qquad\qquad r_t - r_{t-1} = k_2(M_{t-1}^* - M_{t-1})$

Notice that these changes would convert the model into a more general form than the one used in discussing the correspondence principle.† Write the Keynesian model used in the correspondence principle in this matrix form and compare it with (vii).

†See section 1.8.

Example 3.2

Consider the following dynamic formulation of a single market, where the lag structure (again arbitrarily selected) is[†]

(i) $D_t = a_{11}p_t + a_{12}p_{t-1} + a_{13}p_{t-2} + a_{14}\lambda_1^t$

(ii) $S_t = a_{21}p_t + a_{22}p_{t-1} + a_{23}p_{t-2} + a_{24}\lambda_2^t$

(iii) $P_t - P_{t-1} = \lambda(D_{t-1} - S_{t-1}) \quad \lambda > 0$

where $D = $ demand

$S = $ supply

$P = $ price

Notice the assumptions that demand and supply will increase each period by $(\lambda_1 - 1)$ per cent and $(\lambda_2 - 1)$ per cent, respectively, due to the influence of unspecified exogenous factors.[‡]

Again advancing all variables forward two periods and letting E be the shift operator, we can write this model in matrix form as

$$\begin{bmatrix} -E^2 & 0 & a_{11}E^2 + a_{12}E + a_{13} \\ 0 & -E^2 & a_{21}E^2 + a_{22}E + a_{23} \\ \lambda E & -\lambda E & -E^2 + E \end{bmatrix} \begin{bmatrix} D_t \\ S_t \\ P_t \end{bmatrix} = \begin{bmatrix} b_1\lambda_1^t \\ b_2\lambda_2^t \\ 0 \end{bmatrix}$$

where $b_1 = -a_{14}\lambda_1^2$

$b_2 = -a_{24}\lambda_2^2$

A solution to this system will consist of functions of time alone—$D(t)$, $S(t)$, and $P(t)$—which identically satisfy these three equations for $t = 0, 1, \ldots$, and which satisfy specified initial conditions $D(0) = D_0$, $S(0) = S_0$, and $P(0) = P_0$.

In the next three sections we shall develop the mathematical machinery necessary to our exposition of solution techniques for the system expressed in (3.1). We shall examine two methods for solving such systems. The first is the adjoint matrix technique, dealt with in section 3.5. The other technique, the triangularization method, is very similar to the Gaussian method for solving algebraic equation systems, for it also is based on elementary operations; we develop this procedure in section 3.6. In the final section of this chapter, we demonstrate how the system in (3.1) can be transformed into a system of first order difference or differential equations, called the state space (or basic) form. This transformation is important because stability theory and control theory, discussed in Chapters 4 and 5, assume that the system is in state space form.

†See section 1.1 for a discussion of the static version of this model.
‡To see this, set $P_t = P_{t-1} = P_{t-2}$ and solve for $(D_t - D_{t-1})/(D_{t-1})$.

3.2 POLYNOMIALS

Consider the polynomial function

$$f(x) = a_0 x^n + a_1 x^{n-1} + \cdots + a_{n-1} x + a_n$$

where $a_0 \neq 0$. The *degree* of a polynomial is the nonnegative integer n when $a_0 \neq 0$. If $a_0 = 1$, the polynomial is called *monic*. If $f(x)$ cannot be expressed as a product of two polynomials of positive degree, $f(x)$ is said to be *irreducible*. (A polynomial of zero degree is, by definition, a number.) Obviously, any polynomial of degree one, e.g., $x + 7$, is irreducible. If a polynomial can be expressed as a product of two polynomials of positive degree, it is said to be *reducible*; this means that the polynomial can be factored into polynomials of lower degree.

If $f(x)$ and $b(x)$ are polynomials, then $b(x)$ is said to divide $f(x)$ if $f(x) = g(x)b(x)$ for some polynomial $g(x)$. We can also say here that $f(x)$ is *divisible* by $b(x)$. Suppose that $f(x)$ and $g(x)$ are both divisible by $b(x)$ and that any other divisor of $f(x)$ and $g(x)$ divides $b(x)$. We then define $b(x)$ as a *greatest common divisor* (g.c.d.) of $f(x)$ and $g(x)$. If $b(x)$ and $b'(x)$ are two g.c.d.'s of $f(x)$ and $g(x)$, then, by definition of g.c.d., b and b' divide each other. Since a polynomial of a given positive degree cannot divide a nonzero polynomial of smaller degree, b and b' must be of the same degree, and therefore differ only by a multiplicative constant. That is, if $b(x)$ and $b'(x)$ are both g.c.d.'s of two (or more) polynomials, $b(x) = kb'(x)$, where $k \neq 0$ is some constant.

Using these concepts, we wish to demonstrate that any polynomial of nth degree $f(x)$ can be expressed as the constant a_0 times a unique product of n monic polynomials of degree one, that is

$$f(x) = a_0(x - c_1) \cdots (x - c_n)$$

where c_i, $i = 1, \ldots, n$ are real or complex numbers, not necessarily distinct, which are roots of $f(x)$. Several preliminaries are necessary before we can establish this result, which is Theorem 3.10.[†]

THEOREM 3.1

ANY POLYNOMIAL $f(x)$ OF POSITIVE DEGREE IS DIVISIBLE BY AN IRREDUCIBLE POLYNOMIAL.

PROOF:

The proof is by contradiction. Suppose the theorem is false. Then, by the well-ordering principle, there exists an $f(x)$ of smallest positive degree

---

[†]A delightful book which covers some of the material in this section is Uspensky [50, Chaps. 1 and 2]. See also Mostow, Sampson, and Meyer [38, Chap. 6], and Birkhoff and MacLane [9, Chap. 3].

which is not divisible by an irreducible polynomial.† But $f(x)$ is divisible by itself. Therefore, $f(x)$ must be reducible and (by definition of reducible) expressible as the product of two polynomials of positive degree, say $f(x) = g(x)p(x)$. Obviously the degree of $g(x)$ plus the degree of $p(x)$ equals the degree of $f(x)$. Since $f(x)$ is a polynomial of *smallest* degree which is assumed not divisible by an irreducible polynomial, and since the degree of $g(x) <$ the degree of $f(x)$, it follows that $g(x)$ *is* divisible by an irreducible polynomial. Since the latter must also divide $f(x)$, we have a contradiction.

Q. E. D.

THEOREM 3.2   DIVISION ALGORITHM

LET $f(x)$ AND $g(x)$ BE TWO POLYNOMIALS OF POSITIVE DEGREE n AND m, RESPECTIVELY. THEN THERE EXIST TWO POLYNOMIALS $q(x)$ AND $r(x)$ SUCH THAT

$$(3.3) \qquad f(x) = q(x)g(x) + r(x)$$

WHERE DEGREE $r(x) <$ DEGREE $g(x)$ OR $r(x) = 0$ [$q(x)$ IS CALLED THE QUOTIENT AND $r(x)$ THE REMAINDER].

PROOF:

We shall use the second principle of finite induction. Suppose

$$f(x) = a_0 + a_1 x + \cdots + a_n x^n \qquad (a_n \neq 0)$$

and $\qquad g(x) = b_0 + b_1 x + \cdots + b_m x^m \qquad (b_m \neq 0)$

Now if $m > n$, the theorem is trivial for

$$f(x) = 0 \cdot g(x) + f(x)$$

where $q(x) = 0$ and degree $r(x)(\equiv f(x)) <$ degree $g(x)$ by assumption. Assume then that $n \geq m$. Form the following polynomial $p(x)$

$$p(x) = f(x) - \left(\frac{a_n}{b_m}\right) x^{n-m} g(x)$$

Clearly $p(x)$ is of degree $< n$, or zero. Transposing gives

$$(3.4) \qquad f(x) = \left(\frac{a_n}{b_m}\right) x^{n-m} g(x) + p(x)$$

†See Theorem A1. 1 for a statement and use of the well-ordering principle to prove the principles of finite induction. The latter are used frequently in this section.

We now bring in the second induction principle and assume that (3.3) is true for any $f(x)$ of degree $k < n$. In particular, then, (3.3) holds for $p(x)$, since it has degree $< n$.† Thus we write from our induction hypothesis

$$(3.5) \qquad p(x) = q_1(x)g(x) + r(x)$$

where degree $r(x) <$ degree $g(x) = m$ or $r(x) = 0$. Substituting (3.5) into (3.4) gives

$$f(x) = \left[\left(\frac{a_n}{b_m}\right)x^{n-m} + q_1(x)\right]g(x) + r(x)$$

Q.E.D.

THEOREM 3.3   EUCLIDIAN ALGORITHM

LET $f(x)$ AND $g(x)$ BE TWO NONZERO POLYNOMIALS. THEN $f(x)$ AND $g(x)$ HAVE A GREATEST COMMON DIVISOR (g.c.d).

PROOF:

By the division algorithm we know that

$$f(x) = q(x)g(x) + r(x)$$

If $r(x) \neq 0$, divide $g(x)$ by $r(x)$, which, by the division algorithm, gives

$$g(x) = q_1(x)r(x) + r_1(x)$$

Continue this process until a zero remainder is obtained.

$$r(x) = q_2(x)r_1(x) + r_2(x)$$
$$r_1(x) = q_3(x)r_2(x) + r_3(x)$$
$$\vdots \qquad\qquad \vdots$$
$$r_{k-2}(x) = q_k(x)r_{k-1}(x) + r_k(x)$$
$$r_{k-1}(x) = q_{k+1}(x)r_k(x) + 0$$

We know that a zero remainder must occur eventually by this process because the division algorithm states that if the remainder is not zero

$$\deg r(x) < \deg g(x)$$
$$\deg r_1(x) < \deg r(x)$$
$$\deg r_2(x) < \deg r_1(x)$$
$$\vdots \qquad\qquad \vdots$$

---

†Clearly the theorem is true for $n = 1$, $n > m$, in which case $q(x) \equiv f(x)$, $g(x) = 1$, and $r(x) = 0$.

Hence, where m is the degree of $g(x)$, this repeated division would have to be performed, at most, m times to obtain $r_m(x) = 0$.

From these identities we can deduce that $r_k(x)$ is a common divisor of $f(x)$ and $g(x)$, and that any common divisor of $f(x)$ and $g(x)$ divides $r_k(x)$. That is, we can establish that $r_k(x)$ satisfies the definition of a g.c.d. of $f(x)$ and $g(x)$.

To prove the first part of the definition (deleting the x for simplicity), observe that r_k must divide r_{k-1}, hence it also divides

$$r_{k-2} = q_k r_{k-1} + r_k$$

Since r_k divides both r_{k-1} and r_{k-2}, it must divide r_{k-3} and, by induction, it will divide f and g.

To prove the second part of the definition, let p be any polynomial which divides both f and g, that is, $f = s_1 p$ and $g = s_2 p$. Then from the first identity

$$f = qg + r$$

we obtain $s_1 p = q s_2 p + r$, or $r = (s_1 - q s_2)p$. That is, p divides r, and by the same sort of argument, the second identity

$$g = q_1 r + r_1$$

shows that p divides r_1. Therefore, by induction, p is shown to divide r_k.

Q.E.D.

Remark. We have just proved that *every* common divisor of f and g divides the common divisor r_k. Hence, r_k is a common divisor of highest degree. If p is any other common divisor of the same degree, it divides r_k and the quotient is a constant. Thus, there are infinite g.c.d.'s of f and g, and, as we pointed out at the beginning of this section, they are all of the form $k r_k$, where k is an arbitrary constant. If it turns out that r_k is itself a constant, we then say that f and g are *relatively prime* polynomial functions. It should be pointed out that a g.c.d. will usually not be monic.

THEOREM 3.4

LET $f(x)$ AND $g(x)$ BE TWO NONZERO POLYNOMIALS, AND LET $p(x)$ BE A g.c.d. THEN THERE EXIST POLYNOMIALS $s(x)$ AND $t(x)$ SUCH THAT

$$p(x) = f(x)s(x) + g(x)t(x)$$

PROOF:

Consider the following set of equations generated by the Euclidian algorithm, where we assume $a_0(x)$ is divided by $a_1(x)$. This gives (deleting the x's)

$$a_0 = q_1 a_1 + a_2$$
$$a_1 = q_2 a_2 + a_3$$
$$\cdots\cdots\cdots\cdots$$
$$a_{k-3} = q_{k-2} a_{k-2} + a_{k-1}$$
$$a_{k-2} = q_{k-1} a_{k-1} + a_k$$
$$a_{k-1} = q_k a_k + 0$$

Then

$$\begin{aligned}
a_k &= a_{k-2} - q_{k-1} a_{k-1} \\
&= a_{k-2} - q_{k-1}(a_{k-3} - q_{k-2} a_{k-2}) \\
&= (1 + q_{k-1} q_{k-2}) a_{k-2} - q_{k-1} a_{k-3}
\end{aligned}$$

Continuing the substitutions up the list, we eliminate a_{k-2} as we did a_{k-1}, and so on, and finally we get

$$a_k = a_0 \bar{s} + a_1 \bar{t}$$

where $\bar{s}$ and $\bar{t}$ are polynomials, and a_0 and a_1 are playing the role of $f(x)$ and $g(x)$. Recalling that all g.c.d.'s of $f(x)$ and $g(x)$ differ by only a constant, any g.c.d. $p(x) = ca_k(x)$ where c is a constant. Letting $s(x) = c\bar{s}(x)$ and $t(x) = c\bar{t}(x)$, the theorem is proved.

Q. E. D.

THEOREM 3.5

IF $f(x)$ IS OF DEGREE $n > 0$ AND $g(x)$ IS OF DEGREE $m > 0$, AND IF $f(x)$ AND $g(x)$ ARE RELATIVELY PRIME, THEN THERE EXIST A POLYNOMIAL $s(x)$ OF DEGREE $<$ m AND A POLYNOMIAL $t(x)$ OF DEGREE $< n$ SUCH THAT

$$1 = s(x)f(x) + t(x)g(x)$$

PROOF:

From Theorem 3.4 and the assumption that $f(x)$ and $g(x)$ are relatively prime, we know that there exist $s_1(x)$ and $t_1(x)$ such that

$$1 = s_1(x)f(x) + t_1(x)g(x)$$

By the division algorithm we may write

$$s_1(x) = Q_1(x)g(x) + s(x)$$
$$t_1(x) = Q_2(x)f(x) + t(x)$$

where degree of $s(x) < m$ and degree of $t(x) < n$.
Substituting the last two expressions into the preceding one, we have that

$$1 = Q_1(x)g(x)f(x) + s(x)f(x) + Q_2(x)f(x)g(x) + t(x)g(x)$$
$$= [Q_1(x) + Q_2(x)]f(x)g(x) + s(x)f(x) + t(x)g(x)$$

Thus

$$1 - s(x)f(x) - t(x)g(x) = [Q_1(x) + Q_2(x)]f(x)g(x)$$

Unless $[Q_1(x) + Q_2(x)]$ is zero, the right side must be of degree $\geq m + n$ and the left side is of degree $< m + n$. Hence, $[Q_1(x) + Q_2(x)] = 0$.

Q. E. D.

THEOREM 3.6

SUPPOSE THAT $p(x)$ IS AN IRREDUCIBLE POLYNOMIAL, AND THAT $p(x)$ DIVIDES $f(x)g(x)$. THEN $p(x)$ DIVIDES EITHER $f(x)$ OR $g(x)$.

PROOF:
Since $p(x)$ is irreducible, it cannot, by definition, be factored into a product of two polynomials of positive degree. It therefore is divisible by no polynomial of positive degree except itself or some suitable constant times itself. Thus, a g.c.d. of $p(x)$ and $f(x)$ is either some multiple of $p(x)$ or some constant, say 1. If $p(x)$ is a g.c.d. of $p(x)$ and $f(x)$, then $p(x)$ divides $f(x)$. If $p(x)$ is not a g.c.d. of $p(x)$ and $f(x)$, then, by definition, $p(x)$ and $f(x)$ are relatively prime and, by the previous theorem

$$1 = s(x)f(x) + t(x)p(x)$$

Multiplying by $g(x)$ gives

$$g(x) = s(x)g(x)f(x) + g(x)t(x)p(x)$$

and since by assumption $p(x)$ divides $g(x)f(x)$, $p(x)$ divides the right side, hence $p(x)$ divides $g(x)$.

Q.E.D.

THEOREM 3.7   UNIQUE FACTORIZATION THEOREM

ANY POLYNOMIAL $f(x)$ OF POSITIVE DEGREE CAN BE EXPRESSED AS A CONSTANT TIMES A PRODUCT OF MONIC AND IRREDUCIBLE POLYNOMIALS. THUS

$$f(x) = ap_1(x)p_2(x) \cdots p_m(x)$$

WHERE a IS A CONSTANT AND $p_1(x), \ldots, p_m(x)$ ARE MONIC AND IRREDUCIBLE POLYNOMIALS OF POSITIVE DEGREE. THIS EXPRESSION IS UNIQUE EXCEPT FOR THE ORDER IN WHICH THE $p_i(x)$ APPEAR.

PROOF:

First we will show that $f(x)$ of degree $n > 1$ is factorable in at least one way into a product of irreducible monic polynomials of positive degree multiplied by a constant. To do this, assume that there exists a set T of polynomials of degree > 1 which cannot be so factored. We want to show that T is empty. Let a polynomial of minimum degree of T be of degree n, and suppose we label this polynomial $f(x)$. Now $f(x)$ cannot be irreducible and still belong to T, for by factoring out its leading coefficient it would immediately be in the required form. So if $f(x) \in T$, it must be reducible. By Theorem 3.1, any polynomial of positive degree is divisible by an irreducible polynomial. Hence we may divide $f(x)$ by an irreducible polynomial—which in this case must be of positive degree—say, $\bar{p}_1(x)$. Thus

$$f(x) = \bar{p}_1(x)g(x)$$

Next, consider $g(x)$. We know its degree must be less than the degree of $f(x)$, and since $f(x)$ is assumed to be a polynomial of minimum degree belonging to T, it follows that $g(x) \notin T$. Hence, $g(x)$ is factorable as the theorem says, that is, assuming the degree of $g(x) > 1$,

$$g(x) = a_0 p_2(x) \cdots p_m(x)$$

where $p_i(x)$, $i = 2, \ldots, m$, are monic and irreducible polynomials and a_0 is a constant. Factoring out the leading coefficient of $\bar{p}_1(x)$ gives

$$\bar{p}_1(x) = a_1 p_1(x)$$

Substituting the last two expressions into the expression for $f(x)$ establishes that

$$f(x) = ap_1(x) \cdots p_m(x)$$

where $a = a_0 a_1$. Thus, $f(x)$ is factorable in at least one way as the theorem says, and we have contradicted the assumption that $f(x) \in T$, hence, T

is empty. On the other hand, if the degree of $g(x) = 1$, it is already irreducible and can be written as $a_0 p_2(x)$, which means that

$$f(x) = a p_1(x) p_2(x)$$

again leading to the conclusion that T is empty.
It remains to be demonstrated that

$$f(x) = a p_1(x) \cdots p_m(x)$$

is unique, apart from the order of the factors. Assume that the factorization is not unique, and that there exists a set T of polynomials of degree > 1 which cannot be uniquely factored. Let a polynomial of minimum degree of this set be of degree $n > 1$, and call this polynomial $f(x)$. It follows from these assumptions that $f(x)$ has at least two different factorizations. Let two of these be

$$f(x) = a p_1(x) \cdots p_m(x) = b g_1(x) \cdots g_s(x)$$

It is immediately obvious that $a = b$, since they are both the coefficient of the highest degree term of $f(x)$. Since $p_1(x)$ divides $f(x)$, $p_1(x)$ must, by the preceding theorem, divide *some* $g_i(x)$. But, since $g_i(x)$ and $p_1(x)$ are both irreducible, they can differ only by a constant. Since they are monic, this constant must be one, and therefore $p_1(x) = g_i(x)$. Rearrange the factors on the right so that $g_i(x)$ becomes $g_1(x)$.
Now, divide through the last equation by $a p_1(x)$ and define the result as $g(x)$; thus

$$g(x) = p_2(x) \cdots p_m(x) = g_2(x) \cdots g_s(x)$$

Clearly, since $p_1(x)$ is of positive degree, $g(x)$ has a smaller degree than $f(x)$. Therefore, $g(x)$ does not belong to T, and by definition $g(x)$ has only one factorization. Hence, the factors in $p_2(x) \cdots p_m(x)$ are identical to the factors in $g_2(x) \cdots g_s(x)$, apart from order. It follows that if we multiply the last equation by $p_1(x) = g_1(x)$, we retrieve $f(x)$, but find that the two factorizations are not different as assumed; rather, they are identical except for order. It follows that $f(x)$ does not belong to T, hence T is empty. If $f(x)$ is of degree 1, the proof is trivial.

Q.E.D.

THEOREM 3.8   REMAINDER THEOREM

THE REMAINDER OF A POLYNOMIAL $f(x)$ WHEN DIVIDED BY $x - c$ IS $f(c)$.

PROOF:

By Theorem 3.2, for two polynomials, $f(x)$ and $g(x)$,

$$f(x) = q(x)g(x) + r(x)$$

where degree of $r(x) <$ degree of $g(x)$ or $r(x) = 0$. Let $g(x) = x - c$, in which case $r(x)$ is either a constant or is zero. And

$$r = f(x) - q(x)(x - c)$$

Setting $x = c$,

$$r = f(c)$$

Q.E.D.

Corollary. If c is a root of $f(x)$, then $x - c$ divides $f(x)$.

PROOF:

By Theorem 3.8, $r = f(c)$. But if c is a root of $f(x)$, then $f(c) = 0$, thus

$$f(x) = q(x)(x - c)$$

Q.E.D.

At this point we shall assume the truth of the following theorem.†

THEOREM 3.9   FUNDAMENTAL THEOREM OF ALGEBRA

A POLYNOMIAL $f(x)$ OF POSITIVE DEGREE HAS A ROOT, WHICH MAY BE COMPLEX.

THEOREM 3.10

A POLYNOMIAL $f(x)$ OF DEGREE n CAN BE FACTORED UNIQUELY INTO

$$f(x) = a_n(x - c_1)(x - c_2) \cdots (x - c_n)$$

WHERE a_n IS THE COEFFICIENT OF x^n AND WHERE $c_1, c_2, \ldots, c_n$ ARE REAL OR COMPLEX ROOTS OF $f(x)$ AND ARE NOT NECESSARILY DISTINCT.

PROOF:

We shall use induction on the degree of $f(x)$. If $f(x)$ is of degree one, the theorem is trivial. So *assume* that the theorem is true for any polynomial $q(x)$ of degree $n - 1$ (where $n > 1$). By Theorem 3.9, we know that $f(x)$ has at least one root c_1. By the remainder theorem and its corollary we know that

†For a proof, see any standard text on the theory of functions of a complex variable.

(3.6) $$f(x) = q(x)(x - c_1)$$

By the induction hypothesis $q(x)$, which is of degree $n - 1$, can be written as

(3.7) $$q(x) = a(x - c_2)(x - c_3) \cdots (x - c_n)$$

where a is the coefficient of x^{n-1} of $q(x)$. Substituting (3.7) into (3.6), the theorem is proved, for it is obvious that $a = a_n$. Uniqueness follows from Theorem 3.7.

Q.E.D.

Remark. Obviously, some or all of the roots may appear more than once. We may thus write $f(x)$ as

$$f(x) = a(x - c_1)^{k_1}(x - c_2)^{k_2} \cdots (x - c_r)^{k_r}$$

where $r \leq n$, $k_i \geq 1$, $(i = 1, \ldots, r)$, and $\sum_{i=1}^{r} k_i = n$, and we say that the root c_i has multiplicity k_i $(i = 1, \ldots, r)$. This analysis clearly implies that the number of distinct roots of $f(x) \leq$ degree of $f(x)$.

THEOREM 3.11

Suppose that each element of an $n \times n$ matrix A is a function of a scalar variable x. Then

$$\frac{\partial |A|}{\partial x} = \sum_{i=1}^{n} \sum_{j=1}^{n} A_{ij} \frac{\partial a_{ij}}{\partial x}$$

where A_{ij} is the cofactor of a_{ij}.

(This can be verbalized in two ways. The derivative of a determinant with respect to a scalar is a linear combination of *all* of the $n - 1$ order cofactors of A, with A_{ij} multiplied by $\partial a_{ij}/\partial x$; or, equivalently, the derivative of $|A|$ with respect to a scalar is the sum of n determinants, of order n, the ith one being $|A|$ except for the ith row, which contains $\partial a_{ij}/\partial x$ instead of a_{ij} for all j from 1 to n,)

Proof:

Since $|A| = \sum_{j=1}^{n} a_{ij} A_{ij}$, it follows that

$$\frac{\partial |A|}{\partial a_{ij}} = A_{ij}$$

By applying the chain rule

$$\frac{\partial |A|}{\partial x} = \sum_{i=1}^{n} \sum_{j=1}^{n} \frac{\partial |A|}{\partial a_{ij}} \frac{\partial a_{ij}}{\partial x} = \sum_{i=1}^{n} \sum_{j=1}^{n} A_{ij} \frac{\partial a_{ij}}{\partial x}$$

Q.E.D.

THEOREM 3.12

If r IS A ROOT OF THE POLYNOMIAL $f(x)$ OF MULTIPLICITY $k \geq 1$, THEN r IS A ROOT OF THE DERIVATIVE OF $f(x), f'(x)$, OF MULTIPLICITY $k - 1$. [SINCE EVERY DIFFERENTIATION OF $f(x)$ REDUCES THE MULTIPLICITY OF THE ROOT r BY ONE, IT FOLLOWS THAT THE FIRST $k - 1$ DERIVATIVES OF $f(x)$ HAVE r AS A ROOT OF APPROPRIATE MULTIPLICITY, AND ALL DERIVATIVES OF $f(x)$ HIGHER THAN $k - 1$ DO NOT HAVE r AS A ROOT.]

PROOF:

By Theorem 3.10, if r is a root of multiplicity $k \geq 1$ of the polynomial $f(x)$, we may express $f(x)$ uniquely as

$$f(x) = a(x - r)^k (x - c_1) \cdots (x - c_p)$$

where $k + p = n$. Clearly $c_i \neq r, i = 1, \cdots, p$, for if $c_i = r, r$ would be of multiplicity $> k$ contrary to hypothesis.† Let

$$(x - c_1) \cdots (x - c_p) \equiv g(x)$$

and note that $(x - r)$ does not divide $g(x)$, i.e., $g(r) \neq 0$. Then

$$f(x) = a(x - r)^k g(x)$$

hence

$$f'(x) = ak(x - r)^{k-1} g(x) + a(x - r)^k g'(x)$$

That is

$$f'(x) = a(x - r)^{k-1} [kg(x) + g'(x)(x - r)]$$

Clearly, therefore, r is a root of $f'(x)$ of multiplicity at least $(k - 1)$. But evaluating the term in brackets at $x = r$, we see that it is equal to $kg(r) \neq 0$, and thus the root r is not of multiplicity k.

Q.E.D.

THEOREM 3.13

If $f'(x)$ HAS A ROOT r, THEN $f(x)$ NOT ONLY SHARES THE ROOT BUT HAS THE ROOT TO A MULTIPLICITY ONE GREATER THAN $f'(x)$.

†The case where $k = n$ is trivial, hence we assume $k < n$.

PROOF:

Consider a root c of $f(x)$. Then

$$f(x) = a(x - c)g(x)$$

and

$$f'(x) = a(x - c)g'(x) + ag(x)$$

Now suppose that $f'(x)$ possesses the root $r \neq c$ with a multiplicity of k, thus

$$f'(x) = a(x - c)g'(x) + ag(x) = a(x - r)^k p(x)$$

Observe that $(x - r)^k$ divides both $g(x)$ and $g'(x)$. Therefore, $f(x)$ also possesses r as a root of multiplicity k, and we may write $f(x)$ as

$$f(x) = a(x - r)^k s(x)$$

Thus

$$f'(x) = a(x - r)^k s'(x) + ak(x - r)^{k-1} s(x)$$

Now, by assumption, $(x - r)^k$ divides $f'(x)$, therefore $(x - r)$ divides $s(x)$. If $f(x)$ possesses no root other than r, the theorem is trivial.

Q.E.D.

Theorems 3.12 and 3.13 together establish the following:

THEOREM 3.14

GIVEN A POLYNOMIAL $f(x)$, r IS A ROOT OF MULTIPLICITY $k \geq 1$ *if and only if* r IS A ROOT OF $f'(x)$ OF MULTIPLICITY $k - 1$.

THEOREM 3.15

SUPPOSE THAT A IS AN $n \times n$ MATRIX WHOSE ELEMENT ARE FUNCTIONS OF A SCALAR VARIABLE x. IF r IS A SIMPLE ROOT OF $|A(x)|$, THEN $A(r)$ HAS RANK $n - 1$. (A SIMPLE ROOT MEANS A ROOT OF MULTIPLICITY ONE.)

PROOF:

By Theorem 3.11

$$\frac{\partial |A(x)|}{\partial x} = \sum_{i=1}^{n} \sum_{j=1}^{n} A_{ij}(x) a'_{ij}(x)$$

where

$$a'_{ij}(x) \equiv \frac{\partial a_{ij}(x)}{\partial x}$$

Since r is a simple root of $|A(x)|$, then, by Theorem 3.14, the derivative of $|A(x)|$ does not possess r as a root, thus

$$\sum_{i=1}^{n}\sum_{j=1}^{n} A_{ij}(r)a'_{ij}(r) \neq 0$$

Hence, at least one of the cofactors $A_{ij}(r)$ is not zero. Therefore, $A(r)$ has rank $n - 1$. [Clearly $A(r)$ cannot have rank n, since $|A(r)| = 0$.]

Q.E.D.

EXAMPLE:

Let

$$A(x) \equiv \begin{bmatrix} x - 2 & 0 & 1 \\ 1 & x - 1 & 0 \\ 0 & 0 & x - 3 \end{bmatrix}$$

Thus

$$|A(x)| = (x - 2)(x - 1)(x - 3)$$

Let $r = 2$, which is clearly a simple root of $|A(x)|$. Then

$$A(r) = \begin{bmatrix} 0 & 0 & 1 \\ 1 & 1 & 0 \\ 0 & 0 & -1 \end{bmatrix}$$

which has rank 2.

As our final result in this section, we present a theorem on complex roots which ties up a loose end in our discussion of the correspondence principle in section 1.8.

THEOREM 3.16

CONSIDER THE POLYNOMIAL EQUATION

$$f(x) = a_0 x^n + a_1 x^{n-1} + \cdots + a_n = 0$$

WHERE $a_i, i = 0, 1, \ldots, n$ ARE REAL. IF THIS EQUATION HAS A COMPLEX ROOT $a + bi$ OF MULTIPLICITY k, IT ALSO HAS THE CONJUGATE ROOT $a - bi$ OF THE SAME MULTIPLICITY.

Before proving this theorem, we establish a few facts about complex numbers.

1. The sum of the conjugates of two complex numbers equals the conjugate of the sum of the complex numbers. Let the complex numbers be $a + bi$ and $c + di$; the conjugates of these numbers are $a - bi$ and $c - di$. Adding the conjugates gives $(a + c) - (b + d)i$. Adding the complex numbers gives $(a + c) + (b + d)i$. Clearly, the conjugate of the latter sum equals the sum of the conjugates.

2. The product of the conjugates of two complex numbers is equal to the conjugate of their product. The product of the conjugates $(a - bi)$ and $(c - di)$ is $(ac - db) - (ad + bc)i$. The product of the complex numbers $(a + bi)$ and $(c + di)$ is $(ac - db) + (ad + bc)i$. Clearly, the conjugate of the latter product equals the product of the conjugates.

By repeated application of the rules, we can see that any finite collection of complex numbers obeys the properties that the sum (product) of the conjugates equals the conjugate of the sum (product) of the complex numbers. Put differently, if we perform a set of operations involving addition and/or multiplication on a set of complex numbers, we obtain a complex number whose conjugate equals the number obtained by applying the same set of operations to the conjugates of the set of complex numbers. In compact notation:

$$z : c \rightarrow x$$
$$z : \bar{c} \rightarrow \bar{x}$$

This reads z sends c into x and $\bar{c}$ into $\bar{x}$, where

c is a set of complex numbers

$\bar{c}$ is the set of conjugates of c

z is a set of operations involving addition and multiplication

x is a complex number

$\bar{x}$ is the conjugate of x

All sets are finite. We can now prove Theorem 3.16.

PROOF:

Since $f(x) = 0$ is assumed to have the complex root $(a + bi)$ with multiplicity k, it follows from Theorem 3.10 that we can write $f(x)$ as

$$f(x) = [x - (a + bi)]^k g(x)$$

where $g(a + bi) \neq 0$.

It follows from Theorem 3.14 that f and the first $(k-1)$ derivatives of f, evaluated at $x = a + bi$, are zero, and that the kth derivative of f at $(a + bi)$ is not equal to zero. That is,

$$f(a + bi) = 0, \frac{df(a + bi)}{dx} = 0, \ldots, \frac{d^{k-1}f(a + bi)}{dx^{k-1}} = 0, \text{ and}$$

$$\frac{d^k f(a + bi)}{dx^k} \neq 0$$

The first equality says that

$$a_0(a + bi)^n + a_1(a + bi)^{n-1} + \cdots + a_n = 0$$

By the properties of conjugate numbers, and the fact that the a_i are real numbers, it follows that the conjugate of the last equation is

$$a_0(a - bi)^n + a_1(a - bi)^{n-1} + \cdots + a_n = 0$$

that is

$$f(a - bi) = 0$$

It is similarly established that

$$\frac{df(a - bi)}{dx} = 0, \ldots, \frac{d^{k-1}f(a - bi)}{dx^{k-1}} = 0$$

and it only remains to prove that

$$\frac{d^k f(a - bi)}{dx^k} \neq 0$$

We have established that

$$\frac{d^k f(a + bi)}{dx^k} \equiv A + Bi \neq 0$$

Thus, again by the properties of complex numbers, it follows that

$$\frac{d^k f(a - bi)}{dx^k} \equiv A - Bi \neq 0$$

Q.E.D.

3.3 BASIC NOTIONS IN MATRIX ALGEBRA†

Recall that a collection of vectors G called a *vector space* has the properties that, for any vectors x and y belonging to G, $(x + y) \in G$, and for any $x \in G$ then $(\alpha x) \in G$, where α is a real or a complex scalar. Indeed, a vector space is always defined with reference to the number system to which the scalars belong. For our purpose, we may assume that the scalars are real numbers. Any subset of G which is a vector space is called a subspace; thus, any non-empty subset S of G is a subspace if and only if the sum of any two vectors in S is a vector which lies in S, and if the product of any vector in S by a scalar is a vector which lies in S. It is an obvious application of the definition of a vector space that *any* linear combination of a set of vectors in a vector space G is a vector which lies in G, that is, if $(x_1, \ldots, x_m)$ is a set of vectors which lie in G, then $\sum_{i=1}^{m} \alpha_i x_i$ is a vector which lies in G, where $\alpha_1, \ldots, \alpha_m$ are scalars.

Consider now *any* collection of vectors in vector space G, and *all* linear combinations of this set of vectors. This set of all linear combinations of a given collection of vectors in G is a subspace of G. The proof of this statement is immediate. Choose from G the set of vectors $(x_1, \ldots, x_m)$ and consider the following two identities:

$$(3.8) \qquad (\alpha_1 x_1 + \cdots + \alpha_m x_m) + (\beta_1 x_1 + \cdots + \beta_m x_m) = (\alpha_1 + \beta_1)x_1 \\ + \cdots + (\alpha_m + \beta_m)x_m$$

and

$$(3.9) \qquad \beta(\alpha_1 x_1 + \cdots + \alpha_m x_m) = (\beta\alpha_1)x_1 + \cdots + (\beta\alpha_m)x_m$$

where α_i, β_i and β are scalars.

In (3.8) we have on the left side the sum of two vectors in G which is equal to another vector in G. In (3.9) we have a vector in G multiplied by a scalar which is equal to another vector in G. This proves the following theorem.

THEOREM 3.17

THE SET OF ALL LINEAR COMBINATIONS OF ANY COLLECTION OF VECTORS IN A VECTOR SPACE G IS A SUBSPACE OF G.

Since all linear combinations of any set of vectors in a vector space G generates a vector space S, we say that S is *spanned* by the chosen set of vectors.

---

†We assume in this section that the reader has a background in the fundamentals of matrix algebra. See, for example, Yamane [51, Chap. 11] or Allen [3, Chaps. 12 and 13]. At a more advanced level, see Hadley [21, Chaps. 1–5] and Mirsky [36, Chap. 5].

The vectors $(x_1, \ldots, x_m)$ are defined as linearly independent if and only if for all scalars α_i, $\sum_{i=1}^{m} \alpha_i x_i = 0$ implies that $\alpha_1 = \alpha_2 = , \ldots, = \alpha_m = 0$. Vectors which are not linearly independent are defined as linearly dependent.

THEOREM 3.18

THE VECTORS $x_1, \ldots, x_m$ ARE LINEARLY DEPENDENT IF AND ONLY IF AT LEAST ONE OF THESE VECTORS CAN BE EXPRESSED AS A LINEAR COMBINATION OF THE OTHER VECTORS.

PROOF:

Suppose the vectors are linearly dependent; then $\sum_{i=1}^{m} \alpha_i x_i = 0$ implies that at least one $\alpha_i \neq 0$. Suppose a nonzero α_i is α_k where $1 \leq k \leq m$; then x_k clearly can be solved for as a linear combination of the other vectors. Conversely, suppose

$$x_k = \alpha_1 x_1 + \cdots + \alpha_{k-1} x_{k-1} + \alpha_{k+1} x_{k+1} + \cdots + \alpha_m x_m$$

then, by transferring x_k to the right side, it becomes obvious that these vectors are linearly dependent, since at least one scalar ($\alpha_k = -1$) is not zero.

Q.E.D.

It follows from this theorem that if a set of vectors is linearly dependent, there exists a smaller subset of these vectors which generates the same vector space. The reason is that at least one of the vectors is expressible as a linear combination of the other ones. This vector can thus be dropped from the set, and the smaller set must span the same vector space as the original set. If the new set is still linearly dependent, repeat the process, and the same space will still be generated. This process can only come to an end when we are left with a linearly independent set, where by definition it is impossible to express any vector in the set as a linear combination of the others. We have thus established the following.

Corollary. Any finite set of vectors contains a linearly independent subset which spans the same vector space. (This assumes that the finite set is not simply a zero vector.)

THEOREM 3.19 FUNDAMENTAL THEOREM ON LINEAR DEPEND-ENCE

SUPPOSE THAT m VECTORS SPAN THE VECTOR SPACE G, AND THAT G CONTAINS n LINEARLY INDEPENDENT VECTORS. IT IS IMPOSSIBLE THAT $n > m$. THAT IS, $n \leq m$.

PROOF:

Let $(x_1, \ldots, x_m)$ span G, and let $(y_1, \ldots, y_n)$ be linearly independent in G. Now consider the set $(y_1, x_1 \ldots, x_m)$, which obviously spans G and is linearly dependent. By Theorem 3.18, one of these vectors can be expressed as a linear combination of the other ones. Suppose that vector to be x_i.† Then consider the set with x_i dropped

$$(y_1, x_1, \ldots, x_{i-1}, x_{i+1}, \ldots, x_m)$$

which still spans G. Add y_2 to this set

$$(y_2, y_1, x_1, \ldots, x_{i-1}, x_{i+1}, \ldots, x_m)$$

and the set spans G and is linearly dependent. Now since y_1 and y_2 are linearly independent, it must be true that one of the x-vectors is expressible as a linear combination of the other vectors. (Why?) Drop this x-vector and add the next y to create a new set. Continue this process of dropping x-vectors and adding y-vectors. Should we run out of x-vectors along the way, we have a contradiction. To see this, suppose that we have just dropped x_2 and added y_m, yielding a set which, by the above reasoning, must span G and be linearly dependent

$$(y_m, \ldots, y_1, x_1)$$

Again it must be true that x_1 is a linear combination of the other vectors, since $(y_m, \ldots, y_1)$ is a linearly independent set. Dropping x_1, we still have a set $(y_m, \ldots, y_1)$ which spans G. If any more y-vectors exist we have a contradiction, for if $(y_m, \ldots, y_1)$ spans G, then $(y_{m+1}, y_m, \ldots, y_1)$ not only spans G but is linearly dependent. Therefore, it is not possible for $n > m$, and we conclude that $n \leq m$.

Q. E. D.

By the corollary of Theorem 3.18, a minimum set of vectors which spans a vector space must be linearly independent. We call this minimum spanning set a *basis* of a vector space. A vector space is finite-dimensional if and only if it possesses a finite basis. By Theorem 3.19, it can be immediately established that *all bases of a finite dimensional vector space‡ have the same number of vectors*. The proof is simple. If vector set A with m-vectors and set B with n-vectors are both bases of G, they both span G and are linearly independent sets. Since A spans G and B is linearly independent, $m \geq n$ by Theorem 3.19; since B spans G and A is linearly independent, $n \geq m$ by Theorem 3.19, thus

†There must be at least one such x_i. Why?
‡The discussion will be limited to *finite* dimensional spaces.

$n = m$. The number of elements in any basis of a vector space is defined as the *dimension* of the vector space. We shall denote the dimension of the vector space G as $d(G)$. A further implication here is that *if the dimension of a vector space is* m, *any* m $+$ 1 *vectors in the space must be linearly dependent*. This follows from the definition of a basis.

THEOREM 3.20

ANY LINEARLY INDEPENDENT SET OF VECTORS OF A VECTOR SPACE G IS A PART OF A BASIS OF G.

PROOF:

Suppose that $(x_1, \ldots, x_n)$ is a basis of G, and that $(y_1, \ldots, y_r)$ is a linearly independent set of vectors belonging to G. From the definition of a basis, $r \leq n$. Consider the set of vectors

$$(y_1, \ldots, y_r, x_1, \ldots, x_n)$$

which spans G and is linearly dependent. By the corollary of Theorem 3.18, a linearly independent subset of these vectors which spans G exists. We arrive at this new basis by dropping vectors from this set which are expressible as linear combinations of other vectors. This process allows us to drop just x-vectors, since $(y_1, \ldots, y_r)$ is a linearly independent set. Therefore, the new basis will contain $(y_1, \ldots, y_r)$.

Q. E. D.

Next, consider the set of all x-vectors which satisfy the set of equations $Ax = 0$, where A is an $n \times n$ matrix. The collection of such vectors is obviously a vector space. (Why?) We call this vector space the *solution space* of $Ax = 0$. It is sometimes called the *null space* of A. This solution space will have a dimension, which is sometimes denoted the *nullity* of A.

The next theorem establishes a connection among the rank of A, the nullity of A, and the order of A. It says that the nullity plus the rank of A equals the order of A.

THEOREM 3.21   DIMENSIONALITY THEOREM FOR HOMOGENE-OUS SYSTEMS

THE SOLUTION SPACE OF $Ax = 0$, WHERE A IS AN $n \times n$ MATRIX AND x IS AN n-VECTOR, HAS DIMENSION $n - r(A)$. [WHERE $r(A)$ IS THE RANK OF A AND n IS THE ORDER OF A].

PROOF:

Let G be the set of solution vectors of $Ax = 0$. Clearly G is a vector space. The theorem states that $d(G) = n - r(A)$.

Suppose $d(G) = k$. Now if $r(A) = n$, the only solution of $Ax = 0$ is the null vector, and $d(G) = k = 0$ and the theorem holds. Next, suppose $r(A) = 0$. This means that A is a null matrix, and $d(G) = k = n$ in this case, and the theorem holds.

Now suppose $d(G) = k, 0 < k < n$. Let $r(A) = r$ and $(x_1, \ldots, x_k)$ be a basis of G. By Theorem 3.20, $(x_1, \ldots, x_k)$ forms part of a basis of n-space, which can be written

$$(x_1, \ldots x_k, x_{k+1}, \ldots, x_n)$$

Next, consider the set of vectors Ax, and suppose that we call this vector space G^*. Since x can be written as

$$x = \alpha_1 x_1 + \cdots + \alpha_k x_k + \cdots + \alpha_n x_n$$

it follows that
$$Ax = \alpha_1(Ax_1) + \cdots + \alpha_k(Ax_k) + \cdots + \alpha_n(Ax_n)$$

Since $Ax_1 = Ax_2 = , \cdots, = Ax_k = 0$, we have that

$$Ax = \alpha_{k+1}(Ax_{k+1}) + \cdots + \alpha_n(Ax_n)$$

Thus, $(Ax_{k+1}, \ldots, Ax_n)$ spans G^*. Is this set a basis for G^*? If the set is linearly independent, the answer is yes. Consider then

$$\alpha_{k+1}(Ax_{k+1}) + \cdots + \alpha_n(Ax_n) = 0$$
$$= A(\alpha_{k+1} x_{k+1} + \cdots + \alpha_n x_n) = 0$$

The vector in parentheses is part of G, the solution space of $Ax = 0$, and can therefore be expressed as a linear combination of the basis $(x_1, \ldots, x_k)$ of G, hence

$$\alpha_{k+1} x_{k+1} + \cdots + \alpha_n x_n = \alpha_1 x_1 + \cdots + \alpha_k x_k$$

but $(x_1, \ldots, x_k, \ldots, x_n)$ is a linearly independent set, so the only way for this last equality to hold is for $\alpha_1 = \ldots = \alpha_k = \ldots = \alpha_n = 0$. This tells us that $(Ax_{k+1}, \ldots, Ax_n)$ is a linearly independent set and a basis of G^*, the set of vectors Ax. Therefore, $d(G^*) = n - k$. But G^* is the set of all linear combinations of the columns of A and must have dimension equal to the number of linearly independent columns of A, which is equal to $r(A)$, which is assumed to be r. It follows that $n - k = r$, and since $d(G) = k$, the theorem is proved.

Q. E. D.

THEOREM 3.22

THE RANK OF THE PRODUCT OF TWO SQUARE MATRICES IS NOT GREATER THAN THE RANK OF EITHER FACTOR, THAT IS, $r(AB) \leq \{r(A), r(B)\}$.

PROOF:

Let G^* be the vector space of vectors x such that $Bx = 0$, and let $\hat{G}$ be the vector space of vectors x such that $ABx = 0$. Clearly, if $x \in G^*$, then $x \in \hat{G}$, but not vice versa. That is, any x which satisfies $Bx = 0$ must satisfy $ABx = 0$, but there could be x vectors which satisfy $ABx = 0$ but not $Bx = 0$. Thus, the vector space G^* is included in $\hat{G}$, and $d(G^*) \leq d(\hat{G})$. By the dimensionality theorem

$$n - r(B) = d(G^*)$$
$$n - r(AB) = d(\hat{G})$$

Thus

$$n - r(B) \leq n - r(AB)$$
$$- r(B) \leq - r(AB)$$
$$r(B) \geq r(AB)$$

Since the rank of a matrix and the rank of its transpose are identical, we can infer from the last result that

$$r(AB) = r(B'A') \leq r(A') = r(A)$$

Q. E. D.

THEOREM 3.23

SUPPOSE THAT A AND B ARE $n \times n$ MATRICES.[†] THEN THE DIMENSION OF THE SOLUTION SPACE G OF $Ay = 0$, WHERE $y \equiv Bx$, IS EQUAL TO $r(B) - r(AB)$, THAT IS

$$d(G) = r(B) - r(AB)$$

PROOF:

Let

$$G \equiv \{y | Ay = 0, y \equiv Bx\}$$
$$G^* \equiv \{x | Bx = 0\}, d(G^*) = k$$
$$\hat{G} \equiv \{x | ABx = 0\}, d(\hat{G}) = r$$

[†]The theorem does not require that A and B be square, and the proof proceeds along identical lines if they are not.

Then, by Theorem 3.21

$$n - r(B) = k$$

and

$$n - r(AB) = r$$

thus

$$r(B) - r(AB) = r - k$$

By Theorem 3.22, $r(AB) \leq r(B)$, hence

$$0 \leq k \leq r$$

First we consider the case where $0 < k < r$. Let a basis for the solution space G^* be $(x_1, \ldots, x_k)$, and let a basis for $\hat{G}$ be $(x_1, \ldots, x_k, \ldots, x_r)$. If $x \in \hat{G}$, then x can be expressed as

$$x = \alpha_1 x_1 + \cdots + \alpha_k x_k + \cdots + \alpha_r x_r$$

Observe that $x \in \hat{G}$ if and only if $y \equiv Bx \in G$. Hence, any $y \equiv Bx \in G$ can be expressed as

$$Bx = \alpha_1 Bx_1 + \cdots + \alpha_k Bx_k + \cdots + \alpha_r Bx_r$$

or

$$Bx = \alpha_{k+1} Bx_{k+1} + \cdots + \alpha_r Bx_r$$

since $Bx_1 = , \ldots, = Bx_k = 0$. The last expression tells us that $(Bx_{k+1}, \ldots, Bx_r)$ spans G. Are these vectors also linearly independent, hence a basis for G? Consider

$$\alpha_{k+1}(Bx_{k+1}) + \cdots + \alpha_r(Bx_r) = 0$$

or

$$B(\alpha_{k+1} x_{k+1} + \cdots + \alpha_r x_r) = 0$$

For this equation to hold, the vector in parentheses must belong to G^*, and therefore must be expressible as a linear combination of the basis vectors of G_*, $(x_1, \ldots, x_k)$; that is, for appropriate scalars $\alpha_1, \ldots, \alpha_k$ we may write

$$\alpha_{k+1} x_{k+1} + \cdots + \alpha_r x_r = \alpha_1 x_1 + \cdots + \alpha_k x_k$$

But $(x_1, \ldots, x_k, \ldots, x_r)$ is a basis for $\hat{G}$, hence these vectors are linearly independent. Therefore, the last expression, together with the linear independence of the x's, implies that the α's are zero and $(Bx_{k+1}, \ldots, Bx_r)$ is thus a linearly independent set and a basis for G. We have established that if $0 < k < r$

$$d(G) = r - k = r(B) - r(AB)$$

The other cases present no difficulty. If $0 = k = r$, then $r(B) = r(AB) = = n$, and the only vector that satisfies $Ay = 0$ is the null vector, $y = Bx = 0$. Thus

$$d(G) = 0 = r(B) - r(AB)$$

If $0 < k = r$, then a basis for G* is also a basis for $\hat{G}$. Hence, $x \in G^*$ if and only if $x \in G$, that is, $Bx = 0 \longleftrightarrow ABx = 0$. Therefore, if $y \in G$ it must be the null vector, since $Ay = ABx = 0 \longleftrightarrow Bx = y = 0$. This says that

$$d(G) = 0 = r(B) - r(AB)$$

The final case, where $0 = k < r$, is left for the reader.

Q. E. D.

THEOREM 3.24

IF A AND B ARE $n \times n$ MATRICES, THEN

$$r(AB) \geq r(A) + r(B) - n$$

Remark. This result can also be expressed in terms of the nullities of these matrices. Denoting the nullity of A as $n(A)$, recall from Theorem 3.21 that $n - r(A) = n(A)$. Similarly, $n - r(AB) = n(AB)$ and $n - r(B) = n(B)$. Therefore, by subtracting n from both sides of the inequality, we can restate Theorem 3.24 as[†]

$$n(AB) \leq n(A) + n(B)$$

PROOF:

By the previous theorem

$$d(G) = r(B) - r(AB)$$

where

[†]This theorem, together with Theorem 3.22, is known as Sylvester's law of nullity.

$$G = \{y|Ay = 0, y \equiv Bx\}$$

Consider now the null space of A, U, where

$$U = \{y|Ay = 0\}$$

Clearly, any $y \in G$ must belong to U, but the reverse need not hold. [Example: imagine that B is the null matrix and that $r(A) < n$; then there is a $y \neq 0$ belonging to U that could not belong to G.] Therefore,

$$d(G) = r(B) - r(AB) \leq d(U)$$

But the dimension of U, which is the nullity of A, equals $n - r(A)$. Hence

$$r(B) - r(AB) \leq n - r(A)$$

or

$$r(AB) \geq r(A) + r(B) - n$$
$$\text{Q. E. D.}$$

THEOREM 3.25

IF $A(x)$ IS AN $n \times n$ MATRIX WHERE EACH ELEMENT IS A FUNCTION OF THE SCALAR x, AND IF p IS A SIMPLE ROOT OF $|A(x)|$, THEN $r(A^*(p)) = 1$, WHERE A^* IS THE ADJOINT MATRIX OF A. (THE ADJOINT OR ADJUGATE MATRIX OF A IS THE TRANSPOSE OF THE MATRIX OF COFACTORS OF THE ELEMENTS OF A.)

PROOF:
Suppose that B is also an $n \times n$ matrix, and that AB is the null matrix. Then by the preceding theorem

$$r(AB) = 0 \geq r(A) + r(B) - n$$

so that $n \geq r(A) + r(B)$. Now suppose that B is the adjoint of A, that is, $B = A^*$, then

$$A(x)A^*(x) = I|A(x)|$$

Setting $x = p$, where p is a simple root of $|A(x)|$, we have

$$A(p)A^*(p) = 0$$

Therefore

$$n \geq r(A(p)) + r(A^*(p))$$

By Theorem 3.15, we know that $r(A(p)) = n - 1$, hence

$$r(A^*(p)) \leq 1$$

But A^* is made up of all the $(n - 1)$ minors of A, and $r(A(p)) = n - 1$, which means that at least one $(n - 1)$ minor of $A(p)$ is not zero, thus

$$r(A^*(p)) = 1$$

that is, the nonzero columns of $A^*(p)$ will differ only by a constant.

Q. E. D.

3.4 A FUNDAMENTAL SOLUTION SET

In section 3.6 we demonstrate that the system $A(Q)y = f(t)$ is equivalent to a single nonhomogeneous linear nth order differential or difference equation $p(Q)y_i = g(t)$, assuming that $|A(Q)|$ is a polynomial of degree $n > 0$ in the operator. Therefore, the theory of the single equation can be invoked to guarantee that the complete or general solution of $A(Q)y = f(t)$ exists and is unique for any set of n initial conditions. We now investigate the theory of the single equation, and establish that the general solution contains n linearly independent solutions; that is, every solution can be expressed as a linear combination of n linearly independent solutions.†

In many applications of differential or difference equations, it is desired to find a specific solution of the equation such that certain initial conditions are satisfied.‡ Suppose that we have a differential or difference equation of order n

$$(3.10) \qquad p(Q)y = a_n Q^n y + a_{n-1} Q^{n-1} y + \cdots + a_0 = f(t)$$

where a_i are real constants and Q is the differential or shift operator, together with the initial conditions at the point $t = 0$

---

†A set of functions $y_1(t), \ldots, y_n(t)$ are defined as linearly independent if the statement

$$\sum_1^n C_i y_i(t) = 0$$

identically on some nonzero interval of time implies that the constants C_i are all zero. If some collection of C_i, not all zero, can make the equation true throughout the interval, then the set of functions are linearly dependent.

‡In Chapter 5 we will deal with a problem where initial and terminal conditions are present. For sources on the material in this section, see almost any text on differential equations.

(3.11) $\qquad y(0) = K_0, Qy(0) = K_1, \ldots, Q^{n-1}y(0) = K_{n-1}$

where $K_0, \ldots, K_{n-1}$ are specified constants. Recall that for a differential equation $Q \equiv D$ and $D^\alpha y(0) \equiv d^\alpha y/dt^\alpha$ evaluated at $t = 0$; while for a difference equation $Q \equiv E$, so that $E^\alpha y(0) = y(\alpha)$, that is, the value of y in period α, for $0 \le \alpha \le n - 1$.

The equation (3.10) together with the initial conditions (3.11) constitute an *initial value problem*. The following theorem is basic for initial value problems associated with linear difference or diffrential equations. We present the theorem without proof.[†]

THEOREM 3.26 EXISTENCE AND UNIQUENESS

GIVEN (3.10) AND (3.11), WITH $a_n \neq 0$ AND $f(t)$ REAL AND CONTINUOUS, THERE EXISTS ONE AND ONLY ONE SOLUTION OF (3.10) WHICH SATISFIES (3.11).

Consider the homogeneous form of (3.10). Any set of n linearly independent solutions of this equation is called a *fundamental set* of solutions. The importance of being able to find a fundamental set is that it can be established that every solution of $p(Q)y = 0$ is expressible as a linear combination of the fundamental set of solutions. We want to prove this, as well as the fact that a fundamental set always exists.

Intimately related to the question of whether or not a set of functions $y_1(t), y_2(t), \ldots, y_n(t)$ are linearly independent is the determinant called the *Wronskian* of the set of functions. It is defined as the determinant of

$$W(t) \equiv \begin{bmatrix} y_1(t) & y_2(t) & \cdots & y_n(t) \\ Qy_1(t) & Qy_2(t) & \cdots & Qy_n(t) \\ \vdots & \vdots & & \vdots \\ Q^{n-1}y_1(t) & Q^{n-1}y_2(t) & \cdots & Q^{n-1}y_n(t) \end{bmatrix}$$

(When the operator is E, the determinant is sometimes called the Casorati determinant). We shall refer to it as $|W(t)|$. The theorem which gives the Wronskian its importance follows.

THEOREM 3.27

LET THE FUNCTIONS $y_i(t)$, $i = 1, \ldots, n$, BE SOLUTIONS OF $p(Q)y = 0$, THEN:
(a) IF THESE FUNCTIONS ARE LINEARLY DEPENDENT, $|W(t)| = 0$ FOR ALL $t \ge 0$.

[†]All the theorems in this section apply to some interval of time. It is convenient for us to make this interval the set of all $t \ge 0$. The theorems also hold if the coefficients in (3.10) are continuous functions of time on this interval. For a proof of Theorem 3.26, see almost any text on differential equations.

(b) If $|W(t)| = 0$ for any $t \geq 0$, the functions are linearly dependent.[†]
(c) Either $|W(t)|$ is identically zero on the interval and the n functions are linearly dependent, or $|W(t)| \neq 0$ for some $t \geq 0$ and the n functions are linearly independent.

Proof:
(a) By hypothesis, the n functions are linearly dependent, therefore, there exist constants C_i, $i = 1, \ldots, n$, not all zero, such that

$$\sum_{i=1}^{n} C_i y_i(t) = 0$$

for all $t \geq 0$. Since the quantity on the left is identically zero for $t \geq 0$, it follows that

$$Q^j \left[\sum_{i=1}^{n} C_i y_i(t) \right] = 0 \qquad 0 \leq j \leq n - 1$$

for $t \geq 0$, hence we have the n relations

$$W(t)C \equiv 0$$

where $C = (C_1, \ldots, C_n)$. Letting $t \geq 0$ assume any specific value, this system becomes an algebraic system of n equations. Since $C \neq 0$, the system has a nontrivial solution but this can be the case only if the determinant of the system vanishes at every $t \geq 0$. Statement (a) is thus proved.
(b) Consider again

$$W(t)C = 0$$

where, by assumption, $|W(t)| = 0$ for some value of t, say, $t = t^* \geq 0$. Hence, the system of algebraic equations

$$W(t^*)C = 0$$

has a nontrivial solution. Select some $C^* \neq 0$ such that $W(t^*)C^* = 0$ and define a function $y^*(t)$ as

$$y^*(t) \equiv C_1^* y_1(t) + \cdots + C_n^* y_n(t)$$

where $C^* \equiv (C_1^*, \ldots, C_n^*)$ and where the $y_i(t)$ are solutions to $p(Q)y = 0$.

[†]Statement (a) applies to an arbitrary set of functions, while (b) only holds if the functions are solutions of the same equation.

This function $y^*(t)$ is also a solution of $p(Q)y = 0$. Moreover, for $t = t^*$, $W(t^*)C^* = 0$ implies that

$$y^*(t^*) = Qy^*(t^*) = \cdots = Q^{n-1}y^*(t^*) = 0$$

Thus, the initial values of $y^*(t)$ at $t = t^*$ are all zero. Moreover, the identically zero function satisfies $p(Q)y = 0$. By the uniqueness part of Theorem 3.26, it follows that $y^*(t)$ must be the identically zero function. Therefore

$$C_1^* y_1(t) + \cdots + C_n^* y_n(t) \equiv 0$$

on the interval, and since C_i^* are not all zero, we conclude that the functions $y_i(t)$ are linearly dependent.

(c) The functions are either linearly dependent or linearly independent. If they are dependent, then, by (a), $|W(t)|$ vanishes at all $t \geq 0$. If they are independent, $|W(t)|$ cannot vanish at any t; if it did, we know from (b) that the functions would be dependent.

$$Q. \ E. \ D.$$

Example 3.3

Suppose that $p(Q)y \equiv (Q^2 + 7Q + 6)y = 0$. If $Q = E$, then we have the the second order difference equation

$$y_{t+2} + 7y_{t+1} + 6y_t = 0$$

and two solutions are

$$y_1(t) = (-1)^t$$
$$y_2(t) = (-6)^t$$

To evaluate whether these solutions are linearly independent, form the Wronskian

$$|W(t)| = \begin{vmatrix} (-1)^t & (-6)^t \\ (-1)^{t+1} & (-6)^{t+1} \end{vmatrix}$$

$$= (-1)^t(-6)^t \begin{vmatrix} 1 & 1 \\ -1 & -6 \end{vmatrix}$$

$$= -5(-1)^t(-6)^t$$

which is not equal to zero for $t \geq 0$. Actually, by virtue of (c) in Theorem

(3.27), all we have to establish to guarantee linear independence is that $|W(t)| \neq 0$ for *some* t. So, setting $t = 0$, we see that

$$|W(0)| = \begin{vmatrix} 1 & 1 \\ -1 & -6 \end{vmatrix} \neq 0$$

If $Q = D$, we have the second order differential equation

$$\ddot{y} + 7\dot{y} + 6y = 0$$

and two solutions are

$$y_1(t) = e^{-t}$$
$$y_2(t) = e^{-6t}$$

The Wronskian is

$$|W(t)| = \begin{vmatrix} e^{-t} & e^{-6t} \\ -e^{-t} & -6e^{-6t} \end{vmatrix}$$

and again we find that

$$|W(0)| = \begin{vmatrix} 1 & 1 \\ -1 & -6 \end{vmatrix} \neq 0$$

It is now an easy matter to demonstrate that a fundamental solution set always exists, and to establish that such a set forms a basis for a general solution to $p(Q)y = 0$.

THEOREM 3.28

A FUNDAMENTAL SOLUTION SET FOR $p(Q)y = 0$ ALWAYS EXISTS.

PROOF:

Let $y_i(t), i = 1, \ldots, n$, be solutions of the equation which satisfy the following n sets of initial conditions:

$$\begin{array}{lll} y_1(0) = 1, & y_2(0) = 0, \ldots, & y_n(0) = 0 \\ Qy_1(0) = 0, & Qy_2(0) = 1, \ldots, & Qy_n(0) = 0 \\ \vdots & \vdots & \vdots \\ Q^{n-1}y_1(0) = 0, & Q^{n-1}y_2(0) = 0, \ldots, & Q^{n-1}y_n(0) = 1 \end{array}$$

The existence of each of these n solutions is guaranteed by Theorem 3.26. Clearly,

$$|W(0)| = 1$$

Hence, by Theorem 3.27, these solutions are linearly independent.

Q. E. D.

THEOREM 3.29

A FUNDAMENTAL SOLUTION SET FOR $p(Q)y = 0$ FORMS A BASIS FOR A GENERAL SOLUTION OF THE EQUATION. THAT IS, IF $y_i(t), i = i, \ldots, n$, IS A FUNDAMENTAL SOLUTION SET, THEN EVERY SOLUTION OF THE EQUATION IS OF THE FORM

$$C_1 y_1(t) + \ldots + C_n y_n(t)$$

WHERE THE QUANTITIES C_i ARE CONSTANTS.

PROOF:

Let $y(t)$ be any solution of $p(Q)y = 0$, and assume that

$$y(0) = K_0, Qy(0) = K_1, \cdots, Q^{n-1}y(0) = K_{n-1}$$

where $K_0, \ldots, K_{n-1}$ are specified constants. If $y(t)$ is to be expressible in the form $C_1 y_1(t) + \ldots + C_n y_n(t)$, then the constants C_i must be such that

$$C_1 y_1(0) + \cdots + C_n y_n(0) = K_0$$
$$C_1 Q y_1(0) + \cdots + C_n Q y_n(0) = K_1$$
$$\vdots \qquad \qquad \vdots$$
$$C_1 Q^{n-1} y_1(0) + \cdots + C_n Q^{n-1} y_n(0) = K_{n-1}$$

This system of equations has a unique solution for the constants C_i, since its determinant is the Wronskian evaluated at $t = 0$, which is guaranteed not to be zero. Let us select those values of the constants which satisfy this system, and call them C_i^*. Then the corresponding function

$$C_1^* y_1(t) + \cdots + C_n^* y_n(t)$$

is a solution of $p(Q)y = 0$ [since each $y_i(t)$ is a solution] and has the some initial values at $t = 0$ as does the solution $y(t)$. Hence, this function is identical to $y(t)$, by Theorem 3.26.

Q. E. D.

THEOREM 3.30

LET $y_1(t), \ldots, y_n(t)$ CONSTITUTE A FUNDAMENTAL SOLUTION SET FOR $p(Q)y = 0$, AND LET $y_p(t)$ BE ANY ONE PARTICULAR SOLUTION OF $p(Q)y = f(t)$. THEN EVERY SOLUTION OF $p(Q)y = f(t)$ MUST BE OF THE FORM

(3.12) $$C_1 y_1(t) + \cdots + C_n y_n(t) + y_p(t)$$

WHERE THE QUANTITIES C_i ARE CONSTANTS.

PROOF:

It is obvious that any solution of this form solves $p(Q)y = f(t)$, so we wish to show that any solution of the nonhomogeneous equation must look like (3.12). Let $y(t)$ be any solution of the nonhomogeneous equation. Then $y(t) - y_p(t)$ is a solution of the homogeneous equation. Hence, by the previous theorem†

(3.13) $$y(t) - y_p(t) = C_1 y_1 + \cdots + C_n y_n(t)$$

or

$$y(t) = C_1 y_1(t) + \cdots + C_n y_n(t) + y_p(t)$$
$$\text{Q.E.D.}$$

3.5 ADJOINT MATRIX TECHNIQUE‡

We are now ready to investigate a technique for constructing the solution for a system of linear difference or differential equations. Recall that in (3.2) we wrote such a system in the form

$$A(Q)y = f(t)$$

where Q is either the differential or the shift operator, A is an $m \times m$ matrix, with each element a polynomial of any degree in the operator, $y = (y_1, \ldots, y_m)$, with each element a function of time, and $f(t) = (f_1(t), \ldots, f_m(t))$. Before presenting the first theorem, we state the following preliminary result.

---

†Notice that the left side of (3.13) is the difference between two particular solutions of the nonhomogenous equation. Since the C_i are arbitrary constants and $(y_1(t), \ldots, y_n(t))$ is a linearly independent set, it follows that the two particular solutions will not be identical. This is the reason we speak of *a* particular solution, and not *the* particular solution.

‡See Baumol [7, Chaps. 15 and 16], Frazer, Duncan, and Collar [17, Chap. 5], and Ince [27, Chap. 6].

Lemma. $p(E)x^t = x^t p(x)$, where $p(E)$ is a polynomial in the operator E, and $p(x)$ is the polynomial with x in place of E. Also, $p(D)e^{xt} = e^{xt} p(x)$, where D is the differential operator.

PROOF:

Let

$$p(E) = a_m E^m + a_{m-1} E^{m-1} + \cdots + a_1 E + a_0$$

Then

$$p(E)x^t = a_m x^{t+m} + a_{m-1} x^{t+m-1} + \cdots + a_1 x^{t+1} + a_0 x^t$$
$$= x^t(a_m x^m + a_{m-1} x^{m-1} + \cdots + a_1 x + a_0)$$
$$= x^t p(x)$$

The proof for the differential operator is similar.

Q. E. D.

It follows from this lemma that $A(E)x^t = A(x)x^t$, since each element of the matrix A is a polynomial in the operator. Similarly, $A(D)e^{xt} = A(x)e^{xt}$.

THEOREM 3.31

IN THE HOMOGENEOUS SYSTEM OF LINEAR DIFFERENCE EQUATIONS $A(E)y_t = 0$, IF $|A(x)| = 0$ HAS NO REPEATED ROOTS, THEN A SOLUTION OF THIS SYSTEM IS[†]

$$y_t = \sum_{j=1}^{n} K_j x_j^t A_i^*(x_j)$$

WHERE K_j IS AN ARBITRARY CONSTANT, x_j IS THE jTH ROOT OF $|A(x)|$, AND $A_i^*(x_j)$ IS THE iTH COLUMN OF $A^*(E)$, THE ADJOINT MATRIX OF $A(E)$, WITH x_j IN PLACE OF E. NOTICE THAT THE CHOICE OF THE COLUMN DOES NOT MATTER, SINCE $r(A^*(x_j)) = 1$ BY THEOREM 3.25.

PROOF:

Let

$$y_t = \sum_{j=1}^{n} K_j x_j^t A_i^*(x_j)$$

[†]This technique must be modified to handle multiple roots. See Frazer, Duncan, and Collar [17]. The technique developed in the next section covers such cases without modification.

Then, since $A(E)$ is a linear operator

$$A(E)y_t = \sum_{j=1}^{n} K_j A(E)x_j^t A_i^*(x_j)$$

By the lemma, $A(E)x_j^t = x_j^t A(x_j)$, thus

$$A(E)y_t = \sum_{j=1}^{n} K_j x_j^t A(x_j)A_i^*(x_j)$$

Since

$$A(x_j)A^*(x_j) = I|A(x_j)| = I \cdot 0$$

if x_j is a root of $|A(x)|$; it follows that $A(E)y_t = 0$ if each x_j is a distinct root of $|A(x)|$.

$$Q.\ E.\ D.$$

Example 3.4

Consider the system

$$2y_{1t} - y_{1,t+1} + y_{2t} = 0$$
$$2y_{1t} + 3y_{2t} - y_{2,t+1} = 0$$

In matrix form we may write the system as

$$\begin{bmatrix} 2-E & 1 \\ 2 & 3-E \end{bmatrix}\begin{bmatrix} y_{1t} \\ y_{2t} \end{bmatrix} = \begin{bmatrix} 0 \\ 0 \end{bmatrix}$$

where for this problem

$$A(E) = \begin{bmatrix} 2-E & 1 \\ 2 & 3-E \end{bmatrix}$$

$$y_t = \begin{bmatrix} y_{1t} \\ y_{2t} \end{bmatrix}$$

First we need the roots of $|A(x)|$, the characteristic function

$$|A(x)| = \begin{vmatrix} 2-x & 1 \\ 2 & 3-x \end{vmatrix}$$
$$= (x-4)(x-1)$$

so that $x_1 = 4, x_2 = 1$ are the roots. Now substitute these roots into $A^*(x)$ to obtain the two adjoint matrices needed

$$A^*(x) = \begin{bmatrix} 3 - x & -1 \\ -2 & 2 - x \end{bmatrix}$$

$$A^*(4) = \begin{bmatrix} -1 & -1 \\ -2 & -2 \end{bmatrix}$$

$$A^*(1) = \begin{bmatrix} 2 & -1 \\ -2 & 1 \end{bmatrix}$$

As the theory indicated, the columns of $A^*(4)$ and $A^*(1)$ are proportional, so we may choose either one we wish for a solution. We thus have the following solution

$$\begin{bmatrix} y_{1t} \\ y_{2t} \end{bmatrix} = K_1(4)^t \begin{bmatrix} -1 \\ -2 \end{bmatrix} + K_2(1)^t \begin{bmatrix} 2 \\ -2 \end{bmatrix}$$

where K_1 and K_2 are arbitrary constants.

Consider the system $A(D)y = 0$, where $A(D)$ is an $m \times m$ matrix each of whose elements is a polynomial in the differential operator D. We then have the analogue of Theorem 3.31 for a homogenous differential equation system.

THEOREM 3.32

IF THERE ARE NO REPEATED ROOTS, A SOLUTION OF $A(D)y = 0$ IS

$$y = \sum_{j=1}^{n} K_j e^{x_j t} A_i^*(x_j)$$

WHERE K_j IS AN ARBITRARY CONSTANT, x_j IS THE jTH ROOT OF $|A(x)|$, AND $A_i^*(x_j)$ IS THE iTH COLUMN OF $A^*(D)$, WITH x_j IN PLACE OF D.

PROOF:

Let

$$y = \sum_{j=1}^{n} K_j e^{x_j t} A_i^*(x_j)$$

Then, since $A(D)$ is a linear operator

$$A(D)y = \sum_{j=1}^{n} K_j A(D) e^{x_j t} A_i^*(x_j)$$

It follows from the lemma that

$$A(D)y = \sum_{j=1}^{n} K_j e^{x_j t} A(x_j) A_i^*(x_j) = 0$$

for all x_j which are roots of $|A(x)|$.

Q.E.D.

Example 3.5

Consider

$$\begin{bmatrix} 1 & D-1 \\ D-1 & D+5 \end{bmatrix} \begin{bmatrix} y_1 \\ y_2 \end{bmatrix} = \begin{bmatrix} 0 \\ 0 \end{bmatrix}$$

The characteristic function $|A(x)|$ is

$$\begin{vmatrix} 1 & x-1 \\ x-1 & x+5 \end{vmatrix} = -x^2 + 3x + 4$$

and the roots are $x_1 = 4, x_2 = -1$. Next, substitute the roots into $A^*(x)$ to obtain $A^*(4)$ and $A^*(-1)$

$$A^*(x) = \begin{bmatrix} x+5 & -x+1 \\ -x+1 & 1 \end{bmatrix}$$

$$A^*(4) = \begin{bmatrix} 9 & -3 \\ -3 & 1 \end{bmatrix}$$

$$A^*(-1) = \begin{bmatrix} 4 & 2 \\ 2 & 1 \end{bmatrix}$$

As required, the columns of $A^*(4)$ and $A^*(-1)$ are proportional. The solution is

$$\begin{bmatrix} y_1(t) \\ y_2(t) \end{bmatrix} = K_1 e^{4t} \begin{bmatrix} -3 \\ 1 \end{bmatrix} + K_2 e^{-t} \begin{bmatrix} 2 \\ 1 \end{bmatrix}$$

Remark. We will demonstrate in section 3.6 that this method does generate a *general* solution of the homogeneous system. We prove in Thorem 3.36 that the basis for a general solution of $A(Q)y = 0$ consists of n linearly independent m-vectors, where m is the order of A and n is the degree of the characteristic function or polynomial $|A(Q)|$.

So far, we have derived the general solutions of the homogeneous forms of the following nonhomogeneous systems:

(3.14) $A(E)y_t = f(t)$ [Difference equation system]

(3.15) $A(D)y = f(t)$ [Differential equation system]

where $A(E)$ or $A(D)$ is an $m \times m$ matrix whose elements are polynomials in
the shift or differential operator, respectively, y_t or y is an m-vector in the
dependent variables, and $f(t)$ is an m-vector of constants or functions of time;
that is, we have derived the complete solution of (3.14) and (3.15) in the case
where $f(t) \equiv 0$.

The complete solution of the homogeneous form is called the *complementary
function* of (3.14) or (3.15). To complete the problem, we must now find any
particular solution of the nonhomogeneous system and add this particular
solution to the complementary function. This yields the complete solution of
the nonhomogeneous system. The argument which establishes this result is
similar to the analogous result for a single equation (Theorem 3.30), so we leave
it for the reader.

Before examining how this matrix technique can be used to obtain
particular solutions, it will be useful to define the *inverse operator*. Consider
the single equation $p(Q)y = f(t)$, where $p(Q)$ is a polynomial in either the
differential or the shift operator. Then the inverse operator of $p(Q)$, written as
$p^{-1}(Q)$ or $1/p(Q)$, is defined as an operator which, if it exists, operates on $f(t)$
to yield a particular solution of $p(Q)y = f(t)$. For the definition to make sense,
it is necessary that a particular solution not contain any constant multiples of
a term in the complementary function. (This point will become clear in the
following discussion of particular solutions.) With this definition, we can now
define the inverse of the matrix $A(Q)$, designated as $A^{-1}(Q)$, as the adjoint
matrix $A^*(Q)$ multiplied by the inverse operator of $|A(Q)|$, when it exists. We
can establish from the lemma that, when $A^{-1}(E)$ and $A^{-1}(D)$ exist,

$$A^{-1}(E)x^t = A^{-1}(x)x^t$$

and

$$A^{-1}(D)e^{xt} = A^{-1}(x)e^{xt}$$

where x^t and e^{xt} are scalars. To demonstrate this, observe that from the lemma
we know that

$$A^*(E)x^t = A^*(x)x^t$$

Multiply the right side by the inverse operator of $|A(E)|$, which we denote by
the matrix

$$W \equiv \frac{A^*(x)x^t}{|A(E)|}$$

By the definition of the inverse operator, this expression is a set of particular solutions of

$$|A(E)|W = A^*(x)x^t$$

As a trial solution of this system, let $W = Kx^t$, where K is a matrix of constants. Then, from the lemma and the last expression, we have that

$$|A(E)|Kx^t = |A(x)|Kx^t = A^*(x)x^t$$

Thus

$$K = \frac{A^*(x)}{|A(x)|}$$

and

$$W = \frac{A^*(x)x^t}{|A(x)|} = \frac{A^*(x)x^t}{|A(E)|}$$

We can now see that

$$A^{-1}(E)x^t = \frac{A^*(E)x^t}{|A(E)|} \text{ [by definition of } A^{-1}(E)]$$

$$= \frac{A^*(x)x^t}{|A(E)|} \text{ [since } A^*(E)x^t = A^*(x)x^t]$$

$$= \frac{A^*(x)x^t}{|A(x)|} \text{ [by solution for } W]$$

$$= A^{-1}(x)x^t \text{ [by definition of } A^{-1}(x)]$$

Moreover, it is evident that this procedure fails whenever $|A(x)| = 0$. By similar reasoning, it can be shown that

$$A^{-1}(D)e^{xt} = A^{-1}(x)e^{xt}$$

We may now denote particular solutions for (3.14) and (3.15) as

(3.16) $z_t = A^{-1}(E)f(t)$

(3.17) $z = A^{-1}(D)f(t)$

The following discussion gives methods for obtaining the right-hand sides (3.16) and (3.17) for special forms of $f(t)$. To begin, consider a simple case which frequently arises in Economics, that of a constant percentage growth rate.† This assumption would convert (3.16) and (3.17) to

†See Example 3.2.

(3.18) $z_t = A^{-1}(E)K\lambda^t$, where $(\lambda - 1)$ is the growth rate per period

(3.19) $z = A^{-1}(D)Ke^{\lambda t}$, where λ is the instantaneous growth rate

and where K is a vector of constants, and $e^{\lambda t}$ and λ^t are scalars. But we know that

$$A^{-1}(E)\lambda^t = A^{-1}(\lambda)\lambda^t$$

and

$$A^{-1}(D)e^{\lambda t} = A^{-1}(\lambda)e^{\lambda t}$$

Therefore, particular solutions are

(3.20) $$z_t = \lambda^t A^{-1}(\lambda)K = \frac{\lambda^t A^*(\lambda)}{|A(\lambda)|} K$$

(3.21) $$z = e^{\lambda t} A^{-1}(\lambda)K = \frac{e^{\lambda t} A^*(\lambda)}{|A(\lambda)|} K$$

These solutions fail only in the unusual case where $|A(\lambda)| = 0$, that is, where λ coincides with one of the roots of $|A(x)| = 0$.[†] We discuss this case below.

Consider the simple case where $f(t)$ is a vector of constants. This is a special case of (3.18) and (3.19), where $\lambda = 1$ in (3.18) and $\lambda = 0$ in (3.19). In this event, (3.20) and (3.21) would be written with $\lambda = 1$ in (3.20) and $\lambda = 0$ in (3.21), that is, (3.20) would appear as

$$z_t = \frac{A^*(1)}{A(1)} K$$

and (3.21) would be written as

$$z = \frac{A^*(0)}{A(0)} K$$

These solutions would fail only in the unusual event that 1 and 0, respectively, were roots of $|A(x)|$.

By a simple extension of this argument, we can handle the case where $f(t)$ has the form

$$\lambda^t \equiv (K_1\lambda^t_1, \ldots, K_m\lambda^t_m)$$

in (3.16) and

[†]That is, where the inverses of the operators $|A(D)|$ and $|A(E)|$ are not defined.

$$e^{\lambda t} \equiv (K_1 e^{\lambda_1 t}, \ldots, K_m e^{\lambda_m t})$$

in (3.17), where the K's are constants. The easiest way to handle this is to rewrite λ^t as

$$\lambda^t \equiv \begin{bmatrix} K_1 \lambda_1^t \\ 0 \\ \vdots \\ 0 \end{bmatrix} + \begin{bmatrix} 0 \\ K_2 \lambda_2^t \\ 0 \\ \vdots \\ 0 \end{bmatrix} + \cdots + \begin{bmatrix} 0 \\ \vdots \\ 0 \\ K_m \lambda_m^t \end{bmatrix}$$

assuming $\lambda_i \neq \lambda_j, j \neq i$. We can then solve for a particular solution for each of these vectors by itself, using the method just described, and then sum the m particular solutions, with the result being a particular solution of the full problem. A similar argument holds for $e^{\lambda t}$. It is easy to justify this procedure. Rewrite the nonhomogeneous system in (3.14) or (3.15) as

$$A(Q)y = f_1(t) + f_2(t)$$

where

$$f(t) \equiv f_1(t) + f_2(t)$$

Then, find particular solutions for the two problems

$$A(Q)y = f_1(t)$$
$$A(Q)y = f_2(t)$$

Suppose z_1 and z_2 are particular solutions for these problems. Thus

$$A(Q)(z_1 + z_2) = A(Q)z_1 + A(Q)z_2 = f(t)$$

and the procedure is justified. This procedure is known as the *principle of superposition*. The extension to the case where $f(t) = \sum_1^m f_i(t)$, as in our example with λ^t, is obvious. Thus, a particular solution when $f(t)$ is of the form λ^t or $e^{\lambda t}$ can be written as

(3.22)
$$z_t = \sum_1^m \frac{\lambda_i^t A^*(\lambda_i) C_i}{|A(\lambda_i)|}$$

(3.23)
$$z = \sum_1^m \frac{e^{\lambda_i t} A^*(\lambda_i) C_i}{|A(\lambda_i)|}$$

with $C_i \equiv K_i e_i$, where e_i is the ith unit vector. The particular solutions (3.22) and (3.23) contain (3.20) and (3.21) as the special case where all the λ's are the same. Again we see that the solution fails where any λ_i in the nonhomogeneous term happens to coincide with a root of $|A(x)|$.

Consider another form of $f(t)$. Suppose that

$$(3.24) \qquad\qquad A(E)y_t = Kt\lambda^t$$

$$(3.25) \qquad\qquad A(D)y = Kte^{\lambda t}$$

where K is a vector of constants, and t, λ^t, and $e^{\lambda t}$ are all scalars. Let us write particular solutions for (3.24) and (3.25) as

$$(3.26) \qquad\qquad z_t^* = A^{-1}(E)Kt\lambda^t$$

and

$$(3.27) \qquad\qquad z^* = A^{-1}(D)Kte^{\lambda t}$$

Compare these expressions with (3.18) and (3.19), and observe that if we differentiate (3.18) and (3.19) with respect to λ, and multiply the expression resulting from (3.18) by λ, we obtain (3.26) and (3.27). Therefore, if we perform these same operations on (3.20) and (3.21)—which are equivalent to (3.18) and (3.19)—we obtain expressions which are equivalent to (3.26) and (3.27); these are

$$(3.28) \qquad\qquad z_t^* = \lambda \frac{\partial}{\partial \lambda} \left[\frac{\lambda^t A^*(\lambda)}{|A(\lambda)|} \right] K$$

and

$$(3.29) \qquad\qquad z^* = \frac{\partial}{\partial \lambda} \left[\frac{e^{\lambda t} A^*(\lambda)}{|A(\lambda)|} \right] K$$

which may be employed as particular solutions of (3.24) and (3.25), as long as $|A(\lambda)| \neq 0$.

Similar reasoning yields the solutions for (3.24) and (3.25) with t of degree higher than one. Also, setting $\lambda = 1$ in (3.24) and $\lambda = 0$ in (3.25) yields particular solutions when $f(t)$ has the form Kt.

Finally, consider the exceptional case, where $f(t)$ has the form of (3.18) or (3.19), but $|A(\lambda)| = 0$. In such a case, try the particular solutions

$$z_t = \left[\frac{\partial}{\partial x} x^t A^*(x) \right] K^* \qquad \text{at } x = \lambda$$

and

$$z = \left[\frac{\partial}{\partial x} e^{xt} A^*(x)\right] K^* \qquad \text{at } x = \lambda$$

where K^* is a column of constants. Substituting these trial solutions into (3.18) and (3.19) rewritten as†

$$A(E)z_t = K\lambda^t$$

and

$$A(D)z = Ke^{\lambda t}$$

we see, for the difference equation system, that

$$A(E)\left[\frac{\partial}{\partial x} x^t A^*(x)\right]K^* = \frac{\partial}{\partial x}[A(E)x^t A^*(x)]K^*$$

$$= \frac{\partial}{\partial x}[x^t A(x)A^*(x)]K^*$$

$$= \frac{\partial}{\partial x}[x^t |A(x)|I]K^*$$

$$= x^t\left[\frac{\partial}{\partial x} + tx^{-1}\right]|A(x)|K^*$$

Evaluating this at $x = \lambda$, recalling that λ is assumed to be a simple root of $|A(x)| = 0$, and setting the result equal to $K\lambda^t$, we have that

$$\lambda^t \Delta(A(\lambda))K^* = K\lambda^t$$

where

$$\Delta(A(\lambda)) \equiv \left[\frac{\partial}{\partial x}|A(x)|\right]_{x=\lambda}$$

In the last expression, $\Delta \neq 0$ by Theorem 3.14. Therefore,

$$K^* = \frac{K}{\Delta(A(\lambda))}$$

and the particular solution sought is

$$z_t = \frac{\frac{\partial}{\partial x}[x^t A^*(x)]K}{\frac{\partial}{\partial x}|A(x)|}$$

†Equations (3.18) and (3.19) cannot, of course, be written in this case, since the inverse operators do not exist.

evaluated at $x = \lambda$. The result for the differential equation system is the same, except that e^{xt} replaces x^t.

Example 3.6

Find a particular solution of

$$\begin{bmatrix} (2E+1) & (E+2) \\ (E+2) & (E+4) \end{bmatrix}\begin{bmatrix} y_{1t} \\ y_{2t} \end{bmatrix} = \begin{bmatrix} 2^t \\ 3\cdot 3^t \end{bmatrix}$$

where the dot is a multiplication symbol. Using the principle of superposition, we can write the right-hand side as

$$\begin{bmatrix} 2^t \\ 0 \end{bmatrix} + \begin{bmatrix} 0 \\ 3\cdot 3^t \end{bmatrix} = 2^t\begin{bmatrix} 1 \\ 0 \end{bmatrix} + 3^t\begin{bmatrix} 0 \\ 3 \end{bmatrix}$$

Using (3.22), we can write a particular solution as

$$\begin{bmatrix} y_{1t}^* \\ y_{2t}^* \end{bmatrix} = \frac{2^t A^*(2)C_1}{|A(2)|} + \frac{3^t A^*(3)C_2}{|A(3)|}$$

where $C_1 = (1, 0)$, $C_2 = (0, 3)$. Thus

$$\begin{bmatrix} y_{1t}^* \\ y_{2t}^* \end{bmatrix} = 2^t\begin{bmatrix} \frac{3}{7} & -\frac{2}{7} \\ -\frac{2}{7} & \frac{5}{14} \end{bmatrix}\begin{bmatrix} 1 \\ 0 \end{bmatrix} + 3^t\begin{bmatrix} \frac{7}{24} & -\frac{5}{24} \\ -\frac{5}{24} & \frac{7}{24} \end{bmatrix}\begin{bmatrix} 0 \\ 3 \end{bmatrix} = \begin{bmatrix} \frac{3}{7}\cdot 2^t - \frac{15}{24}\cdot 3^t \\ -\frac{2}{7}\cdot 2^t + \frac{21}{24}\cdot 3^t \end{bmatrix}$$

Check this by substituting into the original system of equations.

Example 3.7

Find a particular solution of

$$\begin{bmatrix} (2D+1) & (D+2) \\ (D+2) & (D+4) \end{bmatrix}\begin{bmatrix} y_1 \\ y_2 \end{bmatrix} = \begin{bmatrix} e^t \\ e^{-t} \end{bmatrix}$$

Using the principle of superposition, and (3.23), we can write a particular solution as

$$\begin{bmatrix} y_1^* \\ y_2^* \end{bmatrix} = \frac{e^t A^*(1)C_1}{|A(1)|} + \frac{e^{-t} A^*(-1)C_2}{|A(-1)|}$$

where $C_1 = (1, 0)$, $C_2 = (0, 3)$. Thus

$$\begin{bmatrix} y_1^* \\ y_2^* \end{bmatrix} = e^t \begin{bmatrix} \frac{5}{6} & -\frac{1}{2} \\ -\frac{1}{2} & \frac{1}{2} \end{bmatrix} \begin{bmatrix} 1 \\ 0 \end{bmatrix} + e^{-t} \begin{bmatrix} -\frac{3}{4} & \frac{1}{4} \\ \frac{1}{4} & \frac{1}{4} \end{bmatrix} \begin{bmatrix} 0 \\ 1 \end{bmatrix} = \begin{bmatrix} \frac{5}{6}e^t + \frac{1}{4}e^{-t} \\ -\frac{1}{2}e^t + \frac{1}{4}e^{-t} \end{bmatrix}$$

Check this answer.

Example 3.8

Compute a particular solution for

$$\begin{bmatrix} D+1 & D \\ 1 & 2D+1 \end{bmatrix} \begin{bmatrix} y_1 \\ y_2 \end{bmatrix} = \begin{bmatrix} 2t \\ 3t \end{bmatrix}$$

From (3.29), a particular solution for this case is

$$\begin{bmatrix} y_1^* \\ y_2^* \end{bmatrix} = \frac{\partial}{\partial \lambda} \left[\frac{e^{\lambda t} A^*(\lambda)}{|A(\lambda)|} \right] \begin{bmatrix} 2 \\ 3 \end{bmatrix}$$

evaluated at $\lambda = 0$. Carrying out these operations yields

$$\begin{bmatrix} y_1^* \\ y_2^* \end{bmatrix} = \begin{bmatrix} 2t - 3 \\ t + 1 \end{bmatrix}$$

Work this with E in place of D, using (3.28). Check all answers.

Example 3.9

Construct a particular solution for

$$\begin{bmatrix} 3 & -E+1 \\ E-1 & E-2 \end{bmatrix} \begin{bmatrix} y_{1t} \\ y_{2t} \end{bmatrix} = \begin{bmatrix} 1 \\ 2^t \end{bmatrix}$$

From (3.22), we have as a particular solution

$$\frac{\lambda_1^t A^*(\lambda_1)}{|A(\lambda_1)|} C_1 + \frac{\lambda_2^t A^*(\lambda_2)}{|A(\lambda_2)|} C_2$$

where in this problem $\lambda_1 = 2, \lambda_2 = 1, C_1 = (0, 1), C_2 = (1, 0)$, and

$$A^*(E) = \begin{bmatrix} E-2 & E-1 \\ -E+1 & 3 \end{bmatrix}$$

$$A^*(2) = \begin{bmatrix} 0 & 1 \\ -1 & 3 \end{bmatrix}$$

$$A^*(1) = \begin{bmatrix} -1 & 0 \\ 0 & 3 \end{bmatrix}$$

$$|A(\lambda_1)| = \begin{vmatrix} 3 & -1 \\ 1 & 0 \end{vmatrix} = 1$$

$$|A(\lambda_2)| = \begin{vmatrix} 3 & 0 \\ 0 & -1 \end{vmatrix} = 3$$

Thus

$$\begin{bmatrix} y^*_{1t} \\ y^*_{2t} \end{bmatrix} = 2^t \begin{bmatrix} 0 & 1 \\ -1 & 3 \end{bmatrix}\begin{bmatrix} 0 \\ 1 \end{bmatrix} + 1^t \begin{bmatrix} \frac{1}{3} & 0 \\ 0 & -1 \end{bmatrix}\begin{bmatrix} 1 \\ 0 \end{bmatrix} = \begin{bmatrix} 2^t + \frac{1}{3} \\ 3.2^t \end{bmatrix}$$

Check the solution. Work the problem with D in place of E and e^{2t} in place of 2^t.

3.6 TRIANGULARIZATION METHOD

An elegant alternative method of solving $A(D)y = f(t)$ or $A(E)y_t = f(t)$ is one which is very similar to the methods of solving systems of simultaneous algebraic equations. The technique hinges on the fact that it is possible to triangularize the matrix $A(D)$ or $A(E)$ by elementary row operations *without affecting the solutions of the system.* After converting the matrix into triangular form, the equation containing one dependent variable is solved, and then, working backwards, the solutions for the other variables are found step by step. If the polynomials in the operator are thought of as constants, this technique is similar to the Gaussian method.

Two comments should be made about this technique. First, no modification is required when there are multiple roots. Second, the method can be applied directly to the nonhomogeneous system; it is not essential to first find a complementary function and then a particular solution, although it can be used that way.

We will show that this method can be carried out by means of the following elementary row operations:

1. Interchanging any two rows.
2. Multiplying any row by a nonzero scalar.
3. Adding to any row another row multiplied by a polynomial in the operator.

It is obvious that the first two transformations do not affect the set of solutions, while the validity of the third remains to be established. (See the corollary to Theorem 3.34.)

In order to establish the legitimacy of these elementary operations, we first establish necessary and sufficient conditions for two systems of differential or difference equations to be *equivalent*, that is, to have the same solutions.† Let us write the two systems as follows:

(3.30) $$A_{r1}(Q)y_1 + A_{r2}(Q)y_2 + \cdots + A_{rm}(Q)y_m = f_r(t)$$

(3.31) $$B_{r1}(Q)y_1 + B_{r2}(Q)y_2 + \cdots + B_{rm}(Q)y_m = g_r(t)$$

$$(r = 1, 2, \ldots, m)$$

where $A_{rj}(Q)$ and $B_{rj}(Q)$ are polynomials in the operator, and the equations of both sets are assumed linearly independent. Bringing the right-hand terms to the left side, we can write (3.30) and (3.31) as

(3.32) $$U_r = 0$$
(3.33) $$W_r = 0$$ $$(r = 1, \ldots, m)$$

Suppose we write each equation of (3.33) as a combination of the equations of (3.32), as follows:

(3.34)
$$W_1 = a_{11}U_1 + a_{12}U_2 + \cdots + a_{1m}U_m$$
$$\vdots$$
$$W_m = a_{m1}U_1 + a_{m2}U_2 + \cdots + a_{mm}U_m$$

where a_{ij} are polynomials in Q. It is obvious that if (3.34) holds, every solution of (3.32) must be a solution of (3.33). The reverse may not be true—not every solution of (3.33) may be a solution of (3.32). Now if (3.32) and (3.33) are related as (3.34) indicates, we say that (3.33) is *derived* from (3.32). The matrix of this transformation

$$A(Q) \equiv \begin{bmatrix} a_{11}(Q) & a_{12}(Q) & \cdots & a_{1m}(Q) \\ \vdots & & & \vdots \\ a_{m1}(Q) & \cdots\cdots\cdots & & a_{mm}(Q) \end{bmatrix}$$

is called the *multiplier system* by means of which (3.33) is derived from (3.32). The determinant of A is called the *modulus* of the multiplier system. We may now prove the following theorem.

THEOREM 3.33

A NECESSARY AND SUFFICIENT CONDITION FOR (3.32) AND (3.33) TO BE EQUIVALENT IS THAT THE MODULUS OF THE MULTIPLIER SYSTEM BY MEANS OF WHICH EITHER

†See Ince [27, Chap. 6].

SYSTEM IS DERIVED FROM THE OTHER BE A CONSTANT (A POLYNOMIAL IN THE OPERATOR OF DEGREE ZERO).

PROOF:

Sufficiency. [If $|A(Q)|$ is a constant, then (3.32) and (3.33) are equivalent.] Write (3.34) in matrix form

$$W = AU$$

$$\text{where} \quad W = \begin{bmatrix} W_1 \\ \vdots \\ W_m \end{bmatrix}, \quad U = \begin{bmatrix} U_1 \\ \vdots \\ U_m \end{bmatrix}$$

Multiplying both sides of $W = AU$ by $A^*(Q)$, the adjoint matrix of $A(Q)$, we obtain

$$|A|U = A^* W$$

or

$$(3.35) \quad \begin{aligned} |A|U_1 &= A_{11}^* W_1 + A_{12}^* W_2 + \cdots + A_{1m}^* W_m \\ &\vdots \\ |A|U_m &= A_{m1}^* W_1 + A_{m2}^* W_2 + \cdots + A_{mm}^* W_m \end{aligned}$$

where A_{ij}^* is the ijth element of A^*. If we pick any solution $y(t)$ of (3.33), so that $W_r = 0$ for $r = 1, \ldots, m$, then the right side of (3.35) will vanish, indicating that $y(t)$ is a solution of $|A(Q)|U_r = 0$ for $r = 1, \ldots, m$. But this, by itself, does not mean that $y(t)$ is also a solution of $U_r = 0$. It will be, however, if $|A(Q)|$ is a constant, which is the hypothesis of this part of the proof. We have thus shown that every solution of (3.33) will also be a solution of (3.32), if the modulus of the multiplier system is a constant. As noted earlier, it is obvious that any solution of (3.32) is a solution of (3.33) under the transformation $A(Q)$. Sufficiency is thus established.

Necessity. Assume that (3.33) satisfies (3.32), that is, suppose that (3.32) is derived from (3.33). Then there exists a set of polynomials in the operator Q, b_{ij}, such that

$$(3.36) \quad \begin{aligned} U_1 &= b_{11} W_1 + \cdots + b_{1m} W_m \\ &\vdots \\ U_m &= b_{m1} W_1 + \cdots + b_{mm} W_m \end{aligned}$$

Substitute for $W_1, \ldots, W_m$ from (3.34), which gives

$$U_1 = b_{11}\left(\sum_{s=1}^{m} a_{1s}U_s\right) + \cdots + b_{1m}\left(\sum_{s=1}^{m} a_{ms}U_s\right)$$

(3.37) $\qquad \vdots \qquad\qquad \vdots$

$$U_m = b_{m1}\left(\sum_{s=1}^{m} a_{1s}U_s\right) + \cdots + b_{mm}\left(\sum_{s=1}^{m} a_{ms}U_s\right)$$

Rewriting (3.37) in order to employ the assumed fact that $U_1, \ldots, U_m$ are linearly independent equations gives

(3.38)

$$\left(\sum_{r=1}^{m} b_{1r}a_{r1} - 1\right)U_1 + \left(\sum_{r=1}^{m} b_{1r}a_{r2}\right)U_2 + \cdots + \left(\sum_{r=1}^{m} b_{1r}a_{rm}\right)U_m = 0$$

$$\left(\sum_{r=1}^{m} b_{2r}a_{r1}\right)U_1 + \left(\sum_{r=1}^{m} b_{2r}a_{r2} - 1\right)U_2 + \cdots + \left(\sum_{r=1}^{m} b_{2r}a_{rm}\right)U_m = 0$$

$$\cdots\cdots\cdots\cdots\cdots\cdots\cdots\cdots\cdots\cdots\cdots\cdots\cdots\cdots\cdots\cdots\cdots\cdots\cdots$$

$$\left(\sum_{r=1}^{m} b_{mr}a_{r1}\right)U_1 + \cdots + \left(\sum_{r=1}^{m} b_{mr}a_{rm} - 1\right)U_m = 0$$

which implies that

(3.39) $\qquad \displaystyle\sum_{r=1}^{m} b_{jr}a_{rk} = 0, j \neq k, j, k = 1, \ldots, m$

$$\sum_{r=1}^{m} b_{jr}a_{rj} = 1, j = 1, \ldots, m$$

Now fix j and we have m systems of equations

(3.40) $\qquad b_{j1}a_{11} + b_{j2}a_{12} + \cdots + b_{jm}a_{m1} = 0$

$\qquad\qquad b_{j1}a_{12} + b_{j2}a_{22} + \cdots + b_{jm}a_{m2} = 0$

$\qquad\qquad \vdots \qquad\qquad\qquad \vdots$

$\qquad\qquad b_{j1}a_{1,j-1} + b_{j2}a_{2,j-1} + \cdots + b_{jm}a_{m,j-1} = 0$

$\qquad\qquad b_{j1}a_{1j} + b_{j2}a_{2j} + \cdots + b_{jm}a_{mj} = 1$

$\qquad\qquad \vdots \qquad\qquad\qquad \vdots$

$\qquad\qquad b_{j1}a_{1m} + b_{j2}a_{2m} + \cdots + b_{jm}a_{mm} = 0$

Using vector-matrix notation, the system of m equations in (3.40) can be written as

(3.41) $\qquad\qquad\qquad b_j'A = e_j$

where b_j' is the row vector of polynomials $(b_{j1}, \ldots, b_{jm})$, and e_j is the jth unit vector. Then it is easy to see that the m^2 equations in (3.39) can be written

(3.42) $$BA = I$$

where B is the matrix of the multiplier system in (3.36). From (3.42) it follows that

(3.43) $$|B||A| = 1$$

Since both moduli are polynomials in Q, this last identity can only be satisfied if both $|B|$ and $|A|$ do not contain Q; that is, they both must be constants.

Q.E.D.

THEOREM 3.34

ANY SYSTEM OF INDEPENDENT LINEAR DIFFERENTIAL OR DIFFERENCE EQUATIONS CAN BE TRANSFORMED INTO AN *equivalent* TRIANGULAR SYSTEM. THAT IS, (3.30) CAN BE TRANSFORMED INTO

(3.44)
$$B_{11}(Q)y_1 + B_{12}(Q)y_2 + \cdots + B_{1m}(Q)y_m = g_1(t)$$
$$B_{22}(Q)y_2 + \cdots + B_{2m}(Q)y_m = g_2(t)$$
$$B_{33}(Q)y_t + \cdots + B_{3m}(Q)y_t = g_3(t)$$
$$\cdots\cdots\cdots\cdots\cdots\cdots\cdots\cdots\cdots\cdots$$
$$B_{mm}(Q)y_m = g_m(t)$$

PROOF:

We need only prove that any two equations can be replaced by two equivalent equations with one of the dependent variables eliminated. The theorem then follows by repetition of this process.

Consider two equations from (3.32), say,

(3.45)
$$U_1 \equiv A_{11}(Q)y_1 + \cdots + A_{1m}(Q)y_m - f_1(t) = 0$$
$$U_2 \equiv A_{21}(Q)y_1 + \cdots + A_{2m}(Q)y_m - f_2(t) = 0$$

Now consider the derived equations

(3.46)
$$W_1 = a_{11}U_1 + a_{12}U_2$$
$$W_2 = a_{21}U_1 + a_{22}U_2$$

where a_{ij} are polynomials in Q and

$$\begin{bmatrix} a_{11} & a_{12} \\ a_{21} & a_{22} \end{bmatrix}$$

is the multiplier system of this transformation. By Theorem 3.33, if the two pairs of equations are equivalent, the modulus of the multiplier system must be a constant, thus

$$\begin{vmatrix} a_{11} & a_{12} \\ a_{21} & a_{22} \end{vmatrix} = a_{11}a_{22} - a_{12}a_{21} = k$$

where k is a constant.

Next, let $F(Q)$ be a greatest common divisor of $A_{11}(Q)$ and $A_{21}(Q)$, which appear in (3.45). [$F(Q)$ could of course be a zero degree polynomial.] By the definition of a g.c.d. we can factor A_{11} and A_{21} into

$$A_{11}(Q) = F(Q)H(Q)$$
$$A_{21}(Q) = F(Q)G(Q)$$

where $H(Q)$ and $G(Q)$ are relatively prime (that is, their g.c.d.'s are constants).†

In the multiplier system, let

$$a_{11} = G(Q), a_{12} = -H(Q)$$

It follows from W_1 in (3.46), with these values of a_{11} and a_{12}, that W_1 will have no term in y_1. That is,

$$W_1 = G(Q)[F(Q)H(Q)y_1 + \cdots] - H(Q)[F(Q)G(Q)y_1 + \cdots]$$

All that we need show now is that two polynomials, a_{21} and a_{22}, can be found so that

$$a_{11}a_{22} - a_{12}a_{21} = k$$

Since $G(Q)$ and $H(Q)$ are relatively prime, we know by Theorem 3.5 that the two required polynomials a_{21} and a_{22} can be found.

By induction, it is easy to see that a triangular system equivalent to (3.30) can be generated.

Q.E.D.

This discussion allows us to establish the following corollary.

Corollary. By application of the elementary row operations defined at the beginning of this section, a system of independent linear differential or

---

†If $H(Q)$ and $G(Q)$ had a common factor which was a polynomial of degree greater than zero, then $F(Q)$ would not be a g.c.d. of $A_{11}(Q)$ and $A_{21}(Q)$.

difference equations can always be transformed into an equivalent triangular system.

PROOF:

We shall show that the multiplier system is a set of elementary row operations. We do this by deriving (3.46) from (3.45) by applying elementary row operations to (3.45).

Perform the following elementary operations to obtain W_1. Multiply U_2 by some polynomial b and add to U_1, giving a new U_1

$$U_1^* \equiv U_1 + bU_2$$

Observe that the multiplier system for this elementary operation is

$$\begin{bmatrix} 1 & b \\ 0 & 1 \end{bmatrix}$$

whose modulus is a constant, which by Theorem 3.33 proves the validity of this elementary operation. Next, multiply U_1^* by a_{11} and add to (the so far unchanged) U_2, giving a new U_2.

$$U_2^* \equiv a_{11}U_1 + a_{11}bU_2 + U_2$$

Letting $U_2^* \equiv W_1$, we have

$$W_1 = a_{11}U_1 + a_{12}U_2$$

where $a_{12} \equiv (a_{11}b + 1)$. The multiplier system for this elementary operation can be seen to be

$$\begin{bmatrix} 1 & 0 \\ a_{11} & 1 \end{bmatrix}$$

whose modulus is a constant.

So far, we have transformed (3.45) into an equivalent system consisting of W_1 and U_1^*. To obtain W_2, multiply W_1 by a polynomial c and add to U_1^*, which yields a new U_1^*, called W_2

$$\begin{aligned} W_2 &\equiv cW_1 + U_1^* \\ &= (ca_{11} + 1)U_1 + (ca_{12} + b)U_2 \\ &= a_{21}U_1 + a_{22}U_2 \end{aligned}$$

Where, by definition

$$a_{21} = ca_{11} + 1$$
$$a_{22} = ca_{12} + b$$

The multiplier system for this last elementary operation is

$$\begin{bmatrix} 1 & 0 \\ c & 1 \end{bmatrix}$$

whose modulus is once again a constant.

We have thus derived (3.46) from (3.45) by elementary row operations. If we now employ the reasoning in the proof of the previous theorem, the corollary is established. [That is, by appropriately defining the a_{ij} in (3.46), (3.45) is replaced by the equivalent (3.46) with one of the dependent variables eliminated.]

Q.E.D.

Another form of Theorem 3.33 is now required in order to prove the fundamental theorem which will follow.

THEOREM 3.35

THE CHARACTERISTIC DETERMINANTS OF TWO EQUIVALENT SYSTEMS WILL DIFFER BY A CONSTANT.† [THE CHARACTERISTIC DETERMINANT OF THE SYSTEM $A(D)y = f(t)$ IS THE DETERMINANT OF $A(D)$.]

PROOF:

Consider the homogeneous forms of (3.30) and (3.31). Next, consider (3.34), where we substitude the homogeneous form of (3.30) for the U_i. Deleting the operator for simplicity, this gives the identities

$$W_r = a_{r1}\left(\sum_{j=1}^{m} A_{1j}y_j\right) + \cdots + a_{rm}\left(\sum_{j=1}^{m} A_{mj}y_j\right)$$
$$(r = 1, \ldots, m)$$

Substituting from (3.31) for W_r, and equating the operators on y_j gives for $r = 1, \ldots, m$‡

$$\begin{bmatrix} B_{r1} \\ \vdots \\ B_{rm} \end{bmatrix} = \begin{bmatrix} A_{11} & A_{21} & \cdots & A_{m1} \\ \vdots & & & \vdots \\ A_{1m} & & \cdots & A_{mm} \end{bmatrix} \begin{bmatrix} a_{r1} \\ \vdots \\ a_{rm} \end{bmatrix}$$

†Since these characteristic determinants are polynomials in the operator, this theorem says that the characteristic polynomials (or equations) of two equivalent systems have the same degree.

‡This follows because the last set of equations are identities.

Thus

$$
\begin{bmatrix} B_{11}B_{21} & \cdots & B_{m1} \\ \vdots & & \vdots \\ B_{1m} & \cdots & B_{mm} \end{bmatrix} = \begin{bmatrix} A_{11}A_{21} & \cdots & A_{m1} \\ \vdots & & \vdots \\ A_{1m} & \cdots & A_{mm} \end{bmatrix} \begin{bmatrix} a_{11}a_{21} & \cdots & a_{m1} \\ \vdots & & \vdots \\ a_{1m} & \cdots & a_{mm} \end{bmatrix}
$$

Transposing and taking determinants gives

$$
\begin{vmatrix} B_{11} & \cdots & B_{1m} \\ \vdots & & \\ B_{m1} & \cdots & B_{mm} \end{vmatrix} = \begin{vmatrix} a_{11} & \cdots & a_{1m} \\ & & \\ a_{m1} & \cdots & a_{mm} \end{vmatrix} \begin{vmatrix} A_{11} & \cdots & A_{1m} \\ & & \\ A_{m1} & \cdots & A_{mm} \end{vmatrix}
$$

where the first determinant on the right is the modulus of the multiplier system and the other determinants are the characteristic determinants of systems (3.30) and (3.31). By Theorem (3.33), the modulus is a constant if the two systems are equivalent.

Q.E.D.

By combining these results with the theory of the single equation (section 3.4), we have in fact established a basic result. We state it as the following theorem.

THEOREM 3.36   FUNDAMENTAL THEOREM

THE NUMBER OF LINEARLY INDEPENDENT SOLUTIONS IN THE GENERAL SOLUTION OF THE HOMOGENEOUS FORM OF AN INDEPENDENT SET OF LINEAR DIFFERENTIAL OR DIFFERENCE EQUATIONS IS EQUAL TO THE DEGREE OF THE CHARACTERISTIC DETERMINANT.

PROOF:

Suppose that the homogeneous form of (3.30) has been transformed by elementary operations into an equivalent triangular system (3.44), where $B_{ii}(Q) = 1$ for $i = 1, \ldots, m - 1$.† By Theorem 3.35, these equivalent systems have characteristic equations of the same degree. Suppose the degree of $B_{mm}(Q)$ is n. Thus, the last equation in the triangular system, $B_{mm}(Q)y_m = 0$, can be solved by single equation techniques. By the theory of the single equation discussed in section 3.4, the general solution of this equation will be of the form $C_1 y_1(t) + \cdots + C_n y_n(t)$, where the C_i are arbitrary constants and $(y_1(t), \ldots, y_n(t))$ is a fundamental solution set. Now substitute this solution for y_m into the second last equation and solve for y_{m-1}, which gives

†The argument is similar if $B_{ii}(Q)$, $i = 1, \ldots, m - 1$, are polynomials of positive degree.

$$y_{m-1} = -B_{m-1,m}(Q)[C_1 y_1(t) + , \ldots, + C_n y_1(t)]$$

Since this is not a difference or differential equation in y_{m-1}, no new arbitrary constants are introduced.† Moreover, the right side of this expression is a solution of the last equation. Since the term in brackets satisfies the last equation identically, by definition of a solution, it follows that any polynomial operator multiplying this solution will also satisfy the last equation.‡ Therefore, the solution of the second last equation is a linear combination of the same fundamental solution set as the solution for the last equation. It can thus be written as

$$C_1^* y_1(t) + \ldots + C_n^* y_n(t)$$

where, since there are only n arbitrary constants, C_i^* must be a multiple of C_i for $i = 1, \ldots, n$. We could therefore write the solution for the second last equation as $k_1 C_1 y_1(t) + \cdots + k_n C_n y_n(t)$, where the k_i are *specific* constants. It follows, by applying the same reasoning to the rest of the variables, that the complementary function for $A(Q)y = 0$ will be

$$\sum_1^n C_i K_i y_i(t)$$

where the C_i are arbitrary constants, the K_i are m-vectors of specific constants, and $(y_1(t), \ldots, y_n(t))$ is a fundamental solution set.

Q.E.D.

Remark. There is an interesting difference between differential and difference equations which must be kept in mind when applying this theorem. For difference equations, the degree of the characteristic equation must be computed net of all zero roots of that equation, while the degree of the characteristic equation for differential equations must include zero roots. The reason for this distinction is that, for difference equations, the only solution corresponding to a zero root is zero, which is linearly dependent on any other solution. For differential equations, if the characteristic equation has a zero root of multiplicity r, then there are r linearly independent solutions corresponding to that root, viz., $1, t, t^2, \ldots, t^{r-1}$. (The Wronskian of these solutions at $t = 0$ is the unit matrix.) Thus, for example, if we had a characteristic matrix

---

†Notice that $B_{m-1,m}$ may have a polynomial in its denominator. This does not affect the argument by the definition of an inverse operator, plus the fact that a particular solution involves no arbitrary constants.

‡This assumes that two polynomial operators can be interchanged without affecting the result. Proof of this is left for the reader.

$$\begin{bmatrix} Q^2 & 1 \\ Q^2 & Q \end{bmatrix}$$

we would expect a fundamental solution set with three solutions for $Q = D$, but with only one solution for $Q = E$.

We see then that the triangularization method leads to a single equation, the solution of which leads to another single equation, and so on. Moreover, *the method yields the correct number of arbitrary constants*, since it does not increase the degree of the characteristic polynomial and thus generate redundant solution vectors. This is a practical advantage of the technique, as compared to another elimination method which introduces extraneous constants. We shall consider this other method after Example 3.10, which demonstrates the triangularization method.

Example 3.10

Solve

$$4y_1 + (3D - 1)y_2 = t$$
$$-Dy_1 + Dy_2 = t - 1$$

The degree of the characteristic polynomial is 2, hence, by the fundamental theorem, we should have 2 linearly independent solutions in the complementary function, and two arbitrary constants.

Multiply the first equation by $D/4$ and add to the second equation. This gives the equivalent triangular system

$$4y_1 + (3D - 1)y_2 = t$$
$$\tfrac{3}{4}(D^2 + D)y_2 = t - \tfrac{3}{4}$$

Solving the second equation for y_2 gives, as the general solution

$$y_2(t) = C_1 + C_2 e^{-t} + \tfrac{2}{3}t^2 - \tfrac{7}{3}t$$

where C_1 and C_2 are the arbitrary constants, and $(1, e^{-t})$ is a solution set, whose Wronskian at $t = 0$ is

$$\begin{vmatrix} 1 & 1 \\ 0 & -1 \end{vmatrix} \neq 0$$

which guarantees that these solutions are a fundamental solution set. The term $2/3(t^2) - 7/3(t)$ is a particular solution.†

Substituting $y_2(t)$ into the first equation of the triangular form gives

$$y_1 = -\frac{1}{4}(3D - 1)\left[C_1 + C_2 e^{-t} + \frac{2}{3}t^2 - \frac{7}{3}t\right] + \frac{t}{4}$$

Carrying out the indicated operation yields the general solution for y_1.

$$y_1(t) = \tfrac{1}{4}C_1 + C_2 e^{-t} + \tfrac{1}{6}t^2 - \tfrac{4}{3}t + \tfrac{7}{4}$$

Now we shall try another kind of elimination method that is also similar to the way we eliminate variables from a system of algebraic equation. Consider the algebraic system

$$3x - 2y = 4$$
$$2x + 3y = 7$$

A common procedure for solving such a system is to multiply the first equation by 2 and the second equation by -3 and then add, thus eliminating x. If we apply the same type of operation to $A(Q)y = f(t)$, it will work, but superfluous constants will generally be introduced. The reason is that this operation—multiplying two equations by a polynomial operator and adding—which is *not* one of the elementary operations defined in this section, changes the degree of the characteristic equation, while none of the elementary operations employed in the triangularization method do. Applying this alternative elimination method to Example 3.10, we shall see how additional constants creep in and how we shall have to engage in the tedious and time-consuming task of eliminating them, by determining how they are related—that is, by isolating linearly dependent solution vectors and eliminating them. This exercise will give us a heightened appreciation of the triangularization method, and will serve to emphasize operations that should not be used in eliminating variables, viz., simply multiplying an equation by a polynomial operator or multiplying two equations by same and adding.

To illustrate, multiply the first equation of the system in Example 3.10 by D, which gives

(i)
$$4Dy_1 + (3D^2 - D)y_2 = 1$$
$$-Dy_1 + Dy_2 = t - 1$$

We have just raised the degree of the characteristic equation from 2 to 3. (We

†An easy way to obtain this is to use $At^2 + Bt + c$ as a trial solution and employ the method of undermined coefficients. See Baumol [7, Chap. 10].

emphasize that this operation is not used in the triangularization technique, whose elementary operations do not alter the degree of the characteristic equation.) Next, multiply the second equation by 4 and add, which gives

$$(3D^2 + 3D)y_2 = 4t - 3$$

Solving this equation gives

$$y_2(t) = C_1 + C_2 e^{-t} + \tfrac{2}{3} t^2 - \tfrac{7}{3} t$$

Substituting into the second equation of (i) gives

$$y_1(t) = C_2 e^{-t} + C_3 + \frac{t^2}{6} - \frac{4}{3} t$$

Notice that we have three arbitrary constants, while the theory tells us we should have two. To find the relationship among the three constants, we use the fact that the solution of a system of equations consists of a set of functions which, by definition, satisfies each equation of the system identically. Since $y_1(t)$ was obtained by substituting $y_2(t)$ into the second equation of (i), which is the second equation of the original system, we know that $y_1(t)$ and $y_2(t)$ already satisfy this equation identically. Hence, substitute $y_1(t)$ and $y_2(t)$ into the first equation of the original system. This gives, after performing the indicated operations, the required relationship

$$C_3 = \frac{C_1 + 7}{4}$$

Substituting into $y_1(t)$ gives the corrected solution, which can be seen as identical to that obtained by the triangularization method. The latter is the only method we will use in the examples which follow.

Example 3.11

Solve

$$(E + 1)y_{1t} + (E + 1)y_{2t} = 2^t$$
$$Ey_{1t} - y_{2t} = 4t$$

Subtract the second equation from the first, which gives

$$y_{1t} + (E + 2)y_{2t} = 2^t - 4t$$
$$Ey_{1t} - y_{2t} = 4t$$

Multiply the first equation by E and subtract the result from the second. This yields an equivalent triangular system

$$y_{1t} + (E + 2)y_{2t} = 2^t - 4t$$
$$-(E^2 + 2E + 1)y_{2t} = -2(2)^t + 8t + 4$$

Solving the second equation, we have

$$y_2(t) = C_1(-1)^t + C_2 t(-1)^t + \tfrac{2}{9}(2)^t - 2t + 1$$

Substituting this solution for y_{2t} into the first equation of the triangular form and performing the indicated operation gives

$$y_1(t) = -C_1(-1)^t + C_2(1 - t)(-1)^t + \tfrac{1}{9}(2)^t + 2t - 1$$

The solutions in the complementary function are $(-1)^t$ and $t(-1)^t$, whose Wronskian at $t = 0$ is

$$\begin{vmatrix} 1 & 0 \\ -1 & -1 \end{vmatrix} \neq 0$$

hence these solutions constitute a fundamental set.

To obtain a unique solution for this problem, we must have some boundary conditions for y_{1t} and y_{2t}. Suppose we know the initial values of these variables, that is, that $y_1(0) = y_{10}$ and $y_2(0) = y_{20}$, where y_{10} and y_{20} are specific values. Then, from the general solution $y_1(t)$ and $y_2(t)$, we have that

$$y_{10} = -C_1 + C_2 - \tfrac{8}{9}$$
$$y_{20} = C_1 + \tfrac{11}{9}$$

which can be solved uniquely for C_1 and C_2.

Example 3.12

Solve

$$D^2 y_1 - Dy_2 = 1 - t$$
$$(D - 1)y_1 + 2Dy_2 = 4e^t$$

Multiply the first equation by 2 and add to the second, which gives an equivalent triangular form

$$D^2 y_1 - Dy_2 = 1 - t$$
$$(2D^2 + D - 1)y_1 = 4e^t + 2 - 2t$$

Solving the second equation, we have

$$y_1(t) = C_1 e^{-t} + C_2 e^{1/2t} + 2e^t + 2t$$

Substituting into the first equation of the triangular form and solving gives

$$y_2(t) = -C_1 e^{-t} + \frac{C_2}{2} e^{1/2t} + C_3 + 2e^t + \frac{t^2}{2} - t$$

Check the solution and then work the problem with E in place of D and 2^t in place of e^t. Check the Wronskian at $t = 0$.

Example 3.13

Solve

$$\begin{bmatrix} E-4 & -1 & -2 \\ 1 & E-1 & 1 \\ 3 & 1 & E+1 \end{bmatrix} \begin{bmatrix} y_{1t} \\ y_{2t} \\ y_{3t} \end{bmatrix} = \begin{bmatrix} 3^t \\ 0 \\ 5 \cdot 4^t \end{bmatrix}$$

It will be convenient to write the augmented matrix of the system and operate on it.

$$\begin{bmatrix} E-4 & -1 & -2 & : & 3^t \\ 1 & E-1 & 1 & : & 0 \\ 3 & 1 & E+1 & : & 5 \cdot 4^t \end{bmatrix}$$

Multiply the second row by $E - 4$ and subtract from the first row; then multiply the second row by 3 and subtract from the third row. Next, interchange the second with the new first row. The result of these operations is

$$\begin{bmatrix} 1 & E-1 & 1 & : & 0 \\ 0 & -E^2+5E-5 & -E+2 & : & 3^t \\ 0 & -3E+4 & E-2 & : & 5 \cdot 4^t \end{bmatrix}$$

Divide the last row by 3. We may now replace $-E^2 + 5E - 5$ with 1. To do this, factor this term into something containing $-E + 4/3$. Dividing the latter into $-E^2 + 5E - 5$ gives

$$-E^2 + 5E - 5 = (-E + \tfrac{4}{3})(E - \tfrac{11}{3}) - \tfrac{1}{9}$$

Thus, multiply the last row by $E - 11/3$ and subtract from row two. This gives

$$\begin{bmatrix} 1 & E-1 & 1 & \vdots & 0 \\ 0 & -\dfrac{1}{9} & \dfrac{1}{9}(-3E^2+8E-4) & \vdots & 3^t-\dfrac{5}{9}\cdot 4^t \\ 0 & -E+\dfrac{4}{3} & \dfrac{E-2}{3} & \vdots & \dfrac{5}{3}\cdot 4^t \end{bmatrix}$$

Now multiply the second row by -9. Then multiply the result by $(-E+4/3)$ and subtract from the third row, which yields the triangular form

$$\begin{bmatrix} 1 & E-1 & 1 & \vdots & 0 \\ 0 & 1 & 3E^2-8E+4 & \vdots & -9\cdot 3^t+5\cdot 4^t \\ 0 & 0 & 3E^3-12E^2+15E-6 & \vdots & \tfrac{5}{27}\cdot 4^t+\tfrac{5}{3}\cdot 3^t \end{bmatrix}$$

Solving the last equation gives

$$y_3(t) = C_1 + C_2 t + C_3 \cdot 2^t + \tfrac{5}{1458}\cdot 4^t + \tfrac{5}{36}\cdot 3^t$$

The solutions in the complementary function are $(1, t, 2^t)$. The Wronskian, evaluated at $t = 0$, is

$$\begin{vmatrix} 1 & 0 & 1 \\ 1 & 1 & 2 \\ 1 & 2 & 4 \end{vmatrix} \neq 0$$

which guarantees that these solutions are a fundamental set. The computation of $y_2(t)$ and $y_1(t)$ is left to the reader, along with a check on the solutions.

3.7 ECONOMIC EXAMPLES

Example 3.14   Macroeconomic Model

Consider the following simple Keynesian Model:†

(3.47) $C_t = C_0 + a_{11} Y_t + a_{12} Y_{t-1}$

(3.48) $I_t = I_0 + a_{21} Y_t + a_{22} Y_{t-1} + a_{23} r_t + a_{24} r_{t-1}$

(3.49) $G_t = G_0 \lambda_1^{t-1}$

(3.50) $Y_t = E_t \equiv C_t + I_t + G_t$

(3.51) $M_t^* = a_{31} + a_{32} Y_t + a_{33} Y_{t-1} + a_{34} r_t + a_{35} r_{t-1}$

†For symbols, see section 3.1, and for a discussion of the model see section 1.2.

(3.52) $\qquad M_t = M_0 \lambda_2^{t-1}$

(3.53) $\qquad M_t^* = M_t$

This model might not be realistic. For example, the lag structure arbitrarily assumes that lags of two or more periods do not exist. In addition, both the goods and money markets are always assumed to be in equilibrium, which might not be the case. Making the model more realistic in any of these aspects would increase the size of the characteristic matrix and, usually, the degree of the characteristic polynomial.

Substituting (3.47) through (3.49) into (3.50), and (3.51) and (3.52) into (3.53) gives

(3.54) $\quad (1 - a_{11} - a_{21})Y_t - (a_{12} + a_{22})Y_{t-1} - a_{23}r_t - a_{24}r_{t-1}$

$\qquad\qquad = C_0 + I_0 + G_0 \lambda_1^{t-1}$

(3.55) $\quad a_{32}Y_t + a_{33}Y_{t-1} + a_{34}r_t + a_{35}r_{t-1} = -a_{31} + M_0 \lambda_2^{t-1}$

In matrix form and using the shift operator E, we have

(3.56) $\qquad \begin{bmatrix} (1 - a_{11} - a_{21})E - (a_{12} + a_{22}) & (-a_{23}E - a_{24}) \\ a_{32}E + a_{33} & a_{34}E + a_{35} \end{bmatrix} \begin{bmatrix} Y_t \\ r_t \end{bmatrix}$

$\qquad\qquad = \begin{bmatrix} C_0 + I_0 + G_0 \lambda_1^t \\ -a_{31} + M_0 \lambda_2^t \end{bmatrix}$

Assume that the following values have been estimated for the structural parameters:

$$a_{11} + a_{21} = .5$$
$$a_{12} + a_{22} = .2$$
$$a_{32} = .2$$
$$a_{33} = .1$$
$$a_{23} = -3$$
$$a_{24} = -1$$
$$a_{34} = -2$$
$$a_{35} = -1$$

Substituting into the homogeneous form of (3.56) gives

(3.57) $\qquad \begin{bmatrix} \frac{1}{2}E - \frac{1}{5} & 3E + 1 \\ \frac{1}{5}E + \frac{1}{10} & -2E - 1 \end{bmatrix} \begin{bmatrix} Y_t \\ r_t \end{bmatrix} = \begin{bmatrix} 0 \\ 0 \end{bmatrix}$

The characteristic equation is $|A(x)| = -(8/5)x^2 - (6/10)x + (1/10)$, and the roots are

$$x_1 = -\tfrac{1}{2}$$
$$x_2 = \tfrac{1}{8}$$

Solving (3.57) by the adjoint matrix method, the adjoint matrix is

$$A^*(x) = \begin{bmatrix} -2x - 1 & -3x - 1 \\ -\tfrac{1}{5}x - \tfrac{1}{10} & \tfrac{1}{2}x - \tfrac{1}{5} \end{bmatrix}$$

To find the vector corresponding to the simple root $x_1 = -1/2$, we see that

$$A^*(-\tfrac{1}{2}) = \begin{bmatrix} 0 & \tfrac{1}{2} \\ 0 & -\tfrac{9}{20} \end{bmatrix}$$

and to find the vector corresponding to $x_2 = 1/8$ we have

$$A^*(\tfrac{1}{8}) = \begin{bmatrix} -\tfrac{5}{4} & -\tfrac{11}{8} \\ -\tfrac{1}{8} & -\tfrac{11}{80} \end{bmatrix}$$

which yields the single independent vector we need (the second column is $11/10$ times the first column).

The complementary function is thus

$$\begin{bmatrix} Y_t \\ r_t \end{bmatrix} = C_1(-\tfrac{1}{2})^t \begin{bmatrix} \tfrac{1}{2} \\ -\tfrac{9}{20} \end{bmatrix} + C_2(\tfrac{1}{8})^t \begin{bmatrix} -\tfrac{5}{4} \\ -\tfrac{1}{8} \end{bmatrix}$$

Now we calculate a particular solution. Suppose that the following values have been obtained:

$$C_0 + I_0 = 100$$
$$a_{31} = 100$$

and suppose—to simplify further—that $\lambda_1 = \lambda_2 = \lambda$, and that $G_0 = 75$ and $M_0 = 50$. Using the adjoint matrix technique, and employing the principle of superposition, the expression for a particular solution is†

---

†This assumes that the roots are not equal to 1 or to λ, which is to be expected if the system is stable, as this one is. If both government spending and the money supply grow at 5 per cent, λ would equal 1.05.

Another way of computing a particular solution would be to use the trial solutions $Y_t^* = b_{11} + b_{12}\lambda^t$ and $r_t^* = b_{21} + b_{22}\lambda^t$ and solve for the b's by the method of undetermined coefficients.

$$\begin{bmatrix} Y_t^* \\ r_t^* \end{bmatrix} = \frac{A^*(1)}{|A(1)|} K_1 + \lambda^t \frac{A^*(\lambda)}{|A(\lambda)|} K_2$$

where $K_1 = (100, -100)$, and $K_2 = (75, 50)$. Carrying out these operations, we obtain as a particular solution

$$Y_t^* = \frac{-1000}{21} + \left[\frac{-10(300\lambda + 125)}{(-8\lambda + 1)(2\lambda + 1)} \right] \lambda^t$$

$$r_t^* = \frac{200}{7} + \left[\frac{5(20\lambda - 35)}{(-8\lambda + 1)(2\lambda + 1)} \right] \lambda^t$$

A general solution is obtained by adding this particular solution to the complementary function.

Let us now solve (3.56) by triangularization. The augmented matrix is

$$\begin{bmatrix} \frac{1}{2}E - \frac{1}{5} & 3E + 1 & : & 100 + 75\lambda^t \\ \frac{1}{5}E + \frac{1}{10} & -2E - 1 & : & -100 + 50\lambda^t \end{bmatrix}$$

Subtracting 5/2 the second row from the first gives

$$\begin{bmatrix} -\frac{9}{20} & 8E + \frac{7}{2} & : & 350 - 50\lambda^t \\ \frac{1}{5}E + \frac{1}{10} & -2E - 1 & : & -100 + 50\lambda^t \end{bmatrix}$$

Multiply the first row by $-20/9$. Then multiply the first row by $[(1/5)E + 1/10]$ and subtract from second row. Then multiply the new second row by 9. We thus have the triangular form

$$\begin{bmatrix} 1 & -\frac{20}{9}(8E + \frac{7}{2}) & : & -\frac{20}{9}(350 - 50\lambda^t) \\ 0 & (16E - 2)(2E + 1) & : & 50(-4\lambda + 7)\lambda^t + 1200 \end{bmatrix}$$

We now solve the equation for r_t, which is

$$(16E - 2)(2E + 1)r_t = 50(-4\lambda + 7)\lambda^t + 1200$$

The complementary function can immediately be seen to be

$$K_1(-\tfrac{1}{2})^t + K_2(\tfrac{1}{8})^t$$

As for a particular solution, try

$$r_t^* = a\lambda^t + b$$

where a and b are constants to be determined.

Substituting into the equation for r_t gives

$$(16\lambda - 2)(2\lambda + 1)a\lambda^t + 42b = 50(-4\lambda + 7)\lambda^t + 1200$$

thus

$$a = \frac{50(-4\lambda + 7)}{(16\lambda - 2)(2\lambda + 1)}$$

$$= \frac{25(4\lambda - 7)}{(-8\lambda + 1)(2\lambda + 1)}$$

$$b = \frac{200}{7}$$

A complete solution is

$$r(t) = K_1 \left(-\frac{1}{2}\right)^t + K_2 \left(\frac{1}{8}\right)^t + \frac{25(4\lambda - 7)}{(-8\lambda + 1)(2\lambda + 1)}\lambda^t + \frac{200}{7}$$

Substituting this into the first equation of a triangular form yields the solution for Y_t.

$$Y(t) = \frac{-10}{9} K_1 \left(-\frac{1}{2}\right)^t + 10K_2 \left(\frac{1}{8}\right)^t$$

$$- 10 \left[\frac{300\lambda + 125}{(-8\lambda + 1)(2\lambda + 1)}\right]\lambda^t - \frac{1000}{21}$$

To see that this solution is identical with that obtained by the adjoint matrix method, we rewrite that solution, writing C_1 and C_2 instead of K_1 and K_2.

$$Y_t = \frac{1}{2} C_1 \left(-\frac{1}{2}\right)^t - \frac{5}{4} C_2 \left(\frac{1}{8}\right)^t - 10 \left[\frac{300\lambda + 125}{(-8\lambda + 1)(2\lambda + 1)}\right]\lambda^t - \frac{1000}{21}$$

$$r_t = \frac{-9}{20} C_1 \left(-\frac{1}{2}\right)^t - \frac{1}{8} C_2 \left(\frac{1}{8}\right)^t + 25 \left[\frac{4\lambda - 7}{(8\lambda + 1)(2\lambda + 1)}\right]\lambda^t + \frac{200}{7}$$

letting

$$C_1 = -\frac{20}{9} K_1$$

$$C_2 = -8K_2$$

We can see the two solutions are identical.

Since the modulus of both roots is less than unity, the values of the complementary function will eventually vanish, and the system will converge to a moving equilibrium, involving growth at $\lambda - 1$ per cent. The negative root will serve to impart an oscillatory element into the trajectory of Y and r, which will steadily diminish in amplitude. To obtain precise pictures of the trajectories, it is necessary to give λ a value, and to introduce initial values for Y and r, which will then yield unique values for the C's or K's.

Problem. Let $\lambda = 1.05$, $Y_0 = 600$, and $r_0 = .04$ in the above macroeconomic model. Compute the solution values for Y_t and r_t for the first several periods.

Example 3.15   A Market for a Single Commodity

Consider a single market with the following lag structure:†

$$
\begin{bmatrix}
E^2 & 0 & -(a_{11}E^2 + a_{12}E + a_{13}) \\
0 & E^2 & -(a_{21}E^2 + a_{22}E + a_{23}) \\
-\lambda E & \lambda E & E^2 - E
\end{bmatrix}
\begin{bmatrix}
D_t \\
S_t \\
P_t
\end{bmatrix}
=
\begin{bmatrix}
a\lambda_1^t \\
b\lambda_1^t \\
0
\end{bmatrix}
$$

Assume that we have the following estimates for the structural parameters:

$$\lambda = \tfrac{1}{12}$$
$$a_{11} = -\tfrac{1}{2}$$
$$a_{12} = -\tfrac{1}{3}$$
$$a_{13} = -\tfrac{1}{4}$$
$$a_{21} = \tfrac{1}{2}$$
$$a_{22} = \tfrac{1}{6}$$
$$a_{23} = \tfrac{3}{4}$$

Utilizing these values, let us employ the triangularization method to obtain a general solution. The augmented matrix, after multiplying the first and second rows by $\lambda = 1/12$, is

$$
\begin{bmatrix}
\dfrac{1}{12}E^2 & 0 & \dfrac{1}{12}\left(\dfrac{1}{2}E^2 + \dfrac{1}{3}E + \dfrac{1}{4}\right) & \vdots & \dfrac{a\lambda_1^t}{12} \\
0 & \dfrac{1}{12}E^2 & -\dfrac{1}{12}\left(\dfrac{1}{2}E^2 + \dfrac{1}{6}E + \dfrac{3}{4}\right) & \vdots & \dfrac{b\lambda_2^t}{12} \\
-\dfrac{1}{12}E & \dfrac{1}{12}E & E^2 - E & \vdots & 0
\end{bmatrix}
$$

Add E multiplying the third row to the first row, with the result

†See sections 1.1 and 3.1 for the symbols and a discussion of this model.

$$\begin{bmatrix} 0 & \dfrac{1}{12}E^2 & E^3 - \dfrac{23}{24}E^2 + \dfrac{1}{36}E + \dfrac{1}{48} & : & \dfrac{a\lambda_1^t}{12} \\[2ex] 0 & \dfrac{1}{12}E^2 & -\dfrac{1}{24}E^2 - \dfrac{1}{72}E - \dfrac{3}{48} & : & \dfrac{b\lambda_1^t}{12} \\[2ex] -\dfrac{1}{12}E & \dfrac{1}{12}E & E^2 - E & : & 0 \end{bmatrix}$$

Finally, subtract the second row from the first, and we have the desired triangular form

$$\begin{bmatrix} 0 & 0 & E^3 - \dfrac{11}{12}E^2 + \dfrac{1}{24}E + \dfrac{1}{12} & : & \dfrac{a\lambda_1^t + b\lambda_2^t}{12} \\[2ex] 0 & \dfrac{1}{12}E^2 & -\dfrac{1}{24}E^2 - \dfrac{1}{72}E - \dfrac{1}{16} & : & \dfrac{b\lambda_2^t}{12} \\[2ex] -\dfrac{1}{12}E & \dfrac{1}{12}E & E^2 - E & : & 0 \end{bmatrix}$$

Computing the general solution for P_t, we have†

$$P(t) = C_1 \left(\frac{1}{2}\right)^t + C_2 \left(-\frac{1}{4}\right)^t + C_3 \left(\frac{2}{3}\right)^t + \frac{a\lambda_1^t}{12|A(\lambda_1)|} + \frac{b\lambda_2^t}{12|A(\lambda_2)|}$$

where the C_i are arbitrary constants and $|A(\lambda_i)|$, $i = 1, 2$, is the characteristic function $\lambda_i^3 - (11/12)\lambda_i^2 + (1/24)\lambda_i + 1/12$. Substituting this expression into the second equation and performing the required operations yields the general solution for S_t, which is

$$S(t) = \frac{11}{6}C_1 \left(\frac{1}{2}\right)^t + \frac{137}{12}C_2 \left(-\frac{1}{4}\right)^t + \frac{39}{16}C_3 \left(\frac{2}{3}\right)^t$$
$$+ \left(\frac{3}{4}\lambda_1^{-2} + \frac{1}{6}\lambda_1^{-1} + \frac{1}{2}\right)\left[\frac{a\lambda_1^t}{12|A(\lambda_1)|}\right]$$
$$+ \left(\frac{3}{4}\lambda_2^{-2} + \frac{1}{6}\lambda_2^{-1} + \frac{1}{2}\right)\left[\frac{b\lambda_2^t}{12|A(\lambda_2)|}\right] + b\lambda_2^{-2}\lambda_2^t$$

The solution for D_t is left to the reader. Work this example with the adjoint matrix method and check the answers.

3.8 STATE SPACE FORM

In the final two chapters, we shall explore stability theory and control theory. The theorems in these areas presuppose that the system is in *state space*

---

†Assuming λ_1 and λ_2 do not coincide with any of the roots of the characteristic equation.

(or *basic*) form, that is, that the set of equations consist of *first-order* difference or differential equations. Therefore, it is desirable to have a method for transforming higher order systems into first-order form. We explore such a method in this section.

We can illustrate the method with examples. Consider the system of differential equations

$$(3.58) \qquad \begin{bmatrix} (D^2 - 1) & (D + 2) \\ (D^2 + D) & 2D \end{bmatrix} \begin{bmatrix} y_1 \\ y_2 \end{bmatrix} = \begin{bmatrix} t^2 \\ 1 - t \end{bmatrix}$$

In this pair of equations, the derivatives of highest order for y_1 and y_2, respectively, are $D^2 y_1$ and $D y_2$. The first step in the procedure is to solve the equations for $D^2 y_1$ and $D y_2$ in terms of $D y_1, y_1$, and y_2—that is, in terms of all lower order derivatives (including the zero-order). To do this, we may rewrite (3.58) as

$$\begin{bmatrix} 1 & 1 \\ 1 & 2 \end{bmatrix} \begin{bmatrix} D^2 y_1 \\ D y_2 \end{bmatrix} = \begin{bmatrix} t^2 + y_1 - 2y_2 \\ 1 - t - D y_1 \end{bmatrix}$$

Solving for $D^2 y_1$ and $D y_2$, we have

$$(3.59) \qquad \begin{aligned} D^2 y_1 &= D y_1 + 2y_1 - 4y_2 + 2t^2 + t - 1 \\ D y_2 &= 2y_2 - D y_1 - y_1 - t^2 - t + 1 \end{aligned}$$

Now introduce the auxiliary variable y_3, defined as

$$(3.60) \qquad D y_1 \equiv y_3$$

Substituting (3.60) into (3.59) gives

$$(3.61) \qquad \begin{aligned} D y_3 &= y_3 + 2y_1 - 4y_2 + 2t^2 + t - 1 \\ D y_2 &= 2y_2 - y_3 - y_1 - t^2 - t + 1 \end{aligned}$$

We now have (3.60) and (3.61), which are in state space form and are equivalent to (3.58). Equations (3.60) and (3.61) in matrix form can be written

$$\begin{bmatrix} D & 0 & 0 \\ 0 & D & 0 \\ 0 & 0 & D \end{bmatrix} \begin{bmatrix} y_1 \\ y_2 \\ y_3 \end{bmatrix} = \begin{bmatrix} 0 & 0 & 1 \\ 2 & -4 & 1 \\ -1 & 2 & -1 \end{bmatrix} \begin{bmatrix} y_1 \\ y_2 \\ y_3 \end{bmatrix} + \begin{bmatrix} 0 \\ 2t^2 + t - 1 \\ -t^2 - t + 1 \end{bmatrix}$$

Notice that this transformation hinges on the nonsingularity of the matrix of coefficients of the highest order derivatives

$$\begin{bmatrix} 1 & 1 \\ 1 & 2 \end{bmatrix}$$

If this matrix is singular, we call (3.58) a degenerate system and its reduction to state space form is in general impossible.† If the system is nondegenerate it can always be transformed into state space form.

As another example, consider

$$\begin{bmatrix} (E^2 + E + 6) & 0 \\ 1 & (E^2 + E - 6) \end{bmatrix} \begin{bmatrix} y_{1t} \\ y_{2t} \end{bmatrix} = \begin{bmatrix} f_1(t) \\ f_2(t) \end{bmatrix}$$

Solving for the unknowns with the shift operators of highest order, which in this case means $E^2 y_{1t}$ and $E^2 y_{2t}$, we have

(3.62)
$$E^2 y_{1t} = f_1(t) - E y_{1t} - 6 y_{1t}$$
$$E^2 y_{2t} = f_2(t) - y_{1t} - E y_{2t} + 6 y_{2t}$$

Now introduce the auxiliary variables defined as

(3.63)
$$E y_{1t} \equiv y_{3t}$$
$$E y_{2t} \equiv y_{4t}$$

Substituting (3.63) into (3.62) gives

(3.64)
$$E y_{3t} = f_1(t) - y_{3t} - 6 y_{1t}$$
$$E y_{4t} = f_2(t) - y_{1t} - y_{4t} + 6 y_{2t}$$

where (3.63) and (3.64) are the desired state space form, which in matrix form may be written

$$E \begin{bmatrix} y_{1t} \\ y_{2t} \\ y_{3t} \\ y_{4t} \end{bmatrix} = \begin{bmatrix} 0 & 0 & 1 & 0 \\ 0 & 0 & 0 & 1 \\ -6 & 0 & -1 & 0 \\ -1 & 6 & 0 & -1 \end{bmatrix} \begin{bmatrix} y_{1t} \\ y_{2t} \\ y_{3t} \\ y_{4t} \end{bmatrix} + \begin{bmatrix} 0 \\ 0 \\ f_1(t) \\ f_2(t) \end{bmatrix}$$

As a final example, consider

$$\begin{bmatrix} (Q^2 - 2Q + 1) & (Q - 3) & Q \\ (Q^2 + 1) & (2Q + 1) & (Q - 2) \\ (4Q^2 - 4) & (26Q + 20) & (-19Q - 4) \end{bmatrix} \begin{bmatrix} y_1 \\ y_2 \\ y_3 \end{bmatrix} = \begin{bmatrix} 1 \\ t \\ t^2 \end{bmatrix}$$

†One case of degeneracy is an inconsistent system, for example
$$\begin{bmatrix} D & 2D \\ D & 2D \end{bmatrix} \begin{bmatrix} y_1 \\ y_2 \end{bmatrix} = \begin{bmatrix} 1 \\ 2 \end{bmatrix}$$

For a discussion of other possibilities, see Perlis [43, pp. 138–142].

where Q is either E or D. In this case, we want to solve for $Q^2 y_1$, $Q y_2$, and $Q y_3$. The determinant of the coefficients of these terms is

$$\begin{vmatrix} 1 & 1 & 1 \\ 1 & 2 & 1 \\ 4 & 26 & -19 \end{vmatrix} = -23$$

hence the system is nondegenerate. Solving for these terms, we find that

$$Q^2 y_1 = \frac{1}{23}(128 Q y_1 - 15 y_1 + 211 y_2 - 86 y_3 + t^2 - 45t + 64)$$

$$Q y_2 = -2 Q y_1 - 4 y_2 + 2 y_3 + t - 1$$

$$Q y_3 = \frac{1}{23}(-36 Q y_1 - 8 y_1 - 50 y_2 + 40 y_3 - t^2 + 22t - 18)$$

If we now set $Q y_1 \equiv y_4$ and substitute it into these equations, we obtain the state space form

$$Q \begin{bmatrix} y_1 \\ y_2 \\ y_3 \\ y_4 \end{bmatrix} = \begin{bmatrix} 0 & 0 & 0 & 1 \\ 0 & -4 & 2 & -2 \\ -\dfrac{8}{23} & -\dfrac{50}{23} & \dfrac{40}{23} & -\dfrac{36}{23} \\ -\dfrac{15}{23} & \dfrac{211}{23} & -\dfrac{86}{23} & \dfrac{128}{23} \end{bmatrix} \begin{bmatrix} y_1 \\ y_2 \\ y_3 \\ y_4 \end{bmatrix} + \begin{bmatrix} 0 \\ g_2(t) \\ g_3(t) \\ g_4(t) \end{bmatrix}$$

where
$$g_2(t) \equiv t - 1$$
$$g_3(t) \equiv -t^2 + 22t - 18$$
$$g_4(t) \equiv t^2 - 45t + 64$$

We have demonstrated that a nondegenerate system can always be transformed into state space form. By the analysis of the previous sections, a system in state space form with n variables is equivalent to an nth order equation. Hence, it will have a unique solution with given initial values of the n variables. The general solution will be formed from n linearly independent solutions of the related homogeneous system and one particular solution of the nonhomogeneous system.†

†Notice that the analysis of the correspondence principle in Chapter 1 involves a system in state space form.

4 Stability Theory

In section 3.8 we demonstrated that any nondegenerate system of linear difference or differential equations can be transformed into state space form. We write the system as†

(4.1) $\qquad \dot{x} = Ax + Bu \qquad$ [Differential Equation System]

or

(4.2) $\qquad x_{t+1} = Ax_t + Bu_t \qquad$ [Difference Equation System]

where $\qquad x$ is an n-vector of endogenous variables

$\qquad u$ is an r-vector of exogenous variables

$\qquad A$ is an $n \times n$ matrix of constants

$\qquad B$ is an $n \times r$ matrix of constants

We refer to x as the *state* of the system, and to its elements x_i as the *state variables*. The vector u is called the *control* or forcing function or input of the

---

†It is convenient to dispense with the operator notation from now on, for it leads to confusion with matrix multiplication.

system, and its components u_i are the *control variables*. Both x and u are functions of time. We assume that $t \geq 0$, and that x_0 is the value of x at $t = 0$. If u is identically zero for all t, we say that the system is *free* or unforced. We have been referring to the free system as the homogeneous system.

We may also write (4.1) and (4.2) in general form as

(4.3) $\dot{x} = f(x, u)$

(4.4) $x_{t+1} = f(x_t, u_t)$

where

$$f = (f_1, \dots, f_n).$$

One way of dealing with the stability properties of a linear system is to solve it and look at the roots of the characteristic equation. This will indicate whether, or under what conditions, the complementary function (or the transient solution) converges to zero as $t \to \infty$. A defect in this approach is that, in general, an explicit solution of nonlinear difference or differential equation systems is impossible. This is where the *direct or second method of Liapunov* comes in for this is *a technique for obtaining stability information*

about a linear or nonlinear system, without explicit knowledge of the solutions.†
Intuitively, the idea of this approach is as follows. Suppose the equilibrium state
of the system is the origin, and that the system is perturbed from its equilibrium
state at the origin. The stability question is, will the *motion* or *trajectory* of
the system, that is, the solution of the system, eventually converge to the origin?
Imagine that we have somehow found a scalar function $V(x)$, which is a measure
of the "distance" of the state x from the origin, that is, $V(x) > 0$ when $x \neq 0$
and $V(0) = 0$. If we substitute $x(t)$, the motion of the system, into V, and if
$V(x(t)) \to 0$ as $t \to \infty$, then we know that $x(t) \to 0$ as $t \to \infty$, and the system is
seen to be stable. If such a function can be found, we call it a Liapunov function. This is the idea of the direct method of Liapunov. As is generally the
case with measures of distance, the Liapunov function, $V(x)$, is not unique. Furthermore, at present, there is no general procedure for finding Liapunov functions for nonlinear systems, and ingenuity on the part of the investigator is
often required. There is, however, an algebraic method for obtaining a suitable
Liapunov function for linear systems, as well as a simple technique by Krasovskii
for nonlinear systems which will frequently work.

We shall assume throughout that the vector function f in (4.3) or (4.4) is
sufficiently smooth so that the system has a unique solution starting at any initial
state x_0. Making this notion more precise, imagine that the control function u
in (4.3) or (4.4) is fixed, so that we may consider f as a function only of x. We
assume then that there exists a unique vector function $x(t)$ which identically
satisfies (4.3) or (4.4) for $t \geq 0$, and which equals x_0 at $t = 0$. This vector function
is called a solution (or motion or trajectory) of the system (4.3) or (4.4).‡ If the
motion $x(t)$ equals x_e for all t, we call x_e an *equilibrium state* of the system. In
other words, if a motion passes through an equilibrium state at any time, then
by definition it remains in that state at all times.§

Now imagine that we have selected some fixed motion $x(t)$ of (4.3) or (4.4)
which corresponds to a fixed choice of $u(t)$, and has the initial state x_0. Suppose
that this solution is regarded as an equilibrium path by the economist.‖ Next,

---

†The "first method" of Liapunov involves an explicit representation of the solutions.
We shall not deal with this approach. Liapunov's memoire was published in 1892 in a
Russian journal, translated into French in 1907, and reprinted in America in 1947. It has
only come to be appreciated in the West in the past decade. See Kalman and Bertram
[28], Hahn [23], and LaSalle and Lefschetz [33].

‡For a sufficient condition for the validity of this assumption, see Coddington and
Levinson [11].

§For nonlinear systems there may be more than one equilibrium state. Stability
analysis usually deals with equilibrium states which are isolated from each other. Therefore, in this book, an equilibrium state should be thought of as an isolated equilibrium
state.

‖The choice of an equilibrium path depends on the economics of the model and the
concern of the economist. Thus, the same mathematical model may have a variety of
different stability criteria. For a good discussion on this point, see Lancaster [32, pp.
195-197].

imagine that the system is perturbed from the initial state x_0, and consider the fixed motion $y(t)$ of (4.3) or (4.4), corresponding to the same fixed choice of $u(t)$, but with the initial state $y_0 \neq x_0$. The stability question then is, roughly speaking, will $y(t)$ converge to $x(t)$ as $t \to \infty$? Stability analysis is thus concerned with deviations about some fixed motion, which is considered from the economic viewpoint as an equilibrium motion.

As usually stated, the direct method of Liapunov applies only to free dynamic systems (that is, $u \equiv 0$) with equilibrium state at the origin. It is easy to demonstrate that deviations about some fixed motion are in fact a free dynamic system with equilibrium state at the origin. To see this, let $x(t)$ and $y(t)$ be defined as above, and let $\bar{u}$ be a fixed choice of $u(t)$. We may thus define the deviations about $x(t)$ as $z(t)$, where

$$y(t) \equiv x(t) + z(t)$$

hence

$$\dot{y} = \dot{x} + \dot{z}$$

By (4.3)

$$\dot{y} = f(x(t) + z(t), \bar{u})$$
$$= f(x(t), \bar{u}) + g(z(t), t)$$

where the last equality follows from the theorem of the mean. Since $x(t)$ is a solution of (4.3), it follows that

$$\dot{z} = g(z(t), t),$$
$$0 = g(0, t)$$

for all t. Thus, for fixed $u(t)$, deviations from the motion $x(t)$ are a free dynamic system with equilibrium state at zero. The argument is similar for (4.4).

4.2 STABILITY CONCEPTS

We need to define stability more rigorously than we have done until now. The concept is actually a difficult one.† In fact, there are two major concepts

† We have simplified considerably by excluding t as an additional argument in (4.3) or (4.4), and considering the matrices in (4.1) and (4.2) as consisting of constants rather than functions of t. This simplification is usually made for economic models. If f does not depend explicitly on time, we call the system *stationary*. For a free system, this is equivalent to the assumption that every motion is invariant under a translation in time. Hence, we can always consider the initial time as $t = 0$.

here: *stability* and *asymptotic stability*. Loosely speaking, stability means that for *any* neighborhood of the origin we can find a (nonzero) disturbance of the state from the origin such that the subsequent motion will be contained in that neighborhood for all $t \geq 0$. Notice that this is a local concept, for it refers to disturbances from the equilibrium state which may be very small. Asymptotic stability means that the system is stable, as just defined, and, in addition, that for every sufficiently small disturbance the trajectory will converge to the equilibrium as $t \to \infty$. As just defined, asymptotic stability is also a local concept, for it hinges on motions starting sufficiently near the equilibrium. Finally, we may define, still speaking loosely, the stability concept of greatest interest to the economist, global asymptotic stability, or asymptotic stability in the large. This concept has two aspects: The system is stable, and for *any* disturbance the trajectory converges to equilibrium as $t \to \infty$.

Let us now define these concepts more rigorously.†

Stability

An equilibrium state x_e of a free dynamic system is said to be stable if for every real number $\epsilon > 0$ there exists a real number $\delta > 0$, which depends on ϵ, such that

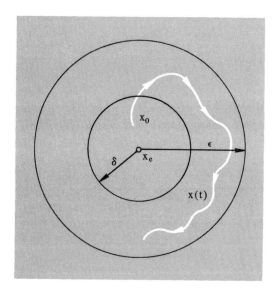

Fig. 4-1

†These definitions apply to systems (4.1), (4.2), (4.3), or (4.4).

$$||x_0 - x_e|| \leq \delta$$

implies that

$$||x(t) - x_e|| \leq \epsilon$$

for all $t \geq 0$ where x_0 is the initial state of the system and $x(t)$ is the solution or motion of the system. Recall that we have taken the origin as equilibrium, so we may simplify by saying that stability means that $||x_0|| \leq \delta(\epsilon)$ implies that $||x(t)|| \leq \epsilon$ for the positive numbers δ and ϵ.† Figure 4–1 illustrates this definition. In the figure, the large circle has radius ϵ and the small circle has radius δ. The representative trajectory starts from the initial state x_0 inside the smaller circle and remains inside the larger circle. Stability means that for every circle of radius ϵ there exists a circle of radius δ such that a picture like Figure 4–1 can be drawn.

Asymptotic Stability

An equilibrium state x_e is asymptotically stable if:

1. It is stable.
2. Every motion starting sufficiently close to x_e converges to x_e as $t \rightarrow \infty$. In other words, there exists some real number $\delta > 0$, and for every real number $\mu > 0$ there exists a T (which depends on μ and δ) such that

$$||x_0 - x_e|| \leq \delta$$

implies that

$$||x(t) - x_e|| \leq \mu \quad \text{for } t \geq T$$

In Figure 4–2, we present a picture of asymptotic stability. In this case, the largest circle has radius ϵ, the next largest has radius δ, and the smallest has radius μ. The representative trajectory starts from the initial state x_0, which is a distance of δ or less from x_e. Then, by stability, this motion remains within the circle of radius ϵ for all time. In addition, the motion must enter the smallest circle — which can be made as small as we like — at time T, and must remain in that circle.

†If the system is not stationary, δ may also depend on the initial time. If, in such a system, δ does not depend on the initial time, we say the system is *uniformly* stable.

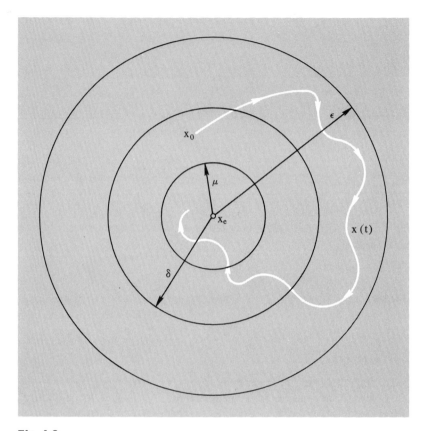

Fig. 4-2

Global Asymptotic Stability

An equilibrium state x_e of a free dynamic system is globally asymptotically stable if:

1. It is stable.
2. *Every* motion converges to x_e as $t \to \infty$. That is, given any fixed but arbitrarily large $\delta > 0$, and any $\mu > 0$, there is some T(which depends on both μ and δ) such that

$$\|x_0 - x_e\| \leq \delta$$

   implies that

$$\|x(t) - x_e\| \leq \mu \qquad \text{for } t \geq T$$

We are now ready for the main Liapunov theorems.

4.3 THE FUNDAMENTAL STABILITY THEOREM

Application of the direct method of Liapunov to problems of stability consists of defining a Liapunov function with appropriate characteristics whose existence can be shown to imply the desired type of stability. The fundamental theorem stemming from the theory of Liapunov is the following.

THEOREM 4.1 LIAPUNOV

CONSIDER THE SYSTEM $\dot{x} = f(x)$, WHICH IS (4.3) WITH $u \equiv 0$, WHERE $f(0) = 0$. ASSUME THAT THERE EXISTS A SCALAR FUNCTION $V(x) \in C^1$ SUCH THAT $V(0) = 0$ AND[†] SUPPOSE THAT:

(i) $V(x) > 0$ FOR ALL $x \neq 0$, THIS IS, $V(x)$ IS POSITIVE DEFINITE. THIS IMPLIES THE EXISTENCE OF A CONTINUOUS, NONDECREASING, SCALAR FUNCTION α SUCH THAT $\alpha(0) = 0$ AND FOR ALL $x \neq 0$

$$0 < \alpha(||x||) \leq V(x)$$

(ii) THE TOTAL DERIVATIVE $\dot{V}$ OF V ALONG A SOLUTION OF THE SYSTEM IS NEGATIVE FOR ALL $x \neq 0$; THAT IS, $\dot{V}(x(t)) < 0$ FOR ALL $x \neq 0$. THIS IMPLIES THE EXISTENCE OF A CONTINUOUS, SCALAR FUNCTION γ SUCH THAT $\gamma(0) = 0$ AND FOR ALL $x \neq 0$

$$\dot{V}(x(t)) \leq -\gamma(||x||) < 0$$

(iii)[‡] THERE EXISTS A CONTINUOUS, NONDECREASING SCALAR FUNCTION β SUCH THAT $\beta(0) = 0$ AND

$$V(x) \leq \beta(||x||)$$

(iv) $V(x) \to \infty$ AS $||x|| \to \infty$. OR or $\alpha(||x||) \to \infty$ AS $||x|| \to \infty$. THEN, THE EQUILIBRIUM STATE $x_e = 0$ IS GLOBALLY ASYMPTOTICALLY STABLE, AND $V(x)$ IS CALLED A LIAPUNOV FUNCTION OF THE SYSTEM.[§]

PROOF:

(a) We first prove stability. Consider any $\epsilon > 0$, and take a δ, which depends on ϵ, such that [see assumptions (i) and (iii)]

(4.5) $$\beta(\delta) < \alpha(\epsilon)$$

It is possible to find such a δ because β is continuous and $\beta(0) = 0$. We picture this in Figure 4–3.

†If f had t as an explicit argument, the Liapunov function would appear as $V(x, t)$.
‡This property is implied by the assumption that $V \in C^1$.
§In the course of the proof, we shall see that if all the assumptions except (iv) are met, then the system is guaranteed to possess only local asymptotic stability.

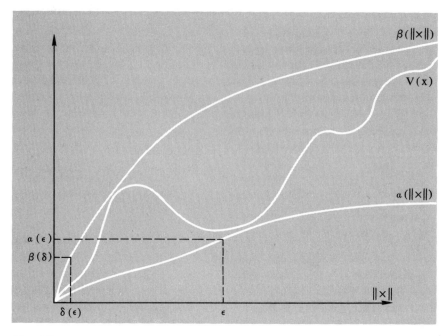

Fig. 4-3

Next, using assumption (ii), we see that V is decreasing along any motion. Thus,

$$(4.6) \qquad V(x(t)) - V(x_0) = \int_o^t \dot{V}(x(\tau))\, d\tau < 0, \qquad t > 0$$

Then, if $\|x_0\| \leq \delta$, we have, using assumption (iii), (4.5), and (4.6), for $t \geq 0$

$$\alpha(\epsilon) > \beta(\delta) \geq \beta(\|x_0\|) \geq V(x_0) \geq V(x(t))$$

From (i) we have $V(x(t)) \geq \alpha(\|x(t)\|)$, thus $\alpha(\epsilon) > \alpha(\|x(t)\|)$. Since α is nondecreasing and positive, it follows that

$$\|x(t)\| < \epsilon$$

when

$$\|x_0\| \leq \delta \qquad \text{for } t \geq 0$$

which is the definition of stability. Notice that hypothesis (iv) has not been used yet; and that it would have been sufficient for $\dot{V}$ to have been nonpositive.

(b) Next we must prove that $||x(t)|| \to 0$ as $t \to \infty$. Take any positive $\mu <$ $||x_0||$. Find an r, which depends on μ, such that

(4.7) $$\beta(r) < \alpha(\mu)$$

The reasoning here is precisely that used in obtaining (4.5). Since $r < \mu$, and μ is *any* positive constant, we can take $r \leq \epsilon$, where ϵ is the number used in part (a) of the proof.

Consider now the function γ [see (ii)] defined on the closed and bounded set $[r, \epsilon]$. Since γ is a continuous function, it will have a minimum on this closed and bounded set.† Call this minimum c. That is,

(4.8) $$c = \min\{\gamma(||x||), r \leq ||x|| \leq \epsilon\}$$

This means that $- c$ is the maximum of $- \gamma(||x||)$ on this interval. Now define T as

(4.9) $$T = \frac{\beta(\delta)}{c}$$

We shall prove this part of the theorem by contradiction. Suppose that $||x(t)|| > r$ on the interval $0 \leq t \leq T$. From this assumption and the definition of α in (i), we have

(4.10) $$0 < \alpha(r) \leq \alpha(||x(T)||) \leq V(x(T))$$

From the definition of the function γ in (ii) and (4.6) and (4.8), we have

(4.11) $$V(x(T)) - V(x_0) \leq - cT$$

or

$$V(x(T)) \leq V(x_0) - cT$$

From the inequalities following (4.6), we know that $\beta(\delta) \geq V(x_0)$; thus, we can alter (4.11) to

(4.12) $$V(x(T)) \leq \beta(\delta) - cT$$

Combining (4.10) and (4.12) and employing the definition of T in (4.9), we have

$$0 < \alpha(r) \leq 0$$

†See Theorem 1.7.

which is a contradiction. Therefore, it is impossible that $||x(t)|| > r$ over the interval $0 \leq t \leq T$. Thus, at some point in the interval it must be true that† $||x(t)|| = r;$ say that this occurs at $t = t_1$. Then

$$||x(t_1)|| = r \qquad 0 \leq t_1 \leq T$$

By (i), we know that

$$\alpha(||x(t)||) \leq V(x(t)) \qquad x \neq 0$$

and since V is assumed to decrease along any motion

$$V(x(t)) < V(x(t_1)) \leq \beta(r) \qquad t \geq t_1$$

Therefore

$$\alpha(||x(t)||) < \beta(r) \qquad t \geq t_1$$

But from (4.7) we know that $\beta(r) < \alpha(\mu)$, thus

$$\alpha(||x(t)||) < \alpha(\mu)$$

for $t \geq t_1$. Since α is nondecreasing and positive, this last strict inequality implies that

$$||x(t)|| < \mu$$

for $t \geq T \geq t_1$, which proves *local* asymptotic stability, for $||x_0|| \leq \delta$, and δ may be very small.

To prove global asymptotic stability, we employ hypothesis (iv) for the first time, that is, the assumption that

$$\alpha(||x||) \to \infty \qquad \text{as } ||x|| \to \infty$$

Observe (4.5). If (iv) is assumed, we can suppose that (4.5) will hold for an arbitrarily large constant δ. That is, for *any* $\delta > 0$ there exists an ϵ, which depends on δ, such that $\beta(\delta) < \alpha(\epsilon)$.

Q. E. D.

This theorem applies intact to difference equation systems. The proof is identical, except for obvious modifications such as replacing integrals with sums, $\dot{V}$ with ΔV, and the continuous t with the discrete t_k.

---

†This follows from the fact that, since a norm is a continuous function, we can invoke the intermediate value theorem. See Theorem 1.14.

As already mentioned, there is no general technique for obtaining Liapunov functions satisfying the requirements of this theorem. Therefore, it is of interest to know whether such a function exists so that one does not search in vain. The converse of the theorem does hold if the f defining the differential equation system is Lipschitzian.† But the converse of the theorem for a difference equation system does not yet appear to have been investigated.

4.4   OBTAINING LIAPUNOV FUNCTIONS

An explicit method for obtaining a Liapunov function does exist for linear systems, such as (4.1) or (4.2). Before proving this theorem, it is necessary that we define the concept *fundamental matrix*.

In the previous chapter we saw that an independent system of equations such as $\dot{x} = Ax$, where A is $n \times n$, will have n linearly independent solution vectors. The matrix X, formed such that its n columns consist of n linearly independent solutions, is called a fundamental matrix. Such a matrix satisfies identically the matrix differential equation $\dot{X} = AX$, by definition of a solution. Observe that fundamental matrices differ from each other by a multiplicative constant matrix. Thus, if X and Φ are fundamental matrices, it must be true that $X = \Phi C$, where C is an $n \times n$ matrix of constants. For a given initial condition, the fundamental matrix is uniquely determined. Define Φ as that fundamental matrix which is the unit matrix at $t = 0$, that is

$$\Phi(0) = I$$

It is now easy to demonstrate that $\Phi(t)x_0$, where $x_0 = x(0)$, is the general solution of $\dot{x} = Ax$, that is

(4.13) $$x(t) = \Phi(t)x_0$$

Clearly, this solution satisfies the initial condition, since $\Phi(0) = I$. Substituting this solution into $\dot{x} = Ax$, we have

$$\dot{x}(t) = \frac{d}{dt}[\Phi(t)x_0] = \dot{\Phi}x_0 = A\Phi x_0 = Ax(t)$$

Thus we have verified that $\Phi(t)x_0$ is a solution of $\dot{x} = Ax$ with initial condition $x(0) = x_0$.

---

†See Massera [35]. If f has t as an explicit argument, then the existence of a Liapunov function as defined in the theorem is necessary and sufficient for *uniform* global asymptotic stability.

We call the unique fundamental matrix $\Phi(t)$ the *state transition matrix*. From (4.13), we can see that it maps x_0 into $x(t)$ at time t. This discussion of the fundamental matrix applies word-for-word to the difference equation system $x_{t+1} = Ax_t$, with obvious modifications.

For the differential equation system, it is a simple matter to demonstrate that the state transition matrix is identical to the matrix exponential†

$$e^{At} \equiv I + \sum_{k=1}^{\infty} \frac{A^k t^k}{k!}$$

Substituting e^{At} for $\Phi(t)$ in (4.13), we can see that $e^{At}x_0$ is the unique solution of $\dot{x} = Ax$, for it follows from the definition of e^{At} that

$$e^{At} = I \quad \text{at } t = 0$$

and

$$\frac{d}{dt}(e^{At}) = Ae^{At}$$

Notice that A and e^{At} commute, that is, $Ae^{At} = e^{At}A$. For the difference equation system, the state transition matrix is A^t, and $A^t x_0$ is the unique solution of $x_{t+1} = Ax_t$. This is also easy to verify.

As a final preliminary to the theorems containing explicit methods for obtaining Liapunov functions, we need the following lemma.

Lemma. The matrix differential equation

$$\dot{X} = A'X + XA \qquad X(0) = Q$$

has the solution

$$X = e^{A't}Qe^{At}$$

PROOF:

Differentiate the proposed solution with respect to t. Then we obtain

$$\dot{X} = A'e^{A't}Qe^{At} + e^{A't}QAe^{At}$$

Since A and e^{At} commute, we have

$$e^{A't}QAe^{At} = e^{A't}Qe^{At}A$$

hence

†The legitimacy of the definition of e^{At} hinges on the fact that the series converges in any finite interval of the time axis.

$$\dot{X} = A'X + XA$$

or $X = e^{A't}Qe^{At}$ is the solution of the given matrix differential equation with the given initial condition.

Q. E. D.

THEOREM 4.2

THE EQUILIBRIUM STATE $x_e = 0$ OF $\dot{x} = Ax$ IS GLOBALLY ASYMPTOTICALLY STABLE IF AND ONLY IF FOR ANY SYMMETRIC POSITIVE DEFINITE MATRIX Q THERE EXISTS A SYMMETRIC POSITIVE DEFINITE MATRIX P, WHICH IS THE UNIQUE SOLUTION OF THE SYSTEM OF ALGEBRAIC EQUATIONS

(4.14) $$A'P + PA = -Q$$

AND $x'Px$ IS A LIAPUNOV FUNCTION FOR $\dot{x} = Ax$.

PROOF:

First we show that if such a P exists, then the system has the asserted type of stability. Define

$$V(x) = x'Px > 0 \qquad \text{when } x \neq 0$$

as a tentative Liapunov function for the system. Then† $\dot{V}$ along any motion is obtained as

$$\dot{V}(x) = (\text{grad } V)'Ax = 2(Px)'Ax$$

hence‡

$$\dot{V}(x) = x'(A'P + PA)x$$

But by (4.14) and the assumptions about Q

$$\dot{V}(x) = -x'Qx < 0 \qquad \text{for all } x \neq 0$$

so that V satisfies (i), (ii), and (iii) of the Liapunov theorem. Therefore, the system is asymptotically stable.

Requirement (iv) of the Liapunov theorem is also satisfied, that is, $V(x) \to \infty$ as $||x|| \to \infty$. To see this, let T be an orthogonal matrix such

---

†As our gradient notation we use here grad rather than ∇.

‡This follows from the assumed symmetry of P plus the easily demonstrable fact that for any square matrix F

$$x'Fx = x'\left(\frac{F + F'}{2}\right)x$$

that $x = Ty$. Then $x'x = y'T'Ty = y'y$. Thus, $||y|| \to \infty$ if and only if $||x|| \to \infty$. But

$$V(x) = x'Px = y'T'PTy$$

If T is such that $T'PT$ equals the diagonal matrix made up of the positive eigenvalues of P, then

$$V(x) = \sum \lambda_i y_i^2 \geq \lambda y'y$$

where λ is a positive constant equal to the smallest eigenvalue $\lambda_i > 0$. Since $y'y \equiv ||y||^2$, we see that property (iv) of the Liapunov theorem is established.

Next we shall prove the converse of what we just proved. That is, we shall demonstrate that if the origin of the system is globally asymptotically stable, then there exists a positive definite symmetric matrix P such that $A'P + PA = -Q$, where Q is any symmetric, positive definite matrix.

Recalling the lemma, integrate both sides of that matrix differential equation from $t = 0$ to $t = \infty$. This gives

(4.15) $$X(\infty) - X(0) = A'\left(\int_0^\infty X dt\right) + \left(\int_0^\infty X dt\right)A$$

Given the stability assumption about $\dot{x} = Ax$, it follows that the transition matrix $e^{At} \to 0$ as $t \to \infty$. Therefore, by the lemma

$$X(\infty) = e^{A't}Qe^{At}|_{t=\infty} = 0$$

and

$$X(0) = Q$$

We thus rewrite (4.15) as

$$-Q = A'\left(\int_0^\infty X dt\right) + \left(\int_0^\infty X dt\right)A$$

Let us define P as†

(4.16) $$P = \int_0^\infty X dt = \int_0^\infty e^{A't}Qe^{At}dt$$

where it is obvious that P is symmetric. We now need to show that P is

†Observe that the elements of the state transition matrix are finite sums of terms like $e^{\lambda_i t}, te^{\lambda_i t}, \ldots, t^{m_i-1}e^{\lambda_i t}$, where m_i is the multiplicity of λ^i. Since the λ_i are assumed to possess negative real parts, the matrix P as defined will exist.

positive definite. Consider the following quadratic form:

$$x'Px = x'\left(\int_0^\infty e^{A't}Qe^{At}dt\right)x$$

Since x is an arbitrary vector of real numbers, we can take x and x' inside the integral sign. Thus

$$x'Px = \int_0^\infty (e^{At}x)'Q(e^{At}x)\, dt$$

But, by assumption, Q is positive definite, hence, by the last expression, P is also positive definite.

We have only one more task. The theorem says that P is unique. We must show that the definition of P in (4.16) is the unique solution of (4.14). Let $\bar{P}$ be any solution of (4.14). Thus

$$A'\bar{P} + \bar{P}A = -Q$$

Substitute this expression into the definition of P in (4.16), which gives

$$P = -\int_0^\infty (e^{A't})(A'\bar{P} + \bar{P}A)(e^{At})\, dt$$

Recalling that A and e^{At} commute, we have

$$P = -\int_0^\infty \frac{d}{dt}[e^{A't}\bar{P}e^{At}]\, dt = -e^{A't}\bar{P}e^{At}\Big|_0^\infty = \bar{P}$$

with the last equality following from the stability assumption.

Q. E. D.

Let us summarize the content of this theorem. To ascertain whether the system $\dot{x} = Ax$ is globally asymptotically stable, set up the algebraic system of equations in (4.14). Solve this system for P. If P is positive definite, the system has the desired stability. That is, the positive definiteness of the P which solves (4.14) is a sufficient condition for the desired stability; it is also a necessary condition. In other words, if the system has the desired stability, then the P which solves (4.14) must be positive definite. Notice that the theorem says that Q may be *any* symmetric, positive definite matrix. Hence, let Q be the unit matrix, and we may rewrite (4.14) as†

$$A'P + PA = -I$$

†For a demonstration that this theorem is equivalent to the Routh-Hurwitz conditions, see Kalman and Bertram [28].

Example 4.1

Determine whether the following system is globally asymptotically stable:

$$\begin{bmatrix} \dot{x}_1 \\ \dot{x}_2 \end{bmatrix} = \begin{bmatrix} -1 & -2 \\ 1 & -4 \end{bmatrix} \begin{bmatrix} x_1 \\ x_2 \end{bmatrix}$$

The equilibrium state is the origin. From Theorem 4.2 we know we must solve the system

$$A'P + PA = -I$$

for P, where P is a symmetric matrix. Then we must examine P to see if it is positive definite. If it is, then $x'Px$ is a Liapunov function and the origin has the desired stability. The above system of equations in this case is

$$\begin{bmatrix} -1 & 1 \\ -2 & -4 \end{bmatrix} \begin{bmatrix} P_{11} & P_{12} \\ P_{12} & P_{22} \end{bmatrix} + \begin{bmatrix} P_{11} & P_{12} \\ P_{12} & P_{22} \end{bmatrix} \begin{bmatrix} -1 & -2 \\ 1 & -4 \end{bmatrix} = \begin{bmatrix} -1 & 0 \\ 0 & -1 \end{bmatrix}$$

This system yields

$$\begin{bmatrix} -2 & 2 & 0 \\ -2 & -5 & 1 \\ 0 & -4 & -8 \end{bmatrix} \begin{bmatrix} P_{11} \\ P_{12} \\ P_{22} \end{bmatrix} = \begin{bmatrix} -1 \\ 0 \\ -1 \end{bmatrix}$$

Solving for the $P's$, we obtain

$$P_{11} = \tfrac{23}{60}, \qquad P_{12} = \tfrac{-7}{60}, \qquad P_{22} = \tfrac{11}{60}$$

thus

$$P = \begin{bmatrix} \tfrac{23}{60} & \tfrac{-7}{60} \\ \tfrac{-7}{60} & \tfrac{11}{60} \end{bmatrix}$$

which is clearly positive definite. A Liapunov function is

$$V(x) = x'Px = \tfrac{1}{60}(23x_1^2 - 14x_1x_2 + 11x_2^2)$$

and

$$\dot{V}(x) = -x_1^2 - x_2^2$$

Theorem 4.2 is altered only slightly when applied to linear discrete systems. We present the analogue of Theorem 4.2 as the following theorem.

THEOREM 4.3

THE EQUILIBRIUM STATE $x_e = 0$ OF $x_{t+1} = Ax_t$ IS GLOBALLY ASYMPTOTICALLY
STABLE IF AND ONLY IF FOR ANY SYMMETRIC, POSITIVE DEFINITE MATRIX Q THERE
EXISTS A SYMMETRIC, POSITIVE DEFINITE MATRIX P, WHICH IS THE UNIQUE SOLUTION
OF THE SYSTEM OF ALGEBRAIC EQUATIONS

$$A'PA - P = -Q$$

AND $x'Px$ IS A LIAPUNOV FUNCTION FOR $x_{t+1} = Ax_t$.

THE PROOF IS COMPLETELY ANALOGOUS TO THE PROOF OF THEOREM 4.2 AND IS
LEFT FOR THE READER.

Perhaps the best result on employing the Liapunov method for nonlinear
systems is the following theorem by Krasovskii.

THEOREM 4.4   KRASOVSKII

CONSIDER THE SYSTEM $\dot{x} = f(x)$ WITH EQUILIBRIUM $x_e = 0$. ASSUME THAT
$f \in C^1$ AND THAT ITS JACOBIAN MATRIX J SATISFIES THE CONDITION THAT

$$x'(J' + J)x < 0 \qquad x \neq 0$$

THEN THE EQUILIBRIUM STATE $x_e = 0$ IS GLOBALLY ASYMPTOTICALLY STABLE AND

$$V(x) = f'(x)f(x)$$

IS ONE OF ITS LIAPUNOV FUNCTIONS.

PROOF:
First, we will show that $f(x) = 0$ only for $x = 0$, from which it immediately follows that the Liapunov function specified by the theorem is positive definite. Let $c \neq 0$ be any constant n-vector. The set of vectors $\{\alpha c:
0 \leq \alpha \leq 1\}$ is a line segment (ray) connecting the origin with c. Consider
$f_i(\alpha c)$, where f_i is an element of the f-vector. Differentiating $f_i(\alpha c)$ with
respect to α gives

$$\frac{df_i(\alpha c)}{d\alpha} = \sum_{j=1}^{n} \frac{\partial f_i}{\partial x_j} c_j$$

where c_j is an element of c. Integrating both sides from $\alpha = 0$ to $\alpha = 1$
yields the identity

$$f_i(\alpha c)\Big|_{\alpha\,=\,0}^{\alpha\,=\,1} = \int_0^1 \sum_{j=1}^{n} \frac{\partial f_i}{\partial x_j} c_j \, d\alpha$$

Since $f(0) = 0$, by assumption, we see that

$$f_i(c) = \int_0^1 \sum_{j=1}^n \frac{\partial f_i}{\partial x_j} c_j \, d\alpha$$

Now, assume that $f(c) = 0$ for some $c \neq 0$. Then

$$0 = c'f(c) \equiv \sum_{i=1}^n c_i f_i(c) = \int_0^1 \left[\sum_{i,j=1}^n c_i \frac{\partial f_i}{\partial x_j} c_j \right] d\alpha$$

But the bracketed term is $c' Jc$, which is easily seen to be negative for $c \neq 0$, because of the assumption of the theorem that $(J' + J)$ is negative definite.† Therefore, the last expression is a contradiction, and it follows that we cannot assume that $f(c) = 0$ for some $c \neq 0$. Hence, $f(x) = 0$ only for $x = 0$; that is, the origin is the only equilibrium state in the entire state space. We deduce from this that

$$V(x) = f'(x)f(x) > 0 \qquad \text{for } x \neq 0$$

We have thus demonstrated that the Liapunov function defined by the theorem is positive definite.

Next, we wish to show that $V(x) \to \infty$ as $||x|| \to \infty$. Again consider $f_i(\alpha c)$ and

$$\frac{df_i(\alpha c)}{d\alpha} = \sum_{j=1}^n \frac{\partial f_i}{\partial x_j} c_j$$

This time integrate both sides from $\alpha = 0$ to $\alpha = m$, where m is any positive constant. This yields

$$f_i(mc) = \int_0^m \sum_{j=1}^n \frac{\partial f_i}{\partial x_j} c_j \, d\alpha$$

Multiply both sides by c_i and sum over i. Thus we obtain

$$\sum_{i=1}^n c_i f_i(mc) \equiv c'f(mc) = \int_0^m \left[\sum_{i,j=1}^n c_i \frac{\partial f_i}{\partial x_j} c_j \right] d\alpha$$

Since the term in brackets is negative for $c \neq 0$, we can assume that the

---

†This follows from the fact that $x'Jx = (x'Jx)'$, hence
$$x'(J' + J)x = x'J'x + x'Jx$$
$$= (x'Jx)' + x'Jx$$
$$= 2x'Jx$$

term $\leq -\epsilon$, for some positive constant ϵ. Hence

$$c'f(mc) \leq -\epsilon m$$

As $m \to \infty$, $c'f(mc) \to -\infty$, for any fixed vector $c \neq 0$. But this can happn only if at least one component of $f(x)$ tends to infinity in absolute value as $||x|| \to \infty$. Hence, $V(x) = f'(x)f(x) \to \infty$ as $||x|| \to \infty$.
Finally, we need to show that $\dot{V}$ is negative definite. Computing $\dot{V}$, we see that

$$\dot{V}(x) = \dot{x}'(\text{grad } V)$$

Given that $V(x) = f'(x)f(x)$, it is readily seen that the ith element of grad V is

$$2\sum_{j=1}^{n} f_j \frac{\partial f_j}{\partial x_i}$$

Thus

$$\dot{V}(x) = 2\sum_{i,j=1}^{n} \dot{x}_i f_j \frac{\partial f_j}{\partial x_i}$$
$$= 2f'(x)J(x)\dot{x}$$
$$= 2f'(x)J(x)f(x)$$

which we know to be negative for $x \neq 0$. Thus, the Liapunov function satisfies all the characteristics spelled out in the fundamental theorem.

Q. E. D.

Example 4.2

Consider the following system with one nonlinearity:

$$\dot{x}_1 = g(x_1) + ax_2$$
$$\dot{x}_2 = x_1 + bx_2$$

where $g(0) = 0$ and $g \in C^1$.
In this example, the Jacobian matrix J is

$$J = \begin{bmatrix} \dfrac{\partial g}{\partial x_1} & a \\ 1 & b \end{bmatrix}$$

Thus

$$J' + J = \begin{bmatrix} 2\dfrac{\partial g}{\partial x_1} & a + 1 \\ a + 1 & 2b \end{bmatrix}$$

Theorem 4.4 says that this system will be globally asymptotically stable at the origin if $J' + J$ is negative definite. A necessary and sufficient condition for the negative definiteness of this matrix is that

$$\frac{\partial g}{\partial x_1} < 0$$

$$4b\frac{\partial g}{\partial x_1} - (a + 1)^2 < 0$$

The analogue of Krasovskii's theorem for difference equation systems hinges on the concept of a *contraction*. A function $f(x)$ is said to be a contraction if

$$\|f(x)\| < \|x\| \qquad f(0) = 0$$

for some $x \neq 0$ and some norm. We may now present the companion to Theorem 4.4.

THEOREM 4.5

CONSIDER THE SYSTEM $x_{t+1} = f(x_t)$ WITH EQUILIBRIUM $x_e = 0$. ASSUME THAT f IS A CONTRACTION FOR ALL $x \neq 0$ AND SOME NORM. THEN THE SYSTEM IS GLOBALLY ASYMPTOTICALLY STABLE AND ONE OF ITS LIAPUNOV FUNCTIONS IS

$$V(x) = \|x\|$$

PROOF:

By definition of a norm, $V(x)$ is positive definite, and obviously $V(x) \to \infty$ as $\|x\| \to \infty$.
Computing ΔV, we see that

$$\Delta V = \|x_{t+1}\| - \|x_t\| = \|f(x_t)\| - \|x_t\|$$

which is negative for all $x \neq 0$ because f is, by assumption, a contraction.

Q. E. D.

There are several functions that satisfy the requirements of a norm. The reader may check that any of the four following functions can be used as a norm.

1. The Euclidian norm.

$$||x|| = (x'x)^{1/2}$$

2. The generalized Euclidian norm.

$$||x|| = (x'Px)^{1/2}$$

where P is any symmetric, positive definite matrix.

3. The absolute value norm.

$$||x|| = \sum_i h_i |x_i|$$

where each h_i is a positive constant.

4. The maximum norm.

$$||x|| = \max_i c_i |x_i|$$

where $c_1, \ldots, c_n$ is a given set of positive numbers.

We shall give some illustrations of the use of these norms as Liapunov functions in the following section, which is devoted to economic examples of stability analysis.

Exercises

Establish whether the equilibrium state $x_e = 0$ of the following systems is globally asymptotically stable.

1.
$$\dot{x}_1 = -3x_1 + x_2$$
$$\dot{x}_2 = x_1 - x_2 - x_2^3$$

Solution. Using Krasovskii's theorem

$$f(x) = \begin{bmatrix} -3x_1 + x_2 \\ x_1 - x_2 - x_2^3 \end{bmatrix}$$

The Jacobian matrix is

$$J(x) = \begin{bmatrix} -3 & 1 \\ 1 & -1 - 3x_2^2 \end{bmatrix}$$

Thus

$$J'(x) + J(x) = \begin{bmatrix} -6 & 2 \\ 2 & -2 - 6x_2^2 \end{bmatrix}$$

which is negative definite, hence the system is asymptotically stable. To prove that it possesses this stability globally, consider the behavior of the Liapunov function prescribed by Krasovskii's theorem as $||x|| \to \infty$. This gives

$$V(x) = f'(x)f(x) = (-3x_1 + x_2)^2 + (x_1 - x_2 - x_2^3)^2$$

which $\to \infty$ as $||x|| \to \infty$.

2.
$$\begin{bmatrix} x_{1,\,t+1} \\ x_{2,\,t+1} \end{bmatrix} = \begin{bmatrix} 1 & -1 \\ 2 & -1 \end{bmatrix} \begin{bmatrix} x_{1t} \\ x_{2t} \end{bmatrix}$$

Solution. By Theorem 4.3 this kind of system possesses the desired type of stability if and only if there exists a symmetric, positive definite matrix

$$P = \begin{bmatrix} P_{11} & P_{12} \\ P_{12} & P_{22} \end{bmatrix}$$

such that

$$A'PA - P = -I$$

where

$$A = \begin{bmatrix} 1 & -1 \\ 2 & -1 \end{bmatrix}$$

Solving for P, we have

$$\begin{bmatrix} 0 & 4 & 4 \\ -1 & -4 & -2 \\ 1 & 2 & 0 \end{bmatrix} \begin{bmatrix} P_{11} \\ P_{12} \\ P_{22} \end{bmatrix} = \begin{bmatrix} -1 \\ 0 \\ -1 \end{bmatrix}$$

which possesses no unique solution, hence the system does not possess the desired stability.

3.
$$\begin{bmatrix} \dot{x}_1 \\ \dot{x}_2 \end{bmatrix} = \begin{bmatrix} 0 & 1 \\ -1 & -1 \end{bmatrix} \begin{bmatrix} x_1 \\ x_2 \end{bmatrix}$$

Answer.

$$P = \begin{bmatrix} \frac{3}{2} & \frac{1}{2} \\ \frac{1}{2} & 1 \end{bmatrix}$$

hence the system has the desired stability.

4.
$$\dot{x}_1 = x_2$$
$$\dot{x}_2 = -x_2 - x_1^3$$

Solution. The Krasovskii theorem does not work, since

$$J'(x) + J(x) = \begin{bmatrix} 0 & 1 - 3x_1^2 \\ 1 - 3x_1^2 & -2 \end{bmatrix}$$

which is not negative definite. But by trial and error, the following turns out to be a suitable Liapunov function for this system:

$$V(x) = x_1^4 + x_1^2 + 2x_1x_2 + 2x_2^2 = x_1^4 + x_1^2 + (x_1 + x_2)^2$$

Clearly, this function is positive definite and $\to \infty$ as $||x|| \to \infty$. Computing $\dot{V}$, we see that

$$\dot{V} = -2x_1^4 - 2x_2^2$$

hence the origin of the system is globally asymptotically stable.

5.
$$\dot{x}_1 = -2x_1 + 2x_2^4$$
$$\dot{x}_2 = -x_2$$

Hint. Try $V(x) = 6x_1^2 + 12x_2^2 + 4x_1x_2^4 + x_2^8$.

6.
$$x_{1,t+1} = x_{1,t}$$
$$x_{2,t+1} = 2x_{1,t} - \frac{1}{2}x_{2,t}$$

Answer.

$$P = \begin{bmatrix} \frac{2204}{405} & \frac{-64}{54} \\ \frac{-64}{54} & \frac{4}{3} \end{bmatrix}$$

which is positive definite.

4.5 ECONOMIC EXAMPLES

Example 4.3 Walrasian Adjustment Process†

Consider a linear approximation to a set of excess-demand functions in a neighborhood of equilibrium, where we assume that the speed of reaction of the price in each market is proportional to the amount of excess demand in that market. By a suitable adjustment of the units of measurement, we can make the speed of reaction in each market equal to unity. This yields the following system.

$$(4.17) \qquad \dot{p} = Ap$$

where $\dot{p}$ is an n-vector of the rates of change of price with respect to time, A is an $n \times n$ matrix of the constant coefficients a_{ij} of the linearized excess-demand equations, and p is an n-vector of prices, measured as deviations from their equilibrium values. If we dealt with discrete time, the system of difference equations corresponding to (4.17) would be

$$(4.18) \qquad p_{t+1} = (A + I)p_t$$

We know from Theorem 4.5 that if $(A + I)$ is a contraction‡ for all p, then (4.18) is asymptotically stable. A well-known condition for the asymptotic stability of (4.18) is that all the eigenvalues of $(A + I)$ be less than unity in absolute value. Since the eigenvalues of $(A + I)$ exceed those of A by one, the asymptotic stability of $(A + I)$ implies that the real parts of the eigenvalues of A are negative, and hence the asymptotic stability of (4.17) is implied by the asymptotic stability of (4.18).

An interesting question is to determine under what conditions $(A + I)$ will be a contraction. One such condition is that A have a *quasi-dominant main diagonal*—that is, that there exists a positive vector h such that either

$$(i) \qquad h_j|a_{jj}| > \sum_{\substack{i \\ i \neq j}} h_i|a_{ij}| \qquad j = 1, \ldots, m$$

or

$$(ii) \qquad h_i|a_{ii}| > \sum_{\substack{j \\ i \neq j}} h_j|a_{ij}| \qquad i = 1, \ldots, m$$

where it is assumed that a_{jj} (or a_{ii}) are all negative.

†See Newman [40], Karlin [29], and Negishi [39].
‡Recall that $(A + I)$ is a contraction if $\|(A+I)p\| < \|p\|$ for some $p \neq 0$ and some norm.

Assume that A is such that condition (i) holds. Now consider the absolute value norm, $||p|| = \sum_i h_i|p_i|$, where the h_i are all positive. We shall use this norm to prove that (i) implies that $(A + I)$ is a contraction. Given (i), and the fact that $a_{jj} < 0$ for all j, we have

$$\sum_{\substack{i \\ i \neq j}} h_i|a_{ij}| + h_j a_{jj} < 0 \qquad \text{for all } j$$

or

(4.19)
$$\sum_{\substack{i \\ i \neq j}} h_i|a_{ij}| + h_j(a_{jj} + 1) < h_j \qquad \text{for all } j$$

By adjusting the units of measurement appropriately, we may assume that

$$\max_j |a_{ij}| \leq 1$$

It is also convenient to define $(A + I)$ as B, where the off-diagonal elements $b_{ij} = a_{ij}$ and where $b_{jj} = a_{jj} + 1$ for all j.

From (4.19), we have

(4.20)
$$\sum_i \frac{h_i}{h_j}|b_{ij}| < 1 \qquad \text{for all } j$$

The absolute value norm $||p|| = \sum_i h_i|p_i|$ implies that

$$||Bp|| = \sum_i h_i \left| \sum_j b_{ij} p_j \right|$$

$$= \sum_i \frac{h_i}{h_j} \left| \sum_j b_{ij} h_j p_j \right|$$

$$\leq \sum_i \frac{h_i}{h_j} \left(\sum_j |b_{ij}| |p_j| h_j \right)$$

$$\leq \left(\sum_i \frac{h_i}{h_j} |b_{ij}| \right) \sum_j |p_j| h_j$$

From (4.20), the expression in parentheses in the last term is less than unity. Hence

$$||Bp|| < \sum_j h_j|p_j| \equiv ||p||$$

We have thus shown that if (i) holds, then $(A + I) \equiv B$ is a contraction. By similar reasoning, it can be shown that if (ii) holds, then $(A + I)$ is a contraction. To prove this, use the maximum norm $||p|| = \max_i c_i|p_i|$, where $c_1, \ldots, c_n$

is a given set of positive numbers. Since the argument is similar to the proposition just proved, we leave the steps to the reader.

Consider system (4.17) again. We can apply Krasovskii's theorem to that system to obtain a sufficient condition for its origin to be asymptotically stable. As our Liapunov function, try the square of the Euclidian norm, $p'p$. Clearly

$$V(p) = p'p$$

is positive definite, and $V(p) \to \infty$ as $\|p\| \to \infty$, so the only remaining question is whether $\dot{V} < 0$ for $p \neq 0$. If it is, we have a sufficient condition for the desired stability. Computing $\dot{V}$, we find that

$$\dot{V}(p) = 2p'\dot{p}$$
$$= 2p'Ap = p'(A' + A)p$$

Therefore, if $A' + A$ is negative definite, then the system has the desired stability.

Let us next employ the square of the generalized Euclidian norm as our Liapunov function for the system in (4.17); that is

$$V(p) = p'Pp$$

where p is any symmetric, positive definite matrix. Again the question of stability hinges on the negative definiteness of $\dot{V}$. Computing $\dot{V}$ gives

$$\dot{V}(p) = 2(Pp)'p$$
$$= 2(Pp)'Ap = 2p'PAp$$
$$= p'(A'P + PA)p$$

Thus, if a symmetric, positive definite P exists such that $(A'P + PA)$ is negative definite, then the system in (4.17) has the desired stability. This reasoning and conclusion is simply a restatement of Theorem 4.2.

Example 4.4   Linear Versus Nonlinear Macro Model

Consider a simple $LM - IS$ version of the Keynesian model,† where we assume that the rates of change in the product and money markets are proportionate to the excess demands in these markets. In differential equation form, we may write

(4.21) $\dot{Y} = \lambda_1(E - Y) \qquad \lambda_1 > 0$
$$\dot{r} = \lambda_2(M^* - \bar{M}) \qquad \lambda_2 > 0$$

†See section 1.2 for a discussion of this model.

where $Y =$ national income

$E =$ aggregate demand

$M^* =$ demand for money

$\bar{M} =$ supply of money

$r =$ interest rate

Assume further that E depends in linear fashion on r and Y, so that, ignoring a constant term

(4.22) $$E = a_{11}Y + a_{12}r \qquad \begin{aligned} a_{11} &> 0 \\ a_{12} &< 0 \end{aligned}$$

Next, let us make two distinct assumptions about the demand for money. First, suppose that it is a linear function of r and Y

(4.23) $$M^* = a_{21}Y + a_{22}r \qquad \begin{aligned} a_{21} &> 0 \\ a_{22} &< 0 \end{aligned}$$

Second, as an alternative, assume that this function has a nonlinearity in it with respect to the interest rate. That is

(4.24) $$M^* = a_{21}Y + g(r)$$

where $g'(r) < 0$ and $g''(r) > 0$, so that the demand for money schedule has the usual convex shape and negative slope.

Substituting (4.22) and (4.23) into (4.21) gives the linear model (setting $\bar{M} = 0$)

(4.25) $$\begin{aligned} \dot{Y} &= b_{11}Y + b_{12}r \\ \dot{r} &= b_{21}Y + b_{22}r \end{aligned}$$

where

$$\begin{aligned} b_{11} &= \lambda_1(a_{11} - 1) \\ b_{12} &= \lambda_1 a_{12} \\ b_{21} &= \lambda_2 a_{21} \\ b_{22} &= \lambda_2 a_{22} \end{aligned}$$

Substituting (4.22) and (4.24) into (4.21) gives a system with the one nonlinearity

(4.26) $$\begin{aligned} \dot{Y} &= b_{11}Y + b_{12}r \\ \dot{r} &= b_{21}Y + \lambda_2 g(r) \end{aligned}$$

Now let us compare the stability properties of systems (4.25) and (4.26) to see what difference the nonlinearity makes. Applying Krasovskii's theorem to both systems, it follows that a sufficient condition for the global asymptotic stability of the origin is, for (4.25) that

$$\begin{bmatrix} 2b_{11} & b_{12} + b_{21} \\ b_{12} + b_{21} & 2b_{22} \end{bmatrix}$$

be negative definitive, and, for (4.26), that

$$\begin{bmatrix} 2b_{11} & b_{12} + b_{21} \\ b_{12} + b_{21} & 2g'(r)\lambda_2 \end{bmatrix}$$

be negative definite. For system (4.25) this condition implies that

$$b_{11} < 0, b_{22} < 0$$
$$4b_{11}b_{22} - (b_{12} + b_{21})^2 > 0$$

or

(4.27) $a_{11} - 1 < 0, \qquad a_{22} < 0$
$$4a_{22}(a_{11} - 1)\lambda_1\lambda_2 - (\lambda_1 a_{12} + \lambda_2 a_{21})^2 > 0$$

For the system (4.26), the condition implies that

(4.28) $a_{11} - 1 < 0, g'(r) < 0$
$$4g'(r)(a_{11} - 1)\lambda_1\lambda_2 - (\lambda_1 a_{12} + \lambda_2 a_{21})^2 > 0$$

For both systems, the marginal propensity to spend, a_{11}, must be less then one and the demand for money must be negatively sloped in order to assure global stability. In addition, the second set of inequalities in (4.27) and (4.28) must hold. The first term in these inequalities will be positive if the marginal propensity to spend is less than one and the demand for money possesses a negative slope. The difference between the stability characteristics of the linear versus the nonlinear model can be seen clearly by the second set of inequalities in (4.27) and (4.28). Since $g'(r)$ becomes a larger negative number as r decreases, by hypothesis, the asymptotic stability of the nonlinear model (4.26) becomes more likely at lower levels of r than at higher levels. Thus, the liquidity trap region of this $LM - IS$ model is more likely to possess the sufficient condition for global asymptotic stability than the classical region. The impact of assumed parameter changes on the likelihood of asymptotic stability can be deduced from (4.27) and (4.28), and is left to the reader. Additional nonlinearities can be handled with Krasovskii's theorem in similar fashion.

5   Optimal Control Theory

5.1 THE CONTROL PROBLEM

Suppose that we have a dynamic economic model in difference equation form

(5.1)
$$x^i_{t+1} - x^i_t = f^i(x_t, u_t) \qquad i = 1, \ldots, n$$
$$x_0 \text{ given} \qquad t = 0, \ldots, T - 1$$

where x_t is an n-vector of variables which describe the state of the system at time t, and u_t is an m-vector of control or policy variables. The behavior of x_t is given by the set of n first order difference equations in (5.1),[†] where the x^i_0 are given.

Next, suppose that the values of u_t are restricted by the relations defined by[‡]

[†]Equation (5.1) is in state space form. See section 3.8 for a description of how a dynamic model is transformed into state space form. We assume that t is not an explicit variable in (5.1), with no effect on the argument throughout.

[‡]Again, t could be an explicit variable in (5.2) without affecting the discussion. Also, x_t could be an argument in (5.2), with obvious modifications in the results presented below.

$$(5.2) \qquad g^i(u_t) \le b_i \qquad \begin{matrix} i = 1, \ldots, m \\ t = 0, \ldots, T - 1 \end{matrix}$$

where the b_i are constants. Any control u_t which satisfies (5.2) we refer to as an *admissible* or *feasible control*.

Now imagine that (5.1), subject to the restraints in (5.2), describes the behavior of a plant or an economy, and that there is a decision maker or policy maker, such as a plant manager or prime minister, charged with the responsibility for the behavior of this system. He is presumed to have control over the inputs, u_t, which in turn affect the state variables according to the relationships posited in (5.1). He must decide how to manipulate these inputs or policy instruments over time. We also suppose that he has some kind of a preference or utility function, and that he would like to manipulate u_t so as to maximize his utility function. In general, we suppose that his utility is a function of all the state variables and policy instrument. That is, we assume that at any time t the scalar valued function

$$(5.3) \qquad F(x_t, u_t)$$

expresses his utility level. Further, assume that our policy maker would like to find that decision vector function or control, u_t, which will maximize the sum of his utility levels over a certain number of time periods, say T periods. Thus, we suppose that the policy maker wants to find that control, u_t, which maximizes

(5.4) $$S \equiv \sum_{t=0}^{T-1} F(x_t, u_t)$$

We refer to S as the *performance* or *objective functional*.† The problem can be stated as one of minimizing instead of maximizing the objective functional, if we define F as disutility instead of utility. The admissible control which optimizes S subject to (5.1) is called the optimal control, and [may be denoted as $\bar{u}_t$. The motion $\bar{x}_t$ corresponding to $\bar{u}_t$ is referred to as the optimal trajectory or motion. We may thus summarize our description of the control problem in the following way. Find that control u_t, satisfying (5.2), for $t = 0, 1, \ldots, T - 1$, which will steer the system whose law of motion is described in (5.1) so as to maximize or minimize S, defined in (5.4).

The control problem can alternatively be expressed in differential equation form. In this case, (5.1) through (5.4) would be written as

(5.5)
$$\dot{x}^i = f^i(x(t), u(t))$$
$$g^i(u(t)) \le b_i$$
$$S \equiv \int_0^T F(x(t), u(t))\, dt$$

We discuss the differential equation form of the control problem in section 5.5.

5.2 THE DISCRETE MAXIMUM PRINCIPLE

In this section, we shall derive a celebrated and powerful technique for solving the difference equation, or discrete, form of the control problem, the maximum principle of Pontriagin.‡ Our method of deriving the maximum principle will be based on Lagrange-Kuhn-Tucker theory developed in Chapter 2.

---

†A functional is a mapping from functions to numbers. It should be stressed that this additive-separable type of intertemporal utility function in (5.4) is a special case; it is used so frequently because it is easy to handle.

‡See Pontriagin [45]. Sometimes the principle is referred to as the minimum principle. For differential equations, it is called the continuous maximum (or minimum) principle.

The discrete form of the control problem described in the previous section is a constrained optimization problem. It is desired to find the mT values of u_t^i for $i = 1, \ldots, m$ and $t = 0, \ldots, T - 1$, which will

$$\text{(5.6)} \qquad \text{optimize } S \equiv \sum_{t=0}^{T-1} F(x_t, u_t)$$

subject to

$$\text{(5.7)} \qquad x_{t+1}^i - x_t^i = f^i(x_t, u_t) + b_t^i \qquad \begin{array}{l} i = 1, \ldots, n \\[4pt] t = 0, \ldots, T - 1 \end{array}$$

$$x_0^i \text{ fixed}$$

$$\text{(5.8)} \qquad g^i(u_t) \leq b_i \qquad \begin{array}{l} i = 1, \ldots, m \\[4pt] t = 0, \ldots, T - 1 \end{array}$$

where T is, for now, assumed given. We have altered (5.1), in writing (5.7), by adding the constants b_t^i, with the understanding that they equal zero unless otherwise stated.†

The Lagrangian expression for this problem may be written

$$\text{(5.9)} \qquad L = \sum_{t=0}^{T-1} \left[F(x_t, u_t) + \sum_{i=1}^{n} \lambda_t^i f^i(x_t, u_t) - \sum_{i=1}^{n} \lambda_t^i (x_{t+1}^i - x_t^i) \right. $$
$$\left. + \sum_{i=1}^{m} \mu_t^i (b_i - g^i(u_t)) \right]$$

where the λ_t^i, and μ_t^i are Lagrange multipliers.

The first two terms in the bracket of (5.9) will turn out to be crucial in the argument which follows. This expression is referred to as the *Hamiltonian*, which we label H, that is,

$$\text{(5.10)} \qquad H(x_t, u_t, \lambda_t) \equiv F(x_t, u_t) + \sum_{i=1}^{n} \lambda_t^i f^i(x_t, u_t)$$

Employing the results of the Kuhn-Tucker theorem,‡ the necessary conditions for the optimization of (5.6) subject to (5.7) and (5.8) are that there exists a unique set of Lagrange multipliers $\bar{\lambda}_t^i$ and $\bar{\mu}_t^i$ such that, at the optimum

---

†Notice that there is no restriction on the terminal values of the state variables, that is, x_t for $t = T$. We shall incorporate some restrictions on x_T below. Also, the constraints on u_t need not equal m, may be made to depend on x_t, and/or may contain a subset of strict equalities. Such alterations lead to obvious modifications in the argument of this section.

‡See section 2.5.

$$(5.11) \qquad \frac{\partial H(\bar{x}_t, \bar{u}_t, \bar{\lambda}_t)}{\partial x_t^j} - \bar{\lambda}_{t-1}^j + \bar{\lambda}_t^j = 0 \qquad \begin{array}{l} j = 1, \ldots, n \\ t = 1, \ldots, T-1 \end{array}$$

which may be rewritten as†

$$(5.12) \qquad \bar{\lambda}_t^j - \bar{\lambda}_{t-1}^j = -\frac{\partial H_t}{\partial x_t^j} \qquad \begin{array}{l} j = 1, \ldots . n \\ t = 1, \ldots, T-1 \end{array}$$

$$(5.13) \qquad \frac{\partial H(\bar{x}_t, \bar{u}_t, \bar{\lambda}_t)}{\partial u_t^j} - \sum_{i=1}^{m} \bar{\mu}_t^i \frac{\partial g^i(\bar{u}_t)}{\partial u_t^j} = 0 \qquad \begin{array}{l} j = 1, \ldots, m \\ t = 0, \ldots, T-1 \end{array}$$

$$(5.14) \qquad \frac{\partial L}{\partial x_T^j} = -\bar{\lambda}_{T-1}^j = 0 \qquad j = 1, \ldots, n$$

$$(5.15) \qquad \begin{array}{ll} \bar{\mu}_t^i \geq 0 & \text{(constrained maximization) } i = 1, \ldots, m \\ \bar{\mu}_t^i \leq 0 & \text{(constrained minimization) } t = 0, \ldots, T-1 \end{array}$$

where the equality holds if $g^i(\bar{u}_t) < b_i$, and where $\geq$ or $\leq$ holds if $g^i(\bar{u}_t) = b_i$. Since (5.7) is a strict equality, it follows that $\bar{\lambda}_t^i \gtreqless 0$.

We shall now use these results to develop a proof of a discrete version of the Pontriagin maximum principle.‡ To do so we shall utilize two assumptions additional to those employed in the Kuhn-Tucker necessary conditions. These new assumptions are as follows:

A1. The set U of u_t which satisfies (5.8) is convex for all t.

A2. For a constrained maximization (minimization) problem, H_t is concave (convex) for admissible u_t.

We may now prove the following lemma, where we assume a constrained maximization problem in (5.6) to (5.8).

Lemma.

$$(u_t - \bar{u}_t)' \nabla_u \bar{H}_t \leq 0$$

for all $u_t \in U$, assuming (5.13) to (5.15) and A1, where $\nabla_u \bar{H}_t$ is the gradient of the Hamiltonian with respect to u_t evaluated at $(\bar{x}_t, \bar{u}_t, \bar{\lambda}_t)$. [The gradient is a column vector, and $(u_t - \bar{u}_t)'$ is a row vector].

---

†In this context the Lagrange multipliers are often referred to as *costate* variables, and (5.12) is referred to as the *auxiliary* system. In addition, (5.12) and (5.1) are called the *canonical* system.

‡The proof is adapted from that given in Holmes [26]. See also Arimoto [5], Halkin [24], and Katz [30]. Some of these papers present stronger versions of the principle than the one we develop here, and they employ more mathematical machinery than we do.

PROOF:

For i such that $g^i(\bar{u}_t) < b_i$, it follows from (5.15) that $\bar{\mu}_t^i = 0$. Hence,

(i) $$\bar{\mu}_t^i(u_t - \bar{u}_t)'\nabla g^i(\bar{u}_t) = 0$$

For i such that $g^i(\bar{u}_t) = b_i$, we have by the Taylor theorem† that

$$g^i[\bar{u}_t + k(u_t - \bar{u}_t)] = g^i(\bar{u}_t) + k(u_t - \bar{u}_t)'\nabla g^i[\bar{u}_t + \theta k(u_t - \bar{u}_t)]$$

for every $k \in [0, 1]$ and some fixed $\theta \in (0, 1)$. The inner product in this expression must be nonpositive, otherwise

$$g^i[\bar{u}_t + k(u_t - \bar{u}_t)] > b_i$$

which violates the assumption that U is a convex set. Therefore, for $0 < k \le 1$ we see that

$$(u_t - \bar{u}_t)'\nabla g^i[\bar{u}_t + \theta k(u_t - \bar{u}_t)] \le 0$$

and by the continuity of ∇g^i it follows that

$$(u_t - \bar{u}_t)'\nabla g^i(\bar{u}_t) \le 0$$

Employing (5.15) and the previous inequality we have, for i such that $g^i(\bar{u}_t) = b_i$

(ii) $$\bar{\mu}_t^i(u_t - \bar{u}_t)'\nabla g^i(\bar{u}_t) \le 0$$

Combining (i) and (ii), we obtain

(iii) $$(u_t - \bar{u}_t)'J_g(\bar{u}_t)\bar{\mu}_t \le 0$$

where $J_g(\bar{u}_t) \equiv (\nabla g^i(\bar{u}_t), \ldots, \nabla g^m(\bar{u}_t))$. Rewrite (5.13) as

$$\nabla_u \bar{H}_t - J_g(\bar{u}_t)\bar{\mu}_t = 0 \qquad t = 0, \ldots, T - 1$$

Premultiply this expression by $(u_t - \bar{u}_t)'$, employ the result in (iii), and we have the statement in the lemma.‡

Q. E. D.

We are now ready to state a discrete version of the Pontriagin maximum principle.

†See section 2.2.
‡The inequality is reversed for a constrained minimization problem.

THEOREM 5.1   THE DISCRETE MAXIMUM PRINCIPLE

IN ORDER THAT $\bar{x}_t$ AND $\bar{u}_t$ MAXIMIZE (MINIMIZE) (5.6) SUBJECT TO (5.7) AND (5.8), GIVEN THE ASSUMPTIONS REQUIRED BY THE KUHN-TUCKER NECESSARY CONDITIONS PLUS A1 AND A2, IT IS NECESSARY THAT THE HAMILTONIAN FUNCTION H_t REACH ITS MAXIMUM (MINIMUM) FOR ADMISSIBLE u_t AT $(\bar{u}_t, \bar{x}_t, \bar{\lambda}_t)$ FOR $t = 0, \ldots, T - 1$.

PROOF:

We shall prove the theorem for a constrained maximum. Since H_t is assumed concave for $u_t \in U$, it follows that

$$(u_t - \bar{u}_t)' \nabla_u \bar{H}_t \geq H_t(\bar{x}_t, u_t, \bar{\lambda}_t) - H_t(\bar{x}_t, \bar{u}_t, \bar{\lambda}_t)$$

for admissible u_t.[†] Combining this inequality with the lemma, we have

$$H_t(\bar{x}_t, \bar{u}_t, \bar{\lambda}_t) \geq H_t(\bar{x}_t, u_t, \bar{\lambda}_t) \text{ for } u_t \in U$$

Q. E. D.

We may also present a set of sufficient conditions for a constrained optimum by following the argument in section 2.7, where sufficient conditions were developed for the Kuhn-Tucker Theorem. If, in addition to the assumptions employed in the previous theorem, we assume that the Hamiltonian is concave (convex) in x, and if the $g^i(u_t)$ are convex (concave) for admissible u_t, then sufficient conditions obtain for the maximization (minimization) of (5.6) subject to (5.7) and (5.8). The proof follows that given in section 2.7.

5.3 AN ECONOMIC INTERPRETATION OF THE MAXIMUM PRINCIPLE

In this section, we shall explore the economic interpretation of the results achieved in the previous section. Does the Hamiltonian, which is so important in the maximum principle, have any economic meaning? What economic interpretation can be placed on the auxiliary system expressed in (5.11) or (5.12)? Finally, what is the significance of the terminal condition on the Lagrange multipliers, or costate variables, expressed in (5.14)?

From the Lagrange-Kuhn-Tucker theory,[‡] we know that

$$(5.16) \qquad \bar{\lambda}_t^j = \frac{\partial \bar{S}}{\partial b_t^j} \qquad \begin{array}{l} j = 1, \ldots, n \\ t = 0, \ldots, T - 1 \end{array}$$

[†]For a proof of this result, see Theorem 2.14.
[‡]See Theorem 2.7 and section 2.5.

and

$$(5.17) \qquad \bar{\mu}_t^i = \frac{\partial \bar{S}}{\partial b_i} \qquad \begin{array}{l} i = 1, \ldots, m \\ t = 0, \ldots, T - 1 \end{array}$$

where the bar indicates that the derivatives are computed at the optimum. Observe that in (5.7) a change in the value of the resource constraint b_t^j implies the same change in x_{t+1}^j, hence in $x_{t+1}^j - x_t^j$. Therefore, $\bar{\lambda}_t^j$ may be interpreted as the shadow price or the marginal utility imputed to x_{t+1}^j, or to $x_{t+1}^j - x_t^j$, at the optimum.

This interpretation of $\bar{\lambda}_t^j$ suggests an economic meaning for the Hamiltonian, defined in (5.10). The term $F(x_t, u_t)$ is the utility level of the optimizer in period t, considering *only* (x_t, u_t) and not the values of the state variables implied by (x_t, u_t) for the period $t + 1$, due to the structure of relationships postulated in (5.7). The value of x_{t+1}^j implied by (x_t, u_t) is expressed by $f^j(x_t, u_t)$, and $\bar{\lambda}_t^j$ is the shadow price of x_{t+1}^j. Therefore, the other term in the Hamiltonian

$$\sum_{i=1}^n \bar{\lambda}_t^i f^i(x_t, u_t)$$

is the marginal utility of the vector x_{t+1}. Hence, we can interpret the Hamiltonian as a measure of the *total* utility experienced by the policy maker in period t. The maximum principle states that, in order to maximize S subject to the constraints in (5.7) and (5.8), it is necessary to maximize the value of this total utility in each period from $t = 0$ to $t = T - 1$ with respect to the policy instruments u_t, given $(\bar{x}_t, \bar{\lambda}_t)$.

The auxiliary system expressed in (5.11) or (5.12) also has a natural economic interpretation. Consider the left side of (5.12). Using (5.16), we can write (5.12) as

$$(5.18) \qquad \bar{\lambda}_{t-1}^j - \bar{\lambda}_t^j = \frac{\partial \bar{S}}{\partial b_{t-1}^j} - \frac{\partial \bar{S}}{\partial b_t^j} = \frac{\partial \bar{H}_t}{\partial x_t^j}$$

To understand (5.18), consider first the difference between $\partial \bar{S}/\partial b_{t-1}^j$ and $\partial \bar{H}_t/\partial x_t^j$. From (5.7) it can be seen that a change in b_{t-1}^j of, say, one unit not only implies a unit change in x_t^j, but also an exogenous unit change in x^j in all future time periods. Thus, a unit change in b_{t-1}^j implies an *exogenous* unit change in $(x_t^j, x_{t+1}^j, \ldots, x_T^j)$ as well as *induced* changes (via the f^i) in all state variables from period $t + 1$ to T. Using this distinction between exogenous and induced, we can see that $\partial \bar{S}/\partial b_{t-1}^j$, or λ_{t-1}^j, expresses the rate at which the optimum value of the objective functional changes with respect to an exogenous change in $(x_t^j, x_{t+1}^j, \ldots, x_T^j)$; while $\partial \bar{H}/\partial x_t^j$ expresses the rate at which the optimal value of the objective functional changes with respect to an exogenous change *only* in x_t^j. (Both measures of course subsume all induced changes in the state variables from period $t+1$ to T.) The second equality in (5.18) now makes sense. The middle term assumes a "small" increase in b_{t-1}^j, hence the same exogenous increase in $(x_t^j, x_{t+1}^j, \ldots, x_T^j)$, plus the same size decrease in b_t^j with the same exogenous decrease in $(x_{t+1}^j, x_{t+2}^j, \ldots, x_T^j)$. Adding these exogenous changes yields only the exogenous increase in x_t^j which is assumed in the right-hand term in (5.18).

Since a change in b_{t-1}^j implies the same exogenous change in $(x_t^j, x_{t+1}^j, \ldots, x_T^j)$, it follows from this discussion that $\bar{\lambda}_{t-1}^j = \partial \bar{S}/\partial b_{t-1}^j$ should equal the sum of the optimal rates of change in the Hamiltonian from period t to period $T-1$ with respect to the exogenous change in x^j of the corresponding period. That is

$$\bar{\lambda}_{t-1}^j = \frac{\partial \bar{H}_t}{\partial x_t^j} + \frac{\partial \bar{H}_{t+1}}{\partial x_{t+1}^j} + \cdots + \frac{\partial \bar{H}_{T-1}}{\partial x_{T-1}^j}$$

and

$$\bar{\lambda}_t^j = \frac{\partial \bar{H}_{t+1}}{\partial x_{t+1}^j} + \frac{\partial \bar{H}_{t+2}}{\partial x_{t+2}^j} + \cdots + \frac{\partial \bar{H}_{T-1}}{\partial x_{T-1}^j}$$

By iterating (5.18), these equalities are easily verified.

The terminal conditions on the Lagrange multipliers in (5.14) express the fact that the rate at which the optimum value of the objective functional changes with respect to changes in the value of any state variable in period T is zero. That is, the decision maker is not concerned with the state of the system in period T, because that is the way we defined S in (5.4). We could redefine S so as to allow the optimizer to be concerned about x_T; for example, we could have defined the objective functional as

$$(5.19) \qquad\qquad S^* = \sum_{t=0}^{T-1} F(x_t, u_t) + F^*(x_T)$$

in which case the terminal condition on the Lagrange multipliers would have been

$$(5.20) \qquad\qquad \bar{\lambda}_{T-1}^j = \frac{\partial F^*(\bar{x}_T)}{\partial x_T^j} \qquad j = 1, \ldots, n$$

where the interpretation is obvious.

From (5.17) we obtain the interpretation of the remaining Lagrange multipliers. As indicated in (5.15), these multipliers are nonnegative for a constrained maximization problem, and are zero if the corresponding constraint in (5.8) is not binding at the optimum. This means that a "small" increase in b_i, which implies an increase in the admissible set of policy instruments, u_t, will increase or leave unchanged the optimal value of the objective functional if the ith constraint is binding at the optimum. The increase in b_i will have no effect on the optimal value of the objective functional if the ith constraint is not binding at the optimum. The reasoning for a constrained minimization problem is similar.

Finally, consider the conditions in (5.13). The first term is simply the marginal utility in period t, at the optimum, of the policy instrument u^j. The expression in (5.17) tells us that the term $\bar{\mu}_t^i$ may be interpreted as the value to the optimizer, at the optimum, of a "small" relaxation of the ith constraint on the policy instruments. Thus, the second term in (5.13) is the sum of the marginal utilities, at the optimum, of u_t^i occasioned by the relaxation of the m constraints on the policy instruments. Therefore, condition (5.13) says that the optimum is characterized by the fact that the marginal utility of u_t^j is equal to the sum of the marginal utilities of u_{ti}^j resulting from the assumed relaxation of the constraints on the policy instruments. The latter of course is zero only if there are no constraints on the policy instruments of if all the constraints are nonbinding at the optimum. In such a case, (5.13) says that the maximum or minimum of the Hamiltonian with respect to the policy variables is characterized by a zero gradient in each time period, since $\bar{u}_t$ occurs at an interior point. On the other hand, if one or more of the constraints on the inputs is binding at the optimum, the maximum or minimum of the Hamiltonian occurs on the boundary of U, where the gradient of the Hamiltonian with respect to u_t may or may not be zero.

5.4 EXTENSION OF THE DISCRETE MAXIMUM PRINCIPLE

In this section we shall consider an extension of the maximum principle. Suppose the optimizer wishes to constrain some or all of the state variables in the final period of time.[†] Consider the simple type of constraints, such as

$$(5.21) \qquad\qquad x_T^i = x_*^i \qquad i = 1, \ldots, r \leq n$$

where x_*^i are fixed values.[‡] In this case we add the constraints in (5.21) to those in (5.7) and (5.8), which adds to the Lagrangian expression in (5.9) the term

[†]We shall not consider constraints on the state variables in other time periods, but the modification in the optimal conditions stemming from these additional restrictions can be derived by straightforward application of the Kuhn-Tucker theorem, as in section 5.2.

[‡]The argument proceeds analogously for the more general form of constraints
$$h_i(x_T) \leq 0 \qquad \text{for } i = 1, \ldots, r \leq n$$

(5.22) $$\sum_{i=1}^{r} \gamma_i(x_T^i - x_*^i)$$

where γ_i are new Lagrangian multipliers. The result is to transform (5.14) to

(5.23)
$$\bar{\lambda}_{T-1}^j = \bar{\gamma}_j \qquad j = 1, \ldots, r$$
$$\bar{\lambda}_{T-1}^j = 0 \qquad j = r+1, \ldots, n$$

where the r new Lagrange multipliers need to be solved for, and the r new conditions in (5.21) replace the loss of the r terminal conditions on $\bar{\lambda}_{T-1}^j$ for $j = 1, \ldots, r$.

5.5 THE CONTINUOUS MAXIMUM PRINCIPLE

A rigorous proof of the continuous maximum principle is beyond the scope of this book.† Instead, we shall derive the continuous maximum principle by applying a limiting process to the difference equations employed in our discussion of the discrete maximum principle.‡

Rewrite the control problem in (5.6) to (5.8) in the following form:

$$\text{optimize } S = \sum_{t=0}^{T-1} F(x_t, u_t) \, \Delta t$$

subject to

$$\frac{x_{t+1}^i - x_t^i}{\Delta t} = f^i(x_t, u_t) \qquad \begin{array}{l} i = 1, \ldots, n \\ t = 0, \ldots, T-1 \end{array}$$

and

$$g^i(u_t) \le b_i \qquad i = 1, \ldots, m$$

where $\Delta t =$ the period of time. As $\Delta t \to 0$, the problem becomes

$$\text{optimize } S = \int_0^T F(x(t), u(t)) \, dt$$

†See Pontriagin [45].

‡We shall assume that the limiting process is valid, without investigating the required mathematical conditions.

subject to

(5.24)
$$\dot{x}_i = f^i(x(t), u(t)) \qquad i = 1, \ldots, n$$
$$g^i(u(t)) \leq b_i \qquad i = 1, \ldots, m$$

The Hamiltonian in (5.10) appears in the continuous time problem as

(5.25) $H(x(t), u(t), \lambda(t)) \equiv F(x(t), u(t)) + \sum_{i=1}^{n} \lambda^i(t) f^i(x(t), u(t))$

The auxiliary system in (5.12), rewritten as

$$\frac{\bar{\lambda}_t^j - \bar{\lambda}_{t-1}^j}{\Delta t} = -\frac{\partial \bar{H}_t}{\partial x_t^j} \qquad \begin{array}{l} j = 1, \ldots, n \\ t = 0, \ldots, T-1 \end{array}$$

becomes in the limit

(5.26) $$\dot{\lambda}^j = -\frac{\partial \bar{H}}{\partial x^j} \qquad j = 1, \ldots, n$$

The terminal condition on the Lagrange multipliers, or costate variables, in (5.14) is transformed at $\Delta t \to 0$ into

(5.27) $$\bar{\lambda}^j(T) = 0 \qquad j = 1, \ldots, n$$

The condition on the costate variables in (5.15) becomes, in the continuous time problem

(5.28)
$$\bar{\mu}^i(t) \geq 0 \quad \text{(constrained maximization)}$$
$$\bar{\mu}^i(t) \leq 0 \quad \text{(constrained minimization)} \qquad i = 1, \ldots, m$$

where $0 \leq t \leq T$, and the equality holds at those moments of time at which $g^i(\bar{u}(t)) < b_i$, and $\geq$ or $\leq$ holds at those instants of time at which $g^i(\bar{u}(t)) = b_i$.

The statement of the continuous maximum principle parallels that for the discrete maximum principle. It states that in order for $\bar{x}(t)$ and $\bar{u}(t)$ to solve the control problem in (5.24), it is necessary, given the assumptions in section 5.2, that there exist a nonzero continuous vector function $\bar{\lambda}(t)$ satisfying (5.26) and (5.27), and that the vector function $\bar{u}(t)$ be selected so that the Hamiltonian in (5.25) is a maximum (minimum) for every t, $0 \leq t \leq T$. The economic interpretation discussed in section 5.3 and the extension developed in section 5.4 apply, with obvious modifications, to the continuous time problem.

5.6 THE TIME-OPTIMAL PROBLEM

Consider an extension of the continuous maximum principle. Suppose that the time horizon T is not fixed, but is considered as an additional variable in the optimization problem. In this case, the optimal T, call it T^*, must be solved for in addition to everything else. To solve for this additional variable, we need an additional condition—the Hamiltonian function at the final moment of time must have a value of zero. Demonstration of this fact is not difficult. Consider the changes in S, under optimal control, due to a change in time from T^* to $T^* + \Delta T$. We may write this as

$$\Delta S = \int_0^{T^* + \Delta T} F(\bar{x}, \bar{u}) \, dt - \int_0^{T^*} F(\bar{x}, \bar{u}) \, dt$$

$$= \int_{T^*}^{T^* + \Delta T} F(\bar{x}, \bar{u}) \, dt$$

From this we may deduce† that

$$\frac{dS}{dt} = F(\bar{x}(T^*), \bar{u}(T^*))$$

By (5.25) and (5.27), we see that the Hamiltonian evaluated at T^* is identical to the right side of this last expression. Since we are optimizing S with respect to t, it is therefore necessary that the Hamiltonian evaluated at T^* be equal to zero.‡

> *Remark.* Under optimal control, it is evident that we have $\bar{u}(t)$ expressed as a function of $\bar{x}(t)$ and $\bar{\lambda}(t)$; therefore, the Hamiltonian may be written as a function of $\bar{x}(t)$ and $\bar{\lambda}(t)$. Differentiating this function with respect to time, and employing (5.26) and (5.27), we see that this derivative is equal to zero. Thus, the Hamiltonian, under optimal conditions, is a constant for $0 \leq t \leq T$. (Clearly, this result only holds if t is not an independent argument in the Hamiltonian function.) It follows that in the time-optimal problem the Hamiltonian, under optimal control, is zero for $0 \leq t \leq T^*$.

> *Remark.* Results which parallel those of this section are not available for the discrete optimization problem. The reason is that in the discrete case t can only take on integer values. Therefore, to optimize S with re-

---

†This deduction follows from the mean value theorem of the integral calculus followed by passage to the limit as $\Delta T \to 0$. The theorem may be applied since by assumption F is continuous and nonnegative. See Courant [13, Vol. I, pp. 126–127].

‡A similar argument establishes this result where some or all of the state variables are fixed at the final moment of time.

spect to t involves a problem in integer programming, and the optimal value of t will not in general imply a zero value for the Hamiltonian.

5.7 PROBLEMS†

1. Find a control u_t for $t = 0, 1, \ldots, T - 1$, which minimizes the objective functional

$$S = \tfrac{1}{2} \sum_{t=0}^{T-1} [\alpha(x_t)^2 + \beta(u_t)^2] \qquad \beta > 0$$

subject to

$$x_{t+1} - x_t = ax_t + bu_t, \qquad x_0 \text{ given}$$

with no constraints on the control and the assumption that T is fixed.

Solution. The Hamiltonian for this problem is

$$H_t = \tfrac{1}{2} [\alpha(x_t)^2 + \beta(u_t)^2] + \lambda_t(ax_t + bu_t)$$

According to the maximum principle, we must minimize H_t with respect to u_t. Since there are no constraints on the control, the extremum of H_t occurs at an interior point of the set of admissible controls. Thus, at the optimum, it is necessary that

$$\frac{\partial H_t}{\partial u_t} = \beta \bar{u}_t + b\bar{\lambda}_t = 0 \qquad t = 0, \ldots, T - 1$$

Thus

(i) $$\bar{u}_t = -\frac{b}{\beta} \bar{\lambda}_t \qquad t = 0, \ldots, T - 1$$

By (5.12), we know that, at the optimum

(ii) $$\bar{\lambda}_t - \bar{\lambda}_{t-1} = -\frac{\partial \bar{H}_t}{\partial x_t} = -\alpha \bar{x}_t - a\bar{\lambda}_t$$

and by (5.14)

(iii) $$\bar{\lambda}_{T-1} = 0$$

†It is easy to check each problem to see that the required assumptions discussed in section 5.2 hold. We leave this verification to the reader.

Substituting (i) into the original constraint gives

$$\bar{x}_{t+1} - \bar{x}_t = a\bar{x}_t - \frac{b^2}{\beta}\bar{\lambda}_t, \ x_0 \text{ given}$$

This equation, along with (ii) and (iii), can now be solved for $\bar{x}_t$ and $\bar{\lambda}_t$. The solution of this system† is

$$\bar{x}_t = \left[\frac{1-\alpha\sigma}{\alpha(1+a)} - \frac{r_1}{\alpha}\right]c_1 r_1^t + \left[\frac{1-\alpha\sigma}{\alpha(1+a)} - \frac{r_2}{\alpha}\right]c_2 r_2^t$$
$$\bar{\lambda}_t = c_1 r_1^t + c_2 r_2^t$$

where r_1 and r_2 are the roots of the characteristic equation, and where $\sigma \equiv -b^2/\beta$ and c_1 and c_2 are constants which can be determined from the boundary conditions on $\bar{x}_t$ and $\bar{\lambda}_t$. The solution for $\bar{x}_t$ yields the optimal trajectory for the state variable of this problem. Substituting the solution for $\bar{\lambda}_t$ into (i) gives the optimal control.

2. Consider the continuous time analogue of problem 1. Find a control $u(t)$ which minimizes the objective function

$$S = \tfrac{1}{2}\int_0^T (\alpha x^2(t) + \beta u^2(t))\, dt \qquad \beta > 0$$

subject to

$$\dot{x} = ax + bu$$
$$x(0) = x_0$$

with no constraints on the control $u(t)$ and with T fixed.

Solution.
The Hamiltonian for this problem is

$$H(t) = \tfrac{1}{2}(\alpha x^2(t) + \beta u^2(t)) + \lambda(t)(ax(t) + bu(t))$$

Minimizing H with respect to u, it is necessary, at the optimum, that (deleting the t's)

$$\frac{\partial \bar{H}}{\partial u} = \beta\bar{u} + b\bar{\lambda} = 0 \qquad 0 \le t \le T$$

Thus

†See sections 3.5 and 3.6 for solution techniques.

(i) $$\bar{u} = -\frac{b}{\beta}\bar{\lambda} \qquad 0 \le t \le T$$

By (5.26) and (5.27), we have at the optimum that

(ii) $$\dot{\lambda} = -\frac{\partial \bar{H}}{\partial x} = -\alpha x - a\lambda$$

and

(iii) $$\bar{\lambda}_T = 0$$

Substituting (i) into the original constraint gives

$$\dot{x} = a\bar{x} - \frac{b^2}{\beta}\bar{\lambda}$$

$$x(0) = x_0$$

This equation, along with (ii) and (iii), is easily solved for the optimal trajectories of the state and costate variables. Substituting $\bar{\lambda}(t)$ into (i) then yields the optimal control.

3. Consider problem 1 with the addition of the terminal condition on the state variable that

$$x_T = x_*$$

The argument is identical with problem 1 except that (iii) is converted to [see (5.23)]

$$\bar{\lambda}_{T-1} = \bar{\gamma}$$

Therefore, the constants c_1 and c_2 in this case must be determined from the boundary conditions on x_t, as contrasted to problem 1, where they were determined from the initial condition on the state variable and the terminal condition on the costate variable. The same modification is made in problem 2 if the terminal condition $x_T = x_*$ is placed on the state variable.

4. Find a control $u(t)$ which sends the state variable from its initial value of x_0 to the value x_* as rapidly as possible subject to

$$\dot{x} = ax + bu \qquad a > 0, b > 0$$

$$N \le u(t) \le M \qquad N > 0, M > 0, M > N$$

Solution. It is possible that there may be no solution to this problem. For example, given the assumptions that the structural parameters a and b are positive, if x_0 has a value such that

$$ax_0 + bM < 0$$

then $\dot{x}$ is always negative, and there will be no solution if $x_* > x_0$. Therefore, to be sure that there is a solution, we must make some additional assumptions. Let us assume that $ax_0 + bM$ and $x_* - x_0$ have the same sign, and that both x_* and x_0 are positive.

The objective functional in this problem can be seen to be

$$S = \int_0^T dt = T$$

which is required to be minimized. The Hamiltonian function is

$$H(x(t), \lambda(t), u(t)) = 1 + \lambda(t)(ax(t) + bu(t))$$

From this expression we can seen that the control which minimizes H at each t will be (omitting the t's)

$$\bar{u} = \begin{cases} N \text{ when } b\lambda > 0 \\ M \text{ when } b\lambda < 0 \\ \text{unspecified when } b\lambda = 0† \end{cases}$$

The auxiliary system is

$$\dot{\lambda} = -\frac{\partial H}{\partial x} = -a\lambda$$

Solving for $\bar{\lambda}$ gives

$$\bar{\lambda}(t) = ce^{-at}$$

where c is an arbitrary constant.

Since b is assumed positive, and $\bar{\lambda}$ is either positive or negative depending on the sign of c, it follows that

$$\bar{u} = \begin{cases} N \text{ if } c > 0 \\ M \text{ if } c < 0 \\ \text{unspecified if } c = 0 \end{cases}$$

---

†The fact that the maximum principle does not specify the optimal control for $b\lambda = 0$ is referred to as "singularity of control."

To obtain the sign of c, recall that the Hamiltonian at the final and optimal moment of time will, under optimal control, equal zero. Thus, using $\bar{\lambda}(t) = ce^{-at}$ in the Hamiltonian and setting $t = T^*$, assuming T^* is optimal, we see that

$$1 + ce^{-aT^*}(ax_* + b\bar{u}) = 0$$

and since $(ax_* + b\bar{u}) > 0$, it follows that $c < 0$, which immediately establishes that the optimal control $\bar{u} = M$.

Differentiating the Hamiltonian with respect to t, evaluated at the optimum, and recalling (5.26), we see that the Hamiltonian is zero for $0 \le t \le T^*$. Thus, writing the Hamiltonian at $t = 0$ and $t = T^*$ yields two equations in two unknowns c and T^*. Finally, to obtain the optimal trajectory, substitute M for u in $\dot{x} = ax + bu$, and solve for $\bar{x}(t)$, using initial condition on the state variable to determine the arbitrary constant.

5.8 ECONOMIC EXAMPLES

Example 5.1   An Inventory Model†

SYMBOLS:

$$P = \text{production}$$
$$M = \text{shipments from the factory}$$
$$U = \text{unfilled orders}$$
$$D = \text{orders received at the factory}$$
$$I = \text{inventory at the factory warehouse}$$

MODEL:

First, we assume that the rate of change of the inventory at the factory warehouse at time t is equal to the rate of production at time t minus the shipment rate from the factory at time t. That is

(5.29) $$\dot{I} = P(t) - M(t)$$
$$I(0) = I_0$$

Next, we assume that the shipment rate from the factory at time t is a simple exponential function of the whole spectrum of past values of unfilled orders. That is

†See Forrester [15] and Connors and Teichroew [12, Chap. 4].

(5.30) $$M(t) = \lambda \int_0^\infty e^{-\lambda\tau} U(t - \tau) \, d\tau$$

By employing the change of variable $x = t - \tau$, (5.30) can be transformed into†

(5.31) $$\dot{M} = \lambda(U(t) - M(t))$$
$$M(0) = M_0$$

Our next assumption is that the rate of change in unfilled orders at time t equals the orders received at the factory at time t minus the shipments from the factory at time t. That is

(5.32) $$\dot{U} = D(t) - M(t)$$
$$U(0) = U_0$$

Suppose that the firm wishes to regulate production so to minimize the sum of inventory holding cost, production cost, and shortage cost over some fixed time interval $[0, T]$. We can then write the performance functional as

(5.33) $$S = \int_0^T [\alpha I(t) + \beta P(t) + \gamma(D(t) - P(t))] \, dt$$

where α = inventory holding cost, assessed against accumulated inventories for the period

β = cost of production, assessed against total production for the period

γ = shortage cost, assessed against the accumulated difference between orders received and production for the period

Finally, we suppose that production, the only control variable in this problem, has some upper and lower limit. That is

(5.34) $$\underline{P} \le P(t) \le \bar{P}$$

†By changing the variable of integration, we have $dx = -d\tau$, giving

$$M(t) = -\lambda \int_t^{-\infty} e^{-\lambda(t-x)} U(x) \, dx$$

Thus

$$\frac{1}{\lambda} e^{\lambda t} M(t) = \int_{-\infty}^t e^{\lambda x} U(x) \, dx$$

Differentiating the last expression with respect to t gives

$$e^{\lambda t} M(t) + \frac{1}{\lambda} e^{\lambda t} \dot{M} = e^{\lambda t} U(t)$$

Dividing by $(1/\lambda)e^{\lambda t} \ne 0$, we can easily obtain (5.31).

The problem is to manipulate $P(t)$ over the time period $[0, T]$ so as to minimize S in (5.33) subject to (5.29), (5.31), (5.32) and (5.34). This is a fixed-time problem with no constraints on the final values of M, U, or I.

To facilitate relating of this problem to the previous sections, we relabel the variables as

$$x_1 = M$$
$$x_2 = U$$
$$x_3 = I$$
$$u = P$$
$$z = D$$

Notice that in this model $D \equiv z$ is an exogenous variable which is not controllable. Therefore, some assumption about its behavior must be made. Let us assume that z grows at σ per cent with initial value equal to one. That is

$$z(t) = e^{\sigma t}$$

We can now restate the control problem as one of finding a $u(t)$ which minimizes the performance functional

$$S = \int_0^T [\alpha x_3(t) + \beta u(t) + \gamma(e^{\sigma t} - u(t))] \, dt$$

subject to

(5.35)
$$\begin{bmatrix} \dot{x}_1 \\ \dot{x}_2 \\ \dot{x}_3 \end{bmatrix} = \begin{bmatrix} -\lambda & \lambda & 0 \\ -1 & 0 & 0 \\ -1 & 0 & 0 \end{bmatrix} \begin{bmatrix} x_1 \\ x_2 \\ x_3 \end{bmatrix} + \begin{bmatrix} 0 \\ 0 \\ 1 \end{bmatrix} u + \begin{bmatrix} 0 \\ 1 \\ 0 \end{bmatrix} e^{\sigma t}$$

with initial conditions

$$x_1(0) = x_{10}$$
$$x_2(0) = x_{20}$$
$$x_3(0) = x_{30}$$

and where $\underline{P} \leq u(t) \leq \bar{P}$. The Hamiltonian in this problem is

$$H = \lambda_1(\lambda x_2 - \lambda x_1) + \lambda_2(-x_1 + e^{\sigma t}) + \lambda_3(-x_1 + u)$$
$$+ (\alpha x_3 + (\beta - \gamma)u + \gamma e^{\sigma t})$$

The auxiliary system is

$$\dot{\lambda}_1 = -\frac{\partial H}{\partial x_1} = \lambda\lambda_1(t) + \lambda_2(t) + \lambda_3(t)$$

$$\dot{\lambda}_2 = -\frac{\partial H}{\partial x_2} = -\lambda\lambda_1(t)$$

$$\dot{\lambda}_3 = -\frac{\partial H}{\partial x_3} = -\alpha$$

with terminal conditions

$$\lambda_1(T) = \lambda_2(T) = \lambda_3(T) = 0$$

Observing the Hamiltonian, which is to be minimized with respect to u, we see that only a few terms in the Hamiltonian contain u. Hence, to minimize the terms in H which contain u is equivalent to minimizing H with respect to u. Writing out just the terms in H which include u, we obtain

$$[\lambda_3(t) + \beta - \gamma]u(t)$$

Substituting into this term the solution of λ_3 from the auxiliary equations, we have

$$(-\alpha t + \beta - \gamma)u(t)$$

It follows that the optimal control is

$$\bar{u} = \begin{cases} \underline{P} \text{ when } (-\alpha t + \beta - \gamma) > 0 \\ \bar{P} \text{ when } (-\alpha t + \beta - \gamma) < 0 \\ \text{unspecified when } (-\alpha t + \beta - \gamma) = 0 \end{cases}$$

The rest of the problem is a straightforward application of the solution techniques developed in Chapter 3. The appropriate value of $\bar{u}$ is substituted into (5.35) and the optimal trajectories are solved for, taking into account the proper boundary conditions. For example, suppose that

$$0 < \frac{\beta - \gamma}{\alpha} < T$$

$$\beta - \gamma > 0$$

$$\alpha > 0$$

Then

$$(-\alpha t + \beta - \gamma)\begin{cases} > 0 \text{ for } 0 \leq t < \dfrac{\beta - \gamma}{\alpha} \\[2mm] = 0 \text{ for } t = \dfrac{\beta - \gamma}{\alpha} \\[2mm] < 0 \text{ for } \dfrac{\beta - \gamma}{\alpha} < t \leq T \end{cases}$$

Thus, we insert $\bar{u} = \underline{P}$ into (5.35) and solve, using the initial conditions $x_1(0) = x_{10}$, $x_2(0) = x_{20}$, and $x_3(0) = x_{30}$. Then, we substitute $\bar{u} = \bar{P}$ into (5.35) and solve, using as our initial conditions the terminal conditions of the solution of (5.35) with $\bar{u} = \underline{P}$. That is, the initial conditions for the solution of (5.35) with $\bar{u} = \bar{P}$ are

$$\bar{x}_1(t^*), \bar{x}_2(t^*), x_3(t^*)$$

$$t^* = \frac{\beta - \gamma}{\alpha}$$

Example 5.2   A Macroeconomic Model

Consider the following standard dynamic Keynesian model with rigid wages and prices and with the monetary sector excluded:†

(5.36)	$C = C_0 e^{r_1 t} + a_1(Y - T^*)$	$0 < a_1 < 1$
(5.37)	$T^* = \bar{T} + nY$	$0 < n < 1$
(5.38)	$I = I_0 e^{r_2 t} + a_2 Y$	$0 < a_2 < 1$
(5.39)	$M = M_0 e^{r_3 t} + mY$	$0 < m < 1$
(5.40)	$X = X_0 e^{r_4 t}$	
(5.41)	$G = \bar{G}$	
(5.42)	$E \equiv C + I + G + X$	
(5.43)	$\dot{Y} = g(E - Y)$	

where
C = consumption spending
I = investment spending
T^* = taxes
G = government spending
X = exports

†For analysis of similar models, see Fox, Sengupta, and Thorbecke [16, Chap. 8].

$M =$ imports

$Y =$ national income

$E =$ aggregate demand (for domestic product)

It is assumed that the exogenous components of C, I, M, and X are expected to grow at rates r_1 to r_4, respectively. To simplify the calculations, we shall assume that $r_1 = r_2 = r_3 = r_4$. Equation (5.43) asserts that the time rate of change in Y depends on the excess demand or supply in the goods market, where g is the speed of response. There are two policy instruments in this model, $\bar{G}$ and $\bar{T}$. These instruments considered as a function of time are the control.†

Next, we consider two preference functions which are assumed to reflect the preferences of the policy maker. Suppose first that the policy maker desires that Y and G follow given trajectories, and that both the budget and the current account in the balance of payments be as close to balanced as possible. We shall write this in quadratic form which asserts that a given deviation from any of these four goals causes the policy maker a greater increase in pain the farther away from the goal he is. The preference function at any moment of time is

$$(5.44) \quad W = \tfrac{1}{2} \left[w_1 (Y - Y_0 e^{\theta_1 t})^2 + w_2 (\bar{G} - G_0 e^{\theta_2 t})^2 + w_3 (X - M)^2 \right.$$
$$\left. + W_4 (\bar{G} - T^*)^2 \right]$$

where w_i, $i = 1, \ldots, 4$, are the weights which the policy maker attaches to the deviation between the actual values of Y, $\bar{G}$, $(X - M)$, and $(\bar{G} - T^*)$ at time t, and the desired values of $Y_0 e^{\theta_1 t}$, $G_0 e^{\theta_2 t}$, 0, and 0 at the same moment of time. The policy maker wishes Y and G to grow at θ_1 and θ_2 per cent, respectively. Y_0 and G_0 are the initial desired values of Y and G. The weights must be non-negative, with at least one being positive. Assuming a given time horizon for the policy maker, his problem then is to minimize

$$(5.45) \qquad\qquad\qquad S = \int_0^T W \, dt$$

with respect to $\bar{G}$, and $\bar{T}$ subject to the model.

Consider next an alternative preference function. Suppose the policy maker wishes to move income to some target level, Y^*, as soon as possible, but still wants the budget and the current account balanced as well as to minimize the deviation of $\bar{G}$ from some desired trajectory. The problem now is to minimize

$$(5.46) \quad S^* = \tfrac{1}{2} \int_0^T \left[w_1 + w_2 (\bar{G} - G_0 e^{\theta_2 t})^2 + w_3 (X - M)^2 \right.$$
$$\left. + w_4 (\bar{G} - T^*)^2 \right] dt$$

---

†For simplicity, we shall assume that the marginal tax rate, n, is a structural parameter for this problem.

where w_1 now expresses the weight which the policy maker attaches to the speed of reaching the target level of Y. In this problem, the time horizon is not given and must be solved for; that is, the optimal T must be found as part of the solution. It should be clear that in both of these cases the optimal control and the optimal trajectory of Y will depend not only on the structural parameters of the model but also on the weights in the preference function.

Substituting equations (5.36) through (5.38) and (5.40) through (5.42) into (5.43) gives

(5.47) $$\dot{Y} = \alpha Y - ga_1\bar{T} + g\bar{G} + ge^{rt}A$$

where

$$\alpha \equiv g(a_1 - a_1 n + a_2 - 1) < 0$$
$$A \equiv C_0 + I_0 + X_0$$
$$r = r_1 = \cdots = r_4$$

The first problem is to minimize (5.45) with respect to $\bar{G}$ and $\bar{T}$, subject to (5.47). The Hamiltonian in this case is

(5.48) $$H = \lambda_1(t)\dot{Y} + W$$

where $\lambda_1(t)$ is the costate variable. We also know that the terminal condition for λ_1 for this problem is

(5.49) $$\lambda_1(T) = 0$$

The auxiliary system is

(5.50) $$\dot{\lambda}_1 = -\frac{\partial H}{\partial Y} = -\lambda_1\alpha - w_1(Y - Y_0 e^{\theta_1 t}) + w_3 m[(X_0 - M_0)e^{rt} - mY]$$
$$+ w_4 n(\bar{G} - \bar{T} - nY)$$

From the maximum principle, it follows that the minimization of H at each point of time with respect to $\bar{G}$ and $\bar{T}$ is a necessary condition for the minimization of S subject to (5.47). This requires that†

(5.51) $$\frac{\partial H}{\partial \bar{G}} = g\lambda_1 + w_2(\bar{G} - G_0 e^{\theta_2 t}) + w_4(\bar{G} - \bar{T} - nY) = 0$$

(5.52) $$\frac{\partial H}{\partial \bar{T}} = ga_1\lambda_1 - w_4(\bar{G} - \bar{T} - nY) = 0$$

---

†Of course, it must be assumed that $\bar{G}(t)$ is nonnegative. Therefore, (5.51) strictly speaking should read $\leq$ rather than $=$, with the equality holding where $\bar{G} > 0$ and $\leq$ holding where $\bar{G} = 0$. In writing (5.51) with the equality, we are simplifying by assuming that the optimal $\bar{G}$ is strictly positive for $0 \leq t \leq T$.

Solving (5.51) and (5.52) for $\bar{G}$ and $\bar{T}$ gives

(5.53) $\qquad \bar{G}(t) = \left(\dfrac{-1 + a_1}{w_2}\right)\lambda_1(t) + G_0 e^{\theta_2 t}$

(5.54) $\qquad \bar{T}(t) = \left(\dfrac{-1 + a_1}{w_2} + \dfrac{a_1}{w_4}\right) g\lambda_1(t) - nY(t) + G_0 e^{\theta_2 t}$

Substituting (5.53) and (5.54) into (5.50) and (5.47) and solving for $Y(t)$ and $\lambda_1(t)$ yields the optimal trajectories for these variables. Carrying out these substitutions yields the following system of differential equations:

(5.55) $\qquad \begin{aligned} \dot{Y} &= a_{11} Y + a_{12}\lambda_1 + a_{13} e^{\theta t} \\ \dot{\lambda}_1 &= a_{21} Y + a_{22}\lambda_1 + a_{23} e^{\theta t} \end{aligned}$

where

$$a_{11} = g(a_1 + a_2 - 1)$$

$$a_{12} = g\left(\frac{a_1 - 1}{w_2}\right) - g^2 a_1\left(\frac{a_1 - 1}{w_2} + \frac{a_1}{w_4}\right)$$

$$a_{13} = [(1 - a_1)G_0 + A]g$$

$$a_{21} = -w_1 - w_3 m^2$$

$$a_{22} = w_4 n\left[\frac{a_1 - 1 - g(a_1 - 1)}{w_2} - \frac{g a_1}{w_4}\right] - \alpha$$

$$a_{23} = w_1 Y_0 - w_3 m M_0 + w_3 m X_0$$

and where we have simplified the nonhomogeneous term by letting all growth rates equal θ.

Solving (5.55), we obtain the optimal motions

(5.56) $\qquad \begin{aligned} \bar{Y}(t) &= \dfrac{c_1(q_1 - a_{22})}{a_{21}} e^{q_1 t} + \dfrac{c_2(q_2 - a_{22})}{a_{21}} e^{q_2 t} + B^* e^{\theta t} \\ \bar{\lambda}_1(t) &= c_1 e^{q_1 t} + c_2 e^{q_2 t} + B e^{\theta t} \end{aligned}$

where q_1 and q_2 are the roots of the quadratic in q

$$q^2 - (a_{11} + a_{22})q + (a_{11} a_{22} - a_{12} a_{21})$$

and where

$$B = \frac{a_{13} a_{21} + a_{23}\theta - a_{23} a_{11}}{(\theta - q_1)(\theta - q_2)}$$

$$B^* = \frac{a_{23} - a_{22}B + \theta B}{a_{21}}$$

and c_1 and c_2 are constants to be determined from the boundary conditions $Y(0) = Y_0$ and $\lambda(T) = 0$. Solving for c_1 and c_2 and substituting (5.56) into (5.53) and (5.54), we have the optimal control.

Next, consider the problem with the performance criterion in (5.46). We follow the same procedure as before, except that there are now two additional unknowns: The optimal period of time, $\hat{T}$, and a boundary condition for λ_1 at $t = \hat{T}$. Recall that two additional conditions exist for this minimum time case which enable us to solve for these additional unknowns: The Hamiltonian function is zero† at $t = \hat{T}$, and $Y(t)$ has the terminal condition that it be equal to Y^*.

The Hamiltonian for this problem is

$$(5.57) \qquad H = \lambda_1(t)[\alpha Y - ga_1\bar{T} + g\bar{G} + ge^{rt}A] + \tfrac{1}{2}[w_1 + w_2(\bar{G} - G_0e^{\theta_2 t})^2$$
$$+ w_3(X - M)^2 + w_4(\bar{G} - T^*)^2]$$

The solution for $\bar{G}(t)$ and $\bar{T}(t)$ has exactly the same form as (5.53) and (5.54). The expression for $\dot{Y}$ is of course the same as in the previous case, but the equation for $\dot{\lambda}_1$ is altered from (5.55) to

$$(5.58) \qquad\qquad \dot{\lambda}_1 = \bar{a}_{21}Y + a_{22}\lambda_1 + \bar{a}_{23}e^{\theta t}$$

where

$$\bar{a}_{21} = -w_3 m^2$$
$$a_{22} \text{ is the same as in } (5.55)$$
$$\bar{a}_{23} = -w_3 m M_0 + w_3 m X_0$$

The remaining labor is straightforward. Solve for $Y(t)$ and $\lambda_1(t)$ from the differential equations in (5.58) and the first equation in (5.55). The constants are then determined from the initial and terminal conditions on Y. This solution represents the optimal motion of Y and λ_1. Substituting these expressions into (5.53) and (5.54) yields the optimal decision rules for $\bar{G}$ and $\bar{T}$. To determine the optimal $T, \hat{T}$, substitute the expressions for the optimal trajectories and the optimal control into the Hamiltonian function in (5.57). Setting t equal to $\hat{T}$, we know that the Hamiltonian function is zero. The only unknown in this equation is then the time period, which can thus be solved for, yielding the optimal time period $\hat{T}$.

---

†It was shown in section 5.6 that, under optimal control, the Hamiltonian is zero for $0 \le t \le T$, if t is not an explicit argument in the Hamiltonian. However, in this case t is an explicit argument, hence the Hamiltonian is only zero at $t = T$.

Example 5.3   Production and Investment of the Firm†

The variables in this model are as follows:

Exogenous Variables

π = profits per unit of output

g = output per unit of capacity

c = price of a unit of capacity

i = market rate of interest

M = upper bound on rate of new capacity purchase

α = depreciation rate

δ = rate of discount

State Variables

x_1 = capacity of the firm

x^2 = net debt of the firm

Control Variables

u^1 = units of capacity used for production

u^2 = rate of purchase of new capacity

It is assumed that the firm wishes to maximize the discounted value of net profits from production minus the interest cost and the cost of new capacity over a fixed interval of time. The objective functional may thus be written‡

$$(5.59) \qquad S = \sum_{t=0}^{T-1} (\pi g u_t^1 - c u_t^2 - i x_t^2) \delta^{-t}$$

This maximization is constrained by two difference equations and two sets of inequalities. These are, for $t = 0, 1, \ldots, T - 1$

$$(5.60) \qquad x_{t+1}^1 - x_t^1 = u_t^2 - \alpha x_t^1$$

$$x_0^1 \text{ given}$$

$$(5.61) \qquad x_{t+1}^2 - x_t^2 = c u_t^2 + i x_t^2 - \pi g u_t^1$$

$$x_0^2 \text{ given}$$

$$(5.62) \qquad 0 \leq u_t^1 \leq x_t^1, \qquad 0 \leq u_t^2 \leq M$$

---

†See Thompson and George [49].

‡We assume that the exogenous variables are constants over the decision making interval. Alternative assumptions as to their behavior do not substantively alter the analysis.

Equation (5.60) says that the change in the capacity of the firm from period t to period $t + 1$ equals the amount of capital purchased less the amount of capital depreciated in period t. Equation (5.61) says that the change in the net debt of the firm from period t to period $t + 1$ equals the cost of capital plus interest payments less profits. The inequalities in (5.62) are self-explanatory.

The control problem is to find values for u_t^1 and u_t^2 for $t = 0, 1, \ldots,$ $T - 1$ which maximize (5.59) subject to (5.60), (5.61), and (5.62).

The Hamiltonian for this problem is

$$(5.63) \qquad H_t = (\pi g u_t^1 - c u_t^2 - i x_t^2) \delta^{-t} + \lambda_t^1 (u_t^2 - \alpha x_t^1)$$
$$+ \lambda_t^2 (c u_t^2 + i x_t^2 - \pi g u_t^1)$$

The auxiliary system is

$$(5.64) \qquad \lambda_t^1 - \lambda_{t-1}^1 = -\frac{\partial H_t}{\partial x_t^1} = \alpha \lambda_t^1$$

$$\lambda_t^2 - \lambda_{t-1}^2 = -\frac{\partial H_t}{\partial x_t^2} = -i\lambda_t^2 + i\delta^{-t}$$

with

$$\lambda_{T-1}^1 = \lambda_{T-1}^2 = 0$$

According to the maximum principle, u_t^1 and u_t^2 must be selected from the admissible values in (5.62) so as to maximize the Hamiltonian for $t = 0, 1,$ $\ldots, T - 1$. From (5.63), we see that the optimal control is thus

$$(5.65)$$
$$\bar{u}_t^1 = \begin{cases} \bar{x}_t^1 & \text{when } \pi g(\delta^{-t} - \bar{\lambda}_t^2) > 0 \\ 0 & \text{when } \pi g(\delta^{-t} - \bar{\lambda}_t^2) < 0 \\ \text{unspecified} & \text{when } \pi g(\delta^{-t} - \bar{\lambda}_t^2) = 0 \end{cases}$$

$$\bar{u}_t^2 = \begin{cases} M & \text{when } c(\bar{\lambda}_t^2 - \delta^{-t}) + \bar{\lambda}_t^1 > 0 \\ 0 & \text{when } c(\bar{\lambda}_t^2 - \delta^{-t}) + \bar{\lambda}_t^1 < 0 \\ \text{unspecified} & \text{when } c(\bar{\lambda}_t^2 - \delta^{-t}) + \bar{\lambda}_t^1 = 0 \end{cases}$$

The remainder of the problem is straightforward. Solve the auxiliary system and substitute into (5.65). Use these values in (5.60) and (5.61) to obtain the optimal time paths for production and investment.

References

1. Ackley, G., *Macroeconomic Theory*. New York: The Macmillan Company, 1961.

2. Allen, R.G.D., *Mathematical Analysis for Economists*. New York: St. Martin's Press, Inc., 1938.

3. _____, *Mathematical Economics*. New York: St. Martin's Press, Inc., 1959.

4. Apostol, T.M., *Calculus*. Vol. 1. Waltham, Mass.: Blaisdell Publishing Company, 1961.

5. Arimoto, S., "On a Multi-Stage Nonlinear Programming Problem," *Journal of Math. Anal. and Appl.*, 17 (January 1967), 161-167.

6. Arrow, K.J., L. Hurwicz, and H. Uzawa, "Constraint Qualification in Maximization Problems," *Office of Naval Research Technical Report No. 64*, Department of Economics, Stanford University, 1958.

7. Baumol, W.J., *Economic Dynamics*. New York: The Macmillan Company, 1951.

8. Bellman, R., *Introduction to Matrix Analysis*. New York: McGraw-Hill Book Company, 1960.

9. Birkhoff, G., and S. MacLane, *A Survey of Modern Algebra*. New York: The Macmillan Company, 1965.

10. Brems, H., *Quantitative Economic Theory: A Synthetic Approach*. New York: John Wiley & Sons, Inc., 1968.

278

11. Coddington, E.A., and N. Levinson, *Theory of Ordinary Differential Equations.* New York: McGraw-Hill Book Company, 1955.

12. Connors, M.M., and D. Teichroew, *Optimal Control of Dynamic Operations Research Models.* Scranton, Pa.: The International Textbook Company, 1968.

13. Courant, R., *Differential and Integral Calculus.* 2 Vols. New York: Interscience, 1936 and 1937.

14. Dorfman, R., P.A. Samuelson, and R.M. Solow, *Linear Programming and Economic Analysis.* New York: McGraw-Hill Book Company, 1958.

15. Forrester, J., *Industrial Dynamics.* Cambridge, Mass.: The M.I.T. Press, 1961.

16. Fox, K.A., J.K. Sengupta, and E. Thorbecke, *The Theory of Quantitative Economic Policy with Applications to Economic Growth and Stabilization.* Amsterdam: North-Holland Publishing Company; Chicago: Rand McNally & Co., 1966.

17. Frazer, R.A., W.J. Duncan, and A.R. Collar, *Elementary Matrices and Some Applications to Dynamics and Differential Equations.* New York: The Macmillan Company, 1946; Cambridge University Press, 1957.

18. Gale, D., and H. Nikaido, "The Jacobian Matrix and Global Univalence of Mappings," *Mathematische Annalen*, 159, No. 2 (1965); reprinted in *Readings*

in Mathematical Economics, Vol. I, ed. P. Newman. Baltimore: Johns Hopkins Press, 1968.

19. Goldberg, S., *Introduction to Difference Equations.* New York: John Wiley & Sons, Inc., 1961.

20. Goursat, E., and E.R. Hedrick, *Mathematical Analysis.* Boston: Ginn and Company, 1904.

21. Hadley, G., *Linear Algebra.* Reading, Mass.: Addison-Wesley Publishing Company, Inc., 1961.

22. _____, *Nonlinear and Dynamic Programming.* Reading, Mass.: Addison-Wesley Publishing Company, Inc., 1964.

23. Hahn, W., *Theory and Application of Liapunov's Direct Method.* Englewood Cliffs, N.J.: Prentice-Hall, Inc., 1963.

24. Halkin, H., "A Maximum Principle of the Pontryagin Type for Systems Described by Nonlinear Difference Equations," *S.I.A.M. Journal on Control*, No. 1 (1966), 90-111.

25. Hansen, A.H., *Monetary Theory and Fiscal Policy.* New York: McGraw-Hill Book Company, 1949.

26. Holmes, W.L., "Derivation and Application of a Discrete Maximum Principle," *Western Economic Journal* (December 1968), 385-394.

27. Ince, E.L., *Ordinary Differential Equations.* London: Longmans, Green & Co. Ltd., 1927; republished New York: Dover Publications, Inc., 1956.

28. Kalman, R.E., and J.E. Bertram, "Control System Analysis and Design Via the Second Method of Liapunov: I. Continuous-Time System; II. Discrete-Time Systems," *ASME J. Basic Engineering*, ser. D, 82 (1960), 371-393; 394-400.

29. Karlin, S., *Mathematical Methods and Theory in Games, Programming, and Economics.* Vol. I. Reading, Mass.: Addison-Wesley Publishing Company, Inc., 1959.

30. Katz, S., "A Discrete Version of Pontryagin's Maximum Principle," *J. Electronics and Control*, 13 (1962), 179-184.

31. Kuenne, R., *The Theory of General Economic Equilibrium.* Princeton, NJ.: Princeton University Press, 1963.

32. Lancaster, K., *Mathematical Economics.* New York: The Macmillan Company, 1968.

33. LaSalle, J.P., and S. Lefschetz, *Stability by Liapunov's Direct Method with Applications.* New York: Academic Press Inc., 1961.

34. Mangasarian, O.L., *Nonlinear Programming.* New York: McGraw:Hill Book Company, 1969.

35. Massera, J.L., "Contributions to Stability Theory," *Ann. Math.*, 64 (1956), 182-206.

36. Mirsky, L., *An Introduction to Linear Algebra.* London: Clarendon Press, 1955.

37. Morishima, M., *Equilibrium, Stability and Growth*. New York: Oxford University Press, Inc., 1964.

38. Mostow, G.D., J.H. Sampson, and J. Meyer, *Fundamental Structures of Algebra*. New York: McGraw-Hill Book Company, 1963.

39. Negishi, T., "The Stability of a Competitive Economy: A Survey Article," *Econometrica*, XXX (October, 1962), 635-669; reprinted in *Readings in Mathematical Economics*, Vol. I, ed. P. Newman. Baltimore: Johns Hopkins Press, 1968.

40. Newman, P., "Approaches to Stability Analysis," *Economica* (February 1961), 12-29.

41. Patinkin, D., *Money, Interest, and Prices: An Integration of Monetary and Value Theory*. New York: Harper and Row, Publishers, 1965.

42. _____, "The Limitations of Samuelson's Correspondence Principle," *Metroeconomica*, IV (1952), 37-43.

43. Perlis, S., *Theory of Matrices*. Reading, Mass.: Addison-Wesley Publishing Company, Inc., 1952.

44. Pfouts, R.W., "The Theory of Cost and Production in the Multiproduct Firm," *Econometrica*, XXIX (October 1961), 650-658.

45. Pontriagin, L.S., *et al.*, *The Mathematical Theory of Optimal Processes*. New York: Pergamon Press, The Macmillan Company, 1964.

46. Protter, M.H., and C.B. Morrey, *Modern Mathematical Analysis*. Reading, Mass.: Addison-Wesley Publishing Company, Inc., 1964.

47. Samuelson, P.A., *Foundatians of Economic Analysis*. Cambridge, Mass.: Harvard University Press, 1948; republished by Atheneum, 1970.

48. Solow, R.M., "On the Structure of Linear Models," *Econometrica*, XX (January 1952), 29-46.

49. Thompson, R.G., and M.D. George, "Optimal Operations and Investments of the Firm," *Management Science*, 15, No. 1 (September 1968), 49-56.

50. Uspensky, J.V., *Theory of Equations*. New York: McGraw-Hill Book Company, 1948.

51. Yamane, T., *Mathematics for Economists*. Englewood Cliffs, N.J.: Prentice-Hall, Inc., 1962.

Index